Globalization and the Gulf

Globalization and the Gulf describes and explains how the strategically situated societies along the Arabian Gulf, in the United Arab Emirates, Qatar, Bahrain, Kuwait, Saudi Arabia and Oman, have embraced the forces of globalization transforming the world into a single market, albeit on their own terms.

While aspects of the Arab world have resisted certain dimensions of globalization, the Gulf societies have by and large welcomed the technological and material aspects of globalization with enthusiasm; small traditional towns of mud-walled communities have been transformed into ultra-modern cityscapes within one short generation. However, despite the familiar "Westernesque" skylines and immaculate physical infrastructure, this is not business as usual where the quest for profits in the most efficient ways dictates business and governmental policy and practice. The local leaders and the now Western educated younger generation of family scions manage the society and have molded an almost unique lifestyle that blends traditional values and attitudes with modern business savvy. While the West has demonstrated a rather poor track record in understanding the Arab world in general, the strategic flow of the world's oil pipeline through these six Gulf countries necessitates a more informed understanding of the workings, meanings, and unique transformations of Gulf society.

Globalization and the Gulf seeks to provide this understanding and includes an analysis of how Arab society and the forces of globalization in economy, ideas and lifestyle have created a unique synthesis of local and global. The contributions in this volume are from leading international scholars that offer a unique insight into the societies of the Arabian Gulf, making this an invaluable volume for those with interests in Middle East politics, political economy, sociology, anthropology, and International Relations.

John W. Fox is Professor of Anthropology at the American University of Sharjah. **Nada Mourtada-Sabbah** is Associate Professor of Political Science and Chair of the Department of International Studies at the American University of Sharjah. **Mohammed al-Mutawa** is Associate Professor of Sociology at the United Arab Emirates University

Globalization and the Gulf

**Edited by
John W. Fox,
Nada Mourtada-Sabbah
and Mohammed al-Mutawa**

Taylor & Francis Group

LONDON AND NEW YORK

First published 2006
by Routledge
2 Park Square, Milton Park, Abingdon, Oxon OX14 4RN

Simultaneously published in the USA and Canada
by Routledge
270 Madison Ave, New York, NY 10016

Routledge is an imprint of the Taylor & Francis Group, an informa business

© 2006 John W. Fox, Nada Mourtada-Sabbah & Mohammed al-Mutawa
for editorial matter; individual contributors their contributions

Typeset in Baskerville by
Newgen Imaging Systems (P) Ltd, Chennai, India
Printed and bound in Great Britain by
Antony Rowe Ltd, Chippenham, Wiltshire

British Library Cataloguing in Publication Data
A catalogue record for this book is available from the British Library

Library of Congress Cataloging in Publication Data
A catalog record for this book has been requested

ISBN10: 0–415–77013–0 (hbk)
ISBN10: 0–415–77014–9 (pbk)

ISBN13: 978–0–415–77013–2 (hbk)
ISBN13: 978–0–415–77014–9 (pbk)

The three co-editors wish to dedicate this volume to the first Chancellor of the American University of Sharjah, Roderick S. French, whose implicit understanding of the academy charted the future direction of AUS as a vigorous blend of scholarship and teaching. We are forever indebted.

Contents

Illustrations

Figures

Tables

Foreword

For centuries, the Arabian Gulf region has been a crossroads where seafaring people and Bedouins alike traveled great distances transacting business. Today the descendants of these merchants and traders oversee ships and aircraft transporting goods to and from all the major ports of the world. Events of the past few years, both good and bad, have directed the world's attention to the Arabian Peninsula, where a rich cultural tradition is rapidly incorporating the latest innovations from around the world. This is the process of globalization.

New economies create enormous potential for humanity as a whole, but like the ships of old globalization can take many courses. If guided wisely, they can be of great benefit to humankind, but it will require great care for the people of the region to steer through a period of profound change. Political and economic interests intent on maintaining the flow of petroleum products, on the one hand, and people in the Gulf region who assess their own interests from quite a different perspective, on the other, exert pressures from conflicting directions. Reconciling these interests in a time of rapid globalization poses enormous challenges.

This timely volume, *Globalization and the Gulf*, brings together the work of scholars from both the Middle East and the West who have the expertise to evaluate the interaction of new ideas, new technologies, and new economies. I am quite pleased to have this cast of authorities on both the processes of globalism and on the traditions of Gulf society and culture offer their views on how these trends interact within the global system. I congratulate the American University of Sharjah and the Sociological Association of the UAE for hosting the conference which brought together this expertise, and I commend the co-editors of this volume for making this expertise accessible.

Sheikh Dr Sultan Bin Mohammed Al Qassimi
Member of the Supreme Council and Ruler of Sharjah
President, American University of Sharjah

Part I

Overview of globalization synchronized with Gulf social norms, *c.*1970–2006

1 The Arab Gulf region

Traditionalism globalized or globalization traditionalized?

John W. Fox, Nada Mourtada-Sabbah, and Mohammed al-Mutawa

No part of the world has come into the global market more rapidly and with more change in material abundance than the oil states along the Arabian Gulf. Within two generations, the peoples of Saudi Arabia, Kuwait, Bahrain, Qatar, the United Arab Emirates, and Oman have turned small desert towns and seaports into urbanized states. The now overwhelmingly ultramodern Gulf societies have grown exponentially to some 33 million persons in all. Based on the rapidity and designed development, all of which has been achieved since the advent of globalization during the 1970s, the Arabian Gulf provides a laboratory *par excellence* to assess and fine tune the theories of globalization.

In these city-states attractive to foreigners, with their high standards of living and mix of traditional and cosmopolitan lifestyles, expatriate residents comprise nearly 33 percent of the total Gulf population. In the UAE, Qatar and Kuwait, the percentage of expatriates is in the majority. This is de facto multiculturalism. However, much of traditional social structure persists and directs the changes, and serves to filter what is acceptable. This is de facto indigenous conservatism with which to face the continually incoming forces of globalization. Unlike cosmopolitan settings elsewhere, market forces do not drive and sculpt cultural norms, although they do impact them. In this volume we attempt to explain why.

First, the traditional familial structure, honed in the earlier days of the desert and sea lifeways, is primary and directs the processes of globalization. This fact renders globalization here distinctive from other regions of the world. While sending petroleum products out, the Gulf monarchies take in capital, goods, information, and skilled labor in percentages not seen elsewhere in the world. The degree of material dependency on the global market is also unprecedented. But these foreign items are placed in separate spaces within Gulf society so that local and global are almost engineered to mix in prescribed ways. In overview, thus, while the Gulf societies are fairly receptive to the material benefits of globalization, on the other hand they deliberately cushion themselves from the negative aspects of market penetration into social life and ideology. This has led to a unique combination of traditional and formal organization, which we examine and explain in this volume.

We focus more on the oil states of the United Arab Emirates, Qatar, Bahrain, and Kuwait, which are in the vanguard of change. Yet on the eve of the oil boom, the Trucial coast as what the forerunner of three of these states was called, was the Middle East's most disconnected area within the European managed world system. The Trucial coast was also the most traditional in tribal norms. Nevertheless, it has developed the most receptive ways of synchronizing localism with globalism within the Middle East as well, which is borne out in many different measures. For example, according to a report issued by the Arab league, economic growth for the Gulf states ranged from about 5 percent to 7 percent for the year 2003, whereas many parts of the Arab world actually "saw the average individual share in GDP decline."[1] Dubai's gross domestic product grew at 16.7 percent in 2004 and posted an astounding 10 percent for the past decade, "which is the highest growth rate in the world."[2] The comparative giant of Saudi Arabia, which is the most culturally controlled of the Gulf oil states has by far the largest oil revenues, the highest unemployment, lowest per capita income, and the highest grow rate (7.1 percent) for 2003. The total gross domestic product for the six Gulf states is about $330 billion with a per capita income of approximately $10,000 per year.[3]

Leadership varies among the Gulf states as well, with some differences in economic results. Like Saudi Arabia, Kuwait also began to pump oil between the world wars. In contrast though, it has secularized most, while also experiencing considerable social disruption from involvement in wars with Iraq. Oman remains the most traditional society today, and has only begun modernizing in earnest since the 1980s and with more modest infusions of petro-dollars. Taken together, the now technologically developed Gulf states provide a vital economic and political link within the global system.

How are these apparent anomalies mixing progressivism and conservatism to be explained? The social sciences almost universally note that economic change impacts and somewhat shapes social organization and ideology. However, the examples listed for the Gulf demonstrate the opposite: social organization and ideology build the economy. As we will see in this volume, much of the ideology and social organization are intact, albeit under constant pressures, but the economy is considerably changed. From the paradigmatic perspective, this "traditional globalization" turns many of the development models upside down. Our volume presents various dimensions of globalization by investigators who have probed deeply to understand its complex processes in a region that is relatively unexplored.

We use the UAE in this introduction to illustrate patterns and trends within the wider region. It seems to be the region's most economically developed and diversified economy and the most culturally diversified between the northern Emirates, which openly entice the forces of globalization, and the southern Emirates (Abu Dhabi) with its more traditional cultural norms and huge oil reserves. Irrespective of these internal poles, the UAE is the Arab world's only viable federation, which is the social organization blueprint for forging closer ties within the six countries of the Gulf Cooperation Council and thus is especially worthy of attention.

As the strategic pipeline of the world economy, the Gulf boasts the world's largest oil reserves. With more than half of the world's population now urbanized and aspiring to or having attained a consumer lifestyle, the Gulf has grown ever more influential in world geopolitics. Arguably, its own political muscle contributed to restructuring world capitalism during the 1970s, especially with the oil embargo and the emergence of a global market. During the Gulf war of the 1980s, Arab nationalism in Iraq met the resurgent Islamic Revolution in Iran; both may be seen within the context of globalization as we will argue in this overview. More or less on this key fracture point, two other Gulf wars have since involved oil, nationalism, and superpowers half a world away. With the new millennium, Western superpowers have asserted their own muscle to catalyze greater participatory government in the traditional monarchies of the Gulf. Internal and external pressures therefore are propelling political and perhaps some ideational change in ways that have yet to be fully discerned. In sum, in less than one lifetime, the Gulf transformed from one of the most disengaged parts of the world to a strategic fracture point of globalization in a regional context where political goals of many local and world players collide with oil as a prize. Together, these contestations have pushed globalization in the Gulf into the center stage of world politics. We attempt in this volume to understand how these changing social formations and processes interrelate.

In this introductory chapter, we: (1) introduce concepts of globalization, and (2) present what the traditional tribal organization was like into the 1960s immediately prior to rapid globalization during the 1970s. The fourteen chapters to follow are authored by some of the leading analysts and theorists on the Middle East. They address dimensions of how globalization and traditionalism mix on this eastern flank of the Middle East across the narrow Arabian Gulf from Central Asia.[4]

Section 1: traditionalism and globalization encountered

Prior to discussing the contributions of fourteen chapters and how they delineate, the forces of globalization have rendered a distinctive synthesis in three tumultuous decades, we first: (1) characterize how the Gulf states market themselves as postmodern and thus as attractive to visit and invest in, (2) argue that the accepted explanatory models of social sciences do not adequately account for globalization in the Gulf, (3) outline some salient features of globalization which converged during the 1970s, (4) sketch the traditional Gulf social organization prior to the profound cultural infusion of new peoples, ideas and technologies, and (5) show how traditional society directs aspects of globalization in this region. This will allow us to see how the time-honored institutions perform new functions in a multi-layered synthesis of local and global.

Promoting postmodern Arab identity

Based on age-old kinship practices that have been retooled for new functions, the Gulf oil-city states have constructed high-tech trading and transshipment ports.

Dubai has risen to third largest re-exporter in the world.[5] Cities with gleaming high-rise architecture are hosts to oil companies, tourism, and shipping to secondary markets in the Middle East and Central Asia. The nationals oversee the society and define what from the rest of the world is acceptable for entry. This is not free marketing but more of traditional social units managing the forces of globalization. To a large extent, foreign residents called guest workers run the technical and managerial aspects of the economy.

In a second phase of development in the 1990s, the Gulf states began to market a lifestyle of leisure on the exotic Arabian Gulf to attract tourism and retailing. Traditional Arabian symbols combined with contemporary design create architectural manifestations of globalization. This synthesis of traditional and ultramodern is emblematic of Gulf society itself as a marriage of the latest in technological innovation with a timeless social structure. The cityscapes are rich mosaics of master-planned communities; neighborhoods of luxurious villas with Arabian, Georgian, Italianate designs; and themed shopping malls. Wide boulevards are lined by flowers during all seasons (and cared for by legions of South Asian workers) and bright lights from the high-rise buildings; flood lights beam colored rays about embellished architectural designs, creating a rich cavalcade of color to contrast with the stark desert sands outside the cities in a kind of iridescent visual ecology. The lightly populated desert interiors starkly hold sway at the city limits, which have become tourist playgrounds for activities such as desert safaris and "dune bashing" (driving four wheel drive vehicles in the soft sand dunes).

These urban showcases have become status symbols marketed to tourists and investors. Post-modern/global "culture industries" advertise the area's architectural wonders, the "fun in the sun" holidays (beach and desert), the shopping festivals, and the marquee sporting events (thoroughbred/Arabian horseracing, golf, tennis, and speedboat racing). To convey the spectacular, the exotic, and the chic, the Gulf cities advertise "consumer style." Dubai, which has made tourism growth one of its major goals, has recently gone to an international level in advertising.

To illustrate, the Dubai-based Emirates Airline has secured the naming rights for the Arsenal football/soccer club's stadium in England. Renamed Emirates Stadium, the site now bears the airline's emblem in both English and in Arabic. Speaking of this transnational merger, Sheikh Mohammed bin Rashid Al Maktoum, the then Crown Prince of Dubai stated, "Sport transcends cultural and language barriers and . . . fosters interaction between the different peoples in the world." The winning record of the Arsenal team should convey the image of a vibrant airline much more vividly to the targeted football/soccer viewing population of Europe. Certainly, sponsoring a European football team helps mitigate the outside perception of the Arabian Gulf as a hotbed of conflict and help makes the Emirates a household word associated with championship sports. And Sheikh Mohammad himself participates in international equestrian events, and is a world class competitor in distance riding, as an exemplary leader exemplifying the new Arab-cosmopolitanism.

The Emirates and other Gulf cities now reflect post-modern place making. They market visual consumption, that is, the acquiring of images and the experience of the exotic and the distinctive places that hold a certain stature in the consumer's imagination. Then, the Gulf cities become the place to be or at least to have visited among a globe-trotting clientele. These post-modern cities interweave the consumption of material goods, images, and experiences. Here, the shopping mall concept has been elevated into a shopping-recreational-hotel district that exudes an exciting ambience for tourists and residents alike. The tourist retail industry has already boosted the northern Emirates well to the front of the region and has shown the other Gulf states the benefits of developing the "chic" niche. Dubai has become linked to other tourist and financial centers – the "global cities" of Tokyo, Milan, Paris, London, New York, and Los Angeles in an East-West axis as stepping-stones in a global archipelago. In a later section of this chapter, we argue that Dubai may in fact have become more closely linked to the global cities elsewhere than to its communities within the country, region or within the Middle East.

The Gulf states are run by a newly enriched social order who see capitalism, quite shrewdly, through the eyes of persons raised by parents who experienced the tribal life. This distinction alone dispels the kin and capitalist modes of production distinguished throughout the literature of sociology, anthropology, and political science. Much of the latest awe-inspiring development projects in Dubai were built or are being built by corporations overseen by Sheikh Mohammed Bin Rashed Al Maktoum. As mentioned, Sheikh Mohammed in many respects epitomizes and leads the entrepreneurial-traditional blend of Gulf business. He was born in a walled extended family-compound built of coral rock covered in plaster, with the only air conditioning during the torrid summers provided by four wind towers (*barjeel*, one in each corner of the compound) along the creek (*khor*) in Dubai and educated in an Arabic primary school and later in language and military schools in Great Britain.[6] "In 1985, Sheikh Mohammed suggested the establishment of Emirates as the official airline, which was launched … In the same year, plans were drawn for the development of the Jabal Ali Free Zone."[7] In 1995 he spear-headed the expansion of the Dubai International Airport and launched the Dubai Shopping Festival, the Dubai Internet City and the Dubai Ideas Oasis, the Dubai Business Bay (2004), and so on. "In the 10 years since he was named Crown Prince, Sheikh Mohammed has built a service-oriented economy and weaned Dubai away from dependence on oil. Oil revenues account for less than 10% of the emirate's GDP."[8]

Quite significantly, local companies are not transnational corporations with the capital and management headquartered in one or more of the G-7 countries, as a hallmark of globalization elsewhere. Dubai has successfully sought outside investment from the private sectors in other Gulf countries. With the oil sector almost depleted in Dubai, foreigners have recently been permitted to own real estate. This change in the code has set in motion a real estate boom, in which tract houses in the desert have been marketed to foreigners as largely investment properties (with plots often changing ownership several times per year). In many respects, Dubai seems to lead the way among the sister Gulf polities in economic diversifying beyond petroleum extraction, although siphoning off petro-dollars from the adjoining states for investment in a cultivated image of Arab cosmopolitanism. Examples abound in other Gulf communities, for example the new policies for privatization in Abu Dhabi, followed this bold and globally oriented lead.[9]

Social explanation of globalization in traditional and oil contexts

How are we to understand these "postmodern" states, which are grounded in traditional structures, but with increasingly stronger ties across the world and within the economic union of the Gulf Cooperation Council? The GCC works to advance the political and economic interests of its six members, who share a cultural heritage, a petroleum export economy, and a basic kinship-based social organization. First, let us ask if these urban social formations, traditional structure-based capitalism, and centralized city-states support or defy the theories of Adam Smith, Max Weber, and Karl Marx, which interlace the theoretical approaches of much of the social sciences? More specifically, can highly localized traditional customs combine with an international consumerist lifestyle to create the modern cultural patterns of the Gulf? Rather than incremental and gradual evolution over long periods of time, which underpins much of social theory, the Gulf represents a dynamic interplay of religion, politics, and economics over a brief period.

In this regard, we attempt to probe beyond the glittering cityscapes and the GCC's alliances with the world's finance institutions and markets to account for the apparent atypical melding of traditionalism and globalism. In method, we probably come closest to the participant observation of anthropology and sociology in answering these questions. Since the Gulf city-states fully developed within a matter of decades, aspects of this interplay are isolated for greater treatment in the chapters to follow. Here, change may sometimes be charted piecemeal, occurring in economics or idea systems prior to the reorganizing of institutions. There is no question that the economic variable of oil extraction set in motion some dynamic processes, which were guided by religious and kinship underpinnings. The political events in the oil embargo of 1974 which drew upon notions of brotherhood, sharing the wealth, and aiding the beleagured Palestinians, also figure prominently.

The early 1970s will be argued as a turnaround point, in both separating modern and postmodern approaches in explaining an emerging globalization in general and as the baseline for globalization of the Gulf specifically. Yet, for the most part, explanation in political science presupposes gradual change of national populations ensconced in territories transpiring through a multitude of rational economic choices. Change is as progressive as it is rational. Following the seminal theorist Adam Smith, who laid out the principles of economic change during the tumultuous social transformation of England's industrial revolution, economics examines the allocation of scarce means to alternative ends.[10] Formalist economics presupposes that scarcity is universal and that people attempt to maximize personal profit over what benefits the interests of the social group. With the bountiful oil revenues, however, scarcity of material products or capital clearly does not figure into how the Gulf and its social groups have survived as the primary social unit of production (in finance).

However, in hindsight now of several decades, it is possible to see that the Gulf Arabs synchronized a traditional ideology, with its own ethos of "knowhow," with a modern lifestyle to create a multilayered cosmology. Religion is embedded in most social relationships here, including the practice of capitalism. Only a small part of Gulf society sees capitalism as antithetical to the strong community values of Islam and have spawned anti-globalism political movements. The leadership constantly strives to show how tolerant Islam is as a religion so that globalization development may continue bereft of indigenous reactions (see below). In many senses, the overwhelming majority of the Gulf populations use indigenous cosmology to incorporate new technologies into a coherent idea system to enact a viable social fabric.

Then, globalization in the Gulf meshes with traditionalism rather than being an imported total package of lifestyle and values. In this view, ideology and kinship are overarching dimensions channeling the day-to-day events creating globalization. With this in mind, the theoretical approach called substantive economics more closely explains how social norms, religion, and economics presently interface in Gulf society. In short, values clearly contrary to maximizing profit guide the normative behaviors in society and the governmental policy and practice. The embedding of religion and economics within society thus renders the Gulf distinctive for much of Western perception, where the profit motive has become deeply embedded in much of the institutional life since the Reagan–Thatcher policies of the 1980s, as well as for the social sciences which purport to explain all societies.

A survey conducted by one of the co-editors defined values more in accord with the substantive approaches of anthropology than with the formalist approaches of economics. The survey showed core values that emphasized the social collectivity over economic achievement more typical of the West.[11] Core values are central to the functioning of any society and help distinguish it from other cultures and societies. Together, these core values contrast sharply with 10 ranked values of American culture listed in the column that follows. The values comparison clearly indicates that Gulf culture and American culture, which is the hearth area for globalization, are quite apart. At the present time at least, there is little probability of the Gulf becoming Western along the new "Gold Coast" of the Middle East with orthodox democratic states, and a laissez-faire economics. The 15 core values of the Arabian Gulf, in order of their frequency of response, are:

1 Priority of family and family dignity/honor; respect for elders
2 Religion provides ultimate meaning, and morality defines face-to-face interactions
3 Transactions focused on influence of kin and friends

4   Hospitality, generosity, sharing
5   Loyalty to family and friends, and patience and mercy
6   Pride of heritage and tradition, and respect for traditional norms and beliefs from the past
7   Sociability; the social group is more important than personal achievements; family councils where issues are discussed
8   Justice, honesty, and compassion for the down-trodden; honest transactions to avoid disgracing one's family name
9   Show of strength and courage; defend one's family, land, and rights at a moment's notice
10 Respect for authority, patriarchy, and gender segregation; deference to the demands of the family/clan/tribal patriarch. Deference to authority (can't question authority)
11 Marriage within the extended family (endogamy)
12 Modesty in dress
13 Religious education, as specified within Islam, to take people from the darkness
14 Material wealth
15 In-group inclusiveness (sometimes associated with ethnic groups as an "in-group out-group dichotomy").

In contrast, the 10 core values of the United States were defined as follows:[12]

1   Equal opportunity
2   Achievement and success
3   Material comfort
4   Activity and work
5   Practicality and efficiency
6   Progress
7   Science
8   Democracy and free enterprise
9   Freedom
10 Group superiority.

Taken together, the American core values, which resonate with Alexis de Tocqueville observations of the American character during the first half of the nineteenth century, seem rather far apart from those of the Gulf. In the Gulf, the individual is submerged within the extended traditional group, obeying its norms and heritage and even marrying within it if possible. If one achieves success, it is also through the efforts of one's kindred, with whom the benefits are shared. In contrast, in the United States, the opportunity for achievement and success, defined as material rewards and money, clearly predominate. Ideally, one reaches his/her goals through individual efforts. In this ideational framework, one cannot blame society or government for the lack of personal success; in fact, in the period since the Reagan days on, the less government the better. Rather than mainly emphasizing personal achievement, the Gulf nationals stress the obligations to redistribute wealth from the community coffers for all to share.

From this brief comparison of core values, it becomes quite apparent that maximizing profit, called rational choice theory, is not as central as in the more market-driven societies of the West. In addition, the official religion of Islam also protects the believers from practices that may undermine adherence to time-honored social codes. There are some inherent censors of ideas and images in Gulf society so as to permit ideas and images approximately concordant with the core cultural values. While this inherent censorship has fared fairly well in the area of television and film, it has failed with the internet.

The oil and trading sectors have strengthened the state rather than reducing it to the vagaries of global business, which is a process of globalization elsewhere. Clearly the free market plays a much reduced role than in the G-7 countries, even though the Gulf states compare favorably in per capita income.

The ruler is ex officio the primary beneficiary of the oil revenues, which he re-allocates as benefits to nationals throughout his country. This redistribution of funds and key benefits thereby reinforces the traditional structure of the state and undermines opposition. Herb writes that "a ruling class which has a mechanism to regulate its own internal conflict (e.g. the lineage elders seeking consensus on choice of ruler) ... and which can attract at least some support within the society is extremely hard to overthrow."[13]

More generally, redistribution invariably characterizes economic circulation in societies with ranked kinship where goods of value or money are paid into a social fund administered by the chief office holder. Marshall Sahlins notes, "Chiefly, redistribution is a centralized, formal organization of kinship-rank reciprocities, an extensive social integration of dues and obligations of leadership ... A leader integrates the economic activity of a localized following: he acts as a shunting station for goods flowing reciprocally between his own and others ... The leader is the central recipient and bestower of favors. So centricity is built into the structure."[14]

In a redistributive economy of a kinship society, the monetary surplus is stored for safekeeping by the leading household. In the case of the Gulf, the ruler would be the sheikh, emir, or sultan as the apex of the kinship web. What motivates social interaction, thus, is not so much maximizing profit but keeping the structure of mutual relations and obligations intact so that revenues may be allocated. Anthropologists term the various sorts of allocations subsistence funds (for roads, bridges, water systems), social funds (for housing, food, health care, education, marriage dowries) and ceremonial funds (for museums, mosques, heritage sites). Again, each fund is provisioned through the central office holder on behalf of the community.

The polity is thus conceptualized as a single interrelated kin group to share and share alike in the corporate means of production. Schematically, the Gulf ruler redistributes the accumulated wealth to members usually based on various factors including seniority of descent. When the oil revenues started to trickle in around 1938, the sheikhs used the money to establish the first schools as part of the social fund. A more modern structure of the traditional state emerged during the 1960s in Abu Dhabi when Sheikh Zayed started to invest this financial bonanza in the social fund. This strategy was a precursor for developing a modern federal state of the UAE a few years later. As oil revenues came pouring in then, Sheikh Zayed used them to provide education and health care, all free of charge, plus electricity, water, and telephones at a very reduced rate to citizens. The civil service, which is the main industry that employs nationals, redistributes funds as entitlements of citizenship.[15]

With this organizational frame in mind, several questions arise that are addressed in this volume: (1) To what extent will the traditional Gulf society embrace the forces of a world market that, in an age of globalization, brings along an unhindered flow of ideas, capital, and people? (2) Will the Gulf states find advantages in forming a stronger economic bloc, which would be more culturally homogeneous than the European Union, to countervail foreign economic and political forces more on its own terms? (3) To what extent can effective union of the GCC proceed with a minimum of economic diversification, since many of the economies are based on oil and gas extraction? And what is currently being done to diversify the economies? (4) Will the current expressions of traditionalism ultimately unfold in, or reveal, an inevitable transition to a full-blown global lifestyle, since global capitalism is thought by some to more strongly determine the course of social form? (5) Will traditional cosmology eventually be replaced with a more individualistic focused one, like that found in many urban settings across the world? (6) Will the extended family and wider community continue to mitigate the forces of globalization and will the values of individualism, personal achievement and success, come to dominate? (7) Will the traditional system, based largely on kinship, or the system of non-Gulf Arab workers, transform into a merit based system more consistent with the exigencies of capitalism? (8) Will the remaining gender divide continue to be mitigated so as to eventually dissipate? And, (9) in response to such considerations as those in the third *Arab Human Development Report: Building a Knowledge Society of the United Nations*, will the states enhance the essential freedoms that strengthen the flow of idea creation within an informational economy, which will become more important as the oil/gas sector diminishes in Dubai, Bahrain, and Oman?

Traditional social structures

In this volume, 16 investigators from across the social and cultural sciences offer various explanatory approaches to enhance understanding of globalization in the Gulf. These contributing authors take two directions: (1) a micro-evolutionary view examines how local populations have melded the new wealth with their lifeways to create new social forms that more or less conform to the basic cosmology inherited from their forebears; (2) a macro approach in which features of Gulf society are compared to a commonly defined global pattern. Some distinguishing features of globalization worldwide are multinational corporations, deregulation of finance for direct foreign investment, liberalization of trade, widespread use of telecommunication technology, and labor flows. While the West has largely created and disseminated globalization, the host societies ultimately determine what should come in and what should not. This is not to say that unintended acculturations of the global and local do not occur. The local societies have built new media industries and universities, staffed largely by expatriate professionals, for creating and disseminating new images and symbols that channel Gulf culture to their populations. And the success of such media outlets as Al Jazeera and Al Arabiya has caused consternation in those Western governments who equate globalization with their penetration into local markets. Recently, the 22-nation Arab League has been developing a pilot program to connect only Arab speakers via the internet. The routing is done simply by adding Arabic characters in the suffix (e.g. rather than com. or org.), which will only require a computer with Arabic letters to get into the system.[16] At present, the coding for internet is controlled by a private corporation in California (i.e. the Internet Corporation for Assigned Names and Numbers); the internet was developed in 1968 by the US government.

While such institutions as the International Monetary Fund and the World Bank have played a major role in facilitating globalization in Asia and Latin America, they had experienced only modest influence in the Middle East. This is even more true in the Gulf, where official and unofficial monitors filter ideas, images, goods, and people coming in. Books and films are examined by customs officials for content that may offend cultural sensitivities. The trading elite, often closely associated with the royal houses, shapes the rules and regulations about how corporations may transact business. Certain sectors are granted exclusive privileges to certain items of business.

In a sense, this suggests a continuity of the traditional structure of privileges granted according to ranking within the wider collectivity. In comparison to the world at large, however, it is unusual to be able to deal with market capitalism strictly on local terms. The question naturally arises: Will Gulf based business ventures be able to compete with international or transnational companies? The Gulf entrepreneurs bring certain advantages into the competition: up-to-date physical infrastructures, no or little taxes and no costly encumbrances of long-term commitments to a foreign labor force. There are disadvantages too, for example an inherent informally stratified system, a yet insufficiently developed national work ethnic and by and large (and although this is progressively changing) a primary and secondary educational system that has vestiges of the rote learning from earlier days. There also exist Islamic banking and finance, which encode principles other than the profit motive.

Yet, there seems to be many locally attuned versions of global forms. Generally, the social structure in the Gulf seems to be, perhaps, the most impervious to change, vis-à-vis economics and ideas. Then, do new ideas precede lifestyle or economic changes? That is, if the primary group manages the resources and is reasonably successful, why change a proven way? On the other hand, have the local societies grown too large and diverse to effectively control undesirable ideas? Does successful capitalism require a broad based tolerance for cultural diversity?

The Gulf states are informally stratified, with nationals, who are safeguarded with significant financial entitlements, followed by workers and employees of various ethnicities ranked by job categories. Since the oil taps were first opened, expatriate workers have undertaken production. Nationals direct the day-to-day distribution of the oil wealth, while the expatriate workers ensure its production. In other parts of the world, the relations between labor and management have changed based on the vagaries of the market (e.g., who works where, job security, minimum health and living standards, the rights of citizenship), and privatization of public production and service has increasingly been subject to the dictates of supply and demand.[17] Moreover, the private sector has increasingly "subordinated the structures of representative democracy to the service of their own interests … Emancipation of capital from labor makes possible the emancipation of the state from legitimization … with a gradual erosion of democratic institutions."[18]

In the Gulf, corporations are often locally owned trading companies that import everything from luxury automobiles to cheap labor. With oil revenues, the merchant families readily became those that owned and managed trading companies of the past generation. Many families almost have monopolies on importing durable goods, and much of the trade is without taxation, which allows a further competitive edge in global marketing.

Among the business class, the basic social unit remains the extended family and its wider networks. The family may in fact shift in and out of a number of different economic enterprises and trading ventures. However, the extended family seems to remain the prime social unit. With economic diversification across a number of business ventures, the wider family can absorb the ups and downs of different businesses along with the international instabilities in the flow of goods and profits. Family self-reliance was not so far in the past that the complete dependence on the market for employment and for one's sense of identity and livelihood does not foster the inherent insecurities and ambivalences more characteristic of market fluctuations elsewhere.

Relatively cheap labor from Asia complements the ready supply of venture capital from oil revenues to provide two key factors of production. The basic social contract is two-tiered: mutually beneficial, informal entitlements for the nationals and tax-free and relatively high salaries for skilled guest workers. The expatriates typically reside for limited contracts. The usual labor relations evade long-term investment, and create conditions in which social relationships are fluid. In contrast to the pace of "just in time production," with its typical 60-hour workweek, a sense of less hurried and harried time seems to pervade social relationships of the national population segments.

A two- or three-tiered classification seems to cross cut many of the institutions (e.g. hospitals, schools), where the most expensive facilities are, by virtue of elevated cost, restricted to nationals and highly paid expatriate professionals. However, broadly speaking, the dictates of capital on the social contract as given in the following quote are not as acute as elsewhere in the world. "Flexible forms of management, relentless utilization of fixed capital, intensified performance of labor, strategic alliances, and inter-organizational linkages, all of which come down to shortening time per operation and speeding up turnover of resources ... what is called 'just in time labor'."[19]

Traditional familial structure remains one way of organizing institutions both big and small. Personnel are often recruited for having not only sufficient skills but for having a particular kinship status. Kinship patronage further cements social life into a fairly strong whole that allows for the persistence of values and customs over the latest fashions promoted by advertising. This again suggests substantive economics, in which some economic surplus must support the social and ceremonial funds for social value rather than for profit alone. Accordingly, the ruler transfers portions of the vast oil revenues to the governmental agencies, which in turn distribute funds in various networks to the population of nationals at large. The authority to allocate benefits conveys enormous power and explains why there is very little social conflict from within these societies.

However, it is interesting to note that the private sector is growing in strength vis-à-vis the public sector. And there is constant discussion about the value of privatization of public-sector industries.[20] Yet, all non-national owned companies must be at least sponsored by locals. In this sense, the "guest workers" are adopted by a national and some of the profits are received by them as a sponsorship fee. According to Zahlan, "Commercial laws protect nations from expatriate competition. Foreigners can only do business by having a partner who is a national; and no foreigner can own more than 49 percent of any company."[21]

Thus far, various strategies aimed at installing suitably trained locals into the positions of skilled expatriate labor have met with limited success. The GCC adopted a policy of raising "minimum wages for nationals to provide incentive to join the public sector and raise its cost of foreign recruitment" so that dependence on foreign workers may be reduced.[22]

Restructuring of institutions

The major transformative events in the recent history of the Gulf seem to have been the pumping of oil, which began first in Saudi Arabia and Kuwait, and dissolving the treaties in which Great Britain militarily protected the regional polities. The extraction of oil throughout the Gulf in the mid-1960s and independence around 1971 propelled the lightly populated Gulf states to global prominence, which coincided with a shift toward globalization elsewhere. Local independence was nested within the forces transforming European colonialism along with the restructuring of market relations.

The epochal changes were variously manifested within the Gulf states during the early 1970s. For example, in 1970 the present Sultan of Oman replaced his father, and within two years Oman began to open its heretofore closed borders to world interaction.[23] Bahrain gained its independence in 1971 and wrote its constitution in 1973, forming an elected national assembly. In 1971, Kuwait elected its first assembly. Qatar became independent in 1971.

The early 1970s showed a rapid crystallization of new approaches to conducting business in the market, in government, and in the social and cultural disciplines as well as the emergence of new technologies for connecting much of the world instantaneously into day-to-day or even moment-by-moment interactions. Computer chip technology proliferated and converged with the corporate shifts to transnationalism and downsizing. In the social sciences, these years also signify the appearance of a new cultural relativism called standpoint theory, the conceptualizing of history within an integrated "world system,"[24] the phenomenological philosophers,[25] the contextual sociologists,[26] and the hermeneutical anthropologists.[27] This pervasive cultural relativity reflected the refiguring of power asymmetries between the Western governments and their former colonies. Just a few years after the oil extraction began, the Bahrainis, Qataris, and Emiratis gained significantly in geopolitical leverage in the world arena. Therefore, the reference point or standpoint changed. The parts of the world system that were once controlled in colonial capitals came to be connected to the rest through economics alone. Direct political control was soon replaced by indirect economic control.

In the early 1970s, converging networks redefined how the nations of the world were connected. We cite several events to show how broad-based and pervasive were the forces that converged:

- Led by Saudi Arabia, OPEC challenged the core nations in an oil embargo in 1973.
- The core states were defeated or seriously challenged by rebellions in Vietnam 1974, and the civil wars in four Central American countries.
- The Pahlavi dynasty of Iran was deposed in an internal Islamic revolution.
- In the West, the hierarchically ordered knowledge of academia was deconstructed in the postmodern challenge.
- The American president was forced to resign or face impeachment (1973).
- The multinational corporations restructured following the recession of 1974–1980.[28]
- The proliferation of telecommunications technology allowed anyone with a personal computer to communicate inexpensively worldwide.
- Financing and investing democratized (i.e., mortgages and junk bonds became available to the small investors through mutual funds), which financed start-up companies bereft of "approval" ratings and bypassed the established financial institutions (e.g., commercial banks, insurance companies).[29]
- The generation socialized with television came into decision-making positions.
- The United States suspended the sales of gold so that the exchange rates of different currencies were fixed to the US dollar, which thereafter opened the door to considerable volatility and speculation in exchange rates.
- The new economy of informationalism began to emerge with capital conceptualized in ideas of advertising rather than as material standards (e.g., gold).
- Network society became more open-ended and less restrained by national borders.[30]

- Corporate organizations downsized followed by the downsizing of the Western governments (in the early 1980s).
- Revitalization or social empowerment movements proliferated (e.g., environmentalism, fundamentalism, feminism).

During those short years, the old world order quickly faded so that a new world order emerged by the end of the 1970s, providing ready access for the new mechanisms of globalization.

Globalization accelerated with "supply-side" capitalism during the early 1980s as production across the globe was restructured for cost-effectiveness. Capitalism out-competed the planned economies of the Soviet and other socialist or communist states. In *The End of History and the Last Man*, Fukuyama argues free market capitalism emerged victorious and spread throughout the world.[31] The value of capital skyrocketed, especially in the equities markets as less costly labor in Eastern Europe became readily available. Global society again restructured: (1) the regional economic blocs solidified (e.g., NAFTA, the European Union, and the Pacific Bloc);[32] (2) the G-7 focused on protecting access to world markets (along with the International Monetary Fund/World Bank of transnational corporations); (3) capital moved throughout the world without much restraint; and (4) after the 1991 Gulf War, the Gulf states separated from the pan-Arab solidarity to come closer to the United States.

In short, basic social relationships, ranging from those within the family household to relationships between countries, reconfigured in the late 1970s and early 1980s and again around 1990. Most fundamentally, capital increasingly connected people with each other. Perhaps the pull of the market eroded the state as the principal institution that organized people into collectivities. In this context, Great Britain realized that continuing its treaties in the Arabian Gulf was no longer sufficiently cost-effective and therefore ended a 150-year liaison with the Gulf states.

Traditional Gulf society

In the Gulf, traditional structure has effectively managed and integrated, where appropriate, the forces of globalization. Traditional Gulf leadership encountered and began dealing with the nascent forces of globalization in the early 1970s almost as a tidal wave – the oil boom, independence, federation, joining the Arab League and the oil embargo all happened within a span of just three years. In this short time, the small states went from highly localized concerns to confronting even the superpowers within the world arena. With the British withdrawal, a larger polity would be necessary for defense and for entry into the United Nations. The UN was seen as a forum in which the boundary disputes involving the regional polities with the giants in the area, especially Saudi Arabia and Iran, could be heard and resolved. To understand the fundamental traditional societal structure that directed these events, we briefly sketch the patterning that has characterized the Gulf for millennia, including the generation of globalization.

The anthropologist Peter Lienhardt, who conducted ethnographic investigations in Kuwait, Bahrain, and the Trucial coast during the late 1950s and early 1960s on the eve of the oil boom, remarked on the "striking number of repetitions of similar situations from time to time and from place to place, in which the ruling families have governed similar governments and similar state communities."[33] This traditional system dealt effectively with the enormous transformation of the economy and accommodated the influx of information from around the world. It continues to organize government and business corporations.

The Gulf society then and now comprises identified lineages that are well known throughout the Middle East and are especially definitive of cultures that have had a pastoralist way of life. Traditional lineages epitomize the adage "me and my brother against my cousin, and we three against the world." Patrilineality is the norm, where descent is traced through the father, grandfather, great-grandfather, etc., through a perceived ancestry to the original founder. Lineage members carry the patronymic *al* to designate descent from the apical or eponymous ancestor, who may have existed sufficiently back in time to be surrounded with legendary events. There is a spatial dimension to the lineage for the prefix *al* also signifies "place of" for the members of the lineage living together (patrilocality).

Based on degree of genealogical distance from the eponymous ancestor, different lineage segments will aggregate in larger units. Division and unification are inherent in the rules of forming larger social groups. First, at the most basic level, "when men marry more than one wife their sons are united in the father but divided in terms of their mothers."[34] In the literature, what is termed complementary opposition unifies: "those who are closer together in descent defend each other against those who are more distant."[35]

Degrees of common descent ideally determine the degrees of social binding and, thus, of obligations owed within kinship networks. Families who descend from a common ancestor tend to recognize greater mutual obligations than those more distantly related. Those who are more closely related also tend to live closer together and usually intermarry (endogamy). Traditionally, closer equates with stronger ties. In this regard, first cousin marriage is the closest degree of proximity allowed and is thus the most idealized. According to Lienhardt, "Marriage with a close agnate is preferred ... [especially if] any sort of kinship connection exists already."[36] Each of the rulers speaks at the roots for a bloc of closely tied families. In traditional societies, multiple wives increase the number of children per father. Marriage adds to the close bound lineage, forming a single economic and political unit. As Lienhardt observed, traditionally, to "sire many children strengthen[ed] the position of a [leader] vis-à-vis competitors within the wider family. Moreover, marriages of the daughters to leading members of the community establishes him in a special relationship, which may be useful to him in politics, and useful also to them."[37] In comparing the kinship structures among the dynastic states of the Gulf, Michael Herb, in his *All in the Family*, notes that "the rule of female endogamy ... establishes a very clear social distance between the ruling dynasty and other lineages. Other families may marry their daughters to men of the ruling dynasties, but their sons will never marry women of the ruling family." This rule "reinforces the separation between the ruling dynasties and other traditional elites," those ones who are allied through marriage.[38]

In a kingdom, the principles of adding successively more distant kindred to the polity headed by the patriarch simply extends the web of the community further and adds more power to the group, but it also adds more complex segments between the internal layers. With regard to the explanatory model, a segmentary state has been likened to a set of Russian nesting dolls by Hoyland, who notes "The smallest units, such as households, are segments of more inclusive units, such as lineages, the lineages in turn segments of larger groups (such as major lineages), and so on. More general issues are handled at higher levels."[39]

Durkheim contrasted such mechanical solidarity binding like segments together with the organic solidarity, which binds together economically differentiated sectors of society into unitary states.[40] However, since the lineages are essentially autonomous and can dissolve the political alliance, it is important for such polities to reach a threshold of mutual interdependence. Mechanical solidarity usually necessitates strong forces such as common religious values and strong leaders to maintain the unification of the structurally similar sectors. In contrast, within the more centralized, unitary, or nation states, power and authority permanently transcend the lineage alliance. In economy, the various regional parts generally produce goods that are distributed throughout the entire state, thereby creating a more economically and ideally interdependent polity.

The revenues from oil that first rolled into Saudi Arabia and Kuwait during the 1930s allowed the Saud dynasty to tighten its grip of centralized control and allowed Kuwait to experiment with a partial parliamentary government. Specifically, at that initial stage of oil benefits, would a parliamentary system adapted from the British or would an indigenous lineage state bind the often competing tribal groups into a larger polity? In the case of the Saudis, they quickly came to "treat their country as their own private property."[41] And the Saudis divvied out the highest state offices to ranking members of the lineage. In contrast, the Kuwaitis experimented with a blend of democracy with a hereditary leader. However, in 1938, the Al Sabah family emir "closed down a legislature set up by Kuwait's merchant notables."[42] The unitary state apparatus was disbanded and the various ministries, offices, and departments were divided among the Al Sabah lineage members – which is the quintessence of a segmentary state.

While traditional family ties build the political body, kinship ties also comprise the basis for decision making. Traditionally, eligibility for succession to a position of authority, either within an extended family or within a kingdom at the other end of the continuum, may be by a brother or by a son or a nephew. Today in the Gulf, the heir designate will carry the title of crown prince. However, within the pool of eligible males of the lineage inner family circle, one member is to be seen as having the best capabilities of making decisions in the interests of the wider community or to be accountable within the primary group at the apex. Approval to assume the rulership as a sheikh or an emir is thus decided by cadre of senior males, who give their consent (*bay'a*).[43] Remember, traditional lineage endogamy tends to increase rapprochement and inherent familial bonds. And the younger lineage males maintain strict decorum in deference to their seniors.

Opportunities to head ministries serve as safety valves in absorbing competition among talented and ambitious siblings and cousins. In the Bedouin past, mobility was inherent in the traditional economies of pastoral activities or fishing and trading in the Gulf. In the desert, the full tribe often relocated and relationships were simply reassembled in new localities. Such mobility is rare since the creation of elaborate physical infrastructures in each city.

Traditionally, lineage fissioning, migration, and fusing of the community according to degrees of genealogical descent are borne out in the histories of the Gulf states. However, these same patterns of lineage fissioning and migration occurred at the threshold of historic cities about two thousand years ago. The Bani Yas maintain oral traditions about how their ancestors departed Yemen when the Marib dam broke, and after an arduous migration they settled around the Liwa Oasis on the edge of the empty quarter (*Rub al-Khali*).[44] Half a millennium ago, they spent half of the year in Liwa and the other on the coast of Abu Dhabi, as observed by Portuguese and Dutch in the 1600s. Other kindred groups migrated from Yemen to Qatar and Bahrain. The latter were known as the Tanukh tribal confederation. Historical references also suggest segmentary lineages, such as *'ashîra*, the term for major lineage, lineage (*âl*), which has been discussed above, and nomad (*a'râb*). Importantly, their mutual ancestry provided a basis for occasional social exchange and political cooperation.[45]

There is evidence that communities in Ras Al Khaimah, UAE, have been in place for two thousand years. Following an age-old pattern, the Al Qassimis' major lineage settled in Sharjah to form a separate but closely allied emirate with separate territory.[46] The present rulers of Sharjah and Ras Al Khaimah are fourth cousins, and their common ancestor was Sultan bin Saqr Al Qassimi (1803–1866). Therefore, we see the alignment of principal lineages in geographically contiguous territories.[47]

Building a traditionally structured confederation/federation

Age-old competition reduced with the avalanche of changes from globalization swirling around these tribal groups – namely, oil extraction and the break-up of the British empire. Traditional rivalries dating back two centuries were glossed over for the mutual advantages of federating in 1971. Since then, lifestyles within the rapidly constructed modern cities soon rendered the traditional mobility patterns all but obsolete. In fact, the reverse seems more common from the 1970s on: the overwhelming percentage of Gulf nationals remain closely tethered to home cities, with the abundance of material benefits, except for vacation travel.

In traditional states like those prior to the oil boom, one lineage came to control the wider kinship alliances and established a ruling dynasty. Such lineage-based organization meshed with an ideology of egalitarianism, in which each kin group considered itself of approximate coeval status to the other groups, maintained its own base of production (autarky), and its own patriarchal leadership. As in generations past, each of the emirates had its own economy centered on its separate estuaries along the Gulf (called *khor* in Arabic and creek in English). These seaside communities closely replicated one another, for each maintained its own facilities to ensure independence. Today, each of the seven emirates still exhibits some of the aspects of the autarky-oriented replication. For example, each emirate maintains an international airport and at least one major institution of higher education.

Unlike contemporaneous political movements in Africa, Southeast Asia, and Latin America, the Gulf Arabs did not gradually evolve to a point of asserting independence. However, in the contexts of the anti-colonialist sentiments of the times, especially those evoked from the wars in Southeast Asia, the newly elected British Labour government announced in 1968 that it intended to withdraw all British presence east of the Suez Canal. At that time, the Western financial markets were particularly unstable and the cost of overseas "protectorates" was deemed expendable. Even after the Tories regained power in 1970, the Gulf states proceeded toward full independence, which was realized for Bahrain, Qatar, and the UAE in 1971. The other Gulf states were affected in other structural ways by the changing political economic milieu of the early 1970s.

The confederation of the emirates along the Gulf coast seemed a good solution to fill the void from the British departure. The population of the emerging UAE was no more than about 150,000 persons at independence. For any nascent state, threats on emerging stability from larger peer polities nearby exist. However, when such emerging states are blessed with bountiful oil reserves, the threats considerably magnify, and the benefits of unity become all the more obvious. In any event, it is important to note that the very model of segmentary lineage emphasizes and enhances closer and stronger unity proportional to the perceived threat. By definition, traditional lineages unite through complementary opposition to form larger and substantial segments (structural relativity). This union most often provides sufficient force to accomplish a desired goal.

Sheikh Zayed of Abu Dhabi (1918–2004) was the architect for creating the UAE federation in 1971, when only two persons had university degrees in the new country. He was a moderate interlocutor who continually deployed generosity to pull together the emirates in the UAE development schemes. There were overwhelming benefits for all in retaining traditional identity, customs, and authority within a federal alliance. Leadership was built across lines of kinship groupings through the institutionalized distribution of economic benefits, which forged reciprocal obligations necessary to pursue new directions of economic development. In a sense, what was created was the best available worldwide in technological infrastructure. However, this did not come in a tidal wave that would have overwhelmed established customs. As the nation's first president, Sheikh Zayed helped promote the development of informationalism and consumerism.

To return to the formative events of the UAE, remnants of old rivalries had to be overcome to unify through complementary opposition in 1971 to build a common defense. Nevertheless, the rulers of the Trucial States knew their counterparts sufficiently well and had ample affinities to consider a beneficial union. Six emirates officially federated in 1971 in an implementation of the motto of "strength in unity." Fujairah joined formally in 1973 as the seventh and final emirate. Each emirate is represented in the national assembly, and the ruler of each emirate has a vote in the Supreme Council, which structurally replicates the council of the senior males of a familial lineage. The Supreme Council, confirms the President, which, has by tradition, been the ruler of Abu Dhabi. The national assembly consists of 40 members: Abu Dhabi and Dubai, in segmentary symmetry, have eight members each; Sharjah and Ras Al Khaimah have six; and each of the three smaller emirates have four.[48] The former Trucial Scouts became the federal military to secure and defend the national boundaries. In essence, this larger traditionally structured state, on a more replicated and inclusive level, essentially retains the same organizational scheme of each of the former Trucial States.

The personal circumstances that united the various states were recalled by the advisor to Sheikh Zayed, Ruler of Abu Dhabi at the time, who initiated and carried out the negotiations. Sheikh Zayed learned of the intended British withdrawal by listening to a broadcast on BBC's Arabic service.[49] Sheikh Zayed approached his counterpart in Dubai, Sheikh Rashid Al Maktoum, to form a federation that was actually more of a confederation initially. They united through complementary opposition within the old rubric of the Bani Yas and the other emirates were invited to join. Each of the emirates could maintain its sovereignty and identity: it was a win-for-all proposition backed up by the oil revenues essentially located in Abu Dhabi.

Sheikh Zayed's advisor further recalled that the daily *majlis* conducted by Zayed was where the decisions of the emirate were made in dialogue with the heads of each of the city's sectors.[50] This model was simply extended to the federation so that the Supreme Council (*Majlis*) involved the sheikhs of the seven emirates – an outgrowth of the former Trucial Council. In this sense, federation for common defense and other benefits followed traditional organizational principles of bringing into alliance further removed blocs or segments. Endowed with the largest oil deposits (fourth largest in the world), Abu Dhabi also has the largest territory and population of the emirates, and seniority within the federal government. Thus, the early federation was more one of fictive aggregating of "equal" and autonomous emirates. At the time of independence, Abu Dhabi accrued ten times the oil revenues of Dubai, and Umm al Quwain was about one-fifteenth the size of Dubai and Abu Dhabi in population.[51] The oil revenues from Abu Dhabi financed a significant part of the government expenditures, especially those in armaments and in education. At that time, the charter members of the UAE modelled their quite forward-looking constitution on that of Bahrain. However, both Bahrain and Qatar opted for greater autonomy as independent states; both were more modernized than the states of the Trucial coast.[52]

The federal union gained strength slowly but surely until about the 1990s. By this time, a generation of Emiratis had had ample time to be raised as nationals and thought of themselves as citizens of the UAE. We may consider that the

UAE, along with Kuwait and probably Bahrain, have recently shifted to an organic federal type of political and economic amalgamation. Trust has overcome the old rivalries between territorially and productively separate emirates.

Another potentially volatile situation was the rise to power of the Baathists in neighboring Iraq, who opposed kingdoms. After building a modern infrastructure in Iraq, Saddam Hussein initiated a draining eight-year war with Iran, which was shortly followed by renewed claims to Kuwait. He asserted the Nasserist mantle to lead the Arab nation, which he stated would include the entire Gulf region.[53] The UAE was one of the principal forces that rallied the other Arab states into a coalition to restore Kuwaiti sovereignty.[54] The Gulf Arab countries contributed to financing the coalition efforts. Further American incursions into Iraq (2003) were part of a policy to stabilize the wider region, to secure the world's second largest reserves, and to bring Iraq into the global market. In this strategy, the neighboring states were and are pressed by the West to undertake liberal democratic reform.

The passing of Sheikh Zayed, the architect in forming and pushing forward the UAE, in November 2004 provided a key juncture at which the functions of a federal government were further centralized over any of the usual rivalries that may be inherent in a traditional familial structure. On the eve of Sheikh Zayed's death, the newspaper headlines proclaimed that "Zayed Reshuffles Cabinet" by federal decree.[55] Of the 21 positions, 10 went to leading members of the Nahyan (Abu Dhabi) and Maktoum (Dubai) families, 2 to members of the Al Qassimi family of Sharjah, 1 to the Al Nuaimi family of Ajman and 8 to ministers of non-royal patrilineages.[56] Sheikh Zayed's eldest son, Sheikh Khalifa, became the President, and his second-born son, Sheikh Sultan, became Deputy Prime Minister. Other main lineage members became the ministers of Foreign Affairs, the Interior, Presidential Affairs, Information and Culture, Education, and Public Works. The three sons of Sheikh Rashid Al Maktoum were confirmed as the Prime Minister (Sheikh Maktoum), Minister of Finance and Industry (Sheikh Hamdan), and Minister of Defense (Sheikh Mohammed). Significantly, the first woman was named to a ministerial position in the UAE: Sheikha Lubna Al Qassimi became the Minister of Economy and Planning. The ministries seem to divide between those of strategic value (foreign relations, defense, and oil, which might be termed ministries of sovereignty, *wizarat al-siyada*), which are headed by individuals in their 50s to early 60s, and those more focused on internal development, which could be headed by ministers as young as in their 30s. Of the 13 members of ruling families, 6 are from the metropolis of Dubai-Sharjah-Ajman, and 7 are from Abu Dhabi. This North–South balance seems to be an updated version of the norm of complementary opposition, basic to segmentary lineage organization.

It seems as though the proportions and strategic ministries follow the same divisions as in the founding arrangements of the UAE. This brief profiling would suggest that the traditional structure of the federal government is ensconced as a kinship-apportioning formula that has proven effective in channeling the uninterrupted growth of the country from the early days into globalization and in dealing with such international crises as wars and fluctuating oil prices. Additionally, an increased economic interdependency among the emirates further guarantees the unity of the federation. It would seem increasingly unlikely that the federation would fragment.

Building a pan-Gulf confederation for future economic diversification

As commercial ventures gain in importance in upcoming years, will there be significant incentive to more closely confederate a larger polity of the six GCC countries? As we have seen, the traditional lineage principles, inherent in society from one end of the Gulf to another, were also used to forge seven separate emirates into the UAE as the most economically viable Gulf state to date on a per capita basis. Accordingly, would it be advantageous to extend the confederation model to weld together a stronger Gulf Cooperation Council? If so, to follow the same principles, the small Gulf coast states could confederate to form one bloc, with the GCC constituting a traditionally premised organizational counterpart to NAFTA, the EU, and the Asian bloc.

Yet, amalgamating the six GCC states into a supra bloc following traditional organizing principles has clearly reached a new threshold and is creating its own developmental trajectory. Heretofore, arrangements between the kinship-based polities were negotiated in councils (cf. *majalis*) in fairly strict confidentiality, so as to preserve the honor and dignity of the various participants. The model of a group of elders discussing and debating what is in the best interests of their individual constituents to countrymen as well as what can be worked out to be in the collective interests of the wider bloc of polities was illustrated when the members of the ruling families of the seven emirates reached an agreement on succession after the passing of Sheikh Zayad.

With the custom of essentially private deliberations in mind, it is relevant to note that Saudi Arabia recently and publicly aired its dissatisfaction with Bahrain over signing a free trade agreement with the US. The Saudis were said to be sending "a strong signal that the old style of hiding inter-GCC problems is being replaced by a newly emerged way of open discussions and criticisms." "News of the controversy over Saudi objections to unilateral agreements . . . would not have been [publicly voiced] a 'few years ago'."[57]

Perhaps wary of the potential of such a power bloc controlling some very strategic oil reserves, the United States has repeatedly refused to negotiate with the GCC as a trade bloc but has attempted to reward the most economically liberal countries with special perquisites. True enough, with a sizeable account surplus of at least $150 billion during the fiscal year 2005, the GCC is a very formidable economic power. This was borne out when a number of Gulf state financiers decided to invest their oil generated capital within the projects of the sister countries rather than in Western financial markets, which had been their custom. To illustrate, the fiscal year 2005 saw an eight-fold increase in the investment of oil revenues within the GCC over the previous five years.[58] The local investment strategy thus sent reverberations throughout the Western financial markets.

Nevertheless, Western powers have also succeeded in forging treaties directly with single Gulf states, as opposed to dealing with them collectively. For example, while the US has asked the UAE "to liberalize commodities trade and open the banking and insurance sectors (controlled by Emiratis), the UAE has sought US access by national investors."[59] Yet, after granting its allies Jordan, Morocco and Bahrain free-trade status, the US has negotiated with the UAE to join this select group. The only stipulation from the US side would be that the labor laws should comply with standards set by the International labor Organization. The US Trade Representative further noted that the legal frameworks of both countries have to be sufficiently "transparent and offering equal treatment for companies and investors" from the respective countries to form workable business partnerships, so as "to ensure that no hidden rules favor some companies over others."[60] Again, the relative giant in the GCC, Saudi Arabia, has taken particular exception to first Bahrain and now the UAE in breaking ranks with their GCC brothers in forging unilateral links outside of the region.[61]

To understand how the traditionally grounded society of the Gulf is dealing with the processes of globalization we next tie together some salient points from the fourteen chapters to follow to present a model of scaled globalization within the Gulf countries. We need to bear in mind all that is traditional and well anchored in these new Gulf cityscapes: the trading orientation, segmentary lineages, redistributive economies, and religious values. It is the primacy of the indigenous traditionalism that renders the Gulf context somewhat unique in attempting comparisons from one region to another to measure manifestations of globalization. Each of the authors ascertains what is new as a result of globalization in describing and explaining this unique cultural blending in the Arabian Gulf.

Section 2: scales of globalism to localism

This second part of our introductory chapter outlines how Gulf society interfaces with globalization on a continuum of scales from global to local. Yet, in considering the distinctiveness of the Gulf within the wider Middle East and from the rest of the non-Muslim world in general, the question is implicit in the chapters to follow: How does the present day Gulf society combine its traditionalism in lineage organization and religious orthodoxy with global practices?

So far in this volume, we have discussed the Gulf from the local view outward, to delineate degrees of articulation between the Gulf with various nodes within the world at large. As we have seen, Gulf norms only recently transformed from traditional structures to synthesize a unique regional expression of globalism. In the remainder of the chapter, therefore, we reverse directions and assess how the findings in the fourteen chapters to follow relate to a scalar path going from the most general expressions of globalization and then sharpening our focus ever inward as we proceed to manifestations of nationalization, regionalization and finally localization. We proceed from the general to the specific and from the global to the local. Accordingly, Part II of the volume deals with the history and dynamics of globalization as a inclusive phenomenon integrating much of the world into a single arena of social, economic and political interaction; Part III focuses on the politics of identity and globalization within the Middle East, and Part IV, comprises chapters that deal specifically with case studies of globalization in the Gulf, and address dimensions of economics, expatriate workers, the Gulf city as an urban type with its own characteristics and the heritage industry, to construct a sense of nationalism in these newly formed countries – nationalism that unites heretofore separate tribal groups into asserting allegience to a larger political entity, the state.

Thus, the Gulf area may be viewed from distinctive levels of scale, with each unit serving to organize peoples at global, national, regional and local levels.[62] In this scheme, a relationality organizes groups of people into successively larger entities, each with its own set of identity symbols, much like Russian dolls contained within successively larger versions of the same figure. But no single level dominates, like that of the national statehood or a sense of tribal identity today. Each of the levels of organization articulate separately with globalization forces. Moreover, to reiterate, the nested units along a scalar path of localism to globalism recall the nested units of traditional lineage organization of the Gulf Arabs, running from the patrilineage itself (*banu*) to the neighborhood (*freij*) with two coupled lineages, to those within a moiety or half of a community to the entire community as an emirate to the moietal grouping of emirates to the pan-regional confederacy.[63] Each level from localism to globalism thus fosters both competition and cooperation like the complementary oppositon inherent in segmentary lineage organization. In organizational comparisons, both globalism and tribalism arise to "organize coherence" at different nested levels within larger crisscrossing networks. To illustrate, we posed the question in the preceding section as to whether the Gulf Cooperation Council will be sufficiently adpative as to confer sufficient advantages on the six member states in its primary function to compete with other pan-national trading blocs, such as the EU or NAFTA.

Gulf society therefore is a multilayered and dynamic system in which its various sectors were and are differently impacted from the global-to-local interaction. As such, globalization relates to separate dimensions of a complex and multi-faceted set of processes in an already variegated cultural tapestry with a majority of foreign workers in half of the Gulf states. Lastly, we note that change in the Gulf has been extremely fast paced while other aspects of social life have remained highly conservative. Taken as a comparative case of regional social evolution, the Gulf did not gradually develop new patterns like those that evolved in the industrial West during one or two centuries. For example, a media blitz promoting a global lifestyle and foreign goods permeated most sectors of Gulf society simultaneously. This opening of the flood gates of globalization there contrasted with the more piecemeal evolution of society in the West. Consequently, the region presents a test case by itself in which to identify the processes of globalization within the different social segments in local, regional, national and pan-Gulf contexts, and then to offer explanation for the patterns.

Part II Globalization: concepts, history dynamics, and consequences, c.1970–2000

As much as anything, globalism refers to how various populations intersect with internationalization along a scaled continuum – running from the macro or global on one end through several intermediate levels to the micro level or local on the other end; each level, such as the regional or national, has its own regulatory mechanisms and symbols for organizing people. Globalization is also an internationalization of national policy to draw on foreign capital and goods, as well as to contribute to the international market. As we have seen, globalism also defines capital flows, images, and products which often emanate in plant or in financing in some of the world's financial centers and are distributed outward throughout the world according to the potential for making the most profits. In this regard, transnational firms seek the most efficient production and marketing throughout the world.

While many of the characteristics that have come to be associated with globalism were evident a century ago, as argued by Roger Owen in Chapter 3, "Globalism at the beginnings of the twentieth and twenty-first centuries," many of the contributing authors herein concur that the forces of globalism converged in the third quarter of the twentieth century to begin to render a new set of relationships between peoples across national boundaries and within national boundaries along a scaled continuum. New idea systems and cosmologies have also rapidly spread through the world, aided by mass media, as a common ground in which to forge the international relationships and networks for doing business. This speaks to global connectivity.

Why would nationally sovereign states with constitutions and governments premised on doing what was best for their citizens permit increasing foreign investment within their national boundaries and more direct control of the labor force? In the early 1970s, some major structural relationships within capitalism, colonialism and modernism faltered, and new, more cost-effective, ways of conducting business were taking root by the early 1980s. What was heretofore the unchallengable truths of social contracts between government and citizens within national statehood, abruptly and cataclysmically transformed, under the guiding principles of trade liberalization and the privatization of basic public services which created a capital-friendly setting meant to attract direct foreign investment. In bold terms, for one function, the national governments were relegated to control labor in the service of capital.

Many institutionalized patterns within the national statehood were quickly recast into more flexible ones, along with the emergence of new models, approaches and even possible paradigms throughout the 1970s. Such simultaneity suggests that some seminal theorists were already reconceptualizing the basic inconsistencies of the emerging social realities with the old explanations of faltering academic models. The major social readjustments continued through the 1970s, when the West experienced double-digit unemployment, stagflation, and strong monetarist policies. By the end of the 1970s, a crisis required more of a fundamental reorganization along new principles of monetarism than attempts to simply patch the old Keynesian relationships between the public and private sectors. During the height of the economic malaise of the 1970s, the prime rate of interest for lending capital had twice peaked above 20 percent and inflation had reached as high as 13 percent.

In the early 1980s, a new set of economic and political principles took hold, largely freeing capital to find the most productive ratios, and some industry relocated to inexpensive labor markets throughout the world. This convergence crystallized a coherent system of free market, deregulation of labor policy, fiscal constraint at home, and the opening of national populations to the imagery and symbolism broadcast from abroad. In succinct terms, new communication and transport technologies, international investment, increased flow of international labor and the relaxing of national protection codes have increasingly destabilized the traditional forms of social organization in the industrialized countries and in what were former colonies.

This section of our volume examines some of the salient dimensions of globalism in which the reader is invited to draw inferences about how they are manifest in the Arabian Gulf area. In Chapter 2 Steve Smith examines new considerations on how security might better safeguard the purveyors of capital, especially as internationally operating terrorist groups target them within a non-convential war against world capitalism, its agents and its ideas. In Chapter 3, Roger Owen argues for antecedents of globalism in the Middle East and South Asia when the British intensified commercial activities there during the late nineteenth century. In Chapter 4, Tim Niblock shows the underlying economic factors in globalization of a single world market. A single world market quickly forged together the transnational production and distribution of products, labor, and ideas. The subsequent deregulation of tariffs, privatization of state-controlled industries, and monetarist economic policies and basic institutional restructuring quickly moved mechanisms of the global system into place in the more metropolitan areas of the world. Finally, in Chapter 5, Ismail Sirageldin deduces the social consequences of globalization, especially as it is linked to political decision-making and its impact on the communitarian idea systems of the Middle East.

To examine more closely the issues of international security in the wake of the September 11 attack on the World Trade Towers as symbols of global capitalism, Steve Smith in "The concept of security in a globalizing world," notes that as the border-keeping function of the state declines, security should be designed to safeguard the non-national residents and capital flows. He visualizes how international and intranational security might be adapted to transnational counter-state forces, such as the networks of terrorism and smuggling. International police will increasingly cooperate in fairly permanent long-term military operations. Given the heavy reliance on tourism within the small Gulf states, acts of terrorism would severely diminish that sector of the economy.

Political groups like Al-Qaeda may use the image-making perfected by the transnational corporations to create their message of overreaction or oppression by the US. For example, the destruction of the World Trade Center Towers may be perceived as a symbol of the hoped-for demise of economic globalism as much as it may be perceived as a blow to the heretofore invincible US; the image of the collapsing towers was graphically etched into the public consciousness across the world and the value of capital was diminished in the aftermath. In a single world market, terrorism undermines investor confidence in international ventures, and thus foreshortens the potentials for future growth and expansion of capital. A major downturn in one of the financial centers could seriously damage the global market, and a further downward spiral in the value of capital could reduce airline travel and tourism, and even the flow of labor from one country to another. The value of capital necessitates investor confidence in future profits, which in turn requires political stability and fairly permeable institutions to accommodate the inflow of capital. Disruptions in oil, or even tourism, the world's largest industry, would seriously impact the wider economy. In short, the intermeshing of the world's productivity and its labor flows could be rolled back by terrorist groups to the once clearly demarcated national and religious boundaries.

The attack on the towers in turn spawned new political doctrines in the West and reactionary policies, notably the Patriot Act, which galvanized world opinion.

Both the Bush and Putin doctrines called for retaliation against the source of terrorism anywhere. Such policy bespeaks more a transnational rooting out of covert networks that spread across a number of states. However, the Patriot Act also appeared to some as an attempt to accentuate the basic American value of isolationism along with making the US an impenetrable fortress. The number of individuals on the so-called "No-Fly-List" has increased one thousand fold since September 11. American installations, particularly embassies and governmental missions, have recently been surrounded by concrete barricades and barbed wire to protect them from trucks bearing explosives.

The increased unilateralism of the United States appears, for a number of commentators, to undermine the trend toward an international civil society for a single world economy.[64] Smith emphasizes the disproportionately large military expenditures of the United States, which rose 14 percent in the year following the September 11 attacks alone. One state "dictating" policy to others is clearly counterproductive to building a wider civil order. To put the degree of this unilaterality in some comparative relief, we need to remember that the military budget of the US is greater than those of the next highest eight countries combined. The sheer size of the military expenditure alone renders the US the world's guarantor of the flow of capital. This amounts to an indirect subsidy from the US taxpayers to the transnational corporations, which generate their profits in the world market. Appropriate justification for the military expenditures would have to be factored into the margins of benefits versus the costs of the military in maintaining the global market. The state provides the maintenance and the private sector reaps the benefits.

Without income taxes and other forms of close scrutiny of business or finance, many of the Arab states once lacked the means to trace money transfers. Throughout the world, such transfers may be routed through a number of financial institutions in quiet succession, so that the money becomes "laundered."

Concerns have been raised regarding the opportunities the absence of taxation and other forms of scrutiny create for a number of states to develop a niche in laundering money, which may be used in counter-state activities such as terrorism.[65] Since the mid-1970s, Bahrain has continued as the only state in the Gulf where it is possible to establish an "offshore bank" devoid of governmental regulation.

While such porosity defines globalism, various states have chartered alliances to thwart the secretive flows of money across state borders. In 2003, the IMF and the World Bank created guidelines to regulate the *hawala* or informal funds transfer (put at $90 billion worldwide). Since the Abu Dhabi Declaration on *Hawala* in 2002, more than 100 *hawaladhars* have been put under regulatory control in the UAE. This procedure attempts to generate greater visibility, accountability, and regulation for outgoing transfers, incoming transfers, and "suspicious" transfers. The Jabal Ali "free trade zone" (i.e., offshore) in Dubai lists 3,860 firms already registered. With the new regulations, only about half (600) of the applicants were accepted in 2004.[66] Thus, the IMF and the World Bank has succeeded in forging a beachhead on this Arab Gold Coast.[67]

In Chapter 4, Tim Niblock surmises that the oneness of the international market is an overriding feature of globalism. In order to lift the world economy out of recession, Reagan and Thatcher put into practice the monetarism advocated by Milton Friedman, which set in motion a number of the new policy features that have come to define globalization.[68]

In putting on the table for wider discussion the negative aspects of economic globalism, Sirageldin (Chapter 5) notes that monetaristic policies undermine some basic-held values of Islamic society. In his thinking, people become mere factors of production and may be discarded by accountant-sensitive managers to maintain or enhance profits. Sirageldin further points out that globalization reduces cultural diversity and thus is disadvantageous to the world at large. This is analogous to the point raised by environmentalists that a reduction in diversity results from the wider forces of globalism. As the biological analogy implies, there must be a sizeable enough segment of society to practice creative cultural diversity; that is, a sufficiently large group (like a gene pool) is necessary so that ways of life may continue and adapt. Ultimately, cultural diversity would be able to provide different viewpoints rather than continually reducing diversity into a cultural homogeneity of consumerism so that most people within a society receive the same messages on a daily basis from the mass media.

Both Sirageldin and Niblock also suggest ways to mitigate the more destructive forces of globalism. The formation of such multi-state economic blocs as the GCC and the EU will provide some regional counterweights to the pressures of immediate profitability from lending institutions. They suggest a number of more humanitarian trade preferences based on capabilities equality, global taxation of the multinational corporations, grassroots advocacy policies fostering "buy local," and empowering international regulatory agencies. Sheltering and promoting the local would, of course, appeal to the communitarian social and religious life in the Gulf, as would redistributing some wealth to the less advantaged.

Part III Globalization, politics, and identity in the Arab world

During the past millennium and a half, the Arab world was welded together in a strong sense of inclusiveness by language, identity within the kinship group and a fairly powerful and homogeneous cosmology. When agents of the West began to broach this fairly sequestered part of the world during the nineteenth century, a genre of images in painting and in literature, termed orientalism, was spawned.[69] Much of the Middle East was under foreign protection prior to the independence movements of the twentieth cenutry. The Ottoman Turks held sway through World War I in much of the area north of Egypt. The successive European hegemons of Portugal, the Netherlands, France briefly, and Great Britain competed for trading networks within the Gulf during two centuries, as detailed in *Power Struggles and Trade in the Gulf, 1620–1820*, by Sultan Bin Mohammed Al Qassimi (1999). What were to become the Gulf states stood apart when under British protection for more than a century after that. The Gulf societies were fragmented into often competing tribal units than were the more metropolitan Levant, Egypt, and Mesopotamia (what was to become Iraq).

Since the 1990s, globalization has created sizeable rifts into what was considered a pan-Arab supra-nationalism. The penetration of global ideas, values and businesses has catalyzed anti-global political action groups as well as greater articulation and development. Thus, on one hand, there seems to be some broad bases of sympathy for the militant organizations which resist the forces of globalism with force of arms in an ever-escalating cultural war, while on the other there is also great receptivity to the material benefits of globalism.

Since globalization is relatively recent, there are also notable generational differences between those who were raised on television with its imagery from across the world and those who were raised more in the home honored traditions of the past. A major fault line also appeared around 1990, which laid to rest the Nasserist-spawned pan-Arabism, which broadly dichotomized states with oil into one group who favored safeguarding their economic bonanza tied to the world market, and those countries without oil who had become the labor providers into another group. The six Gulf monarchies plus that of Jordan became especially supportive of globalization stimulating political and economic initiatives, in contrast to states on the Gulf where the monarchies had been overthrown by populist sentiments (e.g. Iraq and Iran).

This reversed the age-old hierarchy between the more urbane Egypt and the Levant, with their ancient centers of learning in Cairo, Damascus, and Beirut, and the states of the Gulf, with recently settled pastoralists or sea-traders. An underlying egalitarisnism inherent in Muslim thinking was also confronted with the monetarist and pro-capital logic inherent in globalism. In one sense, the Gulf Arabs were at such an inchoate level of their development at the advent of globalization that they were able to bypass many of the entrenched non-growth policies embedded in the older states farther west in the Arab world, who were more embued with the thinking that came to be identified with Nasserism.

In the first two decades of globalism, roughly from 1970 to about 1990, the non-Gulf Arab countries provided a bulk of the educated and skilled labor (e.g. in education, medicine, engineering etc.) to build the infrastructures of the Gulf. After this date, which also marks the watershed of the Western-initiated alliance of Western and Gulf forces to liberate Kuwait, the pan-Arabism began to decline somewhat. And the GCC has increasingly shown at least guarded receptivity of Western initiatives, along with the monarchy of Jordan, geared to strengthen participation in the world market (and to more closely ally with the G-7 countries).

Thus, the Gulf states have entered globalization perhaps more on their own terms than other parts of the Middle East and North Africa, since they controlled so much of the world's petroleum reserves and had ready supplies of capital to purchase what was necessary or desirable.

It is also important to keep in mind that Gulf society retains in many respects its traditional, kinship organized social life, albeit slightly metamorphosed, as bedrock in a sea of tumultuous change from tribal to global in a generation or less. How and what changes transpired for this fairly unique metamorphosis obviously is a complex question in which actors at the government level through the family level evaluate, accept, reject, or modify a wide spectrum of possible behavior-changing ideas, technologies and people.

Within this context, and especially due to the oil bonanza, the Gulf states came to forge new relationships with one another based on aspects of the shared Arab identity and from ancient Arabian social norms of patrilineal lineages that allied into small polities and occasionally into wider confederacies. The alliance of the seven emirates in the UAE provides insight into the process and affords a case in point of the social changes wrought by globalization. Michael Hudson, in Chapter 8, argues that Dubai is the global center point of the Middle East. True enough, Dubai has so embraced globalism that it and its adjoining emirates of Sharjah and Ajman together constitute the closest the Middle East has to a global metropole. It has so embraced the logic underpinning the information age that the Northern Emirates has been rapidly transforming into an idea-generating-center for the Middle East; ideas are thus formulated for presentation throughout the region.

This strategic growth pole in world capitalism has had something of a multiplier effect on areas surrounding the UAE including Qatar and Oman, whose capitals are a short half hour flight from Dubai. In particular, the two emiral states of Qatar and Bahrain are increasingly forming a nucleus with the United Arab Emirates. In this regard, new motor-car causeways have recently been announced to connect Abu Dhabi in the UAE with Doha in Qatar, which will reduce driving to one-third of the present time, and between Qatar and Bahrain.[70] Dubai's success has increasingly galvanized the Arab world. In contrast, the traditional cultural capitals outside of the Gulf remain emersed in the age-old cultural matrix that does not particularly encourage entrepreneurs and idea producers to move into new areas of creativity.

Elsewhere in the Middle East, the forces of globalism have disrupted the balanced factionalism within the endless cycles of competition framed by the egalitarian championing idea systems. To illustrate, attempted change of the traditional authoritarian governments in Afghanistan, Yemen, and Iraq, have accentuated the re-emergence of ethnic and sectarian strife that lay just below the surface. Charismatic and authoritarian personalities in leadership have been necessary to keep this potential strife in check. As we have seen, patriarchal authority in family and religion constitute building blocks of society in each of these states, where strong *pater familia* leadership has readily controlled the rebelling factions in one way or another. One is assisted by one's extended kin through reciprocal duties and obligations, which surfaces as a unit when the state fails. Those who share heritage form a mutual protection group to fend off the incursions from the outside.

In stabilizing the competition among these contending tribal blocs, all of the Gulf states have arrived at governmental formats that may be seen or portrayed by the outside as authoritarian tending. However, in the smaller polities where the distance to the ruler is fairly small, the perception of a more benevolent monarchy where the ruler attempts to act in the best interests of his people, may be more appropriate. Much of the outside criticism relates to the fact that a small cadre of insiders pretty much are the decision makers generation after generation.[71] Closer inspection indicates that the monarchies simply rely on age-old traditional ways of binding groups together. Whether they can withstand the pressures of globalism to create greater multicultural societies, and the pressures to allow the next generation of nationals to be even more exposed to and socialized into global thought, remains a challenge, as does the degree of change in governmental format. However, the success or lack of success of globalization will in the long run be gauged by the degree to which the traditional and sectarian rivalries are channeled into greater economic interdependencies.

Yet it must be considered that the influx of enormous petroleum wealth within the past two generations or so has created disparities within the community of faithful in various countries who adhere to a basic egalitarianism in religion within the Gulf polities. The royal families were the caretakers of this wealth on behalf of the wider community of nationals. The royal families thus have been the recipients and distributors of this unprecedented wealth. The redistribution of the wealth has created welfarism, which intermeshes with the values of the Islamic faith but conflicts with the principles of deregulated capitalism. Therefore, one problem is how to rectify the perceived disparities in disposable income between nationals allied with the royal families and those less closely associated or not at all, such as the recently settled Bedouin in Kuwait and Saudi Arabia.[72] Wealth is redistributed to some degree so that all nationals, notably those of recent and fairly impoverished Bedouin extraction, have experienced radically elevated standards of living in their more basic needs for education, housing, and health care.

The more recent intrusion of a single economic market into a part of the world has been seen by some as contradictory to the guiding principles of religion.[73] This seems so even with the long history of trading within the Gulf. Perceived contradictions have spawned various political responses. On one end of the spectrum are recent attempts to integrate the dynastic structure of Gulf polity with free marketism. Free marketism will thrust into the private sector the less advantaged nationals who have become dependent on the public sector for employment, housing, and reduced rates for water and electricity. On the other end of the spectrum, are political action agendas to attempt reform through increased democratization or even through more militant means.

Within the past generation, the average lifespan has increased along with education (including women), nutrition, health, housing, and per capita income, whereas the rates of infant mortality and births have dropped. In the UAE, the illiteracy rate has declined from about 80 percent at the time of the formation of the country to about 17 percent twenty years later.[74]

Taken as a whole, the formation of the global market coincides with the quest for new forms of collective social identity and ways to involve more segments of the population, who are now better educated, into greater participation in governmental decision making. This is not only true along the Arabian Gulf, which saw the creation of states more or less simultaneously, but throughout the Middle East. The rise of Political Islam may also be seen as an autochthonous retrenchment to globalization. Political Islam in the Middle East and fundamentalism in the United States gain comparative relief as revitalistic or millennarian movements in this increasing destabilization of the old order.

Anthony F.C. Wallace long ago argued that revitalistic fundamentalism intensifies during periods of profound cultural and social change.[75] According to Wallace, to revitalize is to bring back aspects of the old community structure to deal with the contemporary stresses. In these recent manifestations, millennarian movements try to insulate their adherents from the multicultural confusion inherent in globalism. That is, to have to deal daily with the "cultural and religious other" would undermine the basic reciprocities or social exchanges between people with similar backgrounds. Moreover, cultural heterogeneity often fosters the re-examination of one's beliefs and their assumed superiority.[76] However, the daily exposure to satellite television and to expatriate workforces seems to have more broadly created values of tolerance and acceptance of cultural difference.[77]

Political Islam is perceived to interpret Islam to meet political objectives of individuals or groups who feel at odds with the forces of globalization through militant acts to purify or return the community to a more self-contained way. The more idyllic times are remembered prior to the influxes of products and ideas and the less equitable distribution of wealth. The various political activist groups identified with Political Islam, such as the Muslim brotherhood, not coincidentally, rose to prominence during the tumultuous economic and social upheavals of the 1970s that signaled an advent of globalism elsewhere.[78] The Islamic Revolution and militant groups like Al-Qaeda, Hezbollah and Hamas may be seen as counter-globalization activists. Relations between some of the conservative Gulf regimes, notably the Saudis, and the Islamist activists were more symbiotic through the 1980s, but not since the second Iraqi War (2003–present).

The kingdom has been beset by a large birth rate in general, perhaps as a reflection of conservative ideological interpretations, and a high birth rate among the royal patrilineage, whose members were entitled to a fairly sumptuous lifestyle. Even the world's largest oil reserves are insufficient for maintaining an adequate standard of living for all Saudi nationals, so there has been some receptivity for the messages of Political Islam. A number of the recruits to the militant political groups come from Saudi Arabia. However, there have also been attempts to hasten grassroots democractic reform as a counter-measure to the cultural and economic conditions that foster discontent with a broadly gauged change attributed to globalization.

After demands from the United States following the September 11 attacks, the government of Saudi Arabia is in process of abandoning policies of promoting religious conservatism. The Saud dynasty began thwarting the insurgency groups and promoted an atmosphere of greater tolerance and acceptance.[79] In press releases issued during 2004, the Sauds told of how the founder of the Saudi state, King Abdulaziz, pacified the countryside to allow pilgrims to visit Mecca without fear of marauding brigands. This created an atmosphere of tolerance. According to this official stance, the rising tide of current intolerance fomented by the militants goes against the historic "grain of Saudi society and religion."

From the evolutionary perspective, a more tolerant and personalized practice or religion would allow great social heterogeneity more characteristic of an urbanized society more closely in sync with a global economy. There are now articles and editorials in the major Gulf newspapers calling for more tolerance in religious interpretations.

Considering that the Middle East continues to support some of the remaining authoritarian political regimes within the world, Khaldoun Al Naqeeb's Chapter 6, "How likely is democracy in the Gulf," critically examines how liberal reforms proposed by international bodies such as the IMF and by recent Republican administrations would impact Gulf society and culture. Basically, the ideology of free-market capitalism asserts that those who sell the most reap the most; it is the market that ultimately determines worth via the saleability of products and ideas. That is, what is good for business is good for society. To examine the negative side, however, let us consider that the sovereign nation state developed to unify, educate, and militarily protect its populations. The state also economically protected its national workforce through tariffs.[80] As pointed out by Niblock in Chapter 4, these vital functions of the state have appreciably eroded and allowed the penetration of global capital to reorganize local workforces. Privatization increases the efficiencies in production and distribution. During the 1980s, world trade almost doubled and foreign investment quadrupled as local trade barriers tumbled. If we were to follow the implications of Friedmanian economics, the underlying ideological structures would dissolve into liberal democracies that are more protective of the capitalism necessary for production and consumption.

Al Naqeeb points out the inherent contradiction between free marketism and the basic Gulf traditional structures and religious tenets. These serve to counterbalance the pull into the greater marketing of Western lifestyles and values.

To reiterate, however, the Gulf countries do not depend upon capital loaned or authorized by the International Monetary Fund or the World Bank. There is no direct incentive to open their societies to the vagaries of the world capitalism other than for political alliance to the G-7 powers so that the oil deposits may be protected. It is even plausible that a number of Arab ruling families may contribute capital to be loaned by the International Monetary Fund. Nevertheless, countries in the Middle East make little use of the "strings attached" loans of the IMF and World Bank.[81] This may also suggest a healthy skepticism about the intentions of the international financiers, who are allied with hawkish foreign policy by Western governments. An indigenous system of banking through Islamic banks exists side by side with global banks such as the Bank of America and HSBC. As Sirageldin points out in Chapter 5, global capitalism is oriented toward short-term profits and does not factor in the long-term plans necessary for investment in human resources or for the long-term security of labor. Investments in maintaining social structures intact would stabilize family relationships, supporting the first value in Gulf society outlined above.

To promote the greater internal stability, the US has promoted liberal reforms in Saudi Arabia, Kuwait, and Bahrain. Qatar, Bahrain, the UAE, and Oman are apparently seen as sufficiently stable for greater integration into the world market. The US has signed the Trade and Investment Framework Agreement with the UAE and Oman as a prelude to the Free Trade Agreement, which follows the process well underway in Bahrain. The US exports to the UAE $3.5 billion in machinery and vehicles and $259 million in agricultural products, and imports $1.1 billion in oil products and apparel.[82] Additional liberal reforms include such measures as reducing gender stratification and the disparities in the distribution of wealth among citizens and catalyzing democratic political changes. An illustration of recent restructuring of Gulf society is that of Saudi Arabia, where government sanctioned "watch dog" groups of professional women came into being in 2004 to report violations of gender discrimination rules as part of a campaign to eradicate "terrorism and (. . .) fanaticism."[83] The Foreign Minister of the UAE also publicly condemned "all terrorism in the Gulf region, especially in the brotherly Kingdom of Saudi Arabia ... where a number of residential areas were subject to horrific terrorist attacks."[84] Simultaneously, the Prime Minister Sheikh Sabah of Kuwait stated that his government is committed to "granting of political rights to women" and allowing a more open press. Together, these changed policies suggest an orchestrated liberalizing of the normative proscriptions across the Gulf.

To dissipate the conditions fostering Political Islam, Bahrain's *Shura* Council, which is appointed by King Al Khalifa, has undertaken policy initiatives to more fully integrate the less advantaged sectors of Bahraini society with a greater share of the national wealth following a study commissioned by McKensey Global Consultants. The Bahraini council leaders stated that the country needs a "serious national dialogue to address the burning unemployment in the kingdom." "Two out of every three new jobs go to expatriate workers, while one out of eight Bahrainis is out of work." Within a decade the unemployment of nationals could rise to 35 percent, and Bahrain needs to find employment for 100,000 national workers within the next decade, thereby doubling its local labor force.[85] Taken together, the simultaneous policy decrees in Bahrain, Saudi Arabia, and Kuwait indicate a concerted and coordinated effort to engineer changes in the Gulf's wider society for better interrelation with a diversifying economy. The UAE has urged greater reform of the IMF and World Bank to more directly address the heightening Third World poverty going beyond deregulation of the supply-side economics.

As we have seen, the state guarantees internal security for its citizens and guests. In Chapter 10, Abdulkhaleq Abdulla considers the dynastic states anachronistic: they eventually will be pressed into greater liberal reform. In contemplating just how dynastic monarchy and democracy can be forged together, Herb theorizes that democracy gains strength "when authoritarian elites and their challengers can reach a compromise that includes liberalizing elements. The political issue in a liberalizing monarchy is not necessarily the abolition of the throne but instead the incremental increase in the powers of the parliament and a decrease in those of the palace."[86] In this regard, Kuwait has a representative assembly and Bahrain is moving toward greater representative government. Kuwait is strengthen[ing] the bond between people and government. Proposed changes include increasing the number of parliamentary seats for more inclusive participation and increasing the number of cabinet members. Kuwait's constitution, which dates to 1962, states that the emir must be a descendant of the ruler who led until 1915. The positions of crown prince and prime minister were separated in 2003 to decentralize power within the royal family.

Concerns have been raised about the Gulf states being permeable to illegal terrorist organizations and monies to support such organizations.[87] The United States had convergent interests with Saudi Arabia and Iraq in thwarting the spread emanating from the Islamic Revolution under Khomeini in Iran. This political triangulation also developed to balance the power struggle among the three large and powerful states to safeguard the wider Gulf. While the eight-year war raged between Iraq and Iran and again in 1991 when the coalition invaded Kuwait, the small Gulf states created a policy of domestic tranquility, an official pro-Arabism, especially in relation to Palestine, and a necessary pro-West stance in protecting their oil reserves and prosperity. The newspapers and editorials were crafted under the eyes of the local governments to provide a "middle-of-the-road" discourse that reflects the policy stances. As pointed out, however, such official control is slightly antithetical to the laissez-faire marketism, which has spurred much of globalism. The governmental stance of the small Gulf states thus balances the more pro-national broadcasts of Al-Arabiya and Al-Jazeera (discussed below) with the more pro-Western CNN and BBC.

In Chapter 7, Gaber Asfour presents "An argument for enhancing Arab identity within globalization" as a counter to the forces fragmenting the Arab world into oil rich and oil poor blocs. Asfour squarely confronts the cultural issue which is central to understanding the globalization in the Middle East. First, he notes that in Arabic globalization (*awlama*) carries a root for God and apprehension for its degree of profound change; it also is etymologically parallel to *faw'al* meaning falling under coercive power to conform. In order to rectify the two worlds of conforming to tradition or conforming to the values, images and lifeways promulgated by globalism, he takes a statist stance consistent with Nasserist moorings that are especially embedded in Egypt, as he notes. Asfour calls for a body like UNESCO to channel the forces of globalization so as to allow the Arab cultural lifeways as an example of diversity within the world, to persist. The Arab identity would be conceptualized as almost timeless and permanent within the territory of the Middle East.

Asfour's proposal would prompt the intra-Arab inequities to be resolved by accentuating notions of brotherhood and sharing deeply embedded in Muslim thought. To carry forth this social program, the Arab intellectual community, in conjuction with governmental leadership like that of UNESCO or more region-ally like the Arab League, should reshape culture and lifeways so as not to fall prey to the de-humanizing forces of global capitalism in an endless quest for profits. The Arab identity, language and culture would thus be properly managed if change was necessary and desirable.

Yet, relying on a supranational governmental body is generally inconsistent with globalism, whose forces are generally defined as diminishing the authority of the state or of overarching bodies like UNESCO which do not deal with the economies. The few viable governing authorities would be exemplied by the IMF or the World Bank, which function to expedite the flow of capital. And little con-sideration is given to the driving forces of the global economy vis-à-vis the stalled economies of the oil-poor countries.

To further consider the underlying and ingrained practices, it should also be kept in mind whether or not the patronage system, crisscrossing many aspects of institutional life in Egypt, and the Levantine countries be intermeshed with the economic efficiency inherent in global capitalism. Remember, a significant por-tion of the workforces in the Gulf hails from the western flank of the Middle East.[88] Some might argue, in fact, that patronage in Egypt recalls stasis of an entrenched bureaucracy of pharaonic times. This might find voice in notions of brotherhood within the Nasserist and statist position, whereas the Gulf Arabs saw brotherhood as more essentially grounded kinship alliance.

Finally, we note a tie in between the patronage systems, adherence to a social orthodoxy, and self-censorship in the press or in public life in general. An edito-rial in a leading periodical in the Gulf states that the "UAE press is better off than its counterparts in other Arab countries. Journalists are not persecuted or arrested" by the state security apparatuses.[89] While only Kuwait has a "semi-free press," the printed press in the Gulf is reasonably open. Nonetheless, the analysis notes that journalists and public figures tend to "inflict self-censorship" so as not to discuss items inconsistent with the reigning "social and religious values and traditions." Complaints and pressures against free speech may be brought by "social, religious, economic and cultural organizations," along with government officials as patrons who in turn are approached by influential members or patrons of such organizations.

In Chapter 8, Michael C. Hudson assesses how the wider forces of the American-originating imagery promoting a lifestyle of leisure and mass con-sumerism interact with the norms of the extended family as the key building block of Middle Eastern society. What have the Arabs accepted and what have they rejected of this publicly portrayed lifestyle, which is advertised in most media and narratively borne out in films? This interplay of global and local is not the volatile mix envisioned by Benjamin Barber in *Jihad vs. McWorld*.[90] In Barber's reasoning, *jihad* is metaphoric of the aggressive suppression of the consumption lifestyle and its accompanying values by peoples imbued with a contradictory traditionalism. Such a cohort would have been socialized prior to the 1970s and are now passing through their most influential years as leaders or family patriarchs. However, the new avenue to mass consumption made available by the vast oil revenues has indeed impacted basic structures irrespective of the carefully laid plans and programs of the social and political planners. For one, during this rapid metamorphosis from traditional to modern communities, families have become smaller, as predicated by basic demographic transition theory. They have also left the traditional extended family neighborhoods and are now scattered throughout the newly constructed suburbs. This, in effect, is fragmentation to a certain extent of the once all-embracing kinship webs interlocking society. While kinship of the extended family is still important, and one's status depends more than most other places of the world on surname, the normative obligations to all members of the extended family are much reduced to those who are in business or other productive relations. However, the paternalism remains strong and extended kindred forms the cores of many businesses, especially among the old trading families. Marriages arranged by the mothers of a couple are still the ideal among nationals of the old guard. Kinship is also significant in the relationships within the ruling families, in which even the most traditional of customs often holds sway.

Hudson further assesses the Arab receptivity to the American-style consumerism and new technology in the Middle East generally and in the Arab Gulf specifically. First, he observes that communication technologies have spread widely throughout the Gulf, which he labels the "global heartbeat of the Middle East." Local firms have used global technologies to produce films to fit the cultural predilections of the Islamic world. The United Arab Emirates and Qatar have positioned themselves as regional centers for interpreting and presenting news events and media products for a Middle Eastern market. Presumably, Arab producers will create a more culturally attuned product for local audiences than the more established foreign networks. Ideally, the Arab producers, from this perspective, will assert themselves as the main creators of narratives, texts and images more in line with the second set of underlying cultural values mentioned earlier.

Part IV Globalization in the Gulf

We now turn to how manifestations of globalism interface locally, within individual Gulf states. We need to bear in mind the strong traditional factor in these new cityscapes: the trading orientation, segmentary lineages, redistributive economies, and religious values. Each of the contributing authors in this fourth section of the volume ascertains what is new as a result of globalism in describing a rich mosaic of globalism/localism on the Arabian Gulf, that seems to range from (1) cultural juxtapositioning or the spacing of discrete local and foreign parts in separate spaces, to (2) more fully synchretizing the indigenous with the foreign. During the boom years of the 1970s and especially the 1980s, the modern infrastructures of the Gulf countries were built into explosively expanding city-states. The GCC was founded in 1981 to counterbalance superpower manipulation of oil policies in the fairly lightly populated oil states there, and to serve as a traditional council for discussing economic and political issues of mutual interest, and for possible collective action.

In considering how the Gulf region stands apart from the processes of globalism elsewhere, it must be kept in mind that the Gulf countries are not fully dependent on outside capital for development. Significantly, these nations have managed to engineer the impact of outside forces into their own traditional social and symbolic fabrics. Yet, in the first generation of globalism within the Gulf (*c.*1970–2000), much of the cultural production has been from outside the region, especially in the electronically conveyed images that advertise a consumerist lifestyle and its desirable products. The once meagerly provisioned Gulf peoples (outside of Saudi Arabia, Bahrain, and Kuwait, which had undergone a change a generation or two earlier) naturally eagerly embraced the new avalanche of foreign goods and services. Even after two decades of meeting material needs and building an elaborate infrastructure, much of the traditional social organization and the symbolic culture have survived in forms that would have been recognizable several generations ago, albeit with new functions within densely populated multi-ethnic cities. As a whole, however, the Gulf nationals have variously developed quite luxurious lifestyles while producing few goods exportable to other regions of the world except for petroleum products. Since the 1990s, tourists have increasingly flocked to the "Gold Coast" to enjoy its state of the art amenities, the remaining manifestations of a seemingly exotic aboriginal culture (which has been increasingly re-packaged to spur tourism) and a quite agreeable climate for six months of the year.[91]

The seven chapters in this fourth section of the volume offer insights as to how globalism has been recast in an Arabian guise and how society may continue to evolve. The quantitative data and generalizations from the various contributions are woven together here to visualize a society integrating religion with economics. This by itself places the Arabian Gulf apart from other world regions.

In looking into the future, several overarching questions follow from the interdisciplinary studies in this regionally specific portion of the volume: (1) Will the Gulf economic sector develop sufficiently to produce goods and products desirable beyond the GCC? (2) Will the underlying kinship structure increasingly meld into a more "organic" and atomized community organization in which duties and obligations to kindred are less and less factored into government and business, so the most expedient ways to maximizing profit hold sway? (3) Will the fairly centralized forms of government undergo sufficiently liberal reform so that government primarily protects capital and the entrepreneurial sector becomes the impetus shaping society?[92] (4) Will the redistributive functions of the welfare state give way to producing national labor to compete in market-based capitalism? And, (5) will the prevailing ideology accommodate some of the inherent contradictions favoring profit over social obligations and commitments? Presently, kinship and religion seem to still outweigh work and profit as a most significant consideration in directing social interaction.

It is considered axiomatic in sociology that mechanical solidarity, like the segmentary lineage societies of the Gulf, evolves into organic solidarity, with greater economic interdependencies.[93] Religion tends to assume a greater role in welding together the once-competing lineages of mechanical solidarity. The whole is politically simply the sum of its parts, as in the size of armies temporarily assembling to defeat a common foe. In organic solidarity, the whole would be greater than the sum of its parts, and religion often assumes a less overarching function. Following this line of reasoning, thus, the questions arise as to whether the normative codes may be reinterpreted to allow a greater range of behavioral possibilities with the specialized roles and jobs of a more urban and organic society. Alternatively, will basic governing structures sculpt a society unique to the Gulf region, as globalization here enters into a new phase following the building of the modern infrastructure?

Different social sectors construct their cosmologies to interdigitate with their social realities, as do different generations. Cosmology relates how the various disparate and occasionally contradictory elements of one's experiential world are arranged into a coherent ideational whole. Research by el-Aswad shows that older Emiratis tend to view "the oil as a blessing (*ni'mah*) bestowed for their goodness (*khair*) ... for the harsh economic conditions that they and their ancestors endured. ... Yet, their [new] wealth, realized in social cosmology, is sanctified and rationalized in religious terms." The image of the "Unlimited Good" relates to the religious concept of *al-rizq* (livelihood) that belongs to *alam al-ghaib* (divine invisible reality). Metaphorically, *al-rizq* is akin to the rain that unexpectedly revives the desert without intervention of man."[94] Young Emiratis are especially torn between their more sacred home life, in which they practice time-honored traditions and speak Arabic, and their more public life, in which they speak English, eat fast food, drive expensive automobiles, and engage in commerce. In other words, although the luxurious life emulates that of the West and is incorporated as public demeanor, it has not significantly disrupted the basic cosmology and kinship bonding guarded at home.

From a Western perspective, the younger generation of Gulf nationals exhibits a dichotomy between these two fairly separated spheres of life. However, as el-Aswad points out, the Muslim cosmology allows for the two distinctive worlds – the invisible (*alam al-ghaib*) and the visible (*alam ash-shahadah*) – to exist side by side. These worlds have been juxtaposed into a vertical hierarchy of indigenous or national on top, which is holy, and the Western on the bottom, which is secular. This cosmological bipolarity nicely meshes the traditional social organizing principles of segmentary lineages united through complementary opposition. In this case, it becomes "we," the Gulf nationals, opposed in cosmology to the Western and global as the "other"; however, they are united economically and allied politically. In traditional Muslim cosmology, the invisible and the visible comprise a unified universe.

However, the ordering of the invisible and visible worlds differs in the Gulf and the West; in Muslim thinking, the invisible dominates the visible world, and, in rough analogy, the visible (usually economic world) dominates and shapes the invisible world of ideas in Western thinking. Thus, anything becomes possible as instigated from the invisible world, such as the unanticipated oil wealth. However, it is also becoming apparent for those already acculturated to success through personal achievement that equal education in Arabic along with English is a responsibility within an information economy. Since Arabic is considered to be the language bestowed by God, in some respects to downgrade Arabic to merely the language of the home is a realization of the worries raised by Gaber Asfour (Chapter 7). "A language that can only boast about its history brings little comfort to the intellectual challenges of Arab societies seeking to be knowledge-based."[95]

The cosmological categories are borne implicitly in day to day living patterns within the Gulf cities. The established canons, categories, distinctions, and boundaries are quite segregated by ethnicity and status. While the Gulf states are particularly permeable to people and products, the impact of multiculturalism is somewhat cushioned by separate ethnic neighborhoods and distinctive cultural spheres of activities. Yet, local symbols, such as distinctive clothing, indicate the class of nationals in each country. While a basic religious egalitarianism is assumed, and although religious tolerance is the norm, the proprietary class is perceived as superordinate to co-religionists of different ethnicities and to adherents to other religions. This may indicate a subtle national-centrism. In comparison to multicultural cities in other parts of the world, the boundary maintenance functions of dress, friendship, and residence are probably more scrupulously observed by Gulf nationals.

Several theorists in this volume consider globalism to have been largely American spawned, especially in the business reorganization of the mid to late 1970s and the pro-business policies spurred by President Reagan. According to Alan Larson, the US Undersecretary of State for Economic, Business, and Agricultural Affairs, "private enterprise is the basic engine to globalization and development, which interrelates with the American core values and business." Larson theorizes that "private initiatives are the prime movers in any nation's advancement ... and that entrepreneurship, personal responsibility, and property rights ... are development ideals." He states that "free and unfettered trade" spurs economic development.[96] This leads to two questions regarding globalization in the Gulf: (1) How can a traditional kinship-based structure incorporate supply-side economics and deregulated commerce? and (2) What are the changes from this articulation of traditionalism and the global market?

In the chapters of the Gulf case studies, Wilson and Willoughby describe how the Gulf interacts with the world market as the single overriding feature of globalism. At the top end of the economic spectrum in Chapter 9, Wilson examines salient features of the oil economy in Saudi Arabia, whereas Willoughby provides an in-depth study of expatriate labor from India in Chapter 13. We then explore how various segments of society, especially expatriates and nationals, and the changing functions of government relate to one another. In examining changes in political regulation and structure, Abdulla (Chapter 10) and Halliday (Chapter 11) outline changes in governments and their international relations. The geopolitics of these small states so vital to the health of the world economy attract considerable attention and influence from the industrial states. Can these traditional polities be socially engineered to become versions of liberal democracies?

Moreover, Halliday notes that the Arab and Persian populations have intermingled in the Gulf for centuries. Yet for all of this interaction, the Arabian and Iranian governments, he maintains, are woefully ignorant of each other. Moreover, the three large countries in or adjacent to the Gulf region have ongoing claims to territory now within the GCC. It is worth recalling that in 1970 Iran occupied the three small islands off the UAE and still claims Bahrain. Saudi Arabia also earlier claimed Buraimi Oasis on the Oman–UAE border (resolved by Treaty in 1974), and Iraq claimed Kuwait. More recently, Iran and the GCC states have found themselves not only on different sides of the Persian–Arab fault line but on different sides of the *Pax Americana* vision and alliances.

In Chapter 12, "Foreign matter: the place of strangers in Gulf society," Dresch takes a fresh look at how relying on foreign labor has impacted the economy and, to varying degrees, modified the traditional structures. Dresch analyzes how the Gulf nationals, who call themselves *quareeb*, conceptualize the large expatriate workforces as the foreign "other" (*ghareeb*). This binary opposition seems to dovetail with the traditional cosmology outlined above. The foreign communities now range in size from as low as 30 percent in Oman to around 80 percent in Qatar, and just slightly less in Bahrain, the UAE, and Kuwait (see Willoughby's tables in Chapter 13). Before the discovery of oil, never more than a handful of British nationals or other Westerners resided on the Gulf coast.

Dresch observes that the quintessential agnatic (patrilineal) kinship preference of the Gulf nationals has given way to a more cognatic (bilateral) kinship. This system recognizes the families of both mother and father as equally important. Upon closer inspection, though, kinship variation may be more class related. While the middle echelons of Gulf society have tended toward bilaterality, the large extended ruling families still hold cousin marriage as the ideal (patrilineal endogamy). While the first spouse may be a cousin, the other wives may be more of one's own choosing. Just one to two generations ago, it was preferable for brothers and their families to dwell together on their father's property, and cousins would reside on adjoining properties. An entire neighborhood would consist of one or two intermarried families.

That kinship remains of primary importance is also borne out in the marriage norms; it seems more acceptable or preferable to choose a spouse from other Gulf countries, than to select one from among co-religionists from Asia who may be in residence as expatriates. Muslim guest workers generally still lie outside usual marriage bonds. However, nationals from other Gulf countries are perceived as distant kinsmen within the "extended tribe" and are permitted to relocate to the other GCC countries with full rights.

While there has been a viable trade between the Gulf and the Indian subcontinent for millennia, it has never involved the proportions of today, when the immigrants constitute the majority in most Gulf countries. Yet, the workers are usually physically and socially segregated in neighborhoods of their own. There is a continual demographic flux in which the guest workers are shuffled in and out, usually on a three-year visa period. Because they are segregated in specific residential areas, workers can be welcomed or they may leave with little disruption of the community fabric.

In addition to the Saudis considering some guests for possible citizenship, in 2003 Dubai began to allow foreigners to own real estate. These are wealthy expatriates or foreigners who invest in real estate and create capital appreciation within the emirate. The greatest share of capital worldwide comes from domestic savings, which amounts to about $2 trillion a year.[97] The Crown Prince of Dubai, as an entrepreneurial driven aspect of urban governance, has launched construction of a third Palm Island project (off Deira) "to meet increasing requirements of investors, particularly those who could not manage to invest in the two Palm projects in Jumeirah and Jebel Ali."[98] As in Saudi Arabia, the expatriates may stay indefinitely as they contribute to the generation of wealth.

The Gulf states promote a policy variously called Kuwaitization, Emiratization, Saudization, Qatarization, etc. in which the next generation of nationals will replace the managerial and skilled technical expatriate labor. Yet, unemployment remains significantly high for the nationals. However, there remains a strong antipathy toward skilled jobs that restrict personal mobility. Craftsmen have been traditionally recruited from outside of Arabia to live among an Arabian kinship group and were called *hulafa*. Their hosts and protectors were called *jiran*.[99] While locals own 51 percent of any enterprise (called sponsorship), this has not yet brought nationals into the private sector workforce in the numbers predicted. While the oil revenue eventually underwrites the time-honored niche of the Gulf trading company, little hard-core production of goods and services for export has developed to alleviate the primacy of the oil sector.

Trying to increase productivity is a perennial problem and one necessary for continued development. The Kuwaiti Prime Minister has declared "the need to stop employing citizens in the public sector to stop the drain on public expenditure and to give much-needed impetus to the private sector." While "93 percent of the total Kuwaiti workforce is employed in the public sector," about "70 percent of those employed by the Civil Service Commission are not needed."[100] Whether redistributing its entitlements can be re-engineered and privatized to compete internationally is much debated. The Gulf governments are also pressed by the United States to liberalize for greater participation in the world market.

Nevertheless, foreign labor maintains the ultramodern infrastructures and is the mainstay of the economy. In describing the demographics and ranking of the categories of foreign labor, Willoughby, in Chapter 13, "Ambivalent anxieties of the South Asian–Gulf labor exchange," classifies the immigrant guest workers into a four-tiered hierarchy. This ranges from Western professionals at the top to South Asian laborers at the bottom, with workers fairly exclusively distributed to specific sectors. Of the GCC countries, the UAE is one of the most reliant of the Gulf states on expatriate labor (76 percent). Sharjah and Dubai draw foreign workers primarily from Kerala in South India. The Indian experience in the Gulf community is fairly fixed in the public consciousness (through film, novels, newspapers, and television broadcasts). This across-the-Arabian-Sea "economic symbiosis" seems sufficiently beneficial to both sides so that it should continue as a vital linkage of the Asian economy. The labor bridge exemplifies the catalyzing effects of migratory workers.

Labor is recruited through agents working for Gulf sponsors in India. The workers are mostly males in their mid-20s, and about half are married (although the spouse and children usually remain in India) and half are Muslim. They tend to feel cut off from a sense of community since they live apart from their families for several years. Nevertheless, they send sizeable amounts of cash back home to the relatively impoverished Kerala. While the remuneration of basic labor in the Gulf may seem paltry, it allows the families in India to purchase durable goods, "jump-start" businesses, and create capital investments for housing. Examining migratory labor from the supply side, the UN's report *Unleashing Entrepreneurship* calculates that remittances sent home by foreign workers totals some $90 billion worldwide.

This strong labor linkage to South Asia also contributes to dispel the image, of a unified and homogeneous Arab world entity. To generalize from the fairly permanent fixture of Indian labor, it appears that the greater productivity and a lack of long-term obligation to the Indians tend to make them more favored than workers from Egypt, Yemen, Jordan, and Palestine. From this perspective, the desire for pan-Arab nationalism appears quite secondary to the needs of enhanced productivity. While approximately half of the expatriate workers from India are Muslim, many are not. Nevertheless, they are all grouped in the same work camps. The distinction is based on the notion of kindred, ethnicity, and economic class. That is, while core values may emphasize the virtues of fraternal communities and egalitarianism, in practice the economic variable seems to loom weightier.

Let us keep in mind that during the 1970s, the first wave of immigrant labor arrived from the Arab countries, where the cultural values were sufficiently similar to allow homogeneous communities in the Gulf. Workers came predominantly from Egypt and Yemen, as well as from Palestine, Jordan, and Sudan. By the end of the 1970s, these expatriates comprised about 30 percent of the Gulf population. Due to cultural and linguistic compatibilities, they actively contributed in building and managing the basic urban infrastructure of schools, medical facilities, and roads. Following the pan-Arabism movement promulgated by Nasser, the prevailing ideology was one of the Arabs migrating within the wider Arab nation. This, of course, was similar ideology for Gulf Arabs, whose communities were organized through kinship. But cultural similarities did not equate with kinship so that the overwhelming majority of the non-Gulf Arabs would blend into the kinship networked communities. Kapiszewski notes that "Relations between the two groups almost never attain the closeness common among nationals. As a general practice, nationals rarely invite non-local Arabs to their homes, and they tend to discourage them to use local dress in order to prevent them from blending into the population segment of the privileged nationals ... Marriages in which a national marries a non-national Arab woman are usually considered by the local families as misalliances."[101] While the various Gulf governments issued decrees that required a significant percentage of the expatriate workforce to be Arab, a significant percentage were repatriated to their homelands following the Iraqi War in 1990–1991 for publicly supporting Iraq against Kuwait. The percentage of non-Gulf Arabs decreased from 72 percent in 1975 to 25–29 percent in 2002.[102]

Peoples of the Gulf mostly live in urban environs. Today, the three emirates of Dubai, Sharjah and Ajman have forged one metropolitan community of three million persons with mutual economic interdependencies and job specializations more typical of organic solidarity. But how have the traditional norms a short distance below the glistening exteriors of this modern opulence managed the influx of oil wealth and workers from abroad?

In Chapter 14, "The evolution of the Gulf city type," Sulayman Khalaf shows that the modern oil-city is a unique kind of urban community. This should not be surprising, since urban geography simply mirrors society; the Gulf nationals stand apart as overseeing a majority foreign population. The sprawling metropolises starkly give way to open desert at the city limits and almost stand as communities without rural support areas (except for oil fields). The Gulf cities, thus, are city-states with more than 90 percent of the emirate's/country's population. They also show a remarkably parallel ontological cycle when (1) the modern infrastructures were built within about a decade; (2) hospitals, schools, and desalinization plants were constructed into the 1980s; and (3) the cities went global during the 1990s, especially in promoting tourism and wholesaling.

As mentioned, the immigrant workers are segregated into neighborhoods that range from concrete block apartments of up to about six stories to high rises and villas for the more highly paid foreigners. The Gulf city is now a rich mosaic with different ethnic groups maintaining their own cultural spaces, which often feature shops and other commercial establishments that replicate those in their respective homelands. These are fairly segregated neighborhoods – modern manifestations of what we could term "segmental" society. Let us remember, however, that society has long been organized by neighborhoods restricted for those of shared origins.

To illustrate the ethnically segregated neighborhoods today, a part of Dubai is called "Little Bombay/Mumbai." In another a section of Dubai called Jumeirah, the population is largely American/British/Canadian/French and shops are decorated for Halloween, Thanksgiving, and Christmas. A Christmas tree is placed in the Dubai International Airport during December. (One could also argue that some of these celebrations seem to have become global fetes.) There is a full range of primary and secondary schools that follow the American, British, and Indian curricula. Jumeirah also has two business colleges, which have American and British charters. One neighborhood in Sharjah/Ajman houses Russians who are largely involved in the export business. It has its own schools, stores, and recreational areas (mostly in hotels along the beach). Throughout the Gulf recently, American universities have also been established in Kuwait, Bahrain, and in Qatar; American-styled education is seen as providing the foundation to succeed in globalism. Students from all of the ethnic groups enroll at the American universities.

The housing for the nationals also varies by status and social class – from royal palaces and palatial villas for the economic elite to the government-built houses for low-income families. The category *national* was applied in the 1980s as a point of contrast with the "foreign others." However, since the traditional kinship system underlies society, various governments have countered the lure of out-marriage (ethnic exogamy) by offering inducements to marry within the national group. A government-subsidized dowry or "bride wealth" could amount to about 20,000 dirhams in the UAE. Government bestowed marriage funds, begun in 1991, provide about 60,000 to 70,000 dirhams to get newlyweds started in life if both the bride and groom are nationals. About 10,000 persons per year in the UAE have received these marriage grants since 1997. With the declining birth rate among nationals, the government provides a subsidy for each child born. While numbers of marriages were on the decline in the late 1990s, the numbers of weddings have increased 20 percent per year since the price of oil increased dramatically in 2003. One analysis indicates that more disposable income for the Emiratis has resulted in more lavish displays of wealth at weddings, with costs per event in the hundreds of thousands of dollars.[103]

In the final Chapter, 15, "Heritage revivalism in Sharjah," the authors examine how aspects of traditional culture are reconstituted to aid in the concretizing of national identities in the polyglot and multicultural Gulf society. Buildings of the past are resurrected and embellished to assume new functions in promoting nationalism in the countries with greatly significant numbers of resident expatriates. A loose articulation between the Gulf and the English-speaking West dating back two centuries oriented the forces of globalism at the beginning of the 1970s. Prior to that, the Portuguese and Dutch established trading towns at Hormuz and Basrah. Even the Alexandrine Greeks had established an entrepot on Failaka Island *c.*240 BC off of Kuwait (called Ikaros then).[104] However, the mainland was essentially free of outside intrusion for its five millennia so that indigenous social organization remained intact.[105] When the British arrived in the opening years of the nineteenth century, they, too, did not intrude into the affairs of the mainland populations. Nevertheless, the British did serve as the guarantors of political stability within the Gulf as a manifestation of *Pax Britannica* until the early 1970s when they dissolved the long-standing treaties. This vacuum was quickly filled by the United States during the Reagan years, following the recessionary (for the West) 1970s, which ushered in a *Pax Americana*. These were recovery years for the West and boom years for the Gulf, and continued growth depended upon the uninterrupted flow of petroleum.

The spatial arrangements of the highly segmented cities before and after the oil boom are also summarized in Chapter 15. Fox, Mourtada-Sabbah, and al-Mutawa show how the traditional (pre-oil) city was divided into several dozen neighborhoods, or (the *friej*) which are forerunners of the ethnic neighborhoods in the present multicultural Gulf city. During the nineteenth century and earlier, each neighborhood usually contained two intermarried lineages that were joined in the same or related occupations. These were fairly autonomous and complementarily paired segmentary lineages.

Resurrecting the settlement patterns and buildings Old Sharjah not only creates an architectural archifact with the past in a contemporary setting surrounding by high-rise buildings, but it forms a visual sense of collective identity for a time of uprootedness and quickly changing images on the airwaves. The heritage area is also a visual reminder of the social order with the nationals leading on top in a multicultural society. While the families are pretty widely distributed throughout the modern neighborhoods, the foundation of the current social ranking undergirding much of the commercial, service, and government establishment is clearly visible in this heritage area.

In the bustling metropolis of Dubai–Sharjah–Ajman today, the core of the old walled seaport of Sharjah functions as an heirloom with modern meanings accessible to all of the nationals of the UAE, and with meanings as a cultural center for the entire Gulf region. Sharjah has also created seven institutions of higher learning within its University City attempting to make it the educational center for the information economy of the Gulf. For its role in education and in cultural heritage, Sharjah has been recognized accordingly by the Arab League and was designated by UNESCO as the Cultural Capital of the Arab World in 1998.

Sharjah's historical area evidently serves as a counterpart in place-making to Dubai's gleaming skyline and neighborhoods. Together, heritage and post-modernity are two sides of the same token in place making and re-territorialization of the Gulf within its global contexts.

To consider economics and the rentier economies of the oil states, the northern Emirates are also the least petroleum-dependent of the Gulf countries; perhaps these twin emirates have chosen to develop the most in commercial productivity for the wider needs throughout the Gulf in an information age. The Maktoum rulers of Dubai have been entrepreneurs since Shaikha Hussa bint Al-Murr launched a number of commercial endeavors during approximately 1910 to 1930 and her son, Shaikh Rasheed, built the port facilities that pushed Dubai into the forefront of shipping.[106] Until that point, Sharjah was the main sea port of the Northern Emirates. Under the current ruler of Dubai, Sheikh Mohammad bin Rashed, a media and tourism infrastructure has been developed to render Dubai as the media and tourism capital of the Gulf, and probably of the entire Middle East.

The Maktoum family has put into practice a growth oriented strategy for promoting urban development by luring the factors of the global market there, rather than developing through government allocations which was the customary strategy in the state centrism more typical of the Middle East. His brother, Sheikh Hamdan bin Rashid Al Maktoum, the Deputy Ruler and Minister of Finance, stated that "the UAE economy is growing at a healthy pace because it promotes free trade and development and has surged by 30 percent at times."[107] Wholesaling/retailing and tourism have formed twin pillars of the Dubai economy as high performance returns on the architectural marvels that have been built through private investment. The remaking of Dubai provides a subnational city (within the wider UAE), that has as many international interdependencies as it does with the other six emirates within the UAE. The city of Dubai thus has not only jump-started the Northern Emirates, but it perhaps supersedes most of the GCC as a growth pole. This is quintessential globalization, when one city seems to articulate more directly with the global market than with parts of its own nation state. The international dependencies have become all the more important as the oil revenues dwindle into the last decade of oil extraction.

A steady stream of tourists now arrives from Europe and the Islamic world to fill nearly every hotel room during the peak season of November through March. High-profile celebrity events are scheduled during the tourist season, ranging from sporting events to shopping festivals. In fact, the successful one-month-long Dubai shopping festival, was relocated to the edge of the desert and extended from mid-January through March in 2005. The shopping festival is modeled on a world fair, where pavilions from different countries sell their national products and provide entertainment such as folk dancers and food as well. It is not Barber's (1991) newly coined word "infotainment" but more sales-entertainment. The "hospitality industry" is natural for the Gulf Arabs, who have had customs for provisioning travelers in the desert, for the time away from home necessary in seafaring and long distance trading.

Dubai has taken its niche marketing to unseen levels in the Middle East, but invites comparisons to Las Vegas in the US, based on creating built environs that are almost unique for their bold lavishness that stand out from the stark desert landscape like gleaming jewels beckoning the ancient Arab traders. Dubai's architectural splendors are built upon what were only a few years ago such heavily salinated sand dunes that little would grow. New sand was trucked in and new waterways were dug to sculpt harbors and marinas that are lined with high rises fashioned along themes conceptualized by Arabs, designed by Western architects, and constructed by local firms. A significant portion of the new luxury condominiums and villas has been sold recently to European investors to generate Western capital, thus contributing in keeping the "boom" momentum going. Exotic shopping malls in the UAE display the latest in luxury items, adding a special lure for upscale tourism, much like Manhattan or Paris.

In this tourist/shopping magnate, the Gulf in general and Dubai in particular have surpassed present-day Baghdad and Cairo as the metropolitan cores of the Middle East. While some media in the West have portrayed the Middle East as downtrodden and locked in time,[108] a vigorous entrepreneurial leadership has developed an Arab-style cosmopolitanism to draw tourists. The recent designing and promoting of Dubai thus have done much to turn around the stereotype of orientalism made famous by Edward Said. In Dubai, Sharjah, and the UAE, Arabness is chic and not backward.

Although perhaps not to the same degree as Dubai, each of the Gulf states has consciously developed and enhanced its own public identity. Qatar and Abu Dhabi have developed the broadcast networks Al-Jazeera and Al-Arabiya, which present news within the standpoint of the Middle East, and often emphasizing the notion of a pan-Arab brotherhood. Hudson (Chapter 8) shows the influence of

Al-Jazeera television and its website by calculating their market share vis-à-vis such global and competing networks as CNN. Following on the market success of these two networks, the rulers of Dubai launched the adjoining satellite cities of Media City and Internet City as a regional media hub, which house the transnational giants of CNN, Oracle, Dell, and IBM. At the time of this writing, however, the computer companies there were mostly in sales rather than in product development. Dubai's information infrastructure ranks first in the Arab world and eighteenth in the world, as gauged by numbers of personal computers and mobile telephones.[109]

The educational infrastructure within the Gulf has become increasingly more important during the second generation of globalization. First, the Gulf countries have reversed the standings with such an education producer as Egypt during the first generation. Towards the end of the first generation of oil and independence in 1985, moreover, Qatar and Kuwait and Bahrain enrolled significantly higher percentages of students in higher education than the other three Gulf states.[110] By the start of the second generation, the UAE had joined the leaders, and in many respects, had surpassed them. The American University of Sharjah was founded in 1997, in tandem with the American University in Washington, DC, to offer an American-style education in engineering, architecture business and the Arts and Sciences modeled on the successes of the American Unviersity of Beirut. The implicit censorship is noticeably absent in the AUS curriculum, which perhaps sets it apart from most of the other institutions in the Gulf.[111]

A number of institutions have begun to seek US accreditation. Such accreditation is deemed particularly relevant for students seeking graduate and professional programs within the US. Standards of credentials are paramount in a single world organized economically. Accreditations means transferability of experience and education from one country to another. An American-accredited university have subsequently been established in Kuwait, associated with Dartmouth College. In Qatar, the royal family has built branch facilites for the Cornell University school of medicine, Carnegie Mellon in computer technology, University Georgetown University in foreign service and Virginia Commonwealth University in the Arts and Sciences and Texas A and M University in engineering. The concept of inviting various leading insitutions to share a single campus not only bypasses the years of institutional growth necessary to reach that level, but it is a unique concept as well attributed to the ruler of Qatar's wife. The intention is to bring state of the art education, with already existing American accreditation, directly to the Gulf for instilling an informational infrastructure.

However, the traditional duality (structural relativity) of segmentary lineages and gender codes reflected in the ranked values given above lies close to the surface in building modern linkages of economic agglomeration (called "forward lineages" in economic geography).[112] For example, to adapt the university format to the local environment, the University of Sharjah campus has identical separate male and female sections (e.g., two Colleges of Arts and Sciences). The United Arab Emirates University of Al Ain also is divided into halves for males and females.

The University of Sharjah and the United Arab Emirates University enroll primarily nationals, most of whom are from modest backgrounds. The Sociology faculty at UAEU claim that most of their students, who are bussed in daily to the campus in al-Ain, come from small towns and villages where Arabic is the medium of daily speech both inside and outside of the home. It is thus significant that both the national university and the University of Sharjah shifted from classroom instruction in Arabic to English during 2005. This has posed somewhat of a hardship on both the students, who were overwhelmingly monolingual and on the instructional staff, who were largely recruited from the non-oil Arab states. Simply, the leaders of the UAE envision that English will be the language of commerce in the future and thus the basic medium of conversation and public record at least outside the domestic sphere of this Gulf state. To not be fluent in this, the lingua franca, the reasoning runs, is to be far less employable and valuable to Gulf society.

The twin campuses of Zayed University in Dubai and Abu Dhabi also reflect the underlying societal norms. As a federally funded public university, Zayed has developed computer-based education for women as a blend of traditional gender separation with the latest computer-based approaches to learning. Both campuses are surrounded by walls that protect the all-female student bodies, and visitors are screened, which suggests a modern institution has been created to follow the traditional norms for women who would be veiled when in public. Yet, the average Zayed student masters some twenty computer programs by her second year; hardly a scrap of paper is to be found on these largely electronic campuses. This state-of-the-art educational technology is developed for educating Muslim women in a traditional setting. Additionally, a single academic department for each discipline is divided among both campuses; the faculties of these administratively single departments hold joint meetings weekly through video teleconferencing. The fact that Zayed University maintains twin campuses in the capital cities for the two branches of the Bani Yas (Maktoum and Nahyan) also reflects complementary opposition.

In spite of its campuses both in Dubai and Abu Dhabi, Zayed is a single university funded by the federal government, and it is named in honor of the country's first president, who united the seven emirates. The underlying complementary opposition between the Nahyan and Maktoum lineages appear to be borne out in the duality of these institutions which are symbolically united under the rubric of the founding patriach of the federal union.

Lastly we examine the function of retailing and wholesaling. The Gulf cities exhibit some of the largest and most boldly designed malls in the world. Dubai ranks third in the ratio of showroom space per person in the world. Within the past three years Dubai has seen the opening of one mall that replicates the layout of an Italian Renaissance town, another designed as a fortified Moroccan town (*kasbah*) that encloses a man-made lake with a tradtional ship (*dhou*), and a third (Dubailand) with indoor snow-skiing. In these retail show cases, images and identities are appropriated far and wide to entice shoppers from Europe, elsewhere in the Middle East, and more recently from Central Asia. The UAE enhances the symbols of the exotic old Orient to develop and sustain its retailing niche within the global market. The magnitude of retailing along the shores of the Arabian Gulf has yet to be reached. It could also be reasoned that the greater the architectural and themed splendor, the greater proportion of market share that is accumulated for a global virtual world. People come to Dubai in anticipation of unrestrained shopping. The world's tallest building, the Burj Dubai, with 160 floors, is presently under construction as the latest prop in marketing a global city.[113]

Overview and conclusions

To provide a concluding encapsulation of globalization in the Gulf, parts of the region have seen the outward manifestations of tumultuous change within a very short period of time. The local societies ascended from some of the least endowed in the world to some of the wealthiest within mere decades. During an initial stage in the Trucial States in the 1960s and in Kuwait and Saudi Arabia a generation earlier, local Bedouins and fishermen went to work for foreign oil companies in exploring and then pumping oil and gas.[114] A small-scale cash economy developed with local salaried employees who increasingly relied on goods produced elsewhere in the world. By the early 1970s, the embryonic governmental leadership channeled the tide of oil revenues into radically upgrading standards of living. This was a manageable task, for the societies were lightly populated and closely intertwined through kinship. The mode of decision making was simply that of face-to-face negotiations in councils. It was quickly decided to use the new found wealth in building modern infrastructures. Thus, traditional customs have guided the construction of the cities, and not foreign companies geared towards maximizing profits to funnel back to their shareholders. While major social upheavals and wars have taken place in closely bordering regions, the Gulf has experienced unusual stability except for the rarely occurring internal conflict within the royal households when one ruler is replaced by a close relative.

What remains particularly noteworthy in comparison to other parts of the world with high standards of living, is the dominance of traditional kinship practices and religion that act in concert to channel the forces of globalism. More broadly, it remains to be seen how those who advocate an international civil society will deal with the apparent need for new social contracts with their fairly fluid workforces. Alternatively, international civil society could come to mean, in following the reasoning of neo-liberal principles, simply extending principles of supply and demand within the marketplace to how immigrant labor is dealt with. Moreover, certainly Gulf society will continue to ameliorate roles and statuses along the gender divide and along lines of kinship cleavage.

The synchronizing of indigenous and global traditions is quite varied throughout the Gulf. For example, in the UAE, students often say that their dowry payments will be heightened considerably by graduating from a university. The reasons cited include enhancement of a women's prestige, the ability to raise educationally advantaged children and potential earning power should a wife elect to seek employment. Yet, in Qatar, the bride wealth payments have all but disappeared.

In Kuwait, dowry remittances tend to be much lower than in the UAE and perhaps average about 5,000 dinars. Monogamy has become more frequent among the middle and lower classes. This is due as much to cost factors as to the adoption of the nuclear family and employment (usually in the government).

The interplay between kingdom and democracy will perhaps yield new and viable political forms and the strength of the ruling dynasties states will guarantee basic welfare needs – which also eases potential social conflict. The strength of the royal "sector," which distributes wealth, and the strength of the business sector are interrelated to render the Gulf's manifestation of globalization rather unique. There is much more marriage across traditional family lines than a decade or so ago. Surely this trend will continue so that the endogamous unit becomes that of the nationals as one ethnic group. Globalization seems to have blurred the boundaries and statuses of the old social categories which have merged into new ones with new functions. New interpretations will be rendered with existing ideational codes, such as in the law and religion, to address notions of basic human rights which are part of the international discourse and necessary for a global civil society.

By having the key specialists explore some of the most salient dimensions of globalism, we hope to provide the reader with a deeper understanding of this unique region of the world where globalism proceeds under rules somewhat different from the motivations implicit within the literature on global political economy.

Notes

1 "UAE Grow Rate Arab World's Second Highest." *Gulf News*, March 26, 2005.
2 Ali Al Abbar, Director-General of the Dubai Department of Economic Development, in "Dubai's GDP Grows 16.7% in 2004." *Gulf News*, January 2, 2005, p. 33.
3 Per capita income in the UAE for 2004 was $25,000. Reported by the UAE Chambers of Commerce and Industry. *Gulf News*, May 13, 2005, p. 25.
4 The Gulf has been referred to by many names. In recent centuries, the designation Persian Gulf was adopted by European cartographers and became the most prevalent. Since 1958, the Arabs have employed Arabian Gulf so as not to provide justification for Iranian power politics, especially in its claims to Bahrain and to three small islands owned by Sharjah. Cf. Sultan bin Muhammad al-Qasimi. *The Myth of Arab Piracy in the Gulf* (London: Routledge, 1988), *Power Struggles and Trade in the Gulf, 1620–1820* (Exeter, UK: Forest Row, 1999).
5 "Dubai is the World's Third Largest Re-exporter." *Gulf News*, May 13, 2005. Dubai ranks third behind Hong Kong and Singapore according to the Dubai Chamber of Commerce and Industry, and handles 73 percent of the UAE's total foreign trade.
6 "A Decade of Achievement." *Gulf News*, January 6, 2005, p. 10.
7 *Ibid.*
8 "Bold Initiative that Transformed Dubai." *Gulf News*, January 7, 2005, p. 11.
9 "Abu Dhabi Plans to Step Up Privatization." *Gulf News*, December 22, 2004.
10 Adam Smith, *An Inquiry into the Nature and Cause of the Wealth of Nations* (1776).
11 Survey conducted by John W. Fox among a group of students at AUS in October, 2004.
12 Robin Williams, *American Society: A Sociological Perspective* (New York: Knopf, 1970).
13 Michael Herb, *All in the Family* (Albany: SUNY Press, 1999), p. 4.

14 Marshall Sahlins, *Stone Age Economics* (Chicago: Aldine, 1972).

15 See Rosemarie Zahlan, *The Making of the Modern Gulf States* (Reading, UK: Ithaca Press, 1998), pp. 84–87.

16 "In Threat to Internet's Clout, Some Are Starting Alternatives." *The Wall Street Journal*, January 19, 2006, pp. 1, 7.

17 Marvin Harris, *Why Nothing Works: The Anthropology of Daily Life* (New York: Touchstone, Simon and Schuster 1986), p. 157; Morris Berman, *The Reenchantment of the World* (New York: Bantam Books, 1981); Eric R. Wolf, *Europe and the People without History* (Berkeley: University of California Press, 1982); Manuel Castells, "The Rise of the Network Society" in *The Information Age: Economy, Society and Culture*, vol. 1 (Oxford: Blackwell Publishers 1996), pp. 1–2, 61–62.

18 Zygmunt Bauman, "Is There a Postmodern Sociology?" in *The Transmodern Turn*, ed. Steven Seidman, pp. 187–204 (Cambridge: Cambridge University Press, 1994), p. 202.

19 Manuel Castells, *The Rise of the Network Society* (Oxford: Blackwell Publishers, 1996); Cf. Malcolm Waters, *Globalization* (New York: Routledge, 1995). See also Saskia Sassen, *Globalization and its Discontents* (New York: The Free Press, 1998).

20 "National Petroleum Construction Company Set for Privatization." *Gulf News*, January 3, 2005.

21 Rosemarie Said Zahlan. *The Making of the Modern Gulf States* (Reading, UK: Ithaca Press, 1998), p. 87.

22 *Gulf News*, October 13, 2004.

23 Unni Wikan, *Behind the Veil in Arabia* (Chicago: University of Chicago Press, 1982), p. 6.

24 E.g. Fernand Braudel, *Capitalism and Material Life 1400–1800* (New York: Harper and Row, 1973); Immanuel Wallerstein, *The Modern World-system: Capitalist Agriculture and the Origins of the European-world Economy in the Sixteenth Century* (New York: Academic Press, 1974); and Hayden V. White, *Metahistory: The Historical Imagination in Nineteenth Century Europe* (Baltimore: The Johns Hopkins University Press, 1973).

25 E.g. Michel Foucault, *The Archaeology of Knowledge* (New York: Pantheon Books, 1972).

26 Daniel Bell, *The Cult and Contradictions of Capitalism* (New York: Basic Books, 1976).

27 E.g. Clifford Geertz, *The Interpretation of Cultures* (New York: Basic Books, 1973).

28 The year 1974 marked the largest decline in the stock market (24 percent).

29 Thomas L. Friedman, *The Lexus and the Olive Tree* (New York: Anchor Books, 1999), pp. 53–55.

30 As defined by Manuel Castells, *The Rise of the Network Society.* (Oxford: Blackwell Publishers, 1996).

31 London: Hamish Hamilton, 1992.

32 Cf. Leslie A. White, *The Concept of Cultural Systems* (New York: Columbia University Press, 1975), pp. 66–69.

33 Peter Lienhardt, *Shaikhdoms of Eastern Arabia* (New York: Palgrave, 2001), pp. 16–17.

34 *Ibid.*, p. 22.

35 *Ibid.*

36 *Ibid.*, p. 19.

37 *Ibid.*

38 Herb, p. 37.

39 Robert G. Hoyland, *Arabia and the Arabs* (Routledge: London, 2001), p. 114.

40 Emile Durkheim, *The Division of Labor in Society* (New York: Free Press), p. 1964.

41 Herb, pp. 5, 8.

42 *Ibid.*, p. 3

43 *Ibid.*, pp. 22–23. Cf. Frauke Heard-Bey, *From Trucial States to United Arab Emirates* (Dubai: Motivate Publishing, 2004), pp. 22–26.

44 Historically, the breaking of the dam is dated to the first century CE, when groups dispersed throughout Arabia along with the Arab language.

45 Hoyland, p. 233.

46 According to Hoyland, the Qasimis enter the European historical record during the 1600s when they mediated a conflict between the Sultan of Oman and the Portuguese, roughly at the same time as the Bani Yas were reported around Liwa Oasis. The Al Qasimis had an earlier maritime orientation in the Gulf, whereas the Bani Yas emanated from south Arabia and migrated eastward as Bedouins. *Ibid.*

47 Sharjah and Umm al Qaiwain dispute some of the interior tracts of land that lie between Sharjah and Ras al Khaimah.

48 *Gulf News*, November 5, 2004, supplement on Sheikh Zayed, p. 6.

49 *Gulf News*, November 4, 2004, p. 9.

50 *Majlis* is singular and *majalis* is the plural.

51 Frauke Heard-Bey. "The United Arab Emirates: Statehood and Nation-building in a Traditional Society," *Middle East Journal* 59, no. 3 (2005): 360.

52 See Malcolm Peck, "Formation and Evolution of the Federation and its Institutions," in *United Arab Emirates: A New Perspective*, ed. Ibrahim al Abed and Peter Hellyer, pp. 145–160 (London: The Trident Press), p. 149.

53 Fox's interviews with Nizar Hamdoun, Under-Secretary of the Foreign Ministry, Baghdad, Iraq, July 26, 1990. Cf. John W. Fox. "Eye of the Storm." *Waco Tribune Herald.* September 9, 1990, p. 13A.

54 See *Gulf News*, November 9, 2004, p. 9.

55 *Gulf News*, November 2, 2004.

56 *Ibid.*, p. 10.

57 "Open Criticism a Sign of Change in GCC Politics." *Gulf News*, December 21, 2004, p. 15. Cf. "Saudi Arabia and Kuwait in Row Over Exports." *Gulf News*, January 6, 2005, p. 1.

58 "Rising GCC Investments Put Brakes on Capital Outflow." *Gulf News*, February 25, 2005, business section, p. 2.

59 *Gulf News*, October 10, 2004, p. 37.

60 "Trade Agreement by the End of the Year." *Gulf News*, March 10, 2005, p. 1.

61 "Riyadh Threatens to Act Against Unilateral Pacts." *Gulf News*, January 4, 2005, p. 1.

62 D. Delaney and H. Leitner "The Political Construction of Scale," *Political Geography* 12, no. 2 (1997): 93. Neil Brenner, *New State Spaces* (Oxford: Oxford University Press, 2004), pp. 8–9.

63 Lienhardt, for another application of segmentary lineage organization of higher or more inclusive tribal units, see John W. Fox, *Maya Postclassic State Formation* (Cambridge: Cambridge University Press, 1987).

64 See Serge Sur, "An Analysis of American Hegemony," *Journal of Social Affairs* 19, no. 76 (2002): 55–105; Noam Chomsky, *Hegemony or Survival: America's Quest for Global Dominance* (London: Penguin, 2003).

65 See *Netscape News*, September 3, 2004.

66 *Gulf News*, October 10, 2004.

67 E.g. "UAE Gears Up for WTO Regime." *Gulf News*, December 23, 2004, business section, p. 1.

68 Milton Friedman and Rose Friedman. *Free to Choose: A Personal Statement* (New York: Harcourt Brace Jovanovich, 1980).

69 Edward W. Said. *Orientalism* (New York: Vintage Books, 1978).

70 "Causeway to Link Abu Dhabi and Qatar Announced." *Gulf News*, December 22, 2004, p. 1.

71 See Roger Owen, *State, Power and Politics in the Making of the Modern Middle East*, (London: Routledge, 2000), pp. 35–42.

72 See Ali Al Zu'abi, "Modern Urbanization in Kuwait," *Journal of Social Affairs* 21, no. 81 (2004): 13–30.

73 E.g. "Drastic Increase in Rents Is Against Islam, Say Scholars," *Gulf News*, April 13, 2005.

74 "Supplement on Sheikh Zayed," *Gulf News*, November 5, 2004, p. 7.

75 "Revitalization Movements," *American Anthropologist* 58 (1956): 264–281.
76 The Evangelical Right in the United States also inadvertently or consciously contributes to xenophobia perhaps in continuity of America's long-standing geographic isolationism. In this view, there is little need to understand other cultures if one accepts one's views as "ordained by God." Recent polls reveal that half of Americans believe that the country has a special relationship with God, and 60 percent say that the strength and success of the US is a result of religious faith (*Gulf News*, October 4, 2004). The US becomes then a large "gated community" with a highly religious ideology lifestyle called the "gospel of wealth" [G. Ellen, *Southern Baptists: A Culture in Transition* (Knoxville: University of Tennessee Press 1989]. Niblock notes in his chapter (4) in this volume that the richest 20 percent of the world's population at the end of the economic boom of the 1980s earned 150 times that of the world's poorest 20 percent. The world's richest 1 percent owned more than half of the wealth.
77 Mark Tessler and Dan Corstange, "How Should Americans Understand Arab and Muslim Political Attitudes: Combating Stereotypes with Public Opinion Data from the Middle East," *Journal of Social Affairs* 19, no. 76 (2002): 13–34.
78 See Gilles Kepel, *Jihad: The Trail of Political Islam* (Cambridge: Belknap of Harvard University Press, 2002).
79 About the Sauds and the Wahhabi family, see Robert Lacey, *The Kingdom* (New York: Harcourt Brace Jovanovich, 1981), pp. 57–58.
80 See Benedict Anderson, *Imagined Communities* (London: Verso, 1983).
81 Martin Hvidt, "Limited Success of the IMF and the World Bank in Middle Eastern Reforms," *Journal of Social Affairs* 21, no. 81 (2004): 77–103.
82 *Gulf News*, October 15, 2004.
83 Khaled Al Maeena, *Gulf News*, September 22, 2004. Cf. for the UAE, see "Initiative to Empower Women Announced." *Gulf News*, April 20, 2005, p. 1.
84 *Gulf News*, September 24, 2004, p. 7.
85 Reported in the *Gulf News*, September 22, 24, 2004.
86 Herb, 1991, pp. 4–5.
87 See *Netscape News*, September 3, 2004.
88 A similar argument could be drawn from the case of Turkey's entrance into the European Union. Cf. *Gulf News*, October 12, 2004, citing Turkey's ambassador to France, Uluc Ozulker.
89 "Self-censorship Virus Plagues Media." *Gulf News*, May 3, 2005, p. 9.
90 Benjamin Barber. *Jihad vs. McWorld* (New York: Ballantine Books, 1996).
91 See Sulayman Khalaf, "Globalization and Heritage Revival in the Gulf: An Anthropological Look at the Dubai Heritage Village," *Journal of Social Affairs* 19, no. 75 (2002): 13–42.
92 See Zahlan, p. 28.
93 Durkheim 1893.
94 El-Sayed El-Aswad, "Sanctified Cosmology: Maintaining Muslim Identity with Globalism," *Journal of Social Affairs* 20, no. 80 (2003): 65–94.
95 "Who Needs the Arabic Language?" *Gulf News*, December 23, 2004, p. 15.
96 All quotes from *Gulf News*, October 5, 2004.
97 *Unleashing Entrepreneurship: Making Business Work for the Poor*, Commission on the Private Sector and Development, Chaired by Paul Martin and Ernesto Zedillo. New York: United Nations Development Programme.
98 *Gulf News*, October 5, 2004, 1.
99 Hoyland, 118.
100 *Gulf News*, September 24, 2004, p. 13.
101 Andrzej Kapiszewski, "The Changing Status of Arab Migrant Workers in the GCC," *Journal of Social Affairs* 20, no. 78 (2003): 39–60.
102 *Ibid.*, p. 43.
103 "For Oil-rich Brides, Caviar, Crystal, and 1,000 Guests." *The Wall Street Journal.* January 20, 2006, pp. 1, 6.

104 Hoyland, 2001, p. 23.
105 See Fox, p. 92.
106 Zahlan, pp. 112–115.
107 *Gulf News*, October 5, 2004, p. 1.
108 E.g. Said, 1978.
109 "Dubai Leads Arab Cities in Information Infrastructure." *Gulf News*, January 2005, p. 42. Cf. "Region May See Dubai as Research Hub." *Gulf News*, April 17, 2005, p. 6.
110 Herb, p. 12.
111 AUS has grown in numbers and quality of students to 4,000 in six years of its founding, perhaps aided by the swelling of students returning to the Gulf after September 11, 2001, who were enrolled in US universities, and the acquisition of American accreditation in 2003.
112 See M.J. Healey, *Location and Change: Perspectives on Economic Geography* (Oxford: Oxford University Press, 1990).
113 "Burj Dubai to Launch Sale of Business Suites." *Gulf News*, April 1, 2005, business section, p. 1.
114 Frauke Heard-Bey. "An Insider's View of Globalization in the Gulf." *Journal of Social Affairs* 21, no. 83 (2004): 56.

References (excluding newspaper articles)

Al Zu'abi, Ali. "Modern Urbanization in Kuwait." *Journal of Social Affairs* 21, no. 81 (2004): 13–30.

Anderson, Benedict. *Imagined Communities*. London: Verso, 1983.

Barber, Benjamin. *Jihad vs. McWorld*. New York: Ballantine Books, 1996.

Bauman, Zygmunt. "Is There a Postmodern Sociology?" In *The Transmodern Turn*, edited by Steven Seidman, 187–204. Cambridge: Cambridge University Press, 1994.

Bell, Daniel. *The Cult and Contradictions of Capitalism*. New York: Basic Books, 1976.

Berman, Morris. *The Reenchantment of the World*. New York: Bantam Books, 1981.

Braudel, Fernand. *Capitalism and Material Life 1400–1800*. New York: Harper and Row, 1973.

Brenner, Neil. *New State Spaces*. Oxford: Oxford University Press, 2004.

Castells, Manuel. *The Rise of the Network Society*. Oxford: Blackwell Publishers, 1996.

Castells, Manuel. "The Rise of the Network Society." In *The Information Age: Economy, Society and Culture*, Vol. 1. Oxford: Blackwell Publishers, 1996.

Castells, Manuel. *The Power of Identity*. Oxford: Blackwell Publishers, 2004.

Chomsky, Noam. *Hegemony or Survival: America's Quest for Global Dominance*. London: Penguin, 2003.

Delaney, D. and H. Leitner. "The Political Construction of Scale." *Political Geography* 12, no. 2 (1997): 93–97.

Durkheim, Emile. *The Division of Labor in Society*. New York: Free Press, 1964 (1893).

El-Aswad, el-Sayed. "Sanctified Cosmology: Maintaining Muslim Identity with Globalism." *Journal of Social Affairs* 20, no. 80 (2003): 65–94.

Ellen, G. *Southern Baptists: A Culture in Transition*. Knoxville: University of Tennessee Press, 1989.

Foucault, Michel. *The Archaeology of Knowledge*. New York: Pantheon Books, 1972.

Fox, John W. *Maya Postclassic State Formation*. Cambridge: Cambridge University Press, 1987.

Fox, John W. "Solutions to Water Stress in the Middle East." *Journal of Social Affairs* 20, no. 77 (2003): 83–99.

Fox, John W. "Theoretical Approaches on the State, Lineages, and Women in al-Andalus." *Journal of Social Affairs* 20, no. 79 (2003): 87–125.

Friedman, Milton and Rose Friedman. *Free to Choose: A Personal Statement*. New York: Harcourt Brace Jovanovich, 1980.

Friedman, Thomas, L. *The Lexus and the Olive Tree*. New York: Anchor Books, 1999.

Fukuyama, Francis. *The End of History and the Last Man*. London: Hamish Hamilton, 1992.

Geertz, Clifford. *The Interpretation of Cultures*. New York: Basic Books, 1973.

Harris, Marvin. *Why Nothing Works: The Anthropology of Daily Life*. New York: Touchstone, Simon and Schuster, 1986.

Healey, M.J. *Location and Change: Perspectives on Economic Geography*. Oxford: Oxford University Press, 1990.

Heard-Bey, Frauke. *From Trucial States to United Arab Emirates*. Dubai: Motivate Publishing, 2004 (original 1982).

Heard-Bey, Frauke. "An Insider's View of Globalization in the Gulf." *Journal of Social Affairs* 21, no. 83 (2004):53–67.

Heard-Bey, Frauke. "The United Arab Emirates: Statehood and Nation-building in a Traditional Society." *Middle East Journal* 59, no. 3 (2005): 357–375.

Herb, Michael. *All in the Family: Absolutism, Revolution, and Democracy in the Middle Eastern Monarchies*. Albany: State University of New York Press, 1999.

Hoyland Robert, G. *Arabia and the Arabs*. Routledge, London, 2001.

Hvidt, Martin. "Limited Success of the IMF and the World Bank in Middle Eastern Reforms." *Journal of Social Affairs* 21, no. 81 (2004): 77–103.

Kapiszewski, Andrzej. "The Changing Status of Arab Migrant Workers in the GCC." *Journal of Social Affairs* 20, no. 78 (2003): 39–60.

Kepel, Gilles. *Jihad: The Trail of Political Islam*. Cambridge: Belknap of Harvard University Press, 2002.

Khalaf, Sulayman. "Globalization and Heritage Revival in the Gulf: An Anthropological Look at the Dubai Heritage Village." *Journal of Social Affairs* 19, no. 75 (2002): 13–42.

Lacey, Robert. *The Kingdom*. New York: Harcourt Brace Jovanovich, 1981.

Lienhardt, Peter. *Shaikhdoms of Eastern Arabia*. New York: Palgrave, 2001.

Mourtada Sabbah, Nada and John W. Fox. "View from the Prosperous Gulf States." Paper presented at the conference "Bridging the Gap: A Forum on the Crisis in Arab-American Relations," Center for Contemporary Arab Studies, Georgetown University, Washington, DC, April 2005.

Niebuhr, Carsten. *Travels Through Arabia, and the Other Countries in the East*. Edinburgh, 1792.

Owen, Roger. State, *Power and Politics in the Making of the Modern Middle East*. London: Routledge, 2000.

Peck, Malcolm. "Formation and Evolution of the Federation and its Institutions." In *United Arab Emirates: A New Perspective*, edited by Ibrahim al Abed and Peter Hellyer, 145–160. London: The Trident Press.

Al Qassimi, Sultan Bin Mohammed. *The Myth of Arab Piracy in the Gulf*. London: Routledge, 1988.

Al Qassimi, Sultan Bin Mohammed. *Power Struggles and Trade in the Gulf, 1620–1820*. Exeter, UK: Forest Row, 1999.

Rosenberg, Ellen M. *The Southern Baptists: A Subculture in Transition*. Knoxville: The University of Tennessee Press, 1989.

Sahlins, Marshall. *Stone Age Economics*. Chicago: Aldine, 1972.

Said, Edward, W. *Orientalism*. New York: Vintage Books, 1978.

Sassen, Saskia. *Globalization and its Discontents*. New York: The Free Press, 1998.

Smith, Adam. *An Inquiry into the Nature and Cause of the Wealth of Nations*. London, 1776.

Sur, Serge. "An Analysis of American Hegemony." *Journal of Social Affairs* 19, no. 76 (2002): 55–105.

Tessler, Mark and Dan Corstange. "How Should Americans Understand Arab and Muslim Political Attitudes: Combating Stereotypes with Public Opinion Data from the Middle East." *Journal of Social Affairs* 19, no. 76 (2002): 13–34.

Wallace, Anthony, F.C. "Revitalization Movements." *American Anthropologist* 58 (1956): 264–281.

Wallerstein, Immanuel. *The Modern World-System: Capitalist Agriculture and the Origins of the European-world Economy in the Sixteenth Century*. New York: Academic Press, 1974.

Waters, Malcolm. *Globalization*. New York: Routledge, 1995.

Weber, Max. *Economy and Society*, 1921.

White, Hayden, V. *Metahistory: The Historical Imagination in Nineteenth Century Europe*. Baltimore: The Johns Hopkins University Press, 1973.

White, Leslie. *The Concept of Cultural Systems*. New York: Columbia University Press, 1975.

Wikan, Unni. *Behind the Veil in Arabia*. Chicago: University of Chicago Press, 1982.

Williams, Robin. *American Society: A Sociological Perspective*. New York: Knopf, 1970.

Wolf, Eric, R. *Europe and the People without History*. Berkeley: University of California Press, 1982.

Zahlan, Rosemarie Said. *The Making of the Modern Gulf States*. Reading, UK: Ithaca Press, 1998.

Part II

Globalization

Concepts, history, dynamics, and consequences

2 The concept of security in a globalizing world

*Steve Smith**

This chapter[1] was written in the aftermath of the second war in Iraq and was spurred by the challenges to our understanding of security posed by the events of September 11, 2001. My purpose, firstly, is to clear away the conceptual undergrowth surrounding the concept of security, both so that we do not slip into implicit, possibly hidden, assumptions about the nature of international security, and, crucially, to whom and about what security refers. A second aim is to explicitly raise the question of the relationship between our thinking about security and our own social, cultural and even geographical locations. A third and underlying aim is to reflect upon how our theories about international security, both explicit and implicit, relate to the security practices.

In order to accomplish these three goals, I first outline the traditional model of international security, which dominated strategic and security studies from the end of World War II to the end of the Cold War. I then review how the traditional model has been criticized since the end of the Cold War. I examine six alternative approaches and discuss whether these widen and deepen the concept of security to render it more useful for understanding international politics in present contexts. Finally, I highlight how the literature may aid in understanding the nature of international security in a globalizing world.

However, let us keep in mind that the events of September 11, 2001 are claimed to have fundamentally changed the nature of the international security scene. This is mistaken. The security setting for "globalization, civil conflicts, and the national security state" was the same on September 10 as it was on September 12. This requires a bit of telescoping in on the course the events of September 11 with attention on types of actors, on types of rationalities, and on forms of security threat that have largely been ignored in the traditional literature on international security. Putting these factors into comparative relief says more about the myopia and cultural lenses of the mainstream than it does about the nature of security. For the vast majority of the world's population, the events of September 11 represented the "normalization" of the United States' security situation, in that the challenge to the internal security of US (and other) citizens brought the norm to the exception. In other words, much of the reaction to September 11, especially within the United States, reflects the dominance of a culturally specific view of international security, that as essentially the military relationship between national state actors.

A second contextual point is that it is necessary to note that security is not scientifically a neutral definition; all perspectives about "security" and to what it should refer (the state, society, or individual) are views that reflect (often hidden) assumptions about international politics specifically and the social world generally. This critique follows the line of reasoning of "standpoint theory" (e.g. the standpoints of the United States) vis-à-vis "others" and of reflexivity (i.e. reflexive of American interests). This is not the same as simply saying that there are different concepts of international security. I argue that the term can never be defined in some scientific or neutral way since its meaning will always be located within wider, and often conflicting, views about the social world of who is doing the viewing and what national interests are at play. Thus, for example, empirical evidence cannot settle disputes between rival accounts of security since there is no neutral database existing outside of particular theories. For example, to claim that international security is concerned with the military relations between states depends for its explanatory power on a prior and hidden view of the relationship between the internal and external environments of states and about the links between economics and politics. To use the philosopher W.B. Gallie's words, the meaning of terms like *security* is essentially contested.[2] And use of either provides a selection of the data considered relevant. Thus, the data are inextricably tied to the theory or model.

The traditional view of security

I now summarize the main features of the traditional conception of international security to establish a benchmark for our discussion of alternatives. The core assumption of the traditional view is that security relates to the military interactions between nation states. The technical term for such a view is *realism*. Realism is a long-standing account of political life focused on a conservative pessimistic account of human nature that sees individuals as self-interested and potentially aggressive in the face of limited resources. This is also called economic rationalism. This perspective claims a universal motivation for human action, regardless of history, culture, or context. In this line of reasoning, states are motivated by the same basic human drives, whatever their ideology or stated reasons. States are therefore locked in a constant and unavoidable struggle for power. A recent variant of the theory, called neo-realism, downplays the rootedness of the power quest on humans. Instead, the main features of international politics are based on the structure of the international political system.[3] There are 12 core assumptions of this view of international politics:

- States are the major actors in international politics.
- States exist in a structural situation of international anarchy, which creates a self-help system distinct from the kind of politics found within states.
- International anarchy is the main force shaping the behavior of states.
- Domestic factors rarely affect the external behavior of states.
- Non-state actors are of limited importance in world politics, and even where they are, they must work within the rules created by states.

- International anarchy penalizes states that fail to look after their vital interests.
- States possess military forces to protect their most vital interests.
- States tend to behave as instrumentally rational unitary actors.
- States are preoccupied with survival, power, and security.
- States co-exist in a security dilemma whereby it is problematic to find a balance between defensive capability and not threatening one's adversaries.
- Unsure about the motivations and intentions of other states, states tend to be wary of international cooperation even when they have common interests.
- International institutions affect cooperation only marginally, since states will try to shape them to suit their interests; they are thus settings for conflicts between states rather than autonomous actors.

This model of international politics leads to a rigorous and parsimonious account of international security whereby a state's place in the international system will dictate the fundamentals of its foreign and defense policy. The main determinant of this place is the distribution of power within the system, which broadly speaking splits into hegemonic, bipolar, or multipolar systems. This account has been subjected to much criticism. The main criticisms are: (1) the effects outlined above do not logically follow from anarchy, and there are clearly alternatives; (2) neo-realism does not explain change; (3) neo-realism also neglects the beliefs and intentions of state leaders, and these seem to becoming increasingly important in world politics; and (4) neo-realism treats states as unitary actors in a natural, external world of international politics but one that constitutes an external reality for us to observe.

Alternative conceptions of security

However, the traditional model of security increasingly lacks resolution and has been attacked. Alternative accounts are proposed to replace or augment the model. We now examine six main alternative approaches to thinking about international security and although I cannot say much about each, I hope I can give an indication of their main themes.

Constructivist security studies

In constructivist security studies, security is not constructed as existing "out there" waiting for analysts or politicians to discover it. Instead, security is made and re-made by human intersubjective understandings and is embedded in social relations. I note two leading collections of constructivist security studies.[4] The first, edited by Adler and Barnett,[5] proposes that states see security as achievable through community rather than through power. Security, therefore, is something that can be constructed; insecurity or anarchy is not simply the given condition of the international system. As such, security is what states make it and thus believe that: "A constructivist approach, which recognizes the importance of knowledge for transforming international structures and security politics, is best suited to taking seriously how the international community can shape security politics and create the conditions for a stable peace."[6]

Katzenstein[7] edits the second collection, which asserts that national "security interests are defined by actors who respond to cultural factors. This does not mean that power, conventionally understood as material capabilities, is unimportant for an analysis of national security ... but the meanings that states and other political actors attach to power and security help us explain their behavior."[8] Yet, in both cases, the central actor remains the nation-state, and security continues to be defined in military terms. Constructivist security studies are thus criticized as mere supplements to realist and neo-realist security theory. As Kowert and Legro note, constructivist studies do no more than "fill gaps where other perspectives fall short."[9] Similarly for Desch, "The best case that can be made for these new cultural theories is that they are sometimes useful as a supplement to realist theories."[10]

Feminist security studies

Here, international relations are inevitably gendered in their consequences and in their identities and subjectivities. Yet, the discipline is purportedly gender-blind. I see four main strands in feminist security studies. First, Cohn, and Cooke and Woollacott note the masculinized nature of the language used in strategic discourse.[11] Second, Elshtain and Hartsock critique the conventional portrayal of the distinction between men and women as one of the "just warrior" and as the "beautiful soul"; they further note that these myths recreate the roles of women as non-combatants and that of men as warriors.[12] Third, where do women fit into international security? In answer, Enloe is quite influential, and asks, "where are the women?" in international relations. Only by showing where women fit into international relations may we comprehend how power operates and embeds most relations. Thus, Enloe analyzes the roles of women as prostitutes around military bases, at how masculinity is constructed in the military, and examines how women soldiers are treated.[13] Finally, the practical relationship between education, peace research, and feminism is borne out in linkages between militarism and sexism in society. Brock-Utne argues that both are maintained by a similar worldview that men are inherently aggressive and superior whereas women are inherently non-violent and inferior.[14] There are two central criticisms of feminist work. One is that "women" are presented as if there was such a thing as a woman's perspective applicable to all women; another is that feminist perspectives deal with only peripheral aspects of international security.

Post-structuralist security studies

In the most general sense, post-structuralists deny that knowledge in the security studies is through verification. Thus, their approach is commonly attacked for its absence of testable hypotheses and propositions and for the lack of any appeal to a notion of verifiable "truth." Rather, post-structuralist accounts stress the role of identity, discourse, and narrative. To illustrate, the parties involved in conflicts are not merely actors with different values and preferences but instead have fundamentally different identities that lead them to see the world in terms of very distinct narratives. Thus, the traditional discourse of security (above) constructs binary oppositions of "us" and "them," of "inside" and "outside" that present as natural contingent and culturally/historically specific definitions of the participants and issues. For Klein, the core concepts of traditional security studies are constructs "made intelligible to social agents through the medium of language. Instead of presuming their existence and meaning, we should historicize and relativize them as sets of practices with distinct genealogical trajectories. The issue, in short, is not whether they are true or false but how they have acquired their meaning."[15] Campbell, looking at US foreign policy, "offers a non-essentialist account of danger which highlights how the domains of inside/outside, self/other, and domestic/foreign are moral spaces defined by the borders of identity as much as the territorial boundaries of states. These boundaries are constituted through the writing of a threat."[16] For Campbell, "security ... is first and foremost a performative discourse constitutive of political order."[17]

Post-structuralism is criticized for not being open to empirical testing basic in the social sciences. By offering a series of readings or narratives, post-structuralism negates that "truth" is independent of context and too relativistic. In short, a single set of universal principles can be deduced.

Human security

The concept of human security emerged from the 1994 United Nations Development Program (UNDP) report,[18] which proposed to shift from nuclear security to human security. This is also a perspective from the ground up – what is called the social interaction perspective in sociology. To bear out the vantage point of this approach, I cite the various items of concern in day-to-day thinking of the population.

> With the dark shadows of the Cold War receding, one can now see that many conflicts are within nations rather than between nations. For most people, a feeling of insecurity arises more from worries about daily life than from the dread of a cataclysmic world event. Will they and their families have enough to eat? Will they lose their jobs? Will their streets and neigborhoods be safe from crime? Will they be tortured by a repressive state? Will they become victims of violence because of their gender? Will their religion or ethnic origin target them for persecution? In the final analysis, human security is a child who did not die, a disease that did not spread, a job that was not cut, an ethnic tension that did not explode in violence, a dissident who was not silenced. Human security is not a concern with weapons – it is a concern with human life and dignity.[19]

The UNDP report outlines seven basic areas of human security: economic security, food security, health security, environmental security, personal security, community security, and political security. Six main threats to human security are identified: unchecked population growth, disparities in economic opportunities, migration pressures, environmental degradation, drug trafficking, and international terrorism.[20] In 1997, the UNDP refined the concept of human security and introduced the distinction between income poverty and human poverty. Income poverty refers to an income of US $1 a day and less, and human poverty involves factors such as life expectancy and illiteracy.[21] The notion of human security has been taken up by the World Bank and the International Monetary Fund, and the governments of Canada and Japan. In academic synthesis, conflict and security are linked to economic development. Thomas sees that human security shifts focus from the state to the individual and shifts the security of the individual to individual needs.[22] For Thomas, human security requires that basic material needs are met (food, shelter, education, health care, etc.) and that the human dignity is achieved, which allows "personal autonomy, control over one's life, and unhindered participation in the community."[23]

The Copenhagen school and security

The two key theorists from the Copenhagen scholar approach are Barry Buzan and Ole Waever. In 1983, Buzan[24] broadened the definition of security to involve five sectors rather than the traditional focus on military security alone. Buzan added political, economic, societal, and ecological security sectors, although he kept the state as the central reference point. In a series of publications with Waever, Buzan developed "societal security" for understanding security in post-Cold War Europe.[25] Waever worked on "securitization,"[26] which is best understood as a discursive speech act. By labeling something as a security issue, it becomes imbued with importance and urgency that legitimizes special measures outside of the usual political process. In a recent book, Buzan, Waever, and de Wilde assert that "securitization studies aim to gain an increasingly precise understanding of who securitizes, on what issues (threats), for whom (referent objects), why, with what results, and, not least, under what conditions (i.e., what explains when securitization is successful)."[27] Buzan, Waever, and de Wilde then relate this securitization to the five sectors outlined by Buzan's 1983 work as well as to a regional, rather than a state focus. McSweeney criticizes the Copenhagen school, claiming that society is identified in an objectivist, positivistic way. This means that Buzan and Waever treat society and identity as "objective realities, out there to be discovered and analyzed,"[28] rather than being created and re-created by changing social forces. Thus, identity is something "real" that exists for any society, whereas McSweeney argues that identity is negotiated and not discovered. "Who we are is not a matter of fact imposed on individuals who 'belong' to the 'society' of Waever *et al.* Their idea of a collective identity as a social fact projects the image of a collective self to be discovered: we are who we are ... [whereas] we are who we want to be, subject to the constraints of history."[29]

Critical security studies

Finally, critical security studies are the most sustained and coherent critique of the traditional security model. One stream in critical studies is epitomized by the volume *Critical Security Studies*, edited by Krause and Williams.[30] The contributors to this volume share dissatisfaction with orthodox security studies and with the agenda of mainstream security studies after the end of the Cold War. Krause and Williams stress moving from a military dimension of state behavior to a focus on individuals, community, and identity.[31] They propose promoting intellectual pluralism and encouraging a variety of approaches to studying security rather than endorsing one particular approach. Jones locates critical security studies within the tradition of Horkheimer, Honneth, and Habermas, where the emancipation of a genuinely critical theory is emphasized. For Jones, traditional security studies reify the existing order and treat the observer-observed relationship as unproblematic, which is ostensibly neutrally reported.

Booth also reconceptualizes security studies by focussing on human emancipation. Only a process of security covaries with emancipation. He writes, "The next stage of thinking about security in world affairs should be marked by moving it out of its almost exclusively realist framework into the critical philosophical camp."[32] Booth further argues that emancipation "should logically be given precedence in our thinking about security over the mainstream themes of power and order,"[33] and defines it as "the freeing of people (as individuals and groups) from the physical and human constraints which stop them carrying out what they would freely choose to do. War and the threat of war are among those constraints, together with poverty, poor education, political oppression and so on. Security and emancipation are two sides of the same coin. Emancipation, not power or order, produces true security. Emancipation, theoretically, is security."[34]

One criticism of critical security studies is that its focus on emancipation is inappropriate because analysis is confused with morality. An objective analysis of events is replaced with a normative commitment to human emancipation. Eriksson sees critical security studies as "straightforwardly political: the established realism is blamed for the hostility, instability and injustice that unfortunately are a part of world politics ... Like classical idealism, critical security studies open up for discussion how things could and should be rather than how they are."[35] A second concern is with the focus on the emancipation of individuals. Ayoob argues that critical security studies tend to "impose a model of contemporary Western polities ... that are far removed from Third World realities."[36] Adopting an avowedly realist perspective, Ayoob advocates focus on the security of the state: "An explicitly state-centric definition of security is likely to provide an analytical tool of tremendous value that should not be sacrificed at the altar of utopian thinking."[37]

Broadening and deepening the concept of security

The alternative accounts of security broaden the scope of understanding to include a wider range of issues beyond the military dimension, and they deepen the concept with reference to parameters other than the state. But many question whether this undermines its utility. Thus, Baldwin argues that the term *security* now has little analytical usage since it no longer has an agreed upon core meaning.[38] Morgan claims that the coherence of security studies is being eroded: "Broadening security studies to cover other 'harms' – economic, environmental and so forth – is unfortunate for it lumps together deliberate, organized physical harm (or threats thereof) with other threats and pains."[39] Yet, Krause and Williams counter that "It may be necessary to broaden the agenda of security studies (theoretically and methodologically) in order to narrow the agenda of *security*. A more profound understanding of the forces that create political loyalties, give rise to threats, and designate appropriate collective responses could open the way to ... 'desecuritization' – the progressive removal of issues from the security agenda as they are dealt with via institutions and practices that do not implicate force, violence, or the 'security dilemma'."[40]

In short, the concept of security is itself a battleground. Some wish to broaden and deepen it, and some are attempting to reinvigorate the neoclassical realist approach focusing on the military security of nation states. For them the broadening of the meaning of security threatens to undermine the utility of the term. If security refers to any threat then it becomes meaningless. Protagonists contend that the traditional definition is a partial and a one-sided view of the world from the perspective of the powerful. This is reflexive of Western dominance of world politics, which itself relies on a set of prior and implicit binary oppositions between inside and outside, public and the private, society and state, security and development, and between economics and politics.

Security and September 11

While the events of September 11, 2001 did not create epochal change, they nonetheless manifest significance in the future of world politics. The forms of violence used were not new, nor was the role of non-state actors. Neither was this the first time that the United States had faced externally planned terrorism on its own territory (there had been an attempt to destroy the World Trade Center in 1993). But the events significantly changed in the security context of globalization, especially for future civil conflicts and for the make-up of the national security of the state.

The events of September 11, 2001 set in motion a series of major effects on world politics. First, it led to a massive re-assertion of US power. The main indicators are:

- The proposed boost in US defense spending by 14 percent in one year alone, taking the budget to $379 billion. This is the largest percentage increase in 20 years. By 2008, a further $120 billion increase is projected. Remember that even before these proposed increases, the US defense budget is greater than those of the next eight countries combined. With the proposed increases, the United States will outspend the next 15 countries, 13 of which are US allies.
- In January 2002, the United States added Iran, Iraq, North Korea, Syria, and Libya to the list of potential nuclear targets. The United States also

proposed the development of a set of "limited" nuclear weapons for use (presumably pre-emptively) against hardened command posts.

- In January 2002, US President George W. Bush unilaterally announced that an "axis of evil," comprising Iran, Iraq, and North Korea, was intimately involved in terrorism. Since then, a widening of the "war" against Iraq had been discussed in think tanks. However, the troop levels required is quite important and there seems to be little support for it among US allies (with the exception of the United Kingdom).

- The Bush doctrine announced that the United States has a right to act unilaterally against any nation that supports terrorism (as defined by the US). Addressing a group of cadets at West Point, the US military academy, Bush advised, "Our security will require transforming the military you will lead. The military must be ready to strike at a moment's notice in any dark corner of the world. All nations that decide for aggression and terror will pay a price." Paradoxically, Jonathan Steele notes that the Bush doctrine "is hijacking the anti-terrorist agenda and crashing it into the most sacred skyscraper in New York: the headquarters of the UN."[41]

The second effect of the September 11 events has been an increasingly unilateralist reassertion of US power. In the first few weeks after September 11, the Bush administration seemed more multilateralist; building a coalition of allies against terrorism was clearly a prime goal. However, within two months, the United States embarked on an even more vigorously unilateralist foreign policy. For example, to counter political violence in the Middle East, America sided more firmly with Israel at the expense of a fundamental split with many of its European allies. If this split continues, it could presage a major realignment of world power.

Thirdly, the intensification of response also transformed the internal politics of the United States. Before September 11, President Bush was seen as tainted by concerns about the legitimacy of his electoral victory. September 11 instantly changed perceptions of Bush, and his popularity increased. He has grown in stature and has a widespread and deep domestic foundation for his foreign policy actions and for his presidency. US national identity is stronger than it has been in decades, with relatively little in the way of domestic criticism of Bush's foreign and defense policies. Most worryingly, there have been attempts to demonize a list of some forty academics who have spoken out against US foreign policy. These were labeled "traitors" in a deliberate campaign led by the vice president's wife.[42] In short, September 11 has created a more assertive and united public in the US, and this has provided bedrock for an even more unilateralist foreign policy than seen in two generations.

Fourthly, the horrendous and graphic nature of the September 11 attacks has given the Bush administration the moral authority for whatever actions it wishes to take in retaliation since it was portrayed as an innocent victim. I am *not* saying that those who died were anything other than innocent victims, but I am saying that the horror of the attacks makes it difficult to provide any analysis as to why those who planned and undertook them did so. It has also made it difficult to criticize the "war against terrorism" without being seen as condoning the September 11 attacks.

Fifthly, the attacks spurred new security considerations and led to wars in Afghanistan and Iraq. They have made one peace possible (in Northern Ireland) and have severely impacted another (in Palestine/Israel). They have also shown that the state can no longer (if it ever could) guarantee the security of its people: even the United States was unable to prevent the attacks, and it will probably not be able to prevent future attacks of similar or greater magnitude.

Sixthly, the attacks suggest that states are no longer the key actors in world politics. Just as globalization restructures world politics so that most of the most important activities take place between non-state actors, such as the internet, banking, politicized religious groups, and global civil society, so political violence is no longer the preserve of states. Yet, just as globalization undermines the state, it simultaneously is empowered as a crucial agent of globalization. Thus, in the United States, the central state has rarely been more powerful and more legitimate. An interesting reflection of this is the public popularity of organizations such as the New York Police Department and the New York Fire Department. The state is both undermined and central to security in a globalized world. Note also that globalization has developed repressive state structures that represent the greatest threats to the populations of those countries.

Seventhly, the events of September 11 indicate that there is no one underlying logic, such as rationality theory, to world politics and thus no one solution to human security issues. This realization shatters the assumption of the proponents of globalization that the conveyor belts of economic development, liberal democracy, and modernization were in some way universal and irreversible. Remember, there is also no logic to history, and certainly no direction, no teleology. But if September 11 contradicts Fukuyama's "End of History" thesis,[43] please note that it does not vindicate the "clash of civilizations" (i.e. Samuel Huntington).[44] The kinds of "fault-lines" between civilizations outlined by Huntington are not evident in the response to September 11. To cut a long argument short, thus, what is not at stake is a battle between civilizations – the disputes within civilizations are more important. They reveal, for example, that it is misleading, though politically useful, to claim that Islam is a unitary civilization.

Finally, what are the developing security underpinnings of this globalized world? This is both a practical and a moral question. Practically, what will be the security structures to manage a globalized world? Will globalization continue to erode the role of the state in security? Yet, if states are no longer the core actors in security, then who will be? In moral concerns, what will be the source of political legitimacy in a globalized world? To put the problem more precisely: while many interrogate the morality and legitimacy of the United States' foreign and defense policies, how do we interrogate the agendas of non-state actors in world politics and assess the legitimacy of their actions? This raises fundamental issues about the link of politics with morality and also about the form of security structure for the post-Cold War world.

Conclusion

Our discussion of the security environment after September 11 brings us back to the relationship between international security theory and its practice. Some argue vehemently that the events vindicate either realism, with its focus on the inherent aggression in human nature, or neo-realism and its core tenet that if power becomes too concentrated then balancing will occur (in this case via the actions of non-state actors such as Al-Qaeda). My view, however, is that the security theory that we need to make sense of the contemporary world contrasts with the comforting simplicities of realism and neo-realism. Not only this, but we must keep in mind the deeper issue of how our theories help constitute social reality. As such, realism and especially neo-realism are based on positivistic underpinnings and try to explain the social world as a natural scientist explains the physical world. Positivism here is fundamentally misconceived both by using a set of epistemological and methodological lenses inappropriate to the social world and because it fails to take into account the role of theories in creating social interaction. In this light, we need to be particularly careful how we theorize international security, since theory shapes the categories within which we debate the realm of the politically possible. Thus, theories that envision security in narrow military terms and states as the referent object for security and that stress the continuities and regularities of international politics run the risk of re-creating that world. It becomes especially dangerous when this underlying theoretical logic is linked to a simplistic "us versus them" mentality. The notion of an "axis of evil" may play well in US domestic politics, but it fails to comprehend the complexities of world politics generally and of international security specifically. It also depends on a set of assumptions about the nature of security and its referent object that are views from somewhere and ultimately reflect US dominance in world politics.

Thus, how do we develop a theory that is relevant to security in a globalizing world? Security theory needs to understand the nature of contemporary globalization that is decidedly not found in the mainstream literature. That theory defines security too narrowly, and has little to say about the predominant security problems in the world. Globalization has changed the world and has created new security problems, processes, and actors; it is not just that while traditional theory is limited in explaining these new problems, processes, and actors, these theories also interweave and are implicated in attempts by the dominant to control the world. Theory thus creates reality, too. Thus, if we accept these theories uncritically we are in danger of re-constituting the world of the dominant and re-establishing their/our power. Academics should not reinforce power but question it and should try to develop theories that have practical use for more than just the powerful.

Notes

* Vice Chancellor, University of Exeter, Professor of International Politics.
1 An earlier and fuller version of this paper was presented at the 37th Otago Foreign Policy School and will be published in the resulting book *Globalization, Civil Conflicts and the National Security State* edited by Robert Patman (Routledge, forthcoming).

2 W.B. Gallie, "Essentially Contested Concepts," *Proceedings of the Aristotelian Society* 56 (1955–56): 167–198.

3 The classic statement of this perspective is Kenneth Waltz's *Theory of International Politics* (Reading, MA: Addison-Wesley, 1979).

4 See Alastair Iain Johnston, *Cultural Realism: Strategic Culture and Grand Strategy in Chinese History* (Princeton, NJ: Princeton University Press, 1995); Jeffrey Legro, *Cooperation Under Fire: Anglo-German Restraint during World War II* (Ithaca, NY: Cornell University Press, 1995); Elizabeth Kier, *Imagining War: French Military Doctrine between the Wars* (Princeton, NJ: Princeton University Press, 1997); Richard Price, *The Chemical Weapons Taboo* (Ithaca, NY: Cornell University Press, 1997).

5 Emanuel Adler and Michael Barnett, eds, *Security Communities* (Cambridge: Cambridge University Press, 1998).

6 *Ibid.*, 59.

7 Peter Katzenstein, ed., *The Culture of National Security: Norms and Identity in World Politics* (New York: Columbia University Press, 1996).

8 *Ibid.*, 2.

9 Paul Kowert and Jeffery Legro, "Norms, Identity, and Their Limits: A Theoretical Reprise," in Katzenstein, *The Culture of National Security*, 496.

10 Michael Desch, "Culture Clash: Assessing the Importance of Ideas in Security Studies," *International Security* 23 (1998): 142.

11 Carol Cohn, "Sex, Death and the Rational World of Defense Intellectuals," *Signs* 12 (1987): 687–718; M. Cooke and A. Woollacott, eds, *Gendering War Talk* (Princeton, NJ: Princeton University Press, 1993).

12 Jean Elshtain, *Women and War* (New York: Basic Books, 1987); Nancy Hartsock, "The Barracks Community in Western Political Thought," *Women's Studies International Forum* 5 (1982): 283–286.

13 Cynthia Enloe, *Bananas, Beaches and Bases: Making Feminist Sense of International Politics* (Berkeley, CA: University of California Press, 1990); *The Morning After: Sexual Politics at the End of the Cold War* (Berkeley, CA: University of California Press, 1993); *Maneuvers: The International Politics of Militarizing Women's Lives* (Berkeley, CA: University of California Press, 2000).

14 B. Brock-Utne, *Educating for Peace: A Feminist Perspective* (Oxford: Pergamon Press, 1985).

15 Bradley S. Klein, *Strategic Studies and World Order: The Global Politics of Deterrence* (Cambridge: Cambridge University Press, 1994), 10.

16 David Campbell, *Writing Security: United States Foreign Policy and the Politics of Identity* (Manchester: Manchester University Press, 1992).

17 *Ibid.*, 253.

18 United Nations Development Program, *Human Development Report 1994* (New York: Oxford University Press, 1994). Citations that follow are from a reprint of sections of the UNDP report, "Redefining Security: The Human Dimension" in *Current History* (1995): 229–236.

19 *Ibid.*, 229.

20 *Ibid.*, 230–236.

21 United Nations Development Program, *Human Development Report 1997* (New York: Oxford University Press, 1997).

22 Caroline Thomas, *Global Governance, Development and Human Security: The Challenge of Poverty and Inequality* (London: Pluto Press, 2000). See also Caroline Thomas and Peter Wilkin, eds, *Globalization, Human Security and the African Experience* (Boulder, CO: Lynne Rienner, 1999).

23 Thomas, 6.

24 Barry Buzan, *People, States and Fear* (Brighton: Harvester Wheatsheaf, 1983); *People, States and Fear: An Agenda for International Security Studies in the Post-Cold War Era* (Hemel Hempstead: Harvester Wheatsheaf, 1991).

25 Barry Buzan *et al.*, *The European Security Order Recast: Scenarios for the Post-Cold War Era* (London: Pinter, 1990); Ole Waever *et al.*, *Identity, Migration and the New Security Order in Europe* (London: Pinter, 1993); Barry Buzan *et al.*, *Security: A New Framework for Analysis* (Boulder, CO: Lynne Rienner, 1998); Ole Waever *et al.*, *European Polyphony: Perspectives beyond East-West Confrontation* (London: Macmillan, 1990).
26 See Ole Waever, "Securitization and Desecuritization" in *On Security*, ed. Ronnie Lipschutz (New York: Columbia University Press, 1995), 46–86.
27 Buzan *et al*, *Security*, 32.
28 *Ibid.*, 83.
29 *Ibid.*, 90.
30 Keith Krause and Michael Williams, eds, *Critical Security Studies* (Minneapolis, MN: University of Minnesota Press, 1997). See also their work "Broadening the Agenda of Security Studies: Politics and Methods," *Mershon International Studies Review* 40, Supplement 2 (1996): 229–254.
31 *Ibid.*, 33–59.
32 Ken Booth, "Security and Emancipation," *Review of International Studies* 17 (1991): 321.
33 *Ibid.*, 319.
34 *Ibid.*
35 Johan Eriksson, "Observers or Advocates? On the Political Role of Security Analysis," *Cooperation and Conflict* 34 (1999): 318.
36 Mohammed Ayoob, "Defining Security: A Subaltern Realist Perspective," in Krause and Williams, 126–127.
37 *Ibid.*, 128.
38 David Baldwin, "The Concept of Security," *Review of International Studies* 23 (1997): 5–26.
39 Patrick M. Morgan, "Liberalist and Realist Security Studies at 2000: Two Decades of Progress?" *Contemporary Security Policy* (December 1999): 40.
40 Krause and Williams, 249.
41 Jonathan Steele, "The Bush Doctrine Makes Nonsense of the UN Charter," *The Guardian*, June 7, 2002.
42 See the report of her organization on the actions of unpatriotic university professors at http://www.goacta.org/Reports/defciv.pdf.
43 Francis Fukuyama, *The End of History and the Last Man* (New York: Free Press, 1992).
44 Samuel Huntington, *The Clash of Civilizations and the Remaking of World Order* (New York: Simon and Schuster, 1996).

References

Adler, Emanuel and Michael Barnett, eds *Security Communities*. Cambridge: Cambridge University Press, 1998.
Ayoob, Mohammed. "Defining Security: A Subaltern Realist Perspective." In *Critical Security Studies*, edited by Keith Krause and Michael Williams, 126–127. Minneapolis, MN: University of Minnesota Press, 1997.
Baldwin, David. "The Concept of Security." *Review of International Studies* 23 (1997): 5–26.
Booth, Ken. "Security and Emancipation." *Review of International Studies* 17 (1991): 321.
Brock-Utne, B. *Educating for Peace: A Feminist Perspective*. Oxford: Pergamon Press, 1985.
Buzan, Barry. *People, States and Fear*. Brighton: Harvester Wheatsheaf, 1983.
——. *People, States and Fear: An Agenda for International Security Studies in the Post-Cold War Era*, second edition. Hemel Hempstead: Harvester Wheatsheaf, 1991.
Buzan, Barry, Morten Kelstrup, Pierre Lemaitre, Elzbieta Tromer, and Ole Waever. *The European Security Order Recast: Scenarios for the Post-Cold War Era*. London: Pinter, 1990.

Buzan, Barry, Ole Waever and Jaap de Wilde. *Security: A New Framework for Analysis.* Boulder: Lynne Rienner, 1998.

Campbell, David. *Writing Security: United States Foreign Policy and the Politics of Identity.* Manchester: Manchester University Press, 1992.

Cohn, Carol. "Sex, Death and the Rational World of Defense Intellectuals." *Signs* 12 (1987): 687–718.

Cooke, M. and A. Woollacott, eds *Gendering War Talk.* Princeton, NJ: Princeton University Press, 1993.

Desch, Michael. "Culture Clash: Assessing the Importance of Ideas in Security Studies." *International Security* 23 (1998): 142.

Elshtain, Jean. *Women and War.* New York: Basic Books, 1987.

Enloe, Cynthia. *Bananas, Beaches and Bases: Making Feminist Sense of International Politics.* Berkeley, CA: University of California Press, 1990.

——. *The Morning After: Sexual Politics at the End of the Cold War.* Berkeley, CA: University of California Press, 1993.

——. *Maneuvers: The International Politics of Militarizing Women's Lives.* Berkeley, CA: University of California Press, 2000.

Eriksson, Johan. "Observers or Advocates? On the Political Role of Security Analysis." *Cooperation and Conflict* 34 (1999): 318.

Fukuyama, Francis. *The End of History and the Last Man.* New York: Free Press, 1992.

Gallie, W.B. "Essentially Contested Concepts." *Proceedings of the Aristotelian Society* 56 (1955–56): 167–198.

Hartsock, Nancy. "The Barracks Community in Western Political Thought." *Women's Studies International Forum* 5 (1982): 283–286.

Huntington, Samuel. *The Clash of Civilizations and the Remaking of World Order.* New York: Simon and Schuster, 1996.

Johnston, Alastair Iain. *Cultural Realism: Strategic Culture and Grand Strategy in Chinese History.* Princeton, NJ: Princeton University Press, 1995.

Katzenstein, Peter, ed. *The Culture of National Security: Norms and Identity in World Politics.* New York: Columbia University Press, 1996.

Kier, Elizabeth. *Imagining War: French Military Doctrine between the Wars.* Princeton, NJ: Princeton University Press, 1997.

Klein, Bradley S. *Strategic Studies and World Order: The Global Politics of Deterrence.* Cambridge: Cambridge University Press, 1994.

Kowert, Paul and Jeffery Legro. "Norms, Identity, and Their Limits: A Theoretical Reprise." In *The Culture of National Security Norms and Identity in World Politics,* edited by Peter Katzenstein, 496. New York: Columbia University Press, 1996.

Krause, Keith and Michael Williams, "Broadening the Agenda of Security Studies: Politics and Methods." *Mershon International Studies Review* 40, Supplement 2 (1996): 229–254.

——. eds *Critical Security Studies.* Minneapolis, MN: University of Minnesota Press, 1997.

Legro, Jeffrey. *Cooperation under Fire: Anglo-German Restraint during World War II.* Ithaca, NY: Cornell University Press, 1995.

Morgan, Patrick M. "Liberalist and Realist Security Studies at 2000: Two Decades of Progress?" *Contemporary Security Policy* (December 1999): 40.

Price, Richard. *The Chemical Weapons Taboo.* Ithaca, NY: Cornell University Press, 1997.

Steele, Jonathan. "The Bush Doctrine Makes Nonsense of the UN Charter." *The Guardian,* June 7, 2002.

Thomas, Caroline. *Global Governance, Development and Human Security: The Challenge of Poverty and Inequality*. London: Pluto Press, 2000.

Thomas, Caroline and Peter Wilkin, eds *Globalization, Human Security and the African Experience*. Boulder, CO: Lynne Rienner, 1999.

———. *Human Development Report 1994*. New York: Oxford University Press, 1994.

———. "Redefining Security: The Human Dimension." *Current History* (1995): 229–236.

United Nations Development Program (UNDP). *Human Development Report 1997*. New York: Oxford University Press, 1997.

Waever, Ole. "Securitization and Desecuritization." In *On Security*, edited by Ronnie Lipschutz, 46–86. New York: Columbia University Press, 1995.

Waever, Ole, Barry Buzan, Morten Kelstrup, and Pierre Lemaitre. *Identity, Migration and the New Security Order in Europe*. London: Pinter, 1993.

Waever, Ole, Pierre Lemaitre, and Elzbieta Tromer. *European Polyphony: Perspectives Beyond East-West Confrontation*. London: Macmillan, 1990.

Waltz, Kenneth. *Theory of International Politics*. Reading, MA: Addison-Wesley, 1979.

3 Globalization at the beginnings of the twentieth and twenty-first centuries

*Roger Owen**

Introduction

With all the intellectual exuberance for globalism as a phenomenon barely three decades old, I will argue to the contrary that what is usually referred to as globalism actually appeared in the scholarship of the emerging social disciplines during the late nineteenth century. The current era of globalization recalls the end of the nineteenth century. Then came the American empire as an umbrella for the present administration's revolutionary foreign and military policy. And after the regime change in Iraq, we are witnessing a revival of some of the essential features of colonialism. War on Iraq equates with a war on internationalism.

The first wave of globalization which, in my judgment, began sometime around 1870 and lasted through World War I. The latter is often called the Wilsonian "moment' of early internationalism, which then mutated into imperialism when the League of Nations was created along with the mandate system.

And recent events in southern Iraq provide a particularly vivid replay of scenes that occurred during the first British occupation, which are described in Stephen Longrigg's *Iraq 1900 to 1950*.[1] There are the same cast of characters as when the British expeditionary force arrived in Basra in 1914: the sheikhs, the Timimi and Sadun families, and the political officers, such as Sir Percy Cox, struggling to understand local society. There are many of the same events, from looting to the burning of government offices and official records, at a time when Percy Cox announced that no ill will was felt against the civilian population; justice and liberty would be respected and that the troops would behave with complete consideration and friendliness'.[2]

And speeches of General Garner and others recall the British General Maude's liberation address to the people of Baghdad in November 1917. In exuberant prose penned by Sir Mark Sykes, he assured the Iraqi public of British benevolence, suggested an Arab future of "greatness and renown among the peoples of the earth," and invited the public through "your Nobles and Elders" to participate in the management of your civilian affairs.[3]

Today's events in Iraq also parallel the British occupation of Egypt in 1882 and of the similar events in 1956, when a public expressing moral outrage to jingoistic enthusiasm was also asked to believe that these acts were undertaken from a noble desire to protect national and international interests to the basest grab for land, natural resources, and commercial profit.

As such, the events of the past could illuminate the present and provide prescient warnings to the challenges ahead. For example, the problems on how Iraq established a government pliable enough to sign treaties regulating oil and yet legitimate enough to stay in power sufficiently long to honor those commitments once the foreign troops departed; or how America, unable to take its seat at the League of Nations, was still powerful enough internationally to force the British to honor the principle of the "open door" as American oil companies could participate. This is when the Iraq Petroleum Company was created.

Now I would like to pose these questions in reverse, that is, not to have the past to illuminate the present, but to use present concerns to ask new questions of the past in producing a new historiography. I then suggest ways that we might use contemporary constructs such as globalization, imperialism, and internationalism to write the modern history of the Middle East with new questions, new perspectives, and new research strategies. In short, I am advocating a sort of contemporary political ethnography.

General comments

As is well known, the concept of globalization was first popularized by economists who saw it as a technology-driven change that reduced the cost of the movement of people and goods and of interactive communication. It was economists, too, who highlighted the parallels between the present wave and that of the late nineteenth century during a similar explosion of greater economic interconnectedness.

A number of historians have rethought how the first wave coincided with the high tide of Victorian empire, and have linked the two. British historian Anthony Hopkins co-authored the notion of "gentlemanly capitalism" for understanding British imperial expansion.[4] In a chapter entitled "The History of Globalization and the Globalization of History?" in *Globalization in World History*, Hopkins argues that globalization provides a powerful model for increased explanation in history.[5] More specifically, he writes that it should "resurrect some old lines of historical enquiry to open up new ones and to stimulate revision to established interpretations."[6]

According to Hopkins, internationalism was nationalized during nineteenth century. For the national historians, the international arena only entered the national story at times of war and during the expansion and empire. Then, national history proliferated when international connections were expanded.[7] This obviously is the "reflexivity that postmodern social scientists have identified for the past two decades." American history shows the same paradox at work in the present day.

Whereas Hopkins tries to use contemporary themes to re-work the writing of the past, Neil Ferguson's new book, *Empire*, proceeds from the present to the past and then back again to the present, bringing lessons for the modern world.[8]

Ferguson revives the old theme of formal versus informal empire to underpin Anglo-globalization as an integrative form of global institutional development of markets, labor, and capital, as well as for the extension of democratic political practices and of evangelical sects and missionary societies (what he calls "Victorian NGOs").[9] Hopkins, Ferguson, and others also point out a new concern with nineteenth century international institutions, international law, and international society. As Hopkins argues, "links across space and cultures could be sustained only be generating common core values and a lingua franca, and these were put in place by a few dominant nations with the power to spread their own diasporas while inspiring imitation and deference in other societies."[10] The expanded use of the postage stamp, the metric system, and the English language are examples of one set of these nationally engendered internationalizing processes; the spread of European notions of property, commercial law, and business practice are also examples.

Meanwhile, anthropologists and religious historians have called attention to the transnational networks that existed prior to empire but which were then greatly facilitated by it. For example, the Hadrami diaspora, which still has links that stretch from eastern Yemen through the Indian sub-continent to Malaysia and Indonesia. Those international networks had organizational features, based not on imperial institutions but on personal and familial and religious connections.[11]

Such domestic connects also supported the spread of Islam as well as a concerted resistance to colonialism by the Soviets and then the Americans in Afghanistan. However, these new types of historiography – or better yet, interdisciplinary science – also present many challenging problems. While imperialism is identified closely with globalization, it loses much of its ability to describe a system with unequal power, exploitation, racism, and enforced social change. And while it is true that Ferguson acknowledges the dark side of empire and clearly invites the reader to come down on the side of the former,[12] this is reflexive historiography, or history written with a slant from the present day.

Imperialism and globalization do not seem to have anything to say about the way in which the colonial state was seen as a space containing both foreigners and locals in relationships ranging from the adversarial to collaboration and coexistence. The Subaltern school in India suggests situations where large numbers of people live in complete ignorance of the colonial presence. Writing such a history is a task that has only just really begun. This problem is more straightforwardly historiographic. One problem is the danger of simply reinventing and/or re-packaging earlier approaches that stressed the international spread of capitalism (from Marx onwards). This reproduced many of the old problems, for example, the ways in which the spread of capitalism was viewed almost exclusively as from the standpoint of expanding Western influence. Also, which is to be the master-narrative: globalization or the history of formal and informal empire? Another problem is the question of scope: if everything is connected to everything in a global age, and if global forces are present everywhere – in Egyptian villages just as much as the Alexandrian cotton exchange – where should historical analysis begin and end?

While many historians would say that we are no longer contained by national boundaries, Hopkins writes in studying a borderless world, it is not that clear how much further we should move beyond national histories.[13] Hopkins further underlines studying both the qualitative as well as quantitative significance of greater global integration, that is, noting integration not just as measured in numbers – more phones, more boat journeys, etc. – but also in the meaning of this experience in individual lives, which is a much more difficult to gauge.[14] In this borderless world, does it make sense to reductively emphasize economics on one level, politics on another, and society on a third? This may be Eurocentric Cartesianism.

Finally, how can we give the study of capitalism more than two dimensions, focusing not just on accumulation and exploitation, but also identify the actors involved, the impact on lives, the institutional variety, and the different types of social and ecological transformation engendered? In *The Role of Experts*, Mitchell advocates exploring the connections between persons, classes, objects, and practices as capitalists and capitalism, politics, poverty and medicine, human actors, local knowledge, insects (Egypt's invasion by the malaria-carrying mosquito in 1942), water snails, and inanimate forces like the Nile, which was partially harnessed and contained by the international/British irrigation engineers at Aswan in 1898.[15] This, of course, is in the genre of ecological imperialism, which examines more of the totality of transformations from the forces of internationalism.

Middle East

Hopefully, this discussion of some pitfalls and approaches to historiography argues for the need to use the large notions of globalization. This is not to reproduce old orthodoxies or to create new ones but simply to free up the mind. The second is to illustrate this by three different historical examples from my biography of Evelyn Baring, the first Lord Cromer.

The biographical approach provides a way around some of the problems associated with writing about imperialism, internationalism, and globalization. So many of the issues associated with these forces are evidenced in the compass of an individual life. This not only produces many surprises but also makes even the well studied Lord Cromer surprisingly hard to pigeon-hole, since he was active in so many late nineteenth century spheres: the diplomatic, the financial, the administrative, the developmental, and the military among others. From the globalist paradigm, we would say that he participated in numerous overlapping networks. This, of course, answers the question of in a world in which everything is connected to everything else, where do you start and stop? The answer, in this case, is that the study of a life itself is inclusive.

To illustrate these changing views, I offer three examples: The first is the use of a late twentieth-century perspective to interpret the role of late nineteenth-century bankruptcy in structuring an international dynamic. Secondly, I offer Cromer's views about contemporary internationalism in an increasingly interconnected world. And thirdly, I discuss Cromer's participation in Egypt's early twentieth-century "Green Revolution."

International bankruptcy

Let me begin with a brief account of international bankruptcy in Egypt and the Ottoman empire. Egypt's inability to maintain payments on its external debt in 1875 led to the negotiation of a provisional financial settlement by British and French creditors. This created an institutional mechanism for supervising the collection of the revenues for repaying the debt, known as the Caisse de la Dette. One of the representatives of the creditors was the 36-year-old Evelyn Baring. In contrast to those who were anxious to collect the moneys owed by any means possible, there were those such as Baring and others who saw that a commission of inquiry would be necessary to find out what the country could reasonably afford and then what financial reforms were necessary to ensure smooth repayment. At this stage the process was pushed towards "conditionality" – that is, the demand that indebtedness be accompanied by specified changes in financial practice. Some of the conditional terms went beyond simply better financial management to impinge upon the exercise of political power.

In Cairo and in Istanbul local agendas aimed either at using the conditionality to preserve financial independence, or appeared to achieve the same goal by containing the forces for reform. In Egypt the former group was led by Riaz Pasha, an influential government official lent to the 1878 Commission of Inquiry by the ruler, the Khedive Ismail. Riaz Pasha used his position to find ways to contain his master's powers. As we might expect, the leader of the other faction was the Khedive himself. For some months in the spring of 1879 it seemed that Ismail would triumph. But after his deposition in June, the pendulum swung the other way again in Egypt under Riaz. With the encouragement of Baring, Ismail returned to Cairo as one of the two foreign controllers of finance, then moved toward something akin to a constitutional monarchy with a tame ruler, a notion of ministerial responsibility, and a reforming government.

Baring's description of how he and his colleague de Blignières managed the system suggests many parallels to contemporary arrangements featuring the World Bank and the International Monetary Fund. That he and de Blignières had offices contiguous to that of Riaz Pasha, who was then president of the Egyptian Council of Ministers, at the Ministry of Finance meant that they could be in "daily and hourly" conversation with Riaz himself. They also had a "voix deliberative" at the Council of Ministers by which they could give their opinion freely but were unable to vote. And while they left the details of financial management to the ministry, no document of "first-rate importance" could leave without having been prepared under their personal approval.[16]

Meanwhile in Istanbul, the reform party under Midhat Pasha was able to introduce a constitution in 1876, followed by the calling of the first Ottoman parliament in 1877. This was eventually defeated by forces allied with the young Sultan Abdul-Hamid, who also defended the empire's finances by negotiating a settlement. Though requiring the surrender of importance sources of revenue to an international commission, this settlement maintained Ottoman control over the Ministry of Finance.

To draw comparisons to the present day, many groups, either in indebted nations or nations seeking to join international organization such as the World Trade Organization have behaved in much the same manner. The international banking and credit system is also structured to induce such behavior. Then, as now, it is very difficult to have richer nations negotiate with their poorer neighbors strictly on finance. It is likely that the local exercise of power will also soon be introduced. The negotiations should either preserve or expand their positions of the national interest. The persons whose agendas most closely resemble those of the international creditors will become labeled as reformers and those who oppose them as "conservatives," "traditionalists," or simply self-serving reactionaries.

To re-visit the Egyptian and Ottoman history of this period, we refer to Christopher Clay's mammoth account of the Ottoman debt crisis, *Gold for the Sultan*.[17] It should also assume a prominent place in a much-needed biography of Sultan Abdul-Hamid, a man whose own largely unrecognized financial skills would become known.

Internationalism

The managing of Egyptian finances broke down in 1881–1882 as other groups with "nativist" agendas took center stage, which forced the British occupation.[18] This was then followed by the return of Evelyn Baring, soon to become Lord Cromer, who had left the country in 1880 for India. I now draw attention to two further aspects of his biography that throw light on his own views concerning the national and the international.

Through his own experience, Cromer was very well aware of many of the features increasing global integration of his time. Like his countrymen, he also considered the notion that international free trade would bring peace between the nations had been fatally undermined. The growing self-assertion manifested by Britain's European and North American rivals drove them to stake out exclusive positions in the colonial world. Hence he desired to provide Britain with a free hand in Egypt by removing the international control shared with the French after 1882. He also worked to remove the Mixed Tribunals and the Capitulations.

The tensions in his thought between the experience of internationalization and his urgent desire to mitigate many of its political, administrative and legal effects in Egypt is demonstrated by the second volume of his *Modern Egypt* (1908). In it, he also identifies the thinking of orientalism, which Edward Said[19] was to make famous. Cromer writes:

> Of recent years, although there has been no diminution but rather a recrudescence of international rivalry, a tendency towards the international treatment of both European and extra-European questions has become manifest, not only among theorists but among practical statesmen. This tendency is the natural outcome of the circumstances which obtained in the latter part of the nineteenth century. There appears little prospect that the Utopia of the early free-traders will be realized. Trade, with its handmaids, the railway and the

telegraph does not seem to have bound nations together in any closer bonds of amity than existed in the days of slow locomotion and communication.

On the other hand, the European body politic has become more sensitive than heretofore. National interests tend towards cosmopolitanism, however much national sentiments and aspirations may tend towards exclusive patriotism. The whole world is quickly informed of any incident which may occur in any part of the globe. Not only in the cabinet of every Minister, but in the office of every newspaper editor the questions to which its occurrence instantly give rise are, how does this circumstance affect the affairs of my country?

What course should be observed in order to safeguard our interests? It is more difficult than heretofore to segregate a quarrel between two states. In a certain sense, Europeans, in spite of themselves, have become members of a single family, though not always a happy one. They are all oppressed by one common dread, and that is that some accident may perpetuate a general war. If any minor state shows a tendency to light the match which may lead to a general conflagration, the voice of international rivalry is to some extent hushed in presence of the danger, and the diplomatic fire-engine is turned on from every capital in Europe in order to quench the calamity before it can spread.

A certain power of acting together has thus been developed among the nations and governments of Europe and it cannot be doubted that the world has benefited from the change. In all the larger affairs of state, internationalism constitutes a guarantee for peace. It in some measure obliges particular interests to yield to the general good of the European community.[20]

The points mentioned in this lengthy passage raise several interesting issues. Positive internationalism, in Cromer's view, may be seen at work only in a European context. Its function is primarily as a mechanism for preserving Europe's own security in the possibility of inter-state conflict. We may also note that the mechanisms he describes – the diplomatic "fire-engines" uniting to put out a minor conflagration – singularly failed to work in 1914.

Cromer then discusses the case of non-European countries where the rulers sometimes possessed "incomplete" sovereign rights, which opens the way for the development of internationalism. In such countries, he writes, "some European powers have interests which they wish to assert without arousing the jealousy of their rivals by too open an assertion of strength."[21] He adds "cases sometimes arise which involve prolonged supervision and control in the interests of the European powers but which do not justify exclusive action on the part of any one of them, or which, if they (do) justify it, are not of a kind to allow exclusive action without a risk of discord with respect to the particular nation by whom it might be exercised."[22] Here, Cromer is evidently considering Egypt, although there were other parts of the world where the same processes were at work, notably the Ottoman empire and China. Today, on reading these words, most people would immediately be thinking of Iraq.

The results of the experiments in internationalism are not encouraging. Cromer writes, "What has been proved there is that international mechanisms possess admirable negative qualities. They are formidable checks to all action, and the reason why they are so is that, when any action is proposed, objections of one kind or another generally occur to some member of the international body. Hence, for the purposes of action, administrative internationalism may be said to tend towards the creation of administrative incompetence."[23]

This, of course, is just one man's version of the notion of late nineteenth-century internationalism used in support of Lord Cromer's main *idée fixe*: how to reduce its power in Egypt and allow his administration there a freer hand. Yet, he was successful in getting rid of most of the French financial control. However, he was defeated in persuading foreign governments to surrender their capitulatory rights to his Anglo-Egyptian administration. It was only in 1914 that his goal of proclaiming a British protectorate was achieved, as the Ottoman empire entered World War I.

As such, the internationalizing response to late nineteenth-century globalization was contingent on the nature of particular crises as well as on its effectiveness in dealing with particular problems. It should also be clear that, as a result, the nature of internationalism should be subject to a variety of different interpretations.

To return to Lord Cromer, how might one man's approach to late nineteenth-century internationalism in Egypt suggest new avenues for Middle Eastern research? One way already partially explored by Samir Saul in his *La France et l'Egypte* would be to focus on the center of foreign capital in Egypt, particularly that of the French.[24] Cromer was well aware that French private investors were well pleased with his management of Egypt's finances, both in the rise in the value of land and of their shares in the public debt. They were thus able to thwart their own government's obstructionist tactics.

What were the consequences that in the 1870s there was no internationally accepted notion of state bankruptcy? This led Evelyn Baring and de Blignières, to argue that the Egyptian declaration of its bankruptcy contained in the Law of Liquidation of 1880 should be based on a European notion of personal bankruptcy. There is an intriguing glimpse here of international financiers innovating as they went along.

Green revolution

There were also considerable efforts to provide Egypt's farmers with additional water. This goal began with the repair of the Delta Barrage in the 1880s and continued with the completion of the Aswan Dam in 1902. With the Delta Barrage project, productivity increased enormously and saved much manpower and animal power. Instead of having to lift up the water from the system of local canals, simply opening a sluice let the waters rush in.

Meanwhile, the associated introduction of a prolific new strain of cotton, *mit afifi*, allowed yields in the Delta provinces to increase by at least 60 percent from the late 1880s to the late 1890s. The average incomes of the peasant cultivators may have doubled between 1897 and 1907.[25] However, soil fertility eventually deteriorated due to a rise in the water table and lack of adequate drainage. A more intensive form of cultivation so multiplied the number of crops that the various parasites attacked the host cotton itself. Yields tumbled again, losing all previous gains (if measured by the disastrous harvest of 1908). These problems jolted Britain's cotton merchants to look for alternative sources of supply in Sudan.

It would also be possible to connect the green revolution's impact on land prices to the huge increase in foreign investment in Egypt's land and mortgage companies between 1897 and 1907. The lands known as the Daira Saniya were held as security for government debts incurred in the 1870s and were finally sold off at what Cromer himself recognized as a bargain price between 1898 and 1907 to the influential international financier Sir Ernest Cassel.[26]

From the perspective of supply-side economics pushing globalism today, one could see this as early privatization. Some problems that we now recognize more clearly have antecedents in the late nineteenth century, such as setting a fair price for the assets in question, to the drain of state officials into the new private sector thus created, or the attempt to draw up a code of ethical practice for state officials.

Based on Egypt's sudden burst of prosperity, Cromer's reputation increased among the Egyptian elite, reminiscent of successful entrepreneurs today. Ahmad Lutfi al-Sayyid praised the "magnificent results" of Cromer's financial policies while blaming him for his negative impact on educational policy.[27] Interestingly, this point of view persisted in Egyptian school textbooks until the 1930s.[28]

The wider point is that Egypt's place in an integrating world order makes it possible to move in almost any way one chooses. As such, the lack of precision in the notions of globalization, imperialism, and internationalism to get around some within the academy to arrive at a better understanding of the process of greater global integration in a world of unequal power may not have exclusive applicability today but can be shown to have resolution at the turn of the last century.

Now back to the present

In sum, I am not rewriting the history of the Middle East, but rather testing the constructs of globalism in history to access just how unique the current moment is to ward off a tempro-centricism. My aim is to offer how we might use our contemporary concerns with globalization, imperialism, and internationalism to unbind our mental processes from excessive focus on events of the past several decades. Some of my suggestions indicate possible research agendas, for example, the ways in which aspects of late nineteenth-century international relations were structured to produce somewhat similar processes in different parts of the globe.

Others suggest ways in which the almost randomly pursued different types of national and international connections might offer new research strategies. This is a comparative approach basic to anthropology. Nevertheless, the idea of total history has always been somewhat illusive. Yet, it must also be true that we won't really discover both its possibilities and its limitations until we have a range of examples from which to judge. Perhaps somewhat overstated, it seems trite to assume that global forces were present in almost any location, in almost any form, and then pursue the connections you find in any way that seems to make sense.

Many years ago I was much struck by Jacques Berque's attempt to write such a history in what was translated as *Egypt: Imperialism and Revolution.*[29] There he used a kind of pointillist method to build up a picture of life in the Nile valley as it related to occupation, as well as to a variety of projects to develop both its economic and human potential. The project was also informed by a historical sociology by which Berque's extensive knowledge of contemporary Egypt was used to inform a historical reconstruction of the crowded streets to be found, for example, in the Gamalaya quarter of Cairo.

To give another example, Ralph Coury uses his biography of Azzam Pasha to suggest that new ideas were fermented among young Egyptians in London just before the First World War. Then Egyptian, Arab, Ottoman, and Islamic activists networked in Europe. For example, this included Azzam's own project report on the destruction and desecration wrought by the Serbian and other Balkan armies on the new Muslim Albania.[30]

In conclusion, to return to the present political context, we can also entertain ourselves by drawing analogies between past and present. It remains to be seen as to how unique and disjunctive the present day globalism is with the past of a century ago.

Notes

* A.J. Meyer Professor of Middle Eastern History, Harvard University.
1 Stephen Longrigg, *Iraq 1900 to 1950: A Political, Social and Economic History* (London: Oxford University Press, 1953).
2 *Ibid.*, 78.
3 *Ibid.*, 93.
4 P.J. Cain and A.G. Hopkins, *British Imperialism: Innovation and Expansion: 1688–1914* (London: Longman, 1993).
5 Anthony Hopkins, ed., *Globalization in World History* (London: Pimlico, 2002), 14.
6 *Ibid.*, 15.
7 *Ibid.*, 13–14.
8 Neil Ferguson, *Empire: The Rise and Demise of the British World Order and the Lessons for Global Power* (New York: Basic Books, 2002), xii–xxix.
9 *Ibid.*, xxvii.
10 Hopkins, 31.
11 Enseng Ho, "Empire through Diasporic Eyes: A View from the Other Boat" (Department of Anthropology, Harvard University).
12 Ferguson, xx–xxvi.
13 Hopkins, 1–2, 36ff.
14 *Ibid.*, 17.
15 Timothy Mitchell, *The Rule of Experts: Egypt, Techno-Politics, Modernities* (Berkeley: University of California Press, 2002).
16 Evelyn Baring, Memorandum on the Present Situation of Affairs in Egypt, April 30, 1880, enclosed in Malet to Salisbury, May 5, 1880 (London: Public Record Office) FO 78/3142.
17 Christopher Clay, *Gold for the Sultan: Western Bankers and Ottoman Finance 1856–1881* (London: Tauris, 2000).

18 Juan Cole, *Colonialism and Revolution in the Middle East: Social and Cultural Origins of Egypt's 'Urabi Movement* (Princeton, NJ: Princeton University Press, 1992), 13–14, 271ff.
19 Edward Said, *Orientalism* (New York: Vintage, 1979).
20 The Earl of Cromer, *Modern Egypt*, vol. 2 (New York: Macmillan, 1908), 301–302.
21 *Ibid.*, 302–303.
22 *Ibid.*, 303.
23 *Ibid.*, 303–304.
24 Samir Saul, *La France et L'Egypte de 1882 à 1914: Intérêts économiques et implications politiques* (Paris: Ministère de l'économie, des finances et d'industrie/Comité pour l'histoire économique et financière de la France, 1997), passim.
25 Bent Hansen, "Income and Consumption in Egypt 1886/1887 to 1937," *International Journal of Middle Eastern Studies* 10 (1979), 28–30.
26 Cromer to Revelstoke, December 6, 1903, Baring Archive (London), 203076, "Partners' File," Supplementary Set.
27 Ahmad Lutfi al-Sayyid, *Al-Jarida* (Cairo) April 13, 1907.
28 Barak Aharon Salmoni, "Pedagogies of Patriotism: Teaching Socio-political Community in Twentieth Century Turkey and Egypt" (Ph.D. thesis, Harvard University, 2002), 853–854, 918.
29 Jacques Berque, *Egypt: Imperialism and Revolution*, trans. Jean Stewart (London: Faber, 1972), 71–75.
30 Ralph Coury, *The Making of an Egyptian Nationalist: The Early Years of Azzam Pasha, 1893–1936* (Reading: Ithaca, 1998), 63–87.

References

al-Sayyid, Ahmad Lutfi. *Al-Jarida*. Cairo: April 13, 1907.

Baring, Evelyn. Memorandum on the Present Situation of Affairs in Egypt, April 30, 1880, enclosed in Malet to Salisbury, May 5, 1880. London: Public Record Office, FO 78/3142.

Berque, Jacques. *Egypt: Imperialism and Revolution*. Translated Jean Stewart. London: Faber, 1972.

Cain, P.J. and A.G. Hopkins. *British Imperialism: Innovation and Expansion, 1688–1914*. London: Longman, 1993.

Clay, Christopher. *Gold for the Sultan: Western Bankers and Ottoman Finance, 1856–1881*. London: Tauris, 2000.

Cole, Juan. *Colonialism and Revolution in the Middle East: Social and Cultural Origins of Egypt's 'Urabi Movement*. Princeton, NJ: Princeton University Press, 1992.

Coury, Ralph. *The Making of an Egyptian Nationalist: The Early Years of Azzam Pasha, 1893–1936*. Reading: Ithaca, 1998.

Cromer, The Earl of. To Revelstoke, December 6, 1903. Baring Archive, London, 203076. "Partners' File," Supplementary Set.

——. *Modern Egypt*, vol. 2. New York: Macmillan, 1908.

Ferguson, Neil. *Empire: The Rise and Demise of the British World Order and the Lessons for Global Power*. New York: Basic Books, 2002.

Hansen, Bent. "Income and Consumption in Egypt 1886/1887 to 1937." *International Journal of Middle Eastern Studies* 10 (1979).

Ho, Enseng. "Empire through Diasporic Eyes: A View from the Other Boat." Department of Anthropology, Harvard University.

Hopkins, Anthony, ed. *Globalization in World History*. London: Pimlico, 2002.

Longrigg, Stephen. *Iraq 1900 to 1950: A Political, Social and Economic History*. London: Oxford University Press, 1953.

Mitchell, Timothy. *The Rule of Experts: Egypt, Techno-politics, Modernities.* Berkeley: University of California Press, 2002.

Said, Edward. *Orientalism.* New York: Vintage, 1979.

Salmoni, Barak Aharon. "Pedagogies of Patriotism: Teaching Socio-political Community in Twentieth Century Turkey and Egypt." Ph.D. thesis, Harvard University, 2002.

Saul, Samir. *La France et L'Egypte de 1882 à 1914: Intérêts économiques et implications politiques.* Paris: Ministère de l'économie, des finances et d'industrie/Comité pour l'histoire économique et financière de la France, 1997.

4   Globalization as economic phenomenon

A critical interpretation

*Tim Niblock**

Perspective

This chapter is written by a specialist in political economy rather than an economist. Its concerns, therefore, are less with the economic dimensions of globalization *per se*, as with the significance of economic globalization in the international economic and political order. Attention is given to how the processes of economic globalization have been shaped by economic, and associated political, theory. The article first seeks to establish in what sense economic globalization is indeed a new phenomenon. Having identified the key characteristic as lying in the unification of the global market, the article contends that the form taken by market globalization has been tightly shaped by neo-classical economic theory. This raises an important issue as to the relationship between the theory and the practical experience of market globalization: is market globalization bound to exist purely within the framework of neo-classical economics, or are there different forms of national or international economic organization that are compatible with a global market economy? The article concludes by looking at alternatives to the neo-classical economy approach and assesses their viability.

Is economic globalization new?

Some theorists have argued that economic globalization is not a new phenomenon. It has, rather, been a characteristic of the international capitalist economy over a prolonged period, stemming from the steady integration of formerly distant economies into those of the core capitalist world.[1] Hirst and Thompson, in the Introduction to *Globalization in Question*, describe globalization as a "necessary myth," where the necessity is grounded in an attempt "to paralyse radical reforming national strategies, to see them as unfeasible in the face of the judgment and sanction of international markets."[2] Hirst and Thompson put forward a number of reasons why the more extreme claims with respect to globalization need to be treated with some skepticism. The most salient points are summarized below:

1   Global economic relations have been highly internationalized at some earlier conjunctures of the international economy, "ever since an economy based on modern industrial technology began to be generalized from the 1860s." The

current international economy, they claim, "is in some respects less open than the regime which prevailed from 1870 to 1914."

2   There are few genuine transnational companies. Most multinational corporations are in fact nationally based and simply trade internationally.

3   The international economy is not truly global. Capital moves mainly among the advanced industrial economies, together with a small number of newly industrialized countries. Trade and investment follow the same pattern.

4   The global economy is in effect nationally managed. That is to say, the major economic powers (the G3) have the weight and influence, especially if they act in unison, to exert control over global economic trends and developments.[3]

Some of these points are debatable. The 1990s in fact saw quite a substantial shift of investment capital toward countries that are not the traditional "advanced industrial economies." China is a particularly important example of this. With regard to point 1, moreover, the ratio of trade to GDP of developed countries prior to 1914 was in fact substantially lower than at the end of the century. The ratio of exports to GDP in 1913 was 11.2 percent, while in 1985 it was 23.1 percent.[4]

Nonetheless, it is certainly true that the process of capitalist international integration has been underway over an extended period and that an international economy of some kind has been in existence for several centuries. When judged purely in terms of the quantitative measures of trade and investment, it is not difficult to see the justification for using a new term to describe this process of integration. The increases in international trade and investment that have occurred over the last few decades, and especially since the 1990s, could be simply subsumed within the concept of international capitalist integration. This might seem particularly appropriate in view of the disintegration of the Soviet Union and the consequent collapse of non-capitalist approaches to economic organization.

Yet, there is a critical difference between current and earlier forms of international economy. This difference is not quantitative but qualitative. It relates not to the scale of trade and investment but to the dynamics that underlie the economic interchange. It is the qualitative difference that justifies the use of the term "globalization." The section that follows defines this qualitative content.

The qualitative dimension in economic globalization

The qualitative dimension in economic globalization, which differentiates it from the wider process of international capitalist integration, lies in the centrality of the single global market in the contemporary international economic order. The prominent role that the state previously enjoyed in controlling day-to-day economic interaction with other economies has been significantly diluted. International economic contacts are now governed primarily by the dynamics of the impersonal single global market. States have, in effect, been withdrawing from the role of directly promoting their economic interests, and have opened their economies to the global market – believing that in the long term this will accrue more to their benefit. In the past, a large part of international trade, investment, and capital flowed within bounded systems (e.g., between a colonial power and its colonies or among the communist states of eastern Europe) where the system was protected by substantial tariff barriers, practical difficulties of transport and communication, and governmental promotion of national companies/organizations. Now, the activities of economic actors (consumers, producers, investors, etc.) relate directly to the single global market. Decisions on what should be produced, where it should be produced, how much it should be sold for, etc., are made primarily with an eye on conditions in the global market, not on considerations that stem from national policy or state regulation.

It is important to stress that there are policy/ideological as well as technological/infrastructural factors behind this shift in the dynamics of the international economy. As far as technology and infrastructure are concerned, the causes of change are well known: the development of IT communications and of transport networks have enabled producers and traders to gain information on, and respond quickly to, developments in any part of the global economy, taking advantage of easy and cheap means of transportation to satisfy demand wherever that may be.[5] The policy/ideological side, however, has been equally important. The second half of the twentieth century, but in particular the last decade of that century, saw a steady trend toward the reduction of tariffs and the opening up of markets. In the recent phase, this has occurred within a context of strong direction from international financial bodies, where developing countries have been under strong pressure from the International Monetary Fund, the World Bank, and other institutions to reduce the scope of governmental intervention, reduce tariffs, facilitate the flow of private capital, and open their economies to the global market.

The global market that has developed comprises three fields of activity.[6] First, is the global trading market. The lowering of tariffs has, not surprisingly, been a key element here. Largely through the agreements reached through the GATT and WTO, the general level of tariffs in the world economy has declined substantially over the period since World War II. The average world tariff on manufactured goods in 1940 stood at about 40 percent, declining to about 18 percent in 1960, 8 percent in 1980 and 4 percent in 1995.[7] Non-tariff trade barriers continue to play a significant (and in some cases increasing) role, but the impact of tariff reductions on trade has nonetheless been crucial. Since 1950, international trade has increased much more rapidly than production. Total world exports grew by a factor of 14 between 1950 and 1995, while production rose by a factor of 5.[8] Trade rose from 28 percent of world GDP in 1970 to 45 percent in 1998.[9]

Second, is the global investment market. Foreign direct investment has been growing rapidly since the 1970s but with increasing speed since the mid-1980s. It stood at about $12.5 billion in 1970, rose to $55 billion in 1980, to $203 billion in 1990, and $1,492 billion in 2000.[10] There has, moreover, been a qualitative change in the character and composition of this investment. Whereas in earlier times the major part of foreign direct investment in developing countries was in extractive industries and agriculture, more than half of all such investment by the end of the century was going into manufacturing. Most of the production coming from the latter investment, moreover, was for export back to the home country of the investing company.[11]

The character of the investors, moreover, has changed: most of the investment (especially in the manufacturing field) is now undertaken by multinational corporations (MNCs). The impact of this on trade has been very substantial. Todaro and Smith point out that by the late 1990s, the 350 largest corporations controlled more than 40 percent of international trade. They dominated, in particular, the "production, distribution, and sale of many goods from developing countries (e.g., tobacco, electronics, footwear, and clothing)."[12] The scale of the corporations is such that the largest dwarf most of the national economies in which they operate:

> Seven of the top 10 MNCs, and 10 out of the top 40, had worldwide sales in excess of $100 billion in 1999. Any three of them account for more sales than the gross national income of all of sub-Saharan Africa, and any four of them are larger than the economy of India ... The top seven together are larger than China.

In 1993 the sales revenues of General Motors exceeded the GDPs of all developing countries except for seven, and the combined revenues of the five largest MNCs exceeded those of many developed countries (including Australia, Spain, Sweden, and Canada). Of the 150 largest entities (companies and countries) in the world in the mid-1990s, 86 were MNCs.[13]

Third, is the global finance market. Technological changes and the removal of capital controls now enable finance to move around the world at an unprecedented rate. In the course of one day, as recent financial crises in the Far East and in Mexico and Argentina have shown, there can be movements that change fundamentally the prospects for a country's economic prosperity. Currency, equity, and bonds are no longer being acquired simply as an aid to trade and investment but for short-term speculation. In 1977, foreign exchange dealing amounted to $10 billion per day. By the mid-1990s it had increased more than a hundred-fold to $1.3 trillion per day.[14]

In these three different dimensions of the global market, therefore, the critical interaction is that between the trader/investor/financier and the global market, rather than with national institutions at either end. It is this direct interaction with the global market, where individuals are interacting and taking decisions of great economic import outside any framework of tight governmental control, that is new and qualitatively different from the past.

The theoretical underpinning of contemporary economic globalization

As noted above, the move to a single global market has come about in part due to policy/ideological changes. The implications of this need to be recognized and analyzed. All economic agenda are motivated and inspired by an ideology/theory of some kind. A mutually supportive relationship exists between the agenda pursued and the ideology/theory that supports it. The theory provides a rationale and justification for the adoption of the policies concerned, while it is in turn the product of perceptions emanating from the economic experience. While theories may project themselves as the objective reality, based on scientific truth as opposed to false ideology, each does nonetheless carry its own in-built values and assumptions. The adoption and implementation of a theory stems not only from its accuracy in reflecting salient realities, but also from the interests that it serves. In the words of DeMartino:

> it bears emphasis that circumstances and conditions external to the theory play a critical role. Theories are embraced and achieve standing in part by virtue of the salience of the problems they purport to solve. But a theory's success is also influenced by the political and economic interests it serves (and threatens).[15]

The economic theory that has shaped (and been shaped by) the contemporary process of economic globalization is that of neo-classical economics. The practical application of the theory has usually been referred to as neo-liberalism. It must be acknowledged that neo-classical economic theory has been highly successful in shaping the current global economic system. Without the intellectual force of this theory, it is difficult to imagine that a single global market could have come into existence. The theory has come to inspire the policies and strategies of most governments in the world, and of the major financial institutions. This was especially true during and after the Reagan/Thatcher era.

Yet, this raises an important issue. The phenomenon of the single global market may well have been spawned (in part) by neo-classical economic theory, but is the future of globalization necessarily tied to that theory? That, certainly, is the contention of neo-classical economists. But the possibility of there being alternative ways of organizing a globalized economy, according to principles at variance with neoliberalism, needs to be examined.

Before considering whether there are indeed alternative approaches, some attention needs to be given to the central characteristics of neo-classical theory. Neo-classical economics promotes the view that the market constitutes the optimal form of economic organization, in all places and all times, and that regulations that hinder the free operation of this market will lead to diseconomies and a distortion of economic welfare. Under free market conditions, it is contended, companies are bound to use the most efficient means of production (otherwise they will be undercut by competitors who can charge lower prices) and they will allocate resources toward producing the goods that society really needs. Although the market reflects the selfish interests of individuals, it has the overall effect of ensuring that society's scarce resources are used in the most efficient way and thus promoting the social good. Gains from the economic process, moreover, go to those who have contributed most effectively to production and exchange, so the system carries effective incentives. The most productive elements in society will be encouraged to contribute yet more to the process and thereby (it is assumed) enhance further the interests of society as a whole.

There is, in this, a strongly negative view of state "interference" in the economy. Governmental regulation, it is contended, must be kept to a minimum, for it distorts the most beneficial allocation of resources. The driving force behind the economy is the free market, not the government. The governmental role is primarily one of facilitating the efficient operation of the market, especially in such respects as creating the appropriate legal framework necessary for a free market to operate. Government must also ensure the availability of public goods that the private sector cannot itself finance: the appropriate social and physical infrastructure, and essential services such as defense.

Internationally, neo-liberalism entails "replacing state- with market-mediated economic flows and outcomes, within and across all national borders."[16] National borders must cease to be economically significant, with the global economic system constituted by a free flow of trade and resources through the mechanism of the global market. The global intersection of supply and demand will then determine the allocation of income arising from production and exchange. The merits of this system, as seen from the neo-classical viewpoint, are that consumer choice is enhanced (given that a consumer can now acquire products, at the cheapest price, from anywhere in the world); the factors of production move to wherever goods can be produced most cheaply, thus ensuring global economic efficiency; and each country is enabled to "concentrate its efforts on the production of those goods for which it is best suited, while acquiring other kinds of goods from other countries through trade,"[17] thereby enhancing world GDP and creating a higher level of global social welfare.

A key difference between the implications of neo-classical economic theory at the domestic and international levels must be noted. Freeing the domestic market from (perceived) unnecessary governmental regulation does not completely dispense with the role of government. There remains, domestically, a layer of governmental authority whose responsibility it is to limit any damaging effects that come from a market-oriented form of organization. Despite the neo-classical negative view of government, states do retain the ability and responsibility to re-distribute income and resources so as to ensure at least a minimum level of social welfare. At the international level, there is effectively no institution that can play this role. The main concern of the international economic institutions, indeed, is the reverse: to ensure that governments adhere to the norms of the global free market, rather than protect their populations from any damaging effects that follow from reliance on the market. The implications of the free market at the global level, therefore, are rather different–and socially more severe–than at the domestic level.

The "end of history" in global economic theory?

The neo-classical economic theory that has just been outlined is generally put forward within a framework consistent with Fukuyama's "end of history" thesis. In Fukuyama's view, the twentieth century saw the victory of the Western liberal idea over all other ideologies. In the course of the century, liberal democracy was challenged by the forces of fascism and communism, but it ended with the unqualified victory of liberal democracy. In Fukuyama's words:

> the century which began full of self-confidence in the ultimate triumph of Western liberal democracy seems at its close to be returning full circle to where it started: not to an "end of ideology" or a convergence between capitalism and communism, but to an unabashed victory of economic and political liberalism.[18]

The power of the market is central to Fukuyama's thesis: only the free market can deliver the goods populations demand, and only liberal democracy can provide the basis on which a free market can operate effectively. All other systems have been shown to be bankrupt, while only the liberal-democratic/free-market system is free of fundamental internal contradictions. All states, therefore, are bound to converge, sooner or later, around that pattern of economic and political organization, whose triumph marks the end of social evolution.[19]

Neo-classical economic theory similarly projects the global free market, within the framework set by the theory, as the ultimate form of economic organization. All other economic systems, it is suggested, have failed and there is now no alternative to the free market system. Global neo-liberalism, where the benefits of the free market are spread across the world, results in economic organization having reached an end point, where "economic history as the contest among alternative forms of economic system will come to an end."[20]

The trend toward global neo-liberalism, therefore, is put across as an inexorable process. Moves in a different direction are not alternative policies so much as vain attempts to stand in the way of the juggernaut of economic history. Such tactics, it is said, are bound to be ill fated and can do immense damage to a country's economic development. Economic failure is defined almost exclusively in terms of a failure to apply market principles correctly.[21] In this perspective, then, the neo-classical framework creates an ideological block on the pursuit of alternative policies. There is simply no alternative, and all governments have to face up to realities and operate within the ambit of neo-liberalism.

The underside of neo-liberal economic globalization

If neo-liberal economic globalization is indeed the "end of economic history," the world may face the prospect of a disharmonious and divisive future. While neo-liberalism may ensure that resources are used "efficiently" (i.e., they are employed in a way that rewards those who contribute most, and supplies scarce goods to those most able/willing to pay for them) and may maximize world GDP, these are not the only values relevant to an economic system's performance. Distributive justice,[22] social harmony, and the social welfare of the majority of the population must also be valued. Neo-classical economists argue that economic growth enhances social welfare through a trickle-down effect, improving the lot of all parts of society. Critics of neo-liberalism, however, argue that the productivity gains of neo-liberalism come at the expense of levels of inequality that are both morally unacceptable and socially disruptive.[23] These intensified inequalities, they contend, exist both within countries and between them. An "end of economic history" that leaves large parts of society sealed into a fate marked by poverty, relative and absolute, provides a grim prospect for the future.

The impact of neo-liberal globalization on inequality, therefore, now needs to be assessed. It is important to stress that the critics see increased inequalities as stemming from structural factors, not simply short-term or accidental side effects of the neo-liberal globalization process. In the homogenized global market, companies seek the cheapest location in which to produce. Calculations of costing must, no doubt, include the availability of an appropriately skilled workforce and a reasonable level of infrastructure, but wage-levels and social costs will figure prominently in any investor's assessment. There will be a steady tendency, therefore, for investment to move away from countries where governments regulate private economic activity so as to achieve egalitarian social goals.[24] The bargaining power of workers' unions, moreover, is weakened when a multinational company can move production easily in response to pay demands deemed excessive.[25]

Figures from the United Nations Development Program (UNDP) appear to present a clear picture with regard to the growth of inter-state inequalities over the decades of the 1960s, 1970s and 1980s. The 1992 *UNDP Human Development Report* noted that:

> between 1960 and 1989, the countries with the richest 20 percent of world population increased their share of global GNP from 70.2 percent to 82.7 percent. The countries with the poorest 20 percent of world population saw their share fall from 2.3 percent to 1.4 percent.[26]

This had, the report said, dramatic consequences for income inequalities. Whereas in 1960 the top 20 percent received 30 times more than the bottom 20 percent, by 1989 they were receiving 60 percent more.[27] The figures show an increasing rate of inequality: the growth of the gap over the nine years between 1980 and 1989 (in the Reagan/Thatcher era) was approximately equal to the growth of the gap in the preceding 20 years. Even these figures, however, do not reveal the true extent of inequality, in so far as they compare countries rather than people. Domestic inequalities also need to be taken into account. Relatively few countries had at that time published reliable data on income distribution, but on the basis of those that had, the UNDP estimated that the ratio between the incomes of the richest and poorest quintiles of the world's population in 1989 was around 150:1.[28] Such differences were reflected in real consumption levels, with the North (constituting one-quarter of the world's population) consuming 70 percent of the world's energy, 75 percent of its metals, 85 percent of its wood, and 60 percent of its food.[29]

The data from the 1990s is rather more complex and less clear-cut. The rapid growth in the Chinese economy has led some writers to suggest that inter-state income divergence has slowed down, or perhaps even been reversed, over the period since 1990.[30] The flows of private capital to a limited but nonetheless significant group of developing countries do seem to have had some effect in narrowing some inter-state economic inequalities. The rate of economic growth in the East Asia and Pacific Region, bringing per capita income from *c.*$2,300 in 1990 to *c.*$4,500 in 2000, was substantially higher than that in the Organisation for Economic Co-operation and Development (OECD) countries.[31] Per capita income in this region is now one-sixth of the OECD average, whereas it had been one-fourteenth in 1975. Economic growth in Latin America and the Caribbean also exceeded the rate of growth of the OECD countries during the decade of the 1990s. Nonetheless, the 2002 *UNDP Human Development Report* pointed to substantial problems elsewhere. South Asia and the Arab world only registered limited rates of economic growth, well short of that of the developed countries, and Africa and the Central and Eastern European countries registered negative rates of growth (which has been the case in Africa over the whole period since 1975).

A major characteristic of the 1990s, however, was the rising levels of inequality within states. Substantial information on this is now available through the "World Income Inequality Database" at the UNU/WIDER in Helsinki. The database covers 151 countries over the period 1950–1998. Cornia and Court, on the basis of this data, show that the trend toward greater domestic income inequality began in the United States and the United Kingdom in the 1970s and spread elsewhere thereafter as neoliberal economic policies became the international norm. The 2002 *UNDP Human Development Report* comments on the position within OECD countries as follows:

> OECD countries have increased their incomes over the past two decades, but most have seen rising income inequality–most consistently and dramatically in the United Kingdom and the United States. Between 1979 and 1997 US real GDP per capita grew 38 percent, but the income of a family with median earnings grew only 9 percent. So most of the gain was captured by the very richest people, with the incomes of the richest 1 percent of families growing 140 percent, three times the average. The income of the top 1 percent of families was 10 times the median family in 1979 – and 23 times in 1997.[32]

The data on income inequality is more readily available with regard to developed than developing countries, but most data on the latter suggests that intra-country inequalities are wider, and growing even faster than, those in developed countries. The 2003 *UNDP Human Development Report* provides information on inequalities in income for most countries in the world, comparing the income of the richest 10 percent of the population with that of the poorest 10 percent.[33] The ratio in most developed countries is for the richest 10 percent to be earning 5 to 10 times as much as the poorest 10 percent (but with Japan at 4.5, the United Kingdom at 13.4 and the US at 16.6). The range among developing countries is wide, making it difficult to convey a realistic picture concisely. But the ratios for the following key countries (listed according to their overall ranking in the human development index) give some indication of the overall pattern: Mexico 34.6, Malaysia 22.1, Brazil 65.8, Venezuela 44.0, Philippines 16.5, China 12.7, Iran 17.2, South Africa 65.1, India 9.5, Zimbabwe 22.0, Nigeria 24.9, Tanzania 10.8, Zambia 36.6, and Ethiopia 59.7. The highest ratios of all tend to be in southern Africa: Namibia 128.8, Botswana 77.6, and Lesotho 117.8.[34] The only one of the above countries that registered an improvement in the ratio (i.e., a lessening of inequalities) since the 2001 *UNDP Human Development Report* was Zimbabwe.[35] In many cases, the growth in inequality was dramatic.

Taking the inter-state and the intra-state data together, it seems probable that overall inequalities between the world's rich and poor have continued to rise over the period since 1990. A paper produced for the UN Research Institute for Social Development in August 2002 concludes that "the weight of evidence is on the side of those who assert that inequalities are actually increasing."[36] Nor can the rise of inequalities be excused as characteristic of a transitional stage where inequality fosters growth.[37] Recent work has shown that lower levels of inequality in fact promote growth rather than hinder it.[38]

The 2002 report also showed that the absolute numbers of those living on less than $1 a day in sub-Saharan Africa, Latin America, the Middle East and North Africa, Eastern Europe, and Central Asia increased during the decade of the 1990s. In sub-Saharan Africa, moreover, there was substantial slippage in basic services, with many countries regressing in the provision of universal primary education, reducing under-five mortality, and in life expectancy.[39] The report described the level of global inequality as "extremely high", with the world's richest 1 percent of people receiving as much income as the poorest 57 percent. The incomes of the world's richest 5 percent is described as being 114 times that of the poorest 5 percent.

While the trends of the 1990s have not been universally negative, then, inequality has remained a major problem, and the absolute level of poverty remains unacceptable. Neoliberalism has not shown a consistent ability to improve the conditions of the poorest parts of the global community, nor to lessen the gulf between rich and poor. There is, furthermore, considerable evidence of environmental damage stemming from the lack of international control over the activities of multinational corporations.[40]

Globalization on a different basis: toward an alternative to neo-liberalism

The last section has maintained that the neo-liberal approach to globalization creates, and/or fails to resolve, problems that are critical to social harmony and international well-being. This covers issues of social division and also of environmental depredation. Rather than accept that neo-liberalism is indeed "the end of economic history," therefore, consideration must be given to other approaches that may protect populations more effectively against the negative effects of the current pattern of globalization. The merits of five alternative approaches are briefly assessed below. The object is not so much to reach a definitive conclusion on which approach is best as to indicate what options may be viable.

Re-asserting the authority of national governments   An obvious response to the failings in the current framework of globalization, and the absence at the international level of mechanisms that can correct the various imbalances and injustices inherent in it, would be to re-assert national authority. Governments, in this perspective, would be encouraged to hold back the pressures from the international system and act more effectively in defense of socially acceptable principles. The 2002 *UNDP Human Development Report* makes a point that may give credence to such an approach. It points out that some governments have been able to resist the trend toward increased inequality within their own countries: "Canada and Denmark have bucked the OECD trend, registering stable or slightly reduced inequality. This was achieved primarily through fiscal policy and social transfers – indicating that with political will, nothing is inevitable about inequality increasing with rising incomes."[41]

It is certainly true that national governments need to be encouraged not to abandon concern for social equity or environmental protection when no other body can take over responsibility for these issues. In reality, however, it is the stronger and more developed states that alone can take such a stand–and they are usually the ones that, at an international level, are pressing forward the agenda of neo-liberalism.[42] The US's unilateral imposition of tariffs on steel imports in 2002, for example, could not easily be copied by developing countries. The US action was aimed at protecting its own steel industry and was in apparent defiance of the regulations of the World Trade Organization. It is difficult to see this approach, therefore, as helping significantly in the reduction of international inequalities. There is, furthermore, a concern over the motivations that governments have in sealing off their economies from competition. In some countries, especially in the developing world, these measures can have inegalitarian objectives: enabling commercial elites, usually with close governmental connections, to draw benefit from monopoly. The effectiveness and judiciousness of government policy in this context depends much on the nature of the state, and the social basis on which it rests.

Changing the balance of economic power through regional integration   Earlier discussion of the weak position of developing countries, in particular, under the regime of neo-liberal globalization, raises the issue as to whether regional integration could improve their position. This could enable them to increase the size of their local markets and (on the basis of their collective weight) exert more influence on global economic policies. Clearly this would bring benefits, and recent moves in the Arab world to create a common market must be seen positively (as also with ASEAN in the Far East, MERCOSUR in Latin America, etc.).[43] The balance of power, however, may be difficult to shift: the GDP of all of the Arab countries combined is approximately equivalent to that of a middle-ranking EU country.

Returning power to the grassroots: communal organization   The perspective that national government is no longer capable of protecting populations from the ravages of the global system has focused some attention on the promotion of "local power."

Strategies for returning power to local communities include a range of grassroots initiatives, each of which would be adapted to the cultural, economic, and biological context. Among the initiatives that have been attempted to date are the establishment of community banks to increase the capital available locally to be invested locally; holding "buy-local" campaigns to help local businesses to survive against corporate competitors; developing "local currencies" for use only within a communal grouping; instituting community-supported agriculture, where consumers link up directly with nearby farmers; encouraging farmers' markets; creating eco-villages based on local resources and renewable energy; and establishing schools training students in locally adapted agriculture, architecture and artisanal production and technologies suited to local resources.[44] Emphasis in this approach is placed on the need for local democracy, which is seen as basic to any attempt to re-constitute integrated local communities.[45]

While initiatives of this kind are clearly useful and help to create alternative forms of economic organization, it is difficult to see the movement as constituting more than a fringe at the edge of the global economy. The challenge that it poses to neo-liberalism is unlikely to change the direction of global policy.

Achieving global control of the global economy: replacing neo-liberalism with a structure of trade preferences based on capabilities equality, global taxation for MNCs, and international labor mobility   This approach and the one that follows are directed to dimensions of global control. They rest on the assumption that global developments can only be controlled by creating a layer of effective authority at the international level. Just as national governments seek to assuage the social impact of the market economy domestically, so also should there be international institutions geared to performing the same role internationally.

Perhaps the most far-reaching scheme aimed at international re-structuring has been that of George DeMartino, who bases his proposals on Amartya Sen's concept of "capabilities equality."[46] The latter concept refers to the need for labor forces to compete with each other on an equal basis. In order to deter MNCs from directing their investment to areas where workers enjoy the least protection, the lowest material rewards, and the lowest social welfare, DeMartino suggests an international social-index tariff structure. This would be based on the UNDP Human Development Index with a graduated tariff system. Products from countries offering workers the worst conditions would be subject to the highest tariffs. The tariff structure would also reflect the degree of protection given to the environment. Again, the highest tariffs would be imposed on countries with the least environmental protection. DeMartino suggests that this will give foreign investors an incentive to improve the conditions of workers and safeguard the environment, rather than to favor minimal levels. Taxation for MNCs would be standardized and levied globally, so as to prevent countries bidding against each other in providing MNCs with the most favorable tax packages. There would also be an agreement on labor mobility for non-skilled workers so as to foster a commonality of levels of manual pay. The sums raised through the social-index tariffs and the MNC taxation would be put in the hands of newly created international bodies, which would channel them back to developing countries, specifically so as to enhance their capabilities resources.

Well-articulated though this scheme is, the political difficulties in implementing it would be immense. It would, in the short term, run counter to the interests of all of the main parties involved: developing countries would oppose it, in so far as the measures would effectively discourage investment in the developing world; the MNCs would object to restrictions on their ability to utilize cheap labor; and the neoliberal consensus in leading Western governments would shrink away from the interference with the free market.

Achieving global control of the global economy: strengthening, replacing, or re-directing international institutions, and introducing new regulatory frameworks The measures that have been put forward under this heading are widely different in character, ranging from piecemeal reforms within the structure of the existing system,[47] to a radical re-creating of the institutional and regulatory system. Some of the major proposals have been the following:

1 *Re-ordering the priorities of the IMF, or replacing it.* The reformed/new institution would benefit from some citizen participation and would broaden its scope to include regulating financial markets, managing the process of repudiating, and writing off the international debts of low-income countries etc.[48]
2 *Re-ordering or replacing the WTO.* The reformed/new institution would hold responsibility for negotiating agreements regulating transnational corporations and international trade, in accordance with objectives directly geared to increasing local self-reliance and global equity.[49]
3 *Introducing an international financial transactions tax*, collected on all spot transactions in foreign exchange. The objective would be to discourage speculative finance.[50]
4 *Introducing an intensified environmental monitoring system*, with power given to the UN Environment Programme to take appropriate cases to the International Court of Justice and other international judicial bodies.
5 *A global charter for corporate conduct*, laying down a framework for investment. Among the items covered would be citizens' rights, state responsibilities, corporate obligations, fair treatment regulations, social duties to the labor force, investment incentives, etc.[51]

These proposals will not be elaborated upon further here. The intention is simply to show that there is a profusion of ideas about how the international economic system can be reformed. Some of these would involve a radical change to the neo-liberal pattern of globalization by introducing effective controls on how the free market operates. Other options, however, open up the possibility of creating more equity through gradually limiting the harsher effects of globalization. In the light of the neo-liberal consensus that currently dominates international financial policy-making circles, the more radical agendas are unlikely to be feasible in the short term.

Conclusion

While neo-classical economic theory has played a prominent role in bringing the single global market into being, the link between neoliberalism and globalization needs now to be loosened in the interests of social and international harmony. This does not involve a rejection of globalization but rather an insistence that there are alternatives to the neo-liberal model. None of the five approaches mentioned in the last section holds the full solution, but all have a contribution to make. Ultimately, however, the adoption of alternatives requires political determination and political support, both domestically and internationally. Political mobilization will be needed to create the support required.

Notes

* University of Exeter.
1 Some would put the date at which trade became internationalized much earlier than this. The discovery in 1993 that an Egyptian mummy from 1000 BC had threads of Chinese silk in her hair attests to the fact that long-range international trade is of very long-standing. A. MacEwan, *Neo-liberalism or Democracy: Economic Strategy, Markets and Alternatives for the 21st Century* (London: Zed Books, 1999), 25.
2 P. Hirst and G. Thompson, *Globalization in Question* (Cambridge: Polity, 2001), 1.
3 *Ibid.*, 2–3.
4 See J. Perraton, "What Are Global Markets: The Significance of Networks of Trade?" in *Globalization and Its Critics*, ed. R. Germain (London: Macmillan, 2000), 169.
5 A useful discussion of this is to be found in D. Held and A. McGrew, eds, *Globalization/Anti-globalization* (Cambridge: Polity, 2002), 1–8.
6 The tripartite division presented here is taken from G. DeMartino, *Global Economy, Global Justice: Theoretical Objections and Policy Alternatives to Neoliberalism* (London: Routledge, 2000), 11–15.
7 P. Dicken, *Global Shift*, 3rd edn. (London: Paul Chapman Publishing, 1998), 24–25.
8 *Ibid.*, 92–93.
9 World Bank, *World Development Indicators* (Washington, DC: World Bank, 2000), 28.
10 Figures taken from the UNCTAD website at http://r0.unctad.org/en/subsites/dite/fdistats.htm.
11 M. Todaro and S. Smith, *Economic Development*, 8th edn. (London: Pearson Education, 2003), 638.
12 *Ibid.*, 636.
13 M. Todaro, *Economic Development*, 6th edn. (London: Longman, 1997), 535.
14 DeMartino, 14.
15 DeMartino, 36. The analysis in this section draws significantly on the insights of DeMartino.
16 *Ibid.*, 6.
17 *Ibid.*
18 Francis Fukuyama, "The End of History," *The National Interest*, 18 (1989): 2.
19 Francis Fukuyama, *The End of History and the Last Man* (London: Hamish Hamilton, 1992).
20 DeMartino, 2.
21 This required a quick re-evaluation of views during the Asian financial crisis of 1998. The economies of the region had previously been described by neoclassical economists as prime examples of how the free market can transform economies and create growth. The crisis that a number of the economies went through at that time led quickly to a different line of analysis: the states had been subject to "crony capitalism," where the

proper operation of the free market had been distorted by personal links between businessmen and state officials. See V. Mallett, *The Trouble with Tigers* (London: HarperCollins, 1999).

22 The philosophical basis for a critique along these lines can be found in the works of John Rawls, especially *Political Liberalism* (New York: Columbia University Press, 1996).

23 For a very explicit articulation of this view, see D. Korten, *When Corporations Rule the World* (Connecticut: Kumarian Press, 1995). See also J. Brecher and T. Costello, *Global Village v. Global Pillage* (Washington, DC: International Labor Rights Education and Research Fund, 1991).

24 For a perspective that covers this point of view see H. Martin and H. Schumann, *The Global Trap: Globalization and the Assault on Democracy and Prosperity* (London: Pluto Press, 1997). For a counter-view, arguing that globalization has not been the key factor in creating greater wage-inequality, see P. Krugman, "Trade, Jobs and Wages," in *Pop Internationalism*, ed. P. Krugman (Cambridge, MA: MIT Press).

25 For an analysis of this tendency, see A. MacEwan, 4–11. See also A. Wood, *North-South Trade, Employment and Inequality: Changing Fortunes in a Skill-driven World* (Oxford: Oxford University Press, 1994).

26 United Nations Development Program, *Human Development Report 1992* (Oxford: Oxford University Press, 1992), 4.

27 *Ibid.* It should be acknowledged that some writers have taken issue with the basis on which the UNDP HDR figures are calculated. For discussion of alternative approaches, see A. Melchior, "World Income Inequality: Belief, Facts and Unresolved Issues," *World Economics* 2, no. 3 (2001): 87–108, and I. Castles, "The Mismeasure of Nations: A Review Essay on the Human Development Report 1998," *Population and Development Review* 24, no. 4 (1998): 831–845.

28 *Ibid.*

29 *Ibid.*, 35.

30 K. O'Rourke, "Globalization and Inequality: Historical Trends," in World Bank, *Annual Bank Conference on Development Economics* 2001/2, 36–67.

31 All of the statistics in this paragraph are taken from United Nations Development Program, *Human Development Report 2002* (Oxford: Oxford University Press, 2002), 18–20.

32 *Ibid.*, 20.

33 United Nations Development Program, *Human Development Report* 2003 (Oxford: Oxford University Press, 2003), 282–285.

34 Figures for 2001 from United Nations Development Program, *Human Development Report 2001* (Oxford: Oxford University Press, 2001), 182–185.

35 The case of Zimbabwe is, of course, idiosyncratic in the light of political developments in the country, and the rapid shrinkage of GDP that the country has suffered. For some of the countries listed the information for 2003 has not been updated since the 2001 report, but for most of them new information was available.

36 R. Culpeper, "Approaches to Globalization and Inequality within the International System"(paper prepared under the UNRISD project Improving Research and Knowledge on Social Development in International Organizations, August 2002).

37 The contention that developing countries need a transitional period where inequalities grow is associated with the work of Simon Kuznets. See "Economic Growth and Income Inequality," *American Economic Review* 65, no. 1 (1955): 1–28.

38 See P. Aghion and J. Williamson, *Growth, Inequality and Globalization* (Cambridge: Cambridge University Press, 1998).

39 *Ibid.*, 18.

40 The evidence on environmental damage is substantial yet difficult to place within a coherent comparative framework. For a discussion of this see E. Goldsmith, "Global Trade and the Environment," in *The Case Against the Global Economy*, eds J. Mander and E. Goldsmith (San Francisco: Sierra, 1996), 78–91. See also the discussion of the

"Crisis of Ecological Unsustainability," in L. Sklair, *Globalization, Capitalism and its Alternatives* (Oxford: Oxford University Press, 2002), 53–57.

41 UNDP, *Human Development Report 2002*, 20.

42 A possible exception to this should be noted. In the course of the 1998 Asian financial crisis, Malaysia acted rather effectively, and in defiance of the neoliberal consensus, in protecting its economy from the gathering crisis. A draconian package of short-term currency controls was introduced, banning foreign banks from trading in ringgit investments, forbidding Malaysian banks from offering credit facilities to foreign banks and stockbrokers, ordering the repatriation of ringits in circulation outside of the country, insisting that all trade be conducted in foreign currencies, banning foreigners from leaving the country within one year of their selling shares, etc. See *Financial Times*, September 2, 1998.

43 The benefits of the regional integration approach are discussed in A. Hoogvelt, *Globalization and the Postcolonial World* (London: Macmillan, 1997), 216–219 and 242–245.

44 See H. Norberg-Hodge, "Shifting Direction from Global Dependence to Local Interdependence," in Mander and Goldsmith, 404–406.

45 E. Goldsmith, "The Last Word: Family, Community, Democracy," in Mander and Goldsmith, 501–514.

46 DeMartino. For Sen's contribution, see A. Sen, *Inequality Re-examined* (Cambridge, MA: Harvard University Press, 1992).

47 The more limited measures are not covered in what follows. A useful summary of some of the pragmatic policies that could lessen the negative impact of neoliberal policies can be found in Culpeper, 23–25.

48 See Korten, 323; and W. Ellwood, *The No-nonsense Guide to Globalization* (London: Verso, 2001), 108–113.

49 Korten, 324.

50 See J. Tobin, "A Tax on International Currency Transactions," in UNDP, *Human Resources Development Report 1994* (Oxford: Oxford University Press, 1994), 70. James Tobin was the 1981 Nobel Prize winner for economics, and the tax he proposed has become known as the "Tobin Tax."

51 Ellwood, 134–135.

References

Aghion, P. and J. Williamson. *Growth, Inequality and Globalization*. Cambridge University Press, 1998.

Brecher, J. and T. Costello. *Global Village v. Global Pillage*. Washington, DC: International Labor Rights Education and Research Fund, 1991.

Castles, I. "The Mismeasure of Nations: A Review Essay on the Human Development Report 1998." *Population and Development Review* 24, no. 4 (1998): 831–845.

Culpeper, R. "Approaches to Globalization and Inequality within the International System." Paper prepared under the UNRISD project Improving Research and Knowledge on Social Development in International Organizations, August 2002.

DeMartino, G. *Global Economy, Global Justice: Theoretical Objections and Policy Alternatives to Neoliberalism*. London: Routledge, 2000.

Dicken, P. *Global Shift*. 3rd edn. London: Paul Chapman Publishing, 1998.

Ellwood, W. *The No-nonsense Guide to Globalization*. London: Verso, 2001.

Fukuyama, Francis. "The End of History." *The National Interest* 18 (1989).

———. *The End of History and the Last Man*. London: Hamish Hamilton, 1992.

Goldsmith, E. "Global Trade and the Environment." In Mander and Goldsmith, 78–91.

Goldsmith, E. "The Last Word: Family, Community, Democracy." In Mander and Goldsmith, 501–514.

Held, D. and A. McGrew, eds. *Globalization/Anti-globalization*. Cambridge: Polity, 2002.

Hirst, P. and G. Thompson. *Globalization in Question*. Cambridge: Polity, 2001.

Hoogvelt, A. *Globalization and the Postcolonial World*. London: Macmillan, 1997.

Korten, D. *When Corporations Rule the World*. Connecticut: Kumarian Press, 1995.

Krugman, P. "Trade, Jobs and Wages." In *Pop Internationalism*, edited by P. Krugman. Cambridge, MA: MIT Press.

Kuznets, Simon. "Economic Growth and Income Inequality." *American Economic Review* 65, no. 1 (1955): 1–28.

MacEwan, A. *Neo-Liberalism or Democracy: Economic Strategy, Markets and Alternatives for the 21st Century*. London: Zed Books, 1999.

Mallett, V. *The Trouble with Tigers*. London: HarperCollins, 1999.

Mander, J. and E. Goldsmith, eds *The Case Against the Global Economy*. San Francisco: Sierra, 1996.

Martin, H. and H. Schumann. *The Global Trap: Globalization and the Assault on Democracy and Prosperity*. London: Pluto Press, 1997.

Melchior, A. "World Income Inequality: Belief, Facts and Unresolved Issues." *World Economics* 2, no. 3 (2001): 87–108.

Norberg-Hodge, H. "Shifting Direction from Global Dependence to Local Interdependence." In Mander and Goldsmith, 404–406.

O'Rourke, K. "Globalization and Inequality: Historical Trends." In World Bank, *Annual Bank Conference on Development Economics*, 2001/2.

Perraton, J. "What Are Global Markets: The Significance of Networks of Trade?" In *Globalization and Its Critics*, edited by R. Germain, 169. London: Macmillan, 2000.

Rawls, John. *Political Liberalism*. New York: Columbia University Press, 1996.

Sen, A. *Inequality Re-examined*. Cambridge, MA: Harvard University Press, 1992.

Sklair, L. *Globalization, Capitalism and Its Alternatives*. Oxford: Oxford University Press, 2002.

Tobin, J. "A Tax on International Currency Transactions." In United Nations Development Programme, *Human Resources Development Report 1994*, 70. Oxford: Oxford University Press, 1994.

Todaro, M. *Economic Development*, 6th edn. London: Longman, 1997.

Todaro, M. and S. Smith. *Economic Development*, 8th edn. London: Pearson Education, 2003.

United Nations Development Program. *Human Development Report 1992*. Oxford: Oxford University Press, 1992.

———. *Human Development Report 2001*. Oxford: Oxford University Press, 2001.

———. *Human Development Report 2002*. Oxford: Oxford University Press, 2002.

———. *Human Development Report 2003*. Oxford: Oxford University Press, 2003.

Wood, A. *North-South Trade, Employment and Inequality: Changing Fortunes in a Skill-driven World*. Oxford: Oxford University Press, 1994.

World Bank. *World Development Indicators*. Washington, DC: World Bank, 2000.

5 The trends in globalization critiqued

Ismail Sirageldin*

Introduction

GOD Created the universe with humans but a speck in its enormous oceans, left to search for a purpose as they evolve. Organic evolution provides the natural tendency for violence and conquest, while symbolic cultural evolution creates views of nature and 'gods' that justify the consequences of their actions.

This was the opening sentence of a recent paper.[1] Even the "invisible hand" paradigm that, apparently, put faith in the unrestricted guidance of human nature in market and human affairs, and, has been the underlying premise to guide the present phase of globalization needed the help of human authority to keep away its misbehavior, according to its godfather, Adam Smith, although that need has been largely ignored in policy and analysis.[2] Confidence in human nature seems to reach a low point when the domain of interdependence and decision making move from local to global levels especially when globalization, defined as increased interdependence among countries and societies is expected to promote equity and maximize welfare for the majority of humanity.[3] At its best, globalization is expected to develop social, political, and economic institutions, on the local and global levels, that encourage creativeness rather than possessiveness; embody and promote a spirit of reverence between human beings; and preserve self-respect for individuals and societies. But Russell's judgment – more than eighty years ago – about the efficacy of human institutions in achieving the above mentioned goals seem to be as valid today: "in all these ways, the institutions under which we live are far indeed from what they ought to be."[4]

The conflict between "human nature" and global interdependence produces instability, discontinuity, and heightens dependence, with the majority of the world population remaining locked in a global social hierarchy. Other negative consequences are conflict, the lack of both universal justice and the rule of law,[5] a pattern of global finance characterized by abuse and severe instability,[6] and the uncertainty of a global labor market. In this chapter, I discuss four causes of instability – human natures, finance capital, increased uncertainties in labor markets' behavior, and the evolving pattern of global governance. They form integral parts of the global system. Yet, in its present form, the global system is not sustainable and thus requires structural reform.

In overview, this chapter examines the long-term consequences of economic globalization. These trends allow assessment of the developments in the Arabian Gulf region to be placed in wider context in time and space. How will leadership of the Gulf States accentuate the positive effects of globalism and mitigate the negative effects in safeguarding the traditional attributes of Gulf society?

There have been many attempts to evaluate human development in recent years in the context of the evolving global system, including the UNDP's *Human Development Report 1999* and the contributions of Amartya Sen, Jared Diamond, and D.S. Landes, among others.[7] These contributions provide frameworks to examine the status of human development and indicators for assessment and directions for reform. It is felt, however, that the underlying synergies among advances in science and technology, views of nature, culture and institutions – necessary for explicating the dynamic nature of human development, especially in the context of the evolving global environment – are not sufficiently elucidated.[8]

In section 1 of this chapter, I examine briefly the role of human nature within the conceptual framework. In section 2, the destabilizing roles of finance capital, uncertainties in labor markets and the lack of democratic practice in global governance are examined. Section 3 makes some predictions on how the trends of globalization will be manifested in the immediate future.

Section 1: on human nature

Free markets are not designed to maximize the public good and their functioning is often quite variable. As Adam Smith warned, when left on their own, markets tend to produce negative externalities ranging from glaring inequities and poverty to unsustainable environments. When the level of these negative externalities exceeds the tolerance capacity of the prevailing social institutions, both the local and the global social and political systems are threatened. It sends signals questioning the efficacy of existing institutions and the relevance of the prevailing views of nature in the context of current scientific knowledge, thus instigating institutional reform and a re-interpretation of the views of nature to legitimize the evolving social hierarchy. Such re-interpretations do not necessarily provide justice or equitable solutions to the negative externalities of market behavior but often serve the needs of interest groups that profit from the emerging status. Conflict theorists would contend that the financial and political powers resort to force to preserve their privileged positions in the distribution and control of strategic resources. I note the forces that shape "views of nature" and the impact of these views on human development in Figure 5.1.

There are optimists who feel that human societies are increasing their ability to chart and follow a purposeful course of change toward a better life for all, a course in which diversity is welcomed and historical lessons are positively interpreted to provide for better future guidance for equitable development and sustainable environment. Optimists, however, are balanced by an equal, if not

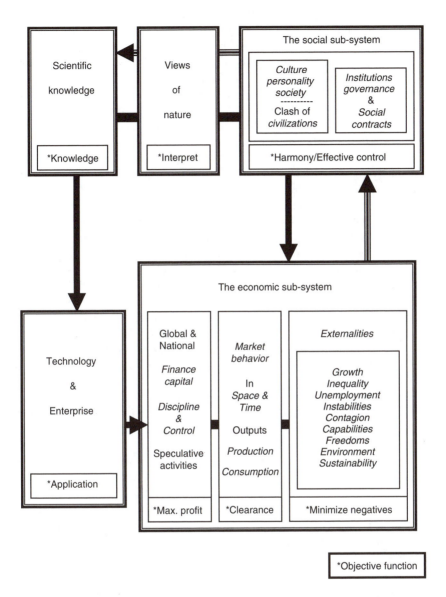

Figure 5.1 Science, views of nature, and development*.

Note
* For a detailed analysis, see Sirageldin, Ismail, "Human Prospects in The 21st Century: Freedom or Serfdom" 2006.

larger, number of pessimists who believe that the inexorable laws of "nature and evolution" will eventually override purpose and cause the human species to decline and disappear, as other animal species have done in the past. Of the 500 million to 1 billion species that existed at one time or another, 97 percent have become instinct, due mostly to their inability to respond to the environmental system. As we approach the earth's carrying capacity, we severely limit human maneuverability in response to change – limits that enforce our species' natural tendency for non-cooperation, violence, irrational values, and unconscionable behavior, the pessimists reason. As population density intensifies, humans invent new paradigms or "views of nature" that legitimize unjust actions and behavior. Teleological explanations, such as the "end of history," "eugenics," "clash of civilizations" or even the "end of the fertility transition," portray contemporary inequities as the inevitable, natural result of the "final cause" or as the ultimate purpose of human history – a view that leads the vast majority of humankind to a state of perpetual poverty, violence, and despair. Today, teleological explanations prevail and guide policies and actions, some evidently harmful to human well-being.

Thus, although for three centuries advances in science provided technological innovations that contributed to human comfort, by the end of the twentieth century, these advances had also provided for the development of the deadliest weapons of mass destruction. Humans never hesitated to use both, especially the latter whenever the existing powerful felt threatened or angry. Just like the Mesopotamian myth when the "gods," who believed that they represented order in the world, heard that all the forces of the past, of the original chaos (or the terrorists, in modern terminology) were making ready to do battle with them, they prepared to battle.

However, none of the students of evolution, whether they believed in chance or design, could have imagined that by the end of the twentieth century the scientific insights and technological knowhow would be in place to make real a vision of a commercial genetic civilization. As Rifkin put it, "the mapping of the human genome, the increasing ability to screen for genetic diseases and disorders, the new reproductive technologies, and the new techniques of human genetic manipulation ... establish the technological foundation for a commercial eugenics civilization."[9] This civilization will be more global with a different view of nature, which is yet to evolve. However, present developments indicate that the evolving views of nature will continue to serve the interest and calculus of the "global" marketplace, with values linked to market behavior.

These dynamics are illustrated in Figure 5.1. Scientific innovations and developments are channeled through corporations into the marketplace as technical applications to satisfy consumer needs and are viewed, if not measured, as enhancement of global welfare. The objective of global finance is to maximize profit through fast relocation of finance capital and speculative activities, and not the longer-term objective of preserving the production structure over time. The result, in most cases is the privatization of risk and increased uncertainties to producers and workers alike; the "disciplinary role" of finance capital to enhance efficiency and promote innovations becomes a tool in the hands of speculators. Thus, in the evolving global system, finance capital becomes the heart of the economy; it stands at the top of the sociopolitical pyramid influencing patterns of production, social values, and views of nature.

The discussion thus far conveys a pessimistic view of human prospect. However, there is also room for optimism. Negative trends may be slowing down.

Technological advances, especially in biotechnology, provide promise for enhanced food production with lower resource use and reduced environmental damage. Meanwhile, the search continues for views of nature that are more rational and less destructive. But for most of humanity, the central challenge remains how to establish a global environment that promotes justice and the rule of law, which will facilitate a sustainable level of development. However, the present evolving global environment seems to have built-in destabilizing forces that require system reform.

Section 2: on destabilizing forces

It can be safely stated that the technological base of globalization is the outgrowth of industrial revolution. As a result, there is a fundamental change in business behavior. The interaction of information technology (e.g., e-commerce) and the global economy induced a need for alliances among multinational corporations to share information, ignoring borders, cultural or language differences, and geography. The only impediments are taxes and government rules. Such apparently cooperative behavior has its limitations. First, maximum returns, mainly short-term, are required for survival in the global marketplace, especially given the discipline of international finance capital. Second, "maximum returns" implies competition in global labor markets and in the acquisition of technological innovations and of vital natural resources, e.g. oil – activities that are more competitive than cooperative in nature. Third, since the privatization of risk in financial transactions took place, short-term speculation accentuated the non-cooperative element of business behavior.

However, not all factors of production allow great mobility. Although global rules free the movement of finance and speculative capital and enhance unrestricted trade including goods and services, they also restrict most labor mobility, especially those in the less skilled occupations in the less developed regions. On the other hand, the phasing out of restrictions on the movement of trade and finance, especially speculative investments, restricted the scope of state powers' actions to exercise and implement effective social and economic policies to reduce the negative effects of market fluctuations. This is especially acute since international regulations and global governance have not developed the necessary framework of standards nor the capacity to control these negative externalities that hamper development. Instead, resorting to arms to resolve conflict is becoming the norm rather than the exception. It is instructive to examine briefly some tangible impacts of these trends.

On finance capital: the invisible hand![10]

Global finance provides for growth beyond the limits of local savings. On the other hand, it tends to increase risk with negative effects for the entire global system. The structure of the present global system seems to differ significantly from previous systems. The present phase is fueled by the rapid development of major innovations in information and communications technology, which instantaneously links global finance capital, while international regulatory institutions are redesigned to provide security for capital movement.

In the boom and bust financial cycles that follow each major innovation, finance capital follows established economic principles for success but eventually gives way to speculative ventures. Economic facts give way to speculative fantasies; share prices become independent of performance, leading to capital flight and eventual stock market collapse. Once the psychological element combines with politics, speculative ventures take over. Such ventures tend to create greater worldwide volatility on a much larger scale and at greater speed, in part because of the efficiency of the information technology itself and partly a result of speculation activities hedging against increased risk. The result has been the recurrence and spread of large economic crises. Meanwhile, workers' security and human well-being could suffer greatly from investing psychology and not necessarily because of weakness in economic fundamentals. In the long run, this situation tends to self-correct, since irrational increases in equity prices cannot be sustained for long without the support of real earnings. Similarly, capital flight would eventually reverse its course once the economic facts override psychological and political forces. However, the economic and social losses could be sizeable and selective in the interim and the interim could be of long duration. Meanwhile, the social role of governments is being compromised in the global environment.

How finance capital and speculative activities create risk with systemic consequences to human development was studied by Eatwell and Taylor, who traced the patterns and consequences of financial developments since the 1960s to infer their expected behavior.[11] They observed the following pattern:

1   A breakdown of national regulatory capacities has occurred as financial liberalization has spread worldwide since the 1960s. Consequences have included high and variable interest rates, increased volatility of asset prices, poor national economic performances, and the spread of market instabilities worldwide.

2   Even in the large and integrated financial markets of the industrialized economies, instability, in the absence of appropriate regulatory procedures to deal with the unleashed financial flows, is associated with currency crises in developing and transitional economies.

3   Changes in exchange rates are driven by speculative activities in the financial markets.

4   Volatility of finance capital flows undermines the integrity of the financial institutions, compromises returns from long-term investments, and introduces instabilities in labor market behavior, but it also undermines governments' abilities to regulate since, in most instances, the routes of volatility are beyond the capacity and authority of governments.

In the present system, the privatization of risk led to the marginalization of existing regulatory agencies. The privatization of risk started when

President Richard Nixon, in 1971, suspended all sales and purchases of gold. This was the end of the Bretton Woods system (founded in 1944) based on fixed exchange rates of the then-major currencies in terms of the US dollars which were tied to gold. Floating rates relaxed the tight control on capital movement that freed the private sector from foreign exchange shocks. The incentive to deregulate international capital flows was driven by the need to hedge against the growing fluctuation of exchange rates. With the extinction of fixed exchange rates, financial risk has been privatized.

Meanwhile, the volume of international capital flows has reached unprecedented high levels. In 1973, daily foreign exchange trading around the world was less than $20 billion and the ratio of foreign exchange trading to world trade did not exceed 2/1. In 1980, average daily trading reached $80 billion and the ratio increased to 10/1. By 1992, daily trading averaged $880 billion with a ratio of 50/1. In 1995, average daily trading in foreign exchange reached $1260 and a ratio of 70/1. The 1995 volume was equal to the entire world's official gold and foreign exchange reserves.[12] These massive volumes dwarf flows into long-term investment. They are short-run speculation designed primarily to hedge against fluctuations in asset prices. The new international financial system is characterized by high volatility, spreading at high speed from one market to other markets across the globe. It has produced interlinked major financial crises.

The freewheeling speculative finance has reduced both government capacity to manage fiscal and monetary policies, while privatizing risk made it more difficult for long-term private sector development. These processes have their impact around the world, but especially in the developing economies. They reduce the potential for development and widen the income and technological gap between rich and poor.[13] The result is instability in the global system and growing resentments of those on the losing side. The emerging situation enhances uncertainty in the financial markets and instability in the global economy. Eatwell and Taylor made, along with many other scholars, a strong case for the need for an international regulatory agency, beyond the present system, which is regarded by many students of international economics and development as biased toward capital.

The privatization of financial risk led to the privatization of risk in labor. Traditionally, labor security systems were domestically based. But the increased global integration of financial and labor markets have reduced governmental capacity to regulate the massive financial flows. The present international regulatory agencies only intervene to protect and hedge finance capital. Thus, safeguards for domestic labor and families have been reduced significantly. The situation created the presence of "absentee governments" on the national and global levels with severe hardships on human development, and with no adequate solutions in sight.

Labor: uncertainty and constrained mobility

The increased global interdependence frees the movement of finance and speculative capital, which creates uncertainty in labor markets. Changes in population size, structure, and movement present opportunities, as well as challenges, for development in every country. World population reached 6.1 billion in mid-2000 and, according to the UN *World Population Prospects: 2000 Revision*, is currently growing at an annual rate of 1.2 percent, resulting in an additional 77 million people per year.[14] By 2050, world population is expected to be 9.3 billion. As illustrated in Figure 5.2, all the growth is contributed by the less developed countries.

Most of the socioeconomic consequences of population growth relate to changes in the age structure. Age groups with different production and saving potential, dependency burden, and reproductive behavior growing at different rates create different opportunities and challenges for development. Figure 5.3 presents growth patterns in 2000 for four age groups (0–14, 15–59, 60+ and 80+); for the world as a whole; and for five broad regions: More Developed Countries (MDCs), Less Developed Countries (LDCs), Least Developed Countries (Least DCs), and separately for Africa and Europe. For all regions, the rates of growth among cohorts younger than 15 were the lowest of all age groups. These growth rates were negative in the case of MDCs, especially for Europe. The rates of growth of the working age groups (15–59) were the second lowest in all regions and were negative in the MDCs. That rate for the Least DCs more than double that of LDCs. These patterns indicate varied socioeconomic

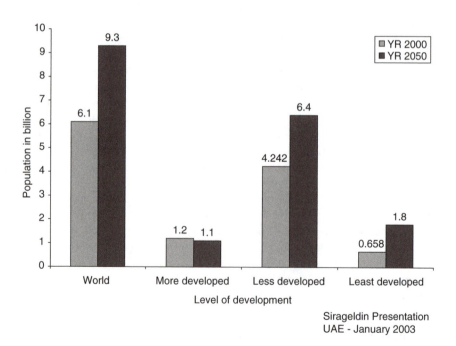

Figure 5.2 World population growth between 2000 and 2050 by level of development.

Source: UN Population Division, "World Population Prospects: 2000 Revision."

prospects for countries and regions depending on their stage in the demographic transition. It indicates that by mid-2000 there was a significant decline in the population in the working age in the more developed countries, and therefore increased dependency of the elderly, compared to a dramatic increase of the working population in the developing countries.

These patterns question some of the popular paradigms in the population and development field, such as the one-time "demographic window of development opportunity." This paradigm provides comfort to those developing countries whose age structure is changing toward a lower dependency pattern and accordingly enhances the potential for saving since the share of the population in the working age increases during this transitional period. Potential savings could then be channeled into investment to improve health, education, and infrastructure. However, as Figure 5.3 indicates, it is only the Least Developed regions that will experience increase in the share of the population in the working ages in conformity with the "Window of Opportunity" paradigm. But the countries of the least developed region have the lowest per capita incomes and highest incidence of poverty, infant mortality, and HIV. In the case of the LDCs, where the bulk of the world's population resides, including much of the Arab world, the percentage of those in the working age cohort will increase significantly and then age into dependency. The demography of the Arab region calls for serious actions to enhance productive investment in human capital. Otherwise, the growing labor force would be a burden rather than an agent for development in the following decades.

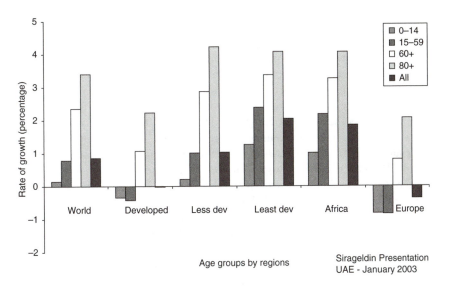

Figure 5.3 Average annual population growth rates by broad regions and age groups (Medium scenario).

Source: UN Population Division, "World Population Prospects: 2000 Revision."

In the case of the MDCs, the relative decline of the working age population is creating potential labor shortages. As the world demography illustrates, policies that restrict labor migration or make it highly selective (i.e., a brain-drain) in the twenty-first century may mitigate population movements created by demographic pressures. The imbalanced world demographic rates are bound to create conflict in both the developed and the developing regions, which will undermine an equitable global village. The less developed countries and the least developed may face severe poverty.[15]

Technological solutions – not all environmentally friendly – combined with population growth and consumption patterns influence the demand for natural resources that ultimately affect their supply and the overall quality of the environment. Yet, labor-saving technological solutions combined with an unstable global economic system do not generate enough employment around the world. A major challenge of the global system is to generate jobs for the 500 million men and women who are expected to enter the labor force over the next ten years. This challenge is intensified by worldwide unemployment figures that increased from 137 million in 1995 to 160 million at the end of 2000, 50 million of whom were in the industrialized countries where population ageing is accelerating. The challenge is further exacerbated by the need to provide support for the growing elderly population, with women constituting the majority of the elderly.[16] As Mark Bruzonsky noted, the world has been "squandering the best of its talent and wealth building ever new generations of ever more frightful weapons, rather than schools and hospitals and food for all."[17] But to stop the "squandering" requires a responsible and effective global governance.

Global governance: how viable?

The role of government and governance in the "new global environment" seems to differ significantly from previous environments. In the past, with the exception of military conquest and occupation, the prevailing environment was one of "interdependence" among states regulated by international institutions. Such organizations as IMF or GATT attempted to set rules for orderly cooperation as interdependence increased among sovereign states. Government sovereignty, especially internal, was not challenged by these regulations, taken mainly as safeguards. The effect of the "new globalization environment" on state sovereignty is subtler. It influences both the external and internal sovereignty of the state, while reducing the interest of national elites in local affairs since global corporate networks challenge a state's internal sovereignty by altering the relationship between the private and public sector. As it integrates markets, globalization fragments the political order.

In one sense, globalization undermines democratic practice and the rule of law. As mentioned above, insecurities in the labor market result from volatility of finance capital, speculative activities and of the volume of foreign exchange. They are also a result of changes in the role of government and institutions as a result of technological innovations. Historically, periods of massive industrial consolidation and dramatic technological innovations have been followed by periods of political, social, and institutional reform. Economic change produces social conditions that conflict with democratic ideals. Clearly the present global system erodes the synergetic relations among "democracy," the "rule of law," and the "role of government" on the national levels. Many political scientists would contend that global governance is being managed more by a dominant power whose culture seems to reject diversity and has a teleological view of historical processes.

Historically, the struggle for freedom has been a struggle between the power of government with arbitrary authority and the rule of the law, or, according to Hume, it is the evolution from a government of will to a government of law. A "government of law," "equality before the law," or "rule of law" are all terms that refer to the ancient Greek concept of isonomy, which identifies a society of human freedom as opposed to an arbitrary government of tyrants. In this view, the law should be obeyed so people could be free from arbitrary rules set for some and not for others. However, although the rule of law provided for individual freedom and for creating and maintaining "trust" in the laws, it erected boundaries and set limits on the freedom of both government and subjects. This was the case in order to limit the power and moderate the dominion of every part and member of society. However, although the ideal of isonomy gave ample power to governments to implement a wide range of measures to enhance human development, from safeguarding values and promoting equality to enhancing individual freedom, it has been on the decline for centuries in all countries of the world.

Concerns about the impact of globalization on government authority are well placed. The impact of the absence of the rule of law on sustainable human development could be negative not only in authoritarian governments but equally in democratic ones, especially those lacking in the ideal of isonomy. For the international system, the adoption of the ideal of isonomy and the development of a global political citizenship seem to be of great urgency. There are authorities who believe that the rule of law is either common to all nations or does not exist. This conditional statement about the rule of law should be at least equally valid in today's globalization environment since global regulations may not be sustainable without it. Rules designed to benefit the few without compensating the losers will be resisted. From this perspective, it is a puzzle as to how a government based on the rule of law and the principle of isonomy could be implemented on the global level, especially if there are many structural factors that tend to inhibit the realization of such an optimistic scenario.[18]

I focus briefly on one factor that stands out as fundamental: namely, the role of human nature in forming associations. What is desired in the relations between states is independence for each regarding internal affairs, and a law rather than private force regarding external affairs. This is similar to what is expected from governance within a single state. But what are the prerequisites to implement such system within the state? Here we need to differentiate between state and nation. According to Russell, what constitute a nation are a sentiment of similarity and an instinct of belonging to the same group or herd.[19] The instinct is "natural," while sentiments refer more to feelings – our ways are right and theirs are wrong; we are virtuous, while many foreigners are full of wickedness. Associations and nations are largely built on differentiating "us versus them." This becomes especially vivid when there is war or danger of war. Standing against the orders of one's own government creates an inner conflict. It is this "natural" conflict based on the "natural" tendency for individual and group violence that a "global" government attempts to suppress. Indeed there are ways to do that by force or persuasion. Force would take away the basic principles and objectives of creating a world government, while persuasion implies the presence of global democratic governance, based in the principle of isonomy, that accepts and respects social and political differentiations. The first seems to be in place while the second has not yet developed in the present system of global governance.[20]

Concluding remarks: the road ahead?

The future of human development in the twenty-first century, characterized by many as the era of globalization, is full of promise and uncertainty. A review of the historical processes that led to the present state of human diversities and differentiations has not been optimistic. Technological changes promote new knowledge as well as new socioeconomic inequalities. It also introduces new views of nature that, in many cases, deepen inequalities and diversities. Historical processes are also reflected in long-term demographic trends that reduce the potential for human development for a large part of humanity. There is room for optimism. Negative trends are slowing down or checked, while technological advances provide promise for enhanced food production at lower resource use. But for the majority of humanity, the central challenge remains unanswered: namely, how can a sustainable level of development be reached? This emerging state of world order is bound to destabilize the global system with unforeseen consequences. For more than three decades, the development establishment has been occupied in efforts and programs around the world to enhance human capabilities, opportunities, and the overall quality of life. Yet, views and paradigms about development processes and strategies have changed little, if any, even while the world system and its political and technological bases have changed dramatically. Also unchanged are the marginal conditions of human life in most of the developing countries, especially the least developed.

I attempted to show that human nature or worldviews are not independent from scientific developments and the externalities of market behavior. Furthermore, the present structure of global government seems to be controlled by finance capital whose interest is to maximize material gains. The synergies are complex. My attempt to elucidate its dynamic nature should be taken as preliminary.

The privatization of risk in financial activities increases risk and makes it harder to regulate. But it is instructive to note that confidence may be affected by changes in confidence in other similar activities. For example, a bank failure may make people think that there is something wrong with all banks and accordingly distrust their own bank, even if it was the best-run institution. This contagious tendency is not confined to the financial sector, although it is more evident there. A government failure somewhere may equally induce distrust in all governments. Or, an unproductive labor performance in a developing country may induce distrust and reduce direct investment in other developing countries. These examples call for more, not less, investment in sound internal sustainable reform (IOSR). It also calls for the development of an innovative and more robust world regulatory authority that is better able to deal with the emerging patterns of international risk that produce serious systemic threats to human development in the developing and emerging economies. Such developments, which are relatively feasible to implement, may lead to a better world system that is more equitable and sustainable. Meanwhile, the development of a new vision for global governance based on equity and transparency is required, a vision in which "freedoms" are gained through reason and not absolutism – people are not forced to be free! The world society should be aware of both the danger of "absolutism" and that of "relativism," especially when there is no clear definition of "reason." As Leo Strauss amply put it:

> For to say in the same breath that our sole protection against war between societies and within societies is reason, and that according to reason 'those individuals and societies who find it congenial to their system of values to suppress and subjugate others' are as right as those who love peace and justice, means to appeal to reason in the very act of destroying reason.[21]

Equally essential is the presence of a rational assessment of the evolving views of nature and their socio-political consequences. This is a tall order and probably against human nature. But the world should be ready for a new vision in which artificially erected walls between civilizations, races, or socioeconomic groups are flattened and peaceful interactions enhanced.

Notes

* Professor Emeritus, Johns Hopkins University. The present essay is based partly on views presented in the author's previous works including "Sustainable Human Development in the Twenty-first Century: An Evolutionary Perspective," in *Encyclopedia of Life Support Systems* (Oxford: UNESCO/EOLSS Publishers, 2001); "Human Prospects in an Age of Uncertainty and the Decline of Rationality," address to the Economic and Research Forum Annual Conference, Sharjah, UAE, 2002.

1 The quotation is from Sirageldin, "Human Prospects," 2002.

2 Adam Smith cautioned, with equal concern, about the misbehavior of both governments and free markets. He emphasized the need for intelligent control of both, in order to maximize the welfare benefit of free markets. However, his emphasis of the negative effects of free markets and the need for control and remedial measures were largely ignored in policy and analysis until very recently.

3 Globalization, defined in this discussion as increased interdependence among countries and communities, is viewed as a process with varied phases, a connected history, rather than any abrupt phenomenon that emerged in the last few decades or even centuries.

However, there are important qualitative differences in the present phase, namely a significant change in communication technology, the presence of institutions to oversee the free flow of finance capital and trade, the evolution of a global labor market, and the attempt to establish a global government in the presence of a hegemonic power that apparently does not accept diversity in views of nature or culture (for details, see Sirageldin "Globalization, Regionalization, and Recent Trade Agreements: Impact on Arab Economies: Rapid Exogenous Change – Slow Endogenous Response," in *New Economic Developments and Their Impact on Arab Economies*, ed. A. Al-Kawaz, 15–56 (Amsterdam: North Holland, 1998); "Global Interdependence, Privatization of Risk and Human Development," The Quad-I-Azam Memorial Lecture in *The Pakistan Development Review* 39, no. 4, Part 1 (2000): 313–336; and I. Sirageldin and S. Serageldin, "Global Interdependence, Privatization of Risk, and Human Insecurity," in *Encyclopedia of Life Support Systems* (Oxford and Paris: UNESCO/EOLSS Publishers, 2002).

4 Bertrand Russell, *Political Ideals* (London: Unwin Paperbacks, 1917/1980), 12–14.

5 The concept of isonomy refers to the stability and certainty of the rule of law. The concept was initiated by ancient Greece and adopted in the early evolution of British democratic institutions. It has been viewed as a prerequisite for the presence of a viable democracy [cf. F.A. Hayek, *The Political Ideal of the Rule of Law*, Fiftieth Anniversary Commemoration Lectures (Cairo: National Bank of Egypt, 1955)].

6 Cf. John Eatwell and Lance Taylor, *Global Finance at Risk: The Case for International Regulation* (New York: The New Press, 2000).

7 Amartya Sen, *Development as Freedom* (New York: Anchor Books–Random House, Inc., 2000); Jared Diamond, *Guns, Germs, and Steel* (New York: W.W. Norton & Company, 1999).

8 See also Sirageldin, "Sustainable Human Development"; "Culture and Development in the Arab World," Public Lecture, Arab Planning Institute, Kuwait, October 2, 2001; "Population Challenges for the 21st Century in the MENA Region: Introduction to the Issues," in *Human Capital: Population Economics in the Middle East*, ed. Sirageldin (2003), and references cited.

9 Jeremy Rifkin, *The Biotech Century: Harnessing the Gene and Remaking the World* (New York: Penguin Putnam, Inc., 1998).

10 This section relies heavily on C.P. Kindleberger, *Manias, Panics and Crashes: A History of Financial Crises* (London: Macmillan, 1978/1996); Emil-Maria Claassen, *Global Monetary Economics* (Oxford: Oxford University Press, 1997); Eatwell and Taylor; and Sirageldin, "Global Interdependence."

11 Eatwell and Taylor.

12 For more details, see Eatwell and Taylor.

13 The distributive impact of the global system was not confined to the developing economies. For example, the spectacular growth of the US economy in the 1980s and 1990s was accompanied by unprecedented increase in income and wealth inequalities. There was no convincing economic explanation for this phenomenon. Paul Krugman of MIT (*New York Times*, October 2002) resorted to non-economic explanations for the dramatic increase in inequality, i.e., change in social norms. But as discussed above, change in norms could be viewed teleologically as part of "nature's" design. Thus, inequalities are deepened, leading to the division of humanity into higher and lower forms, back to the caste system of Plato's Utopia – a serious and unsustainable tendency.

14 United Nations Population Division (New York: United Nations, 2002).

15 The outcomes of these opportunities and challenges vary by country depending on their demographic structures and technological progress. This is illustrated, for example, by the presence of significant inequalities in the production of, access to, and use of digital technology, dubbed the "digital divide." For example, by the end of 1997, there were only 23 internet hosts (a computer connected to the internet that can both access and be accessed) per 1,000 inhabitants in Organization for Economic

Cooperation and Development (OECD) countries as compared to 0.21 per 1,000 inhabitants outside the OECD area. By the end of 2000, the first figure jumped to 82 in the OECD area in contrast to 0.85 in the non-OECD countries. There are signs, however, that the Asian region recorded some increase. The "digital divide" is also a "gender divide." Although the gender-digital divide in internet use has been narrowing in the United States, women make up only 25 percent of the users in the European Union, 18 percent in Japan and the Russian Federation, and 4 percent in the Middle East ["The Digital Divide: Employment and Development Implications," Special Issue, *International Labor Review* 140, no. 2 (2001)].

16 "The Digital Divide: Employment and Development Implications," Special Issue, *International Labor Review* 140, no. 2 (2001); United Nations Development Program, *Human Development Report 1999* (New York: Oxford University Press, for the UNDP, 1999).

17 Mark Bruzonsky, Keynote Address, University of Chicago Model United Nations, January 31, 2002.

18 There are many important factors that tend to inhibit the realization of equitable global governance. These include size, boundaries, repeated interaction, established cultures, and lack of isonomy, justice, and transparency in national governance, which make the spontaneous emergence of systems of cooperative norms unlikely without the helping hand of rational hierarchical authority in the form of government and formal law. I focus, however, on the role of human nature in forming associations (cf. Sirageldin, "Globalization, Regionalization" and "Sustainable Development").

19 Russell, *Political Ideals*, 67.

20 For more details, see Sirageldin (2003).

21 *The Rebirth of Classical Political Rationalism: Essays and Lectures by Leo Strauss* (Chicago: University of Chicago Press, 1989), 12.

References

Ali, A.A. and I.A. Elbadawi. "Poverty in the Arab World: The Role of Inequality and Growth." In *Human Capital: Population Economics in the Middle East*, edited by I. Sirageldin, 2002.

Barbu, Zevedie. *Society, Culture and Personality*. New York: Schooken Books, 1971.

Bongaarts, John. *The End of the Fertility Transition in the Developed World*. Working Paper, 2001, no. 152. New York: Population Council, 2001.

Bruzonsky, Mark. Keynote Address, University of Chicago Model United Nations January 31, 2002.

Claassen, Emil-Maria. *Global Monetary Economics*. Oxford: Oxford University Press, 1997.

Derry, T.K. and Trevor I. Williams. *A Short History of Technology: From the Earliest Times to A.D. 1900*. New York: Dover Publications, 1960.

Diamond, Jared. *Guns, Germs, and Steel*. New York: W.W. Norton & Company, 1999.

"The Digital Divide: Employment and Development Implications." Special Issue, *International Labor Review* 140, no. 2 (2001).

Eatwell, John and Lance Taylor. *Global Finance at Risk: The Case for International Regulation*. New York: The New Press, 2000.

Foucault, Michel. *The Archaeology of Knowledge & the Discourse in Language*. New York: Pantheon Books, 1971.

Gleick, Peter H. "Human Population and Water: Meeting Basic Needs in the 21st Century." In R.K. Pachauri and Lubina F. Qureshy, 105–121.

Hawking, Stephen W. *A Brief History of Time*. London and New York: Bantam, 1988.

Hayek, F.A. *The Political Ideal of the Rule of Law*. Fiftieth Anniversary Commemoration Lectures. Cairo: National Bank of Egypt, 1955.

Ibn Khaldun. *The Muqaddimah: An Introduction to History*. Translated from the Arabic by Franz Rosenthal, abridged and edited by N.J. Dawood. London and Henley: Routledge and Kegan Paul, 1377/1967.

Kindleberger, C.P. *Manias, Panics and Crashes: A History of Financial Crises*. London: Macmillan, 1978/1996.

Morici, Peter. *Reconciling Trade and the Environment in the World Trade Organization*. Washington, DC: Economic Strategy Institute, 2002.

Pachuri, R.K. and L.F. Qureshy, eds. *Population, Environment and Development*. New Delhi: Tata Energy Research Institute, 1997.

Pangle, Thomas L. "Introduction." In *The Rebirth of Classical Political Rationalism: Essays and Lectures by Leo Strauss*. The essays were selected by Pangle.

Reader, John. *A Biography of the Continent Africa*. New York: Vintage Books, a Division of Random House, Inc., 1997.

Rifkin, Jeremy. *The Biotech Century: Harnessing the Gene and Remaking the World*. New York: Penguin Putnam, Inc., 1998.

Russell, Bertrand. *Political Ideals*. London: Unwin Paperbacks, 1917/1980.

——. *Authority and the Individual*. London and New York: Routledge, 1949/1990.

Sen, A. *Development as Freedom*. New York: Anchor Books – Random House, Inc., 2000.

——. "Globalization and its Discontent: Development Thinking in the Millennium." Annual World Bank Conference on Development Economics and Conseil d'Analyse Economique, Paris, June 26, 2000.

Sirageldin, Ismail, "Population Dynamics, Environment, and Conflict." In *Population and Development Transformations in the Arab World*, edited by Sirageldin and Al-Rahmani, 185–217. Greenwich and London: JAI Press, Inc, 1996.

——. "Globalization, Regionalization, and Recent Trade Agreements: Impact on Arab Economies: Rapid Exogenous Change – Slow Endogenous Response." In *New Economic Developments and Their Impact on Arab Economies*, edited by A. Al-Kawaz, 15–56. Amsterdam: North Holland, 1998.

——. "Global Interdependence, Privatization of Risk and Human Development." The Quad-I-Azam Memorial Lecture, *The Pakistan Development Review* 39, no. 4, part 1 (2000): 313–336.

——. "Culture and Development in the Arab World." Public Lecture, Arab Planning Institute, Kuwait, October 2, 2001 (in Arabic).

——. ed. *Human Capital: Population Economics in the Middle East*. London and Cairo: I.B. Tauris and AUC Press, 2002.

——. "Population Challenges for the 21st Century in the MENA Region: Introduction to the Issues." In *Human Capital*, edited by Sirageldin.

——. "Human Prospects in an Age of Uncertainty and the Decline of Rationality." Address to the Economic and Research Forum (ERF) Annual Conference, Sharjah, UAE, 2002. Available on the ERF website.

——. "Human Development in a Century of Population Growth and Scarcity: Prospects and Problems." Address to Johns Hopkins Symposium, "The Coming Crunch: Population, Food and Water in the 21st Century," Baltimore, Maryland, February 21, 2002.

——. "Sustainable Human Development in the Twenty-first Century: An Evolutionary Perspective." In *Encyclopedia of Life Support Systems*. Oxford: UNESCO/EOLSS Publishers, 2001. Also, an edited version of the article is available as a background document for the World Summit Conference in Johannesburg, August 2002.

Sirageldin, I. and S. Serageldin. "Global Interdependence, Privatization of Risk, and Human Insecurity." In *Encyclopedia of Life Support Systems*. Oxford and Paris: UNESCO/EOLSS Publishers, 2002. Also available on the worldwide web.

Squire, Victor. "The Role of Food, Agriculture, Forestry, and Fisheries in Human Nutrition." In *Encyclopedia of Life Support Systems*, 563–577. Oxford and Paris: UNESCO/EOLSS Publishers, 2002.

Stebbins, G. Ledyard. *Darwin to DNA, Molecules to Humanity*. San Francisco: H.W. Freeman and Company, 1982.

Strauss, Leo. *The Rebirth of Classical Political Rationalism: Essays and Lectures by Leo Strauss*. Chicago: University of Chicago Press, 1989.

Swaminathan, M.S. "Sustainable Food and Water Security." In *Encyclopedia of Life Support Systems*, 579–597. Oxford and Paris: UNESCO/EOLSS Publishers, 2001.

Tolba, Mostafa K., ed. *Our Fragile World – Challenges and Opportunities for Sustainable Development*. Two volumes. Forerunner to the *Encyclopedia of Life Support Systems* (EOLSS). Paris and London: UNESCO-EOLSS, 2001.

United Nations Development Program (UNDP). *Human Development Report 1999*. New York: Oxford University Press for the UNDP.

United Nations Population Division. *World Population Prospects: The 2000 Revision*. New York: United Nations, 2002.

West, David. "The Contribution of Continental Philosophy." In *A Companion to Contemporary Political Philosophy*, edited by Robert E. Goodin and Phillip Pettit. Oxford: Blackwell Publishers, 1996.

Williams, Bernard. *Ethics and the Limits of Philosophy*. Cambridge, MA: Harvard University Press, 1985/1998.

Part III

Globalization, politics, and identity in the Arab world

6 How likely is democracy in the Gulf?

Khaldoun Al Naqeeb[1]

Introduction: first principles

Recent developments after 1989's abrupt transformation in world geopolitics have not yet shed enough light on the process that led to the collapse of the communist–West competition and its accompanying world order. On the contrary, the processes of globalization brought about a loss of the traditional meaning in international politics, especially in "the double essence of centrality" (global fragmentation) and of final goals (what will come after capitalism) that seem to characterize the present international system.[2]

In our explanatory models, confusion seems to hold sway. One might argue that the social world is quite fluid now so that the lack of understanding in the conceptual level reflects, to various degrees, the lack of established patterning in a global society and especially in the relations between the amorphous and ever-changing political blocs. Let us consider the following points: (1) while development schemes failed in most of the Third World, a democratization process spread across the world like wildfire; (2) although democratization spread, it did not lead, in most cases, to a regime shift but to a further entrenchment of elite interests and monopolies; and (3) there is abundant evidence to confirm that a cultural shift is taking place in social values and in everyday life. These changes were accompanied by "paradigm" shifts in intellectual orientations from post-colonialism, imperialism dependence, core–periphery relationships in the world systems framework, and primacy of state institutions, to post-structuralism, post-modernism, deconstructionism, and other anti-rational and antirealist approaches.[3]

According to Gills and Rocamora, part of the inapplicability of existing disciplinary approaches to social explanation is a result of deep-seated ideological biases basic to Western thinking. These biases, as exemplified by recent statements in political science, include "political democracy per se, is a goal worthy of attainment" even without social reforms and that "all democracies are to some degree capitalist," and that the failure of development schemes are inherent in the defective Third World "indigenous" political culture.[4] With these sweeping generalizations aside, basically the Third World needs the guidance provided by the international organizations of the Western world.

I would like to contend that the overriding disarray between disciplinary models and social reality cannot be resolved at the geopolitical level of applied politics, for it calls into question the very basic principles of what holds a society together: legal rules and basic reciprocities or the growth of capital. What made the complex social, economic, and political institutional set-up of the Eastern bloc collapse in few months? If such a thing is possible, do we expect that all other former or present authoritarian regimes will collapse with such rapidity and impunity?

The sociologist Emmanuel Wallerstein offered three axioms to address these very basic questions.[5] All sociologists tend to accept these axioms without reservation: (1) that "there exist social groups which have rational structure" (which is derived from Durkheim); (2) that "all social groups contain subgroups that are ranked in a hierarchy and are in conflict with each other" (derived from Marx); and (3) that "to the extent that groups/states contain their conflicts, it is in large part because lower-ranked subgroups accord legitimacy to the authoritative structure of the group on the grounds that this permits the group to survive, and the subgroups see long-term advantage in the group's survival." This is a spin-off of Weberian reasoning.

Furthermore, Wallerstein argues that until the mid-1970s and the onset of post-modernism, sociologists shared these basic propositions. These are, to reiterate: the reality of social "facts" (Durkheim); the perennity of social conflict (Marx); and the existence of legitimization to prevent society from unraveling into chaos (Weber).

These axioms provide guidelines for political sociology. According to Durkheim, there exists a group mind or collective representation that may withdraw legitimacy from the authoritarian regimes if it perceived this to be conductive to group survival. To return to the query above, it is very difficult to time regime collapse and regime shift. I suggest that collapse may be explained by individual minds independent of a group mind. Institutional facts differ from social facts in that they are simple to explain by a concept like collective intention. Having a common purpose is sufficient to explain cooperation, conformity, and revolt.[6] Therefore, the three tenets underlying modernist political sociology may need slight revision when applying orthodox sociological method and theory to contexts beyond the West, such as the Middle East.

Rational vs. traditional authority: the question of control

Let us consider that the second and third propositions (above) may hold the key to our queries as to what holds people together in some semblance of order and what causes collapse. A possible answer provided by Weber's proposition is that although social conflict is perennial, people in a society generally accept a particular order of things to avert chaos and upheaval. I would classify the modes of acceptance into: (1) the form of habitual-traditional, (2) the form of legal-rational institutions, or (3) the form of charismatic leadership. We disregard for the moment Marx's postulation that authority can be imposed by persuasion (false consciousness), co-optation, force, and physical violence.

Yet, Weber's formulation does not solve the problem of authority. On the contrary, it complicates the situation. Basically, Weber intended these three types of legitimacy as analytical tools and ideal types, not as the totality of leadership. However, when these types of models are used to define evolutionary historical stages, they tend immediately to lose their validity.

In this regard, its our hypothesis that traditional authority, rather than disappearing after a century of modernization, is thriving in the Arab world and elsewhere by having a greater capacity to adapt to changing conditions due to assimilating aspects of rational-legal bureaucratic structures. Furthermore, we are discovering that charismatic leadership may not necessarily lead to modernization-democratization; it could bring out the most traditional values with genuine indigenous creativity as opposed to emulating Western, usually secular, forms of leadership and cultural ways.

Contrary to the claims of Fukuyama, the collapse of the authoritarian Eastern bloc did not signal the final victory of liberal constitutional democracy. It ushered in what Fareed Zakaria calls "illiberal" democracy.[7] The real problem is that those who accept Weberian categories as universal historical facts also accept the dichotomy that all aspects of modern society are modern. This is obviously not true. And, traditionalism does not always precede modernism in evolutionary development as subsumed within Western models of evolutionary change. The debate concerning this issue is captured well by Heelas, Lash, and Morris.[8] De-traditionalization processes, as claimed by modernists, do not occur in isolation from other processes such as "tradition-maintenance and construction or reconstruction of traditional forms of life."

One dramatic case in point is the success of authoritarian regimes in legitimizing themselves by means of "authoritarian elections."[9] Another example is the simultaneous resurgence of Christian–Jewish–Muslim religious activism, which Gilles Kepel describes as the revenge of God.[10] When these two phenomena are combined, they tend to reinforce or reproduce the existing ethnic-sectarian-tribal divisions, rather than produce democratic institutions or a secular body politic-constructing institution of nationalism.

Zakaria quotes an expert on ethnic conflict as saying, "in the face of this rather dismal account...of the concrete failure of democracy in divided societies...one is tempted to throw up one's hands. What is the point of holding elections if all they do in the end is substitute a Bempa-dominated regime for a Nyanja regime in Zambia, the two equally narrow, or a southern regime for a northern one in Benin, neither incorporating the other half of the state? In Lebanon elections not only produce ethnic-sectarian divisions as voter blocs, they pave the way for warlords and their cronies to become deputies, ministers, and major political actors."[11]

Democracies are embedded in societies; one presupposes the other. The process of "democratization" involves much more foundational changes than simply a switch to Western-style liberal democracy. In this regard, we note that a transition to a new phase of authoritarianism incorporates elements of new basic forces, or what Geertz calls "primordial sentiments/attachments," as an integral part of a political system taking shape.[12] Geertz further suggests that the trajectories of contemporary post-traditional states often involve a transition to the new phase of authoritarianism. Since so many features are shared, a type seems warranted by the empirical data, to which we now turn.

Major propositions

Authoritarianism: a new phase

In order to establish a structural position within the new world order, a particular political regime may not find a compelling reason to adopt a liberal democratic system. Matters of survival in maintaining and/or imposing a system of efficient control over the population and resources available to them may lead a regime to adopt a more authoritarian system since social control is what holds institutions together. After all, a political system is one of "technology of control."

According to Gibbs, social control is an "overt behavior" by a human (agent) in the belief that (1) the behavior increases or decreases the probability of some subsequent condition, and (2) the increase or decrease is desirable.[13] Social power becomes "the perceived capacity for effective control."[14]

Many sociologists have shown how knowledge and power interface, and Foucault has garnered the limelight among the current generation of theorists. Following Foucault's line of reasoning in particular, knowledge leads to better methods of control.[15] Social power, then, is accentuated by a "technology of control," i.e., information, methods, techniques, and mechanization designed to yield acceptance of authority.

Our main hypothesis is that the relative political, cultural, and economic "openness," which is erroneously called democratization, is taking place globally through advances of technology of control.[16] This is the ability to achieve the effective control of the many diverse cultural and political groups by means other than force and physical violence.

In this context, it is not necessarily class interests or other interests of the elite in power that motivate the new mechanisms of control. The shift in social values – what Haskell describes as "cognitive style"[17] (when citizens accept the authority of sectarian-ethnic leaders) – is partly due to "the expansion of the market, the intensification of market discipline, and the penetration of that discipline into spheres of life previously untouched by it."[18]

Later in this chapter, I demonstrate how the state apparatus has entered a phase of sponsoring or condoning "neo-primordial" solidarity networks of auxiliary forces. I will also provide evidence that state leaders ensure that major decisions are reached outside parliaments and that such practices are adorned with the facade of constitutional-democratic rule. In addition, those constitutions are a series of compromises between the major political actors who uphold the national norms. Therefore, the cultural norms continue to override constitutional rule.

Also, I counter that the insistence by some Western political scientists on classifying political regimes as liberal/democratic or illiberal/undemocratic only further obscures the political processes now operating. Since we do not have a cross-culturally viable criteria of constitutionalism and democracy – other than one that "citizens would enjoy the greatest measure of intellectual freedom, moral autonomy, and political choice," – it is comparatively meaningless to classify political systems as such.

Neither would we anticipate that the constitutional systems of the West, which are themselves recent developments in historical terms, would fit the cultures of other societies. Either the indigenous culture of a given society changes to become more similar to that of the West (to fit the Western notion of liberal democracy), or more inclusive criteria of democracy are developed. Daniel Lazare shows that the Americans themselves speak of their exceptionalism, which would lead to an exclusionary definition of democracy if imposed on non-Western contexts.[19] Zakaria states, "It is odd that the United States is so often the advocate of elections and plebiscitary democracy abroad. What is distinctive about the American system is not how democratic it is but rather how undemocratic it is, placing as it does multiple constraints on electoral majorities."[20]

Even if one accepts the conclusion that many Third World (and most Arab) countries at various intervals during the twentieth century opted for the centralized states (statism) more akin to the French system rather than the decentralized Anglo-American system, this dichotomy does not account for the wide range of "democracies" on the right and left of the political spectrum: liberal, formal, deliberative, associational, communitarianism, etc. Held identifies at least ten variants of democracy.[21] I could define another five types.

Apart from Western "state-sponsored" bestowing of the democratic label on some of their client states, there is still the need for finding a more comparatively objective method of classifying fairly new political regimes emerging from authoritarianism. Nevertheless, by adhering to the "technology of control" governmental strategy through solidarity network-building, which I term *political tribalism*, we seem to be entering into another possible phase of authoritarianism. This new phase of government-directed control is yet to be defined or properly labeled.

New authoritarianism in the Middle East

Concerns about the new wave of democratization[22] coincided with the strategic American doctrine of low-intensity conflict.[23] Under President Ronald Reagan's "Crusade for Democracy" in 1982, the United States began to withdraw its support for dictators whom they had supported. New regimes that replaced these dictators started reform that Gills and Rocamora defined as low-intensity democracy (e.g., Argentina, Guatemala, the Philippines, South Korea, Chile, Congo, and Indonesia).[24]

Almost all of the Arab States followed a trajectory of the despotic rule of the Ottoman empire to colonial rule by Europeans. Later, some Arab states attempted aspects of Western-style "representative" governments, most notably Egypt, Iraq, and Syrian and Maghrib countries.[25] Other states, such as Turkey, Iran, and Pakistan, created semi-fascist regimes.[26] A third group of countries managed, to a large extent, to peacefully transform their traditional authoritarian regimes into "modern" bureaucratic kingdoms, such as the Gulf and Peninsula countries.[27] The basic features of the Middle Eastern countries' transition from the Ottoman and colonial phase to the present phase of authoritarianism are outlined in the table compiled by Posusney.[28] Although none of these countries in the table have fully emerged from military or tribal domination of political life, 12 of the 19 listed (63 percent) have elections of some sort. Most of these countries do not have permanent constitutions.

In this chapter, I compare Turkey and Kuwait as case studies, although both are atypical in some respects. Turkey is the only Middle Eastern country that was not colonized, and, according to Bernard Lewis, it is "the only Muslim democracy."[29] Kuwait is the only Gulf country that is experimenting with participatory democracy. Kuwait may also represent a model of the future for other Gulf countries, which have emulated it in the past.

In both cases, the authoritarianism prior to the 1980s was based on the monopoly by state actors of the sources of wealth and power.[30] As in the economic changes identified above, with the expansion of the market and the penetration of market discipline into new spheres of life "the beneficiary class" of oligarchs also expanded greatly along with the role of auxiliary tribal-sectarian forces upholding the state.[31]

Our brief entry into the power networks of Turkey is based on a 1999 study by Hamit Bozarslan.[32] The starting point for his study was a 1996 car accident near Susurluk in which three of its passengers were members of overlapping power networks who died instantly. The fact that they were working together is instructive of the modern dynamics of a Middle Eastern democracy. The three passengers, who came to be known as the Susurluk Gang, were a "well-known radical-right militant sought by Interpol for 18 years for his involvement in more than a dozen homicides," his second wife, and a high-ranking member of Istanbul police. "The only survivor was a Kurdish tribe leader with very close ties to former Turkish Prime Minister Tansu Ciller (and her husband)" who was also a deputy of her party in parliament. The car was full of sophisticated unlicensed weapons.[33] Despite leads from press reports and testimonies by hundreds of living members of their "gang," or close network, submitted to an ad hoc parliamentary inquiry commission with two official reports, no judicial action resulted against the wider gang. In fact, the official inquiry provided an unusually unobstructed view into how the political regime, with a democratic label and a prospective membership in the European Union, worked. Bozarslan closely followed the biographies of the three members of the Susurluk Gang and was able to identify relationships with the main actors in the current political "democratic" regime in Turkey. What he uncovered was revealing as well as astounding.

Bozarslan's findings support our major proposition that efficient control holds society together. They support our hypothesis that the more efficient the exercise of control by the state the more it allows regional/local actors to operate within it in an auxiliary capacity alone. Therefore, political analysts, as in political anthropology, "should move from analysis of the state towards power structure and relations." By doing so, we will be able to reveal network building as a constant production and re-production of the nationwide power structure, and the processes of state coercion, civil violence, and ethnic and/or tribal relations.[34]

From looking at the data provided by Bozarslan, several networks seem to be operating alongside state institutions:

1　State actors, which included a former president, a former prime minister, former heads of security forces, former ministers, a former head of the metropolitan area police, present and former deputies in parliament, senior officers in the national intelligence organization, former governors, and a former general staff of the air forces.

2　Radical-right militants loyal to the state, mostly members of organized gangs (e.g., Gete) who worked closely with the state security services, and mafia members involved in smuggling, gambling, and sports clubs. These "factions" were protected by the police and the state's security services, and therefore must have protected the interests of persons in more official positions of power.

3　"Non-state" actors such as godfathers and tribal chiefs commanding forces fully armed by security services and the military, ostensibly to fight Kurdish "rebels" such as the Kurdish Workers Party (PKK). Most of the "godfathers" worked closely with radical-right groups and utilized methods of kidnapping, abduction, torture, and murder in a statewide arena, both in rural centers and urban areas.

I attribute to the network-building processes carried out by these actors and factions the following characteristics:

1　Tribal groups are tied together by blood or marriage as a solidarity network, sometimes based on common locality and on shifting tribal alliances and ethnic alliances (such as between some Kurdish tribes and the American government).

2　Such solidarity networks also extend beyond Turkey to Europe and elsewhere. Their activities support international smuggling of humans and commodities, drug trafficking, and other contraband. They channel the financial profits derived from these activities for political purposes. Since international networks are involved with activities tied to many governments, this is a globalizing process.

3　These networks have transformed tribal-sectarian-ethnic relations into a wider patronage system (or *istizlam* system in Arabic), which with its political functions is often quite innovative in practice. Thus, these are new transnational patterns that in some cases are encouraged by the state into a peculiar corporate system.

4　The collusion of the state actors with these factions or auxiliary forces also fosters tension between them. They are, in fact, in constant tension, which means that state security police and the army intervene when necessary. Nevertheless, there are mutual benefits for both parties, such as the increase in the efficiency of state coercion, the privatization of civil violence, the institutionalization of corruption, and the behind-the-scenes manipulations of elections, especially in balloting and in selecting candidates.

Factional corporatism and "designer" democracy in the Middle East

I contend that all four characteristics identified in the Turkish case are present in almost all Arab countries with only minor adjustments. This would tend to support the idea that the trajectory of political developments entering the second phase of Middle Eastern authoritarianism has little to do with point of departure, with whether a particular country was previously colonized. Rather, it suggests that the elite-in-power (a much wider concept than ruling elites) are much more interested in a system of effective control. Therefore, the taxon of democracy used in Western political science and by politicians is an anachronism in relation to the new political formations in the Middle East and elsewhere, which are networked throughout the global arena. In other words, the democracy label is a gloss today with perhaps 15 more accurate subtypes.

To give an example of one of these adjustments, Iraq and Syria differ only from the Turkish case with ruling dictators that hold the balance of power. Another example of a modification of the Turkish model is found in Egypt and Algeria. In these two countries, the PKK is replaced by the militant *salafy* groups. More generally, the similarities in authoritarian practices in the Middle East are far greater than the impression we get from Posusney's table of national elections.

Based on political structures, then, the Gulf countries emerge as the odd case. Their uniformity as a distinctive type is bereft of national elections and political parties, and any legal political opposition to the ruling dynastic kingdom is strictly curtailed. We now turn to our second case in point, Kuwait, to get a more in-depth look at political networking.

Kuwait, unlike other Arabian peninsula countries, has a history of demands for participatory democracy, which were manifested in 1920 and 1938 through fledgling "starts" of democracy. The 1920 attempt failed because the oligarchs disagreed on how to select an amir. Next, the 1938 experiment lasted only six months when the nationalists argued as to who would be the recipient of oil revenue.

However, a turnaround came when a participatory democratic experiment managed to endure constitutional crises (in 1967, 1976, 1985, and 1989). Probing more deeply, the democratic design seems to have been based on a series of compromises and unwritten deals. This is where we first detect the technology of control in full play. The first compromise was to enshrine the rule of one branch of the Al-Sabah family into the fourth article of the constitution. The second and more serious compromise was to give the ruling amir virtual veto power over the parliament so that no legislation could be passed into law without his approval. Furthermore, one "escape" mechanism allowed the amir not to sign an unpopular decree, but if he were to let the one-month deadline required by the constitution lapse without returning the decree to the parliament, it would automatically become law.

In compromise number three, one-fifth of the parliament's members were ministers, who, although unelected, functioned as full members of parliament.

This tempering factor, in essence, entailed a no-confidence vote in the full parliamentary system. The constitution of 1961 provided for a confidence vote in one minister at a time, but it did not give the parliament any provision of a no-confidence vote on the government as a whole. The rationale was that the prime minister would be the heir apparent who acts officially and by convention as a permanent prime minister. Such constitutional arrangements render the parliament powerless to form or dissolve governments, but gives the right to the amir and his heir apparent – the prime minister – to dissolve parliament at their discretion.

Even with all the trappings of democratic rule and political openness, the technology of control exercised by the regime-in-power constitutionally ensures that loyalty is accorded to the ruling family and not to the state and its institutions. The working of this system of controls curtails political opposition, especially organized opposition, in many ways not encoded in the constitution.[35]

To ensure the effectiveness of control, all advantages and privileges are channeled through the parallel system of political tribalism, which includes many of the major public services. For example, if an individual citizen needs a commercial permit, or to finance a business, or to obtain a government-financed house, or a job, he will need an intermediary, someone with influence and/or leverage (*wasta*), to intercede with the officialdom on his behalf. And, if that individual does not belong to a highly ranked family, usually defined as a member of the oligarchy or tribal aristocracy, he is forced to seek a parliamentary deputy who has both the influence and the leverage to dispense the required service to members of his constituency. The vast majority of the members of the Kuwaiti parliaments are selected to function as such intermediaries. They are aptly called in Arabic *Nuwab Al-Khadamat* (services deputies). If a particular deputy is in good standing with the official or unofficial hierarchy, he is rewarded by receiving the required services. However, if he is perceived as a maverick or someone generally not on good terms with government officials (perhaps for criticizing government policies or by opposing a government project), he will be denied any access to those empowered to grant favors. This renders him useless to his constituents. The very few deputies who belong to his oppositional minority are called *Nuwab Al-Mabadi*, the deputies of principles.

The services deputies further divide into the tribal deputies and conservative "independent" deputies. The tribal deputies are selected through a tribal primary or by-election called *Al-Intikhabat Al-Far'iyah*. However, the parliament criminalized this process in 1998 although no one has been found guilty. The "independent" conservative deputies should be considered those loyal to the parliamentary majorities since the first parliament in 1961.

The division between loyalty and opposition is embedded in more complex factional cross ties. The loyalist group, which is the largest, is comprised of the services deputies (27 deputies in the 1992 parliament, and 34 deputies for the 1996 parliament). Within this group the personality of the deputy and his personal networks, not his political or ideological principles, seem to play a major part. When it comes down to the final vote, a deputy will invariably vote for the government, but sometimes it comes after delivering a blistering speech against government policies. This indicates the technology of control over the facade of democracy.

The second group comprises so-called religious movements with 11 deputies in both 1992 and 1996. They present themselves as deputies of principles and occasionally oppose the government, but they invariably avoid a showdown with it. They have persistently resisted allying as a united front with the popular "permanent" opposition. This, too, bespeaks aspects of intimidation of the informal apparatus of governmental control.

The Kuwaiti version of "participatory democracy" exhibits a parliamentary process that cannot form government or override the veto power of the ruling amir. The parliament also has permanent prime minister with changing ministers who continually revolve in and out of office and who maintain a permanent parliamentary majority. Thus, an oppositional movement cannot structurally be confrontational. We see the many workings of the technology of control. While Kuwait may manifest the trappings of democracy, it clearly lacks the participation of a democracy. In fact, these trends have intensified. The government of Kuwait tightened its controls over the population by passing through parliament (having secured a permanent majority) several laws that contradict the constitution. These include the press law, the nationality law, the electoral law (which deprives women from acquiring the right to vote), and free assembly law (which gives the government powers to restrict free assembly, similar to the provisions of martial law).[36]

Beyond that, I call attention to three sources of potential dangers that threaten the system of controls: (1) tribal alliances, (2) tribal–sectarian fundamental alliance, and (3) a free and critical press. The tribal-sectarian alliance was consolidated according to residential patterns. Two groups represented the greatest potential opposition: Al-Awazim tribal group and the Shi'a minority. The old tenth district of Al-Ahmadi represents a third possibility.

Karam and Al-Ali's study graphically shows how the Kuwaiti government gerrymandered and malapportioned to thwart these potential dangers and avert the consolidation of residential districts, which can be translated into electoral gains.[37] The process of malapportioning voters result in a disparity between the number of voters in several electoral districts to the advantage of the government. The redistricting was clearly not undertaken to achieve relative parity in the number of voters per district. To the contrary, it was deliberately designed to avoid consolidation of tribal and/or sectarian voting blocs. The new dividing lines separated the urban "internal districts" (2, 3, and 7) from the settled Bedouins in the "external districts" (13, 16, and 25) while mixing the two groups in district 8.

The second major danger emerged from the alliance between the tribal and fundamentalist forces. This danger was largely averted by the government appropriating the slogans and proposals of the fundamentalists in a series of appeasement policies. The fundamentalist movement has failed to make larger inroads within the external tribal districts, contrary to the predictions of many observers.

However, it did become a vehicle for social protest for the urban Kuwaiti lower middle class. Significantly, the external tribal districts voted even more resolutely according to tribal affiliation rather than by ideological affiliation.[38]

The third and the most potentially undermining danger to governmental control came from the relatively free press. In the past, especially when the parliament was unconstitutionally dissolved (in 1967, 1976, 1985, and 1989), the government attempted to gag the press, which managed on many occasions to mobilize public opinion against government policies.

After the liberation of Kuwait from Iraqi occupation, government loyalists came to own most weekly magazines. At that time, some editors adopted strict self-censorship of their columnists and writers by not allowing criticism of the government. In reaching this point, the government of Kuwait had successfully accomplished a complex and effective technology of control. In this environment defined by latent function reciprocities, the government can tolerate tempered criticism, and the system of truncated participatory democracy can in turn tolerate the curtailment of liberty and constitutional guaranties.

In sum, the Kuwaiti adaptation of participatory democracy to its Gulf context, in which kinship underpins many social institutions, shows that political parties or formal social movements and other institutions of democratic polity are superfluous. Social and political forces function in this particular system of political control in a manner more attuned to the traditional ways of political behavior and social conduct, which are based on kinship and patronage. One could say that Kuwait efficiently adapted some democratic privileges to suit local folkways. To generalize more broadly, it seems plausible that many other Third World countries will have their own interpretation of democracy, perhaps in a similar process of adaptation.

Our main thesis, however, has been supported by the Kuwaiti data. It is how efficiently controlled and managed a society is that matters, and not how it is democratically ruled according to imported Western standards. It is the analysis of the technologies of control and the mechanization of social power that should be the center of our interest and not the process of democratization based on the assumption that we all, some time in the future, will be Western-style citizens with an equal say in the decision-making process of government.

Notes

1 Professor of Sociology, University of Kuwait.
2 Zaki Laidi, *A World Without Meaning: The Crisis of Meaning in International Politics*, trans. J. Burnham and J. Coulon (London: Routledge, 1998), 4–14.
3 Roland Inglehart, *Modernization and Postmodernization: Cultural and Political Change in 43 Societies* (Princeton, NJ: Princeton University Press, 1997), 7–33.
4 Barry Gills and Joel Rocamora, "Low Intensity Democracy," *Third World Quarterly* 13, no. 3 (1992): 502–503.
5 Wallerstein 1993: 3–9.
6 John Searle, *Mind, Language and Society: Doing Philosophy in the Real World* (London: Weidenfeld and Nicolson, 1999), 116–134.

7 Fareed Zakaria 1997: 22–43.
8 Paul Heelas, Scott Lash, and Paul Morris, eds, *Detraditionalization: Critical Reflection on Authority and Identity* (Cambridge: Blackwell, 1996).
9 Marsha Posusney, "Behind the Ballot Box: Electoral Engineering in the Arab World," *Middle East Report* Winter 1998.
10 Gilles Kepel, *The Revenge of God: The Resurgence of Islam, Christianity and Judaism in the Modern World*, trans. Alan Braley (University Park: The Pennsylvania State University Press, 1995).
11 Zakaria, 36.
12 Geertz.
13 Jack P. Gibbs, *Control: Sociology's Central Notion* (Urbana: University of Illinois Press, 1989), 23.
14 *Ibid.*, 67.
15 Mark Haugaard, *The Constitution of Power: A Theoretical Analysis of Power, Knowledge and Structure* (Manchester: Manchester University Press, 1997).
16 James R. Beniger, *The Control Revolution: Technology and Economic Origins of the Information Society* (Cambridge: Harvard University Press, 1986).
17 Thomas L. Haskell, *Objectivity Is Not Neutrality: Explanatory Schemes in History* (Baltimore, MD: The Johns Hopkins University Press, 1998), 237.
18 *Ibid.*, 138.
19 Daniel Lazare, *The Frozen Republic: How the Constitution is Paralyzing Democracy* (New York: Harcourt Brace, 1996); Lazare 2000.
20 Zakaria, 39.
21 David Held, *Models of Democracy* (Stanford, CA: Stanford University Press, 1997), 5.
22 O'Donnel and Schmetter, 1986.
23 Cf. Gills and Rocamora.
24 *Ibid.*
25 Al-Naqeeb, 1998; Hermassi.
26 Simon Bromley, *Rethinking Middle East Politics* (Cambridge: Polity Press, 1994), 119–154.
27 Khaldoun H. Al-Naqeeb, *Society and State in the Gulf Arab Peninsula: A Different Perspective* (London and New York: Routledge, 1990).
28 Posusney, 16.
29 Bernard Lewis, "Why Turkey Is the Only Muslim Democracy," *Middle East Quarterly* (1994).
30 Al-Naqeeb, 1996: 139–144.
31 Al-Naqeeb, 1996: 204–207.
32 Hamit Bozarslan, "Network-building, Ethnicity and Violence in Turkey," *The Emirates Occasional Papers*, no. 33 (Abu Dhabi: The Emirates Center for Strategic Studies and Research, 1999).
33 *Ibid.*, 1.
34 *Ibid.*, 2.
35 Mary Ann Tetrault, "Designer-democracy in Kuwait," *Current History* (January 1997).
36 The electoral law was amended to give women the vote in 2005 after a protracted fierce battle in parliament. In May 2006, the constitutional court struck down the free assembly law as being unconstitutional. A lawsuit was brought forth by a group of lawyers.
37 Jasim Karam and Jasim Al-Ai, "Demarcation of Electoral Districts by the Use of Geographical Data System in Kuwait," [in Arabic]. Kuwaiti University Department of Geography, 1998. The boundaries of the 10 districts in 1962 were district 10, which contained the majority of the Ajam tribe, and the districts 9 and 8, the Awazim and Shi'a. Map 2 shows the effects of dividing Kuwait into 25 electoral districts instead of 10 in 1981. Keep in mind that in 1976 the Shi'a managed to send 10 deputies to the parliament, which was one-fifth of the total. In 1981 the first district, Al-Sharq, lost 3 deputies (from 5 to 2), and the seventh district, which became the fourth, lost 3 deputies

(from 5 to 2). Both of these contained a majority of Shi'a. The old ninth district, which contained a majority of Awazim, was divided into 2 districts (12 and 13) and lost 1 deputy. At the same time, the tenth district was divided into 5 districts (21 through 25), doubling the number of their deputies (from 5 to 10) but becoming a conglomeration of several tribes.

38 In fact, many candidates from the same tribal and ideological affiliation competed against each other, attesting that the fundamentalist label was simply a cover for a tribal affiliation.

References

Al Naqeeb, Khaldoun H. *Society and State in the Gulf Arab Peninsula: A Different Perspective.* London and New York: Routledge, 1990.

——. "Social Origins of the Authoritarian State In the Arab East." In *Statecraft in the Middle East,* edited by Eric Davis and N. Gavrielides. Florida International University Press, 1991.

——. *The Authoritarian State in the Arab Mashriq* [in Arabic]. Beirut: Center for Arab Unity Studies, 1996.

——. *Tribalism and Democracy: The Case of Kuwait* [in Arabic]. London and Beirut: Dar Al-Saqi, 1996.

Al-Sayyed Saeed, M. "The Problematic of Democratic Rule in the Arab World" [in Arabic]. *Al-Zemen* (Kuwait) 15 (1997).

Beniger, James R. *The Control Revolution: Technology and Economic Origins of the Information Society.* Cambridge: Harvard University Press, 1986.

Bozarslan, Hamit. "Network-building, Ethnicity and Violence in Turkey." *The Emirates Occasional Papers,* no. 33. Abu Dhabi: The Emirates Center for Strategic Studies and Research, 1999.

Bromley, Simon. *Rethinking Middle East Politics.* Cambridge: Polity Press, 1994.

Cohen, Jean L. "Exclusiveness of the Geertz Clifford Demos." *International Sociology* 14, no. 3 (1999).

Gibbs, Jack P. *Control: Sociology's Central Notion.* Urbana: University of Illinois Press, 1989.

Gills, Barry and Joel Rocamora. "Low Intensity Democracy." *Third World Quarterly* 13, no. 3 (1992).

Good, James and Irving Velody, eds *The Politics of Postmodernity.* Cambridge University Press, 1998.

Graham, David and Mark Tessler, eds *Democracy, War and Peace in the Middle East.* Indiana University Press, 1995.

Haskell, Thomas L. *Objectivity Is Not Neutrality: Explanatory Schemes in History.* Baltimore, MD: The Johns Hopkins University Press, 1998.

Haugaard, Mark. *The Constitution of Power: A Theoretical Analysis of Power, Knowledge and Structure.* Manchester: Manchester University Press, 1997.

Heelas, Paul, Scott Lash, and Paul Morris, eds *Detraditionalization: Critical Reflection on Authority and Identity.* Cambridge: Blackwell, 1996.

Held, David. *Models of Democracy.* Stanford, CA: Stanford University Press, 1997.

Hirst, P. "Associational Democracy." In *Prospects for Democracy: North, South, East, West,* edited by D. Held. Cambridge: Polity Press, 1993.

Inglehart, Roland. *Modernization and Postmodernization: Cultural and Political Change in 43 Societies.* Princeton, NJ: Princeton University Press, 1997.

Karam, Jasim and Jasim Al-Ai. "Demarcation of Electoral Districts by the Use of Geographical Data System in Kuwait" [in Arabic]. Kuwaiti University Department of Geography, 1998.

Kepel, Gilles. *The Revenge of God: The Resurgence of Islam, Christianity and Judaism in the Modern World*. Translated by Alan Braley. University Park: The Pennsylvania State University Press, 1995.

Laidi, Zaki. *A World Without Meaning: The Crisis of Meaning in International Politics*. Translated by J. Burnham and J. Coulon. London: Routledge, 1998.

Lazare, Daniel. *The Frozen Republic: How the Constitution is Paralyzing Democracy*. New York: Harcourt Brace, 1996.

Lewis, Bernard. "Why Turkey Is the Only Muslim Democracy." *Middle East Quarterly* (1994).

Lipset, Seymour Martin. *American Exceptionalism: A Double-Edge Sword*. New York: Norton, 1966.

Mair, C.S., ed. *Changing Boundaries of the Political: Essays on the Evolving Balance between State and Society, Public and Private in Europe*. Cambridge: Cambridge University Press, 1987.

Morris, Paul. "Community Beyond Tradition." In Heelas *et al.*

Norris, Christopher. *Uncritical Theory: Postmodernism, Intellectuals and the Gulf War*. Amherst: The University of Massachusetts Press, 1992.

Posusney, Marsha. "Behind the Ballot Box: Electoral Engineering in the Arab World." *Middle East Report* (Winter 1998).

Robinson, Glenn E. "Defensive Democratization in Jordan." *International Journal of Middle Eastern Studies* 30, no. 3 (1998).

Rothstein, Robert L. "Democracy in the Third World: Definitional Dilemmas." In Graham and Tessler.

Searle, John. *Mind, Language and Society: Doing Philosophy in the Real World*. London: Weidenfeld and Nicolson, 1999.

Shearer, David. "Outsourcing War." *Foreign Policy* (Fall 1998).

Squires, Judith. "In Different Voices: Deliberative Democracy and Aestheticist Politics." In Good and Velody.

Tetrault, Mary Ann. "Designer-democracy in Kuwait." *Current History* (January 1997).

7 An argument for enhancing Arab identity within globalization

*Gaber Asfour**

Globalization has accelerated modernization in material aspects throughout the world. It has revamped the relations among developing and developed nations as well as rich and poor ones. The processes of globalization have led to the migration of broad segments of the population in Egypt and elsewhere in the non-oil rich parts of the Arab world. This mobilization of human and material resources has dissolved traditional boundaries dividing nations. Advanced technology, new media, and information are harnessed through transnational corporations to promote the flow of labor, commodities, and information. By permeating all aspects of social life, globalization has profoundly impacted cultural revision on the national level. In this chapter, I identify continuities and disjunctions in the culture of Egypt resulting from globalization and the consequent contradictions.

Traditionalists might perceive negative responses to globalization in how Arabic interprets English vocabulary, which is the language of globalism. For several Arab intellectuals, globalization is a new tempero-spatial location constructed by economic, political, and cultural transformations that jointly formulate a new capital/power system encompassing the globe. By and large, these changes are pushed by multinational corporations that, along with advances in information and communication, intervene in the production of knowledge and serve to missionize global values.

To illustrate, the word *'awlama*, the Arabic term for globalization, has gained popularity and new connotations. From a sociolinguistic vantage point, this term reflects Arab apprehension toward this new world order, signifying a powerful center dominating peripheral nations like the many without oil throughout the Middle East. For Arabs focused on the local community and the close-knit social life among extended kindred, globalization can upend their social meanings and thus be frightening. Globalization incorporates nations around the world into one system, molding them into a total structure-dependent entity closely monitored by the business and military interests of the hegemonic United States. In such a rapidly transforming and power-driven context, the anticipated Arab culture would appear sinister; that is, cultural change for the sake of economic control by multinational corporations whose interests are guaranteed by the military might of Western governments. Multi/transnational corporations form a liaison of interests; information exchange – recently commodified – is also hegemony in the global capitalist/power system. Meanwhile, recent political formation of globalism, with its economic and political strength, brought about the demise of the former Soviet Union and the fall of the communist regimes. Basically, the latter failed to live up to their promises and could not compete with American-based globalism. Reflecting this new reality in sociolinguistics, *'awlama*, the Arabic term for globalization, is inflected *faw'al*, an infinitive connotating coercion, and homologous to *qawlaba*, the Arabic for *molding*. Therefore, *'awlama* connotes falling under certain pressure to conform.

If the term *globalization* connotes coercion in Arabic, this stems from attempts to mold nationalities into one global format through vast communication networks related to the new economic order of the production and dissemination of knowledge, or what is termed *informationalism*. As such, information is a top-rate raw material vital to capital flow. Hence, knowledge production reinforces the cultural, economic, and political hegemony.

With the accelerating pace of globalization, many Arab thinkers have re-examined the future of Arab culture in relation to external influences. In the context of crucial changes touching upon the mode of production of knowledge, we must reconsider methods of consolidating what is authentic or original in Arab culture against what may be identified as neo-colonial intervention innovations and cultural syncretisms. They have realized that nations incorporated within the global network have fallen victim to the hegemony of Americanization. The result is a negation of cultural traits, practices, beliefs, and national identities. All this is implemented by advanced communication and transcontinental institutions of acculturation and through proxy institutions disseminating globalized ideas and products.

Globalization may also be interpreted as a historical process, evolving novel economic, political, social, and epistemological constructions. It also connects concepts justifying interrelated material transformations inherent in the word *globalism*. Both interpretations focus on the general, foregrounding its cultural values, while demeaning the particular. All this has endangered the peculiarities of national cultures, arousing the need for redefining identity in the context of globalization.

Such processes and dilemmas should not be restricted to theorization alone, as manifested by some Arab intellectuals. These individuals have explored Arab identity through existentialism, structuralism, deconstruction, modernism, and postmodernism. Yet, there is a pressing need to critique how ongoing changes impact "routine and day-to-day cultural practices" in local culture. Indeed, in a world of accelerated change, Arabs are involved in globalization processes in economy, politics, and culture. Arabs have been relocated into other cultures. This begets issues that need to be framed for analysis and then actions to remove present obstacles, and to successfully face future problems.

This new location requires going beyond effective and redundant solutions. These could be replaced by a free imagination capable of mapping new links in the present globally transformed world. Consequently, anticipation for the impact of globalization on the present and future can be made on sound footing. This would include possible deals with transnational capital generated by the new economic relationships. It also addresses how multicultural people with high-tech experience and advanced communication programs can ethically shape a global consciousness. These interdependent aspects have impacted our world, and Arabs should intervene in the process of their making. In other words, Arabs should not sit idly by as Arab culture is reshaped.

An imaginative plan should involve rational thinking capable of humanizing globalization in order to mitigate its ravages and thereby place it in different contexts. This may diminish polarizing divisions between rich and poor nations or the suppression of firmly rooted cultural identities. I believe that cultural diversity may be protected by Third World nations in the United Nations generally and in UNESCO specifically. Such a collective approach would challenge compulsory globalization by introducing a humanist factor. This would also relieve the underprivileged nations of the south. This model, entitled "Our Creative Diversity," was advocated by the UN's International Committee for Culture and Development in 1995 under the sponsorship of then UN Secretary Javier Perez de Cuellar. This position was presented in book form by the UN as *Crossing the Divide* (2002). Both the report (1995) and the book (2002) identify the threats awaiting creative diversity and call for new mental mappings to thwart the challenges of globalization.

Creative diversity promotes respect for national identities and the particularity of history without prioritizing any. It deflects the centricity of the view based on the possibility of a dialogue between nations, creeds, sects, systems, and ideas. Rather than dominance and ethnocide, tolerance is the rule. Accordingly, the tendency toward creative diversity insures mutuality among nations and cultures, based on economic, political, and cultural interdependence. Thus, the previous relations of dominance are undermined. This also provides independent nations with more scope for interaction with other nations to confront international problems that cannot be dealt with single-handedly. This, in turn, lays the foundation for a unifying human ethics based on equality in a world ideally liberated from discrimination and oppression. It also promotes a civil society and tolerance.

Creative diversity provides counter-values to hegemonic globalization that subverts its centrality and domination. Diversity also contests the political Americanization basic in globalization and provides a chance for other nations to take the lead in a particular endeavor. It also counters transnational corporations through a movement sponsored by international organizations whose objectives are not geared to increasing the economic divide between rich and poor. Implementing creative diversity would involve a thorough critique of globalization, exposing its inherent contradictions. This would also explore globalization from different viewpoints, disclosing how the means of freedom serve to divert the covert goals of hegemony. For example, information banks, advanced communication technology that currently implement globalization, could also subvert globalization if used to foster interdependent scientific research among nations. This can only be achieved through a new consciousness capable of subverting the monolithic viewpoint and constructing positive relations among nations to contest global hegemony. Clearly this calls for a collective effort among the world's citizens to not be "bought off" by the short-term financial inducements of global capitalism. This raises additional challenges for intellectuals in the Arab world to confront neo-colonialism and the negative effects of globalization.

Such strategies would require new rational thinking. In this regard, several conferences in the Arab world have explored the dimensions of globalism in an attempt to offset its hazards. Six conferences were held between 1996 and 1998 to call the Arab intelligentsia to action: (1) "Economic Globalization: Its Directions and Impact on Arab Companies and Organizations," sponsored by the Arab Organization for Administration and Development in Cairo in September 1996; (2) "The Clash of Civilizations, or Cultural Clash," hosted by the Organization for Afro-Asian Solidarity in Cairo in March 1997; (3) "International Development and Social Transformation in the Arab World," held by the Center for Arab Studies in Cairo in co-ordination with the Arab Society for Social Sciences in March 1997; (4) "Globalization and Identity," held by the Moroccan Royal Academy in Rabat in May 1997; (5) "Arabs and Globalization," held by the Center for Arab Unity Studies in Beirut in December 1997; and (6) "Globalization and Cultural Identity Issues," sponsored by the Supreme Council for Culture in Cairo in May 1998. While more conferences are planned, what effect does talk have on the negative impact of globalism, on national sovereignty, economic development, and national culture? Taken as a whole, the conferences convey apprehension toward the impact of globalization on cultural identity rather than meaningful action.

These conferences have emphasized raising a critique of the expected results of globalization. Supposedly, researchers will coalesce through the exchange of knowledge; however, this approach could also be recycled Soviet-styled eradication of false consciousness in the hope that positive collective action could ensue. Yet, in my view, none of these conferences has made any recommendations or offered solutions to the problem. However, their efforts propounded new inquiries into the radical transformations in the global world. Such inquiries offer chances for multiple efforts, novel imaginings, and perceptions, mentally activating the search for rational formulations. Developed thinking would hypothetically problematize the question of identity in relation to globalization. But can such idle-thinking sequestered savants thwart the onslaught of globalization on the rank and file of Arab society, who are lured by short-term material inducements such as purchasing Western products?

This quest needs a critique of consciousness that can act in two contrapuntal directions to attend to identity issues with as much force as globalization issues. As such, the negative aspects in globalization may be remedied by positive aspects inherent in it. By analogy, cultural identity is not an ideal organized set of closed relations but contains negative aspects that are open to critique and, hopefully, revision.

The critique of national culture confronts those who, with religious fervor, idealize nationalism as a new fundamentalism in which globalization is evil impersonated. Such extremism may catalyze a total rejection of tradition. A critique of national culture, on the other hand, is a rational act that re-examines its multiple and competing discourses. One confrontation should be with authoritarian, fundamentalist discourse – under whichever pretext – whose stance toward national culture drives it to negate the other that falls beyond the orbit of its belief, be it Marxist, nationalistic, or religious. A discourse of fundamentalism is put forth by those over-protective of the national culture to the extent of "othering" all that falls beyond its strict parameters. A critical consciousness can also distinguish different discourses of globalization. As such, cultural identity would avoid repeating the past, while national policy would be freed from foreign dependency.

Localism at its extreme may become xenophobic and even violent. When indigenism is paired with religious fundamentalism the result becomes grave, with many innocent victims suffering within the Islamic world first and foremost and then those beyond it. The events of September 11, 2001, are the prime case in point, highlighting that the inverse discourse arouses a dramatic response to globalization. The expansion of globalization has brought about localism to defend against its threats. This in turn has dichotomized cultural identity and globalization as two poles of the economic, political, and cultural interrelational dimensions of same system. This fosters pre-conceived binary divisions as opposite interrelations. It its assumed that isolated communities are incapable of developing the positive aspects in their cultural traditions. This local community is seen as incapable of reaching out to other cultures. The "other" becomes an imagined targeted opponent, since their logic is based on "us" and "them." Presently, immigration, geographical displacements, tourism, and travel have brought peoples of different cultures in contact in an unprecedented manner. In the past, people were more stationary and may not have personally experienced distinct cultures. The merging of the local and the foreign may be a source of specialized knowledge and insight. While citizens today take pride in their national traditions, this should not motivate politics of exclusion. Interaction with other cultures will take place with an awareness of the ethics binding humanity across the ages. The course of academic history reveals that nations are united by a universal humanity rather than divided by the sectarianism of their separate identities. And Islam promotes tolerance as revealed by the following verses:

> O mankind! We created/ You from a single (pair)/ Of male and female/ And made you into/ Nations and tribes, that/ Ye may know each other/ (Not that ye may despise/ (Each other). Verily/ The most honored of you/ In the sight of Allah/ Is (he who is) the most/ Righteous of you. / And Allah has full knowledge/ And is well acquainted/ With all things).[1]

These verses signify a path that does not divide global and local, but one that reveals potentials and related anticipations. It also contradicts the global-local binary since all nations now create world culture.

We must keep in mind that national belonging does not deter access to international cooperation. A cultural identity is formed either in a global context or in contesting it. Both local and global need critique to instill continual renewal of the creative process that resists repetitiveness. Repetitiveness intellectually fosters dependence of the past, while resisting economic dependence.

Many savants see creative diversity in the world of a global village. To use a metaphor here, if one house catches on fire, the fire will spread and endanger all the roofs. Conversely, if one reconstructs an edifice, his efforts require public solidarity. In this respect, I quote Mahatma Gandhi: "I don't want my house to be enclosed from all sides, with blocked windows. I rather want its branches exposed to the winds of the world's cultures without having any of them uproot me from the ground." The novelist Carlos Fuentes adds,

> Capitalism and socialism have both proven their failure in saving our nation (i.e. Mexico) from the claws of misery. The question is: Is there another solution emerging from within us? Do we not possess a tradition, an imagination, intellectual aptitude, enabling us to formulate models for development concomitant to our conditions, concordant with our past, present and the objectives we long to reach in the future?

Indeed, the deep roots of Arab identity need constant revision to stand up to the contemporary challenges of globalization. We should not resort to preserving identity in its form of origin, but rather use it as a potential for creativity. The new can only be generated by re-defining the old in the context of present transformations and in view of future anticipations. Identity can only acquire presence by being a vital process, constancy being a non-essential core that allows the growth of being. Identity is not rigidly steadfast, thwarting transformation, but is a perpetual course, a presence susceptible to change in response to external factors.

As a process, identity may also be viewed as inquiry, based on a creative intellect that probes the self in different contexts. Accordingly, equilibrated identity would stand against discrimination between races, nations, and cultures; would mediate North and South; would lay the seeds for tolerance; and would initiate an intercultural dialogue. Such an Arab identity is an interlocutor. We hope that the times of domination, discrimination, and exploitation are over, especially in an environment that calls for cultural diversity. However, we should keep in mind the difference between the calls for diversity among the intelligentsia and the as-of-yet unabated erosion of diversity by global economic forces. Furthermore, I believe that there is little hope for peace, so long as there is a community, a nation, or a culture exercising political or academic pressure or economic exploitation. Of course, the human condition seems to generate pressure in most contexts. Yet, for a promising future there must be mutual respect for difference, diversity in practices, and emancipation from all forms of racial or sectarian discrimination while resisting domination through globalization. Equally, it would readily be recognized that the negation of cultural particularities is a negation of the dignity of a people and consequently, humanity at large. Otherwise, a bland cultural homogeneity would promote exploitation of those people who attempt to forsake their cultural traditions to become something else.

Globalization and localization are presented as binaries, representing poles of good and evil. However, both actually retain some positive elements that enable them to overlap. Globalization benefits all nations through advanced communication technology, information exchange, and organized campaigns against crime, disease, and ecological ravages. In the meantime, an understanding of local ethnic cultures, national language, and creed is of major importance. If globalization promotes competition in all fields, hopefully it can tap into the boundless human creativity in different cultures. As such, there is a need for the coexistence of globalization and the particularity of localism. Such a coexistence consolidates mutual interaction between universal and particular, a crossing of the divide, transforming opposites to a new synthesis, which transcends both. Therefore, one can be freed from the "either/or," "us/them" mentality and work for an interactive humanity. But let us not lose sight of the capitalist basis of globalism that requires many to work for the few. This is inherent inequality.

But to argue for a new practice of equality and diversity, the proliferation of knowledge through globalization may promote greater interdependence between nations. This, in turn, will transcend prejudice and would promote a belief that national and international progress is mutually sustainable. This kind of knowledge that reaches its destination by transcending the source is reminiscent of the "flash of lightening" mentioned by the medieval Sufi Arab poet, Ibn ʿArabi. I quote from his &265a.eps *Torjomman al-Ashwaq*, written almost eight centuries ago:

> Seeing the lightning Eastwards he pined for the East,
> Had it flashed Westwards, he'd have pined for the West,
> I yearn for that flash of lightning,
> Nor for sites not lands.

Notes

* Head of the Supreme Council for Culture, Egypt.
1 *Holy Qur'an*, English translation revised and edited by the Presidency of Islamic Researchers, IFTA, Call and Guidance, (The Custodian of the Two Holy Mosques King Fahd Complex for The Printing of the Holy Qur'an) 1593.

8 The Gulf engulfed

Confronting globalization
American-style

*Michael C. Hudson**

This chapter places in context the issues of globalization facing the United Arab Emirates, which I describe without too much exaggeration as "the beating heart of globalization" in the Arab world. The Gulf countries in general, and the UAE in particular, have emerged as the Arab region's flagship of globalization. His Highness Sheikh Dr Sultan Bin Mohammed Al Qassimi, Ruler of Sharjah, has taken the lead in developing an educational center in the emirate of Sharjah that connects the Gulf with the global world of research, teaching, scholarship, and decision-making. Others are also working to integrate the Gulf into global networks of finance, trade, media, information technology, culture, and tourism. The results are spectacular and are readily evident in the skylines of cities along the Arabian Gulf.

It is evident that globalization has costs as well as benefits. Nowhere are those costs and benefits as evident as in the Arab world, where the challenges to the citizens of the GCC countries are equally intense. Although the Gulf region developed *sui generis*, in so many ways it remains an organic part of the Arab world and cannot remain indefinitely immune to the problems of the wider region. Moreover, living as we are at a historical watershed – the conjuncture of major new structural trends mixing together in a truly unpredictable manner – the challenges of globalization are particularly daunting. Since the collapse of the Soviet Union and the intensification of global integration in so many fields, the Arab countries have found themselves engulfed by forces over which they seem to have little control. Globalization has stimulated social inequalities and cultural conflict in addition to providing many material benefits. And, the emergence of the United States as the most powerful country in the world has given globalization a certain "American accent" that generates dissonance in a region where some of America's policies are detested. The events of September 11, 2001 traumatized the American public and created a demand for radical, vigorous – indeed preemptive if not preventive – action against what we have come to think of as the global terrorist threat. Today, the US government has little hesitation in bringing to bear all the instruments of its power and influence on countries as it seeks to eradicate what is seen as an unprecedented terrorist menace. To counter the perceived danger of Iraq's "weapons of mass destruction," the Bush Administration has assembled a formidable military force. The use of that force to invade a major Arab country, with unavoidable civilian casualties, is an event with serious consequences.

In an earlier era of Arab national self-assertion, it would have been unthinkable that virtually every government in the region would participate to some degree or other in this enterprise, however reluctant some of them profess to be about doing so. Nonetheless, such is the global reach of the United States that the unthinkable has become the inevitable. But America's global reach is not just military: the present US administration believes that America can also reshape the domestic affairs of Iraq and neighboring countries. Hence the intense criticism from some American media figures and religious leaders of "failed states," "failed economies," "religious bigotry," "educational inadequacy," "governmental incompetence and corruption," etc., in this part of the world – all of which is seen to incubate terrorist threats to America.

Visitors flying into an Arab Gulf state sometimes feel they are entering a kind of splendid bubble, separated from the tensions and miseries of the less-favored world outside. But as the petroleum analyst Vahan Zanoyan recently observed at a conference in Kuwait, this region is not immune from troubles in the wider region. He said:

> September 11 empowered a group of conservative thinkers in the U.S. and, in the absence of a credible response from the region, lent credibility to their ideas. A new vision for the Middle East is being promoted, in which old taboos are broken and old priorities discarded. The long-established special relationship between the U.S. and the moderate Gulf states has no relevance in this vision. The objective of forcing a regime change in Iraq and the down-grading of the Gulf region's strategic role in global energy markets are important cornerstones of this vision.[1]

Is Zanoyan correct in his interpretation of a change in the direction of American policy? One might take issue with particular "objectives" ascribed to the Americans by voices in Washington other than the neo-conservatives, but in general I think that his interpretation is justified. There have indeed been major structural changes in world politics and economics, not all of which lead to a frictionless integration of the less-developed regions into a larger and stable global order. In fact, global disorder seems more pronounced, especially since September 11, 2001. I will now comment briefly on some of these underlying new structures, looking first at the nature of globalization "American-style," then at political and societal changes in the Arab region. Particular attention is given to new information technologies, the construction of new identities, and the development of extremist networks.

Globalization American-style

Globalization has emerged as a conceptual anchor for the post-Cold War world; in Arabic *al-'awlama* denotes globalization. The concept refers to "increasing levels of interdependence over vast distances" along economic, cultural, environmental, and political dimensions.[2] Quantitative evidence shows the acceleration of this trend during the 1990s, although recent indications suggest a retreat from the world economic slowdown and the September 11 attacks.[3] The "global village" metaphor suggests both a general interdependence and awareness of it that at once links economic and societal actors in the Middle East to peoples across the globe. It also reduces the latitude of sovereign governmental authorities in the face of international "regimes." The most powerful sovereign governments are in turn influenced by notions of "empire." In the cultural and political realms, the distinction between Barber's *Jihad vs. McWorld* actually masks a peculiar symbiosis between "traditionalist" establishments like the Saudi state and modern technology: tradition is an instrument for achieving modernity, as Fox and Mourtada illustrate for Sharjah in this volume (Chapter 8).[4] Similarly, Jon W. Anderson notes that pan-Islamist organizations seize upon globalizing technologies like the Internet to advance a mythical traditionalist order (i.e. one that is constructed in the present and which never existed in the past).[5]

However, globalization in the Middle East is divisive as well as integrative. In government, certain heads of state may be more "at home" in the cosmopolitan environment of major world capitals than in their own capital. Computerized intelligence shared among Arab interior ministries after September 11 is now interconnected with their Western counterparts and illustrates lateral globalized integration among governmental and security agencies. Yet, many of these Middle Eastern "globally wired ruling circles" are perhaps more isolated from their people than ever before. While there may be parallel lateral linkages from organizations in Middle Eastern civil society with "global civil society," growing vertical participatory linkages with their own governments is lacking. The term "digital divide" describes the growing distance between elites and masses inside states, and the divide is widening between Africa and the Middle East on the one hand and the industrialized, high-tech societies on the other. If it is true that the "masses" in the Middle East are increasingly left behind in global economic and social development, then the level of discontent will be exploitable by high-tech militant networks. Additional tension derives from the unevenness of globalization across the lower classes in the Middle East: they can also see that they are falling behind. Satellite television is widespread but internet connections are not; neither are frequent opportunities to partake in the global economy.

How has globalization affected the balance of political-military power in the world, and how does this balance affect the Middle East? In constructing a model for this question, Hardt and Negri contend that, yes, there is a new "empire," but it is not merely the US government. We cannot compare the empire of today's post-Cold War, post-industrial world with the classical empires of earlier centuries. Everybody knew what the British empire was and the particular place from which it was governed; its power could be assessed in size and capacity of armed forces, budgetary capacity, and other traditional measures. Today's empire, in contrast, is "decentered":

> Empire is formed not on the basis of force itself but on the basis of the capacity to present force as being in the service of right and peace. All interventions of the imperial armies are solicited by one or more of the parties

involved in an already existing conflict. Empire is not born of its own will but rather is called into being and constituted on the basis of its ability to resolve conflicts ... The first task of Empire, then, is to enlarge the realm of the consensuses that support its own power.[6]

This approach helps us understand the pervasiveness and subtlety of contemporary "imperial" power. Some antagonists in local conflicts such as the Arab-Israeli struggle plead for American intervention. Yet, there is a certain coyness in how Hardt and Negri are indirect about the "reality" of an American-centered empire. As Brooks and Wohlforth observe, America dominates the world by virtually any measure of military, economic, and technological power – proportionally far in excess of any previous empires. As such, "the United States is the country in the best position to take advantage of globalization," attracting disproportionate shares of high-tech manpower and direct foreign investment. For better or worse, America is the center of today's globalized world.[7]

The present US administration does not seem to appreciate that cooperation is now more important than unilateralism in globalization. The place of the Middle East in today's global situation is more complex than the bipolar, superpower Cold War world of little more than a decade ago. When Middle Eastern countries were pieces on a chessboard manipulated by two contending players, the picture was simpler. And, perhaps, the region was more stable than it will be under the influx hegemony of the United States. But whether the contemporary "empire" can engineer global support of its power and prerogatives seems highly debatable as we saw in the prelude to the second war with Iraq.

Globalization and structural change in the Arab world

Let us now elucidate how globalization in various aspects affects Arab society. To illustrate, in the information revolution, the rapid introduction and spread of new information and communications technology (ICT) accelerates the erosion of the state's "monopoly" over framing and ratifying identities and loyalties. It also decentralizes how the public perceives public issues. It blurs established political boundaries and opens the door to transnational action. It profoundly affects the construction of identities, communities, and ideological projects in society. Not only is ICT deepening the effects of the global order on the domestic and regional scene in the Arab world, it is also enhancing the reverse flow of influence from the region to the world at large, including the United States. Whether we refer to the anger in Arab public opinion over American policies, the rise of politicized Islam waging a war of symbols against the West, or the projection of violent and terroristic force against the United States itself, we see clearly that the Gulf area cannot remain isolated from the ferment in the contemporary Arab world. To discuss the changing political terrain in the Arab world, we should focus on challenges to states and regimes, the effervescence in society, and the interventions of an American-dominated global order. In doing so, we note the relative weakening of authoritarian regimes in the face of globalization, Islamist ideologies, and demands for liberalization and democratization. Notwithstanding these trends, authoritarianism is deeply rooted, and authoritarian regimes friendly to the United States have been exempted from Washington's commitment to the expansion of democracy throughout the world. Nevertheless, the interesting and symbiotic coalescence of the new information technologies with the rise of networks as a response to ingrained authoritarianism is exerting a great influence.

The information revolution in the Arab world

Within the Arab region's information and communications technology revolution, the number of users of satellite television and the internet has reached impressive levels. Granted that reliable numbers are hard to come by, viewership of the Al-Jazeera Satellite Channel is estimated at 35 million, although the audience for specific programs may run in the low to mid hundreds of thousands depending on time of day and the "newsworthiness" of events. Al-Jazeera is a global as well as Arab world media outlet, with tens of thousands of viewers in North America alone. An increasing proportion of viewers – perhaps 30 percent – is female. While its audience share trails that of entertainment-oriented satellite channels such as LBC (Lebanese Broadcasting Company) and the state-run channels in many Arab countries, Al-Jazeera has a significant if not predominant presence within its targeted audience of educated, professionally oriented individuals in or near the circles of political influence. Anecdotal evidence suggests that Al-Jazeera is "required" watching for leaders, high officials, politicians, diplomats, the intelligentsia, business leaders, and "opinion-makers" across the region. It also has a high degree of saturation among Arab communities of the diaspora, especially in the United States and Europe. Please bear in mind that Al-Jazeera is a news and opinion media platform a scant half-decade old comparable to the traditional print news media and much more inclusive. Also remember that Al-Jazeera has also been imitated by region-wide satellite channels such as LBC and Al-Mustaqbil (Future Television) from Lebanon, Abu Dhabi and Dubai channels, Saudi-owned MBC (Middle East Broadcasting Center), Nile and ESC (Egyptian Satellite Channel) from Egypt, and local government-operated stations. Moreover, Al-Jazeera and its imitators are significantly more interactive with their audiences than traditional television outlets. This is evident in the volume of on-screen polls and e-mail responses to particular programs as well as in Al-Jazeera's stated policy of providing a forum for "the other opinion."

There has been a recent proliferation of Arab portals on the internet. According to Jon W. Anderson, more than 50 portals are operating, with most functioning in Arabic as well as or instead of English. As one of the Arab world's busiest websites, the recently launched Al-Jazeera.net receives some 300,000 visits a day.[8] When Al-Jazeera.net invites online polling on current affairs, sports, or Islam, it registers 20,000–35,000 "votes." The interactive behavior of the web audience is also a factor in constructing identity and communal solidarity.

Consider, too, that similar "publicly oriented" websites, such as those established by major print newspapers, compete with portals catering to a particular ideological tendency or material interest. For example, portals ranging from Islam and youth culture to pop music, fashion, and business are also establishing active online communities.

The Arab Information Project, established at Georgetown University in 1995 under the direction of Michael C. Hudson and Jon W. Anderson, has been studying the implantation of the internet in Egypt, Jordan, Syria, and Saudi Arabia. Despite initial hypotheses that those nations' regimes, which have tendencies toward authoritarianism in varying degrees, would seek to inhibit intrinsically pluralistic ICT development, it was found that the top leadership in all cases took the lead in encouraging it. Even though the more controlling regimes (Syria and Saudi Arabia) sought to centralize and censor internet availability, they acknowledged the necessity of internet access for economic and business development. They also recognized the practical obstacles to suppression of unwanted access and material. Even in Jordan, with its particularly delicate internal situation, the economic benefits of a liberal ICT policy clearly outweighed the political security costs. Even though Islamist groups have quickly grasped the political significance of ICT, governments with a relatively secular orientation perceive the countervailing benefits of a liberal ICT and media policy that helps socialize young people into a culture of globalization.

The changing political terrain

The state steadily emerged as the dominant organizing body of Arabs from the post-World War II period almost up to the present. It grew dramatically in terms of size, revenues, and coercive capacity. It also enjoyed certain legitimacy derived from the successful struggle against Western imperialism. One group of states embarked on a nationalist-reformist direction, led mainly by military officers and a professional, reform-minded middle-class stratum. The authoritarian-populist regimes in these states framed the public priorities in terms of economy developed through import-substitution-industrialization, land reform, and emasculation of the very wealthy. Populations were mobilized to unify the Arab nation, redress the grievous *nakba* (catastrophe) of Palestine, and prevent Western neo-imperialism. For them, the Soviet Union balanced Western encroachment and, to some extent, modeled political and economic development. Egypt, Algeria, Tunisia, Libya, Syria, Iraq, and North and South Yemen pursued this course in various ways. A second group, while passively accepting nationalism including the leading role of the state, featured regimes with "traditional" and "patriarchal" character. These included Saudi Arabia, the eastern Arabian states, Jordan, Lebanon, and Morocco. Unlike the "nationalists" these regimes celebrated Islamic authenticity rather than relegating it to a lower priority. Many were rentier-states – major oil exporters in which vast revenues accrued directly to the dynastic state. Their well-to-do classes were coopted rather than suppressed and harnessed to non-socialist development plans. Their external orientation favored the West as a bulwark against the challenges of the transnational ideological appeal of the "progressive" states. Both groups of states, however, mobilized a broad-based populism. Political liberalization leading to pluralistic democracy was not on the agenda. The state framed the public agenda and society followed, deferentially and passively. The post-colonial Arab state was subordinate after World War II, when bipolar superpowers dominated global order. As pan-Arabism waned following the defeat of Egypt's Gamal Abdel-Nasser in the 1967 war with Israel, some Middle East specialists theorized a "maturing" of the Arab states in general. Individual states were becoming more autonomous, self-contained, self-interested, Weberian, and Westphalian along the format of the post-Enlightenment states of the West. The states of the region were behaving as structural-realist international relations theory would have them behave: rational, trying to maximize development, and pragmatic to the global distribution of power.[9] For the two rival superpowers, the Middle East was a contested region where each constructed client blocs that mimicked their patrons in an "Arab cold war."[10]

The global and regional relationships defining the world system began to shift in earnest in the 1980s. States that seemed dominant over their societies began to falter, unable to deliver on the socioeconomic promises that had fostered political passivity. Decades of considerable economic growth ended with the collapse of oil prices in the mid-1980s. The oil-rich rentier regimes experienced huge revenue declines. The nationalist-progressive ideological formulas of regimes faded. Additionally, the bipolar global order ended with the demise of the Soviet Union, leaving the United States the hegemon of an increasingly integrated global economy informed by an ideology of liberalism. International financial institutions, heavily influenced by the United States, intervened in the most sensitive domestic policy issues in countries around the world, including most of those in the Islamic and Arab worlds. Westphalian sovereignty was being undermined everywhere. In the military world, where only the United States possessed a global reach, "humanitarian interventions" served notice on dictators that "the international community" might intrude militarily against regimes whose internal practices egregiously violated international standards.

Across the Arab world, then, states began to weaken. At the same time, societies displayed greater vitality than before. NGOs emerged during the 1980s to articulate alternative agendas and priorities, although they rarely participated in the policy-making process. Political scientists produced a number of studies depicting the growth of what Norton described as more "vibrant" political studies, while also subjecting the once all-powerful, stable "*mukhabarat* (national security police) state" to revisionist interpretations.[11] Perhaps the most cogent revisionist model was Nazih Ayubi's *Over-Stating the Arab State*.[12] Where would the new societal energy lead? While intellectuals and business leaders advanced projects of political liberalization and democratization, they did not reap a broad popular constituency. The Islamists garnered deeply rooted societal tendencies. And, as leader of a new global order, the United States during the 1990s struggled to define its role, whether as "umpire" (i.e. a neutral evaluator) during the Clinton administration, or perhaps as "empire," as George W. Bush has favored to date. With America's overarching presence in the Middle East after the collapse of the Soviet Union, its oil connection, and its support for Israel, American policy could only have a major impact both on states and societies. However, developments in the region could not be ignored in Washington, especially were they to penetrate the United States itself. With the weakening states, social ferment, and the new global order, the developments of transnational information technologies and political networking in the Arab world in tandem accelerate sociopolitical change, contestation, and uncertainty.

Networks and new modalities of contestation

In today's Information Age, says Castells, "Networks constitute the new social morphology of our societies, and the diffusion of networking logic substantially modifies the operation and outcomes in processes of production, experience, power, and culture."[13] He continues:

> A network is a set of interconnected nodes. A node is the point at which a curve intersects itself. What a node is, concretely speaking, depends on the kind of concrete networks of which we speak . . . . Networks are open structures, able to expand without limits, integrating new nodes as long as they are able to communicate within the network, namely as long as they share the same communication codes (for example, values or performance goals).[14]

Inherent in the network experience is the potential for the production, consumption, and investment of social capital. In a definitive article, Coleman defines social capital by its productive function, i.e., "the achievement of certain ends that in its absence would not be possible." He continues, "Unlike other forms of capital, social capital inheres in the structure of relations between actors and among actors."[15] Examples of culturally networked communities are the wholesale diamond market or the Cairo bazaar, in which a sense of community engenders trust and thus promotes collectively productive action. The informal *hawala* money-transfer networks thought to support Al-Qa'ida constitute another example. Remember, however, that social capital and networking are not confined to modern societies with formal rules and institutions; they also operate in what Rose (referring to Russia) calls anti-modern societies, providing channels for "getting things done" when formal institutions do not work.[16]

This brings us to the contemporary Arab world. Our current preoccupation with high-tech networks and "netwars" (as Ronfeldt and Arquilla use the term) notwithstanding, Arab society is and was permeated with networks.[17] In his comparison of informal networks in Egypt, Iran, and Lebanon, Denoeux generalizes that networks promote either political stability or instability.[18] They absorb the dysfunctional social atomization and personal anomie that might otherwise cause disruptions in rapidly modernizing societies with repressive governments. But such social dislocations can also form networks as alternatives to the official vision of society and thus challenge the political order. We now examine the tipping-point from one to the other in various episodes of recent Arab history.

The development of the post-colonial Arab state was authoritarian almost everywhere. While socioeconomic development began to establish the infrastructure that might support a vibrant civil society, insecure regimes, avaricious elites, ideologues, and international influences converged to create a *mukhabarat* state suspicious of societal autonomy, pluralism, and alternative agendas. Consequently, political parties other than the regime-sponsored single parties were weak, elections were usually rubber-stamp affairs, and interest groups and labor unions came under constant government surveillance and interference. The mass media, with certain exceptions, was coopted into helping frame the regimes' political agendas. In addition, the rule of law was too feeble to protect civil and political relationship; and the bureaucracies of state-driven economies were opaque, inefficient, and corrupt. In short, the political structures of a vibrant and participant civil society were truncated at best. Significant opposition was forced to be clandestine or at least low profile. Is it surprising, then, that alternative groups that survived adopted network structures (formal and informal) and cultures?

In Nasserite Egypt, political parties were banned, and the two main opposition groups, the Muslim Brotherhood and the Communist Party, were forced to be clandestine. Bereft of formal political organizations, powerful families and social networks (*shillas*) were the key factions.[19] Beneath the surface of High Politics (oriented around the central government), informal political networks formed in the poor quarters of Cairo and elsewhere and in the villages of Upper Egypt to cope with the important issues of family and marriage, employment, education, and social services.[20]

In "Bilad al-Sham" and Mesopotamia, "new" states were constructed mostly from the outside, namely Syria, Transjordan, and the non-state national community of Palestine, Lebanon, and Iraq. Some political networks were transnational as well: the Ba'th was found in all these countries (before it became a ruling party in Syria and Iraq); the Muslim Brotherhood spun off into satellites of the original Egyptian organization; the Arab Nationalists' Movement; the Communists; the Syrian Social National Party of "Greater Syria;" and the Palestinian resistance movement, with its numerous factions, in its early incarnation from the mid-1950s to the late 1960s. Lebanon, the one relatively non-authoritarian Arab state, featured legal parties and regular elections. Yet, even there, perhaps owing to Lebanon's highly plural society, formal political parties were weak and were organized as informal factional networks of notables and their clienteles, usually within a sectarian or regional framework. The Lebanese (Maronite) Phalange Party emerged out of a quasi-fascist youth organization. The (Druze) Progressive Socialist Party derived its cohesion and influence from dominant family networks (i.e. the Junblats and Arslans). When the state collapsed into a civil war (with significant transnational features) from 1975 to 1990, Lebanon became a "republic" of networked militias.

In the Arabian peninsula, where family and tribal-based patrimonial systems framed the political agenda, political parties were illegal and elections almost non-existent. Yet, social pluralism existed through the political, kinship-based networks of the *diwaniyya* in Kuwait, the *majlis* in Saudi Arabia, and the *mafraj* in Yemen. Arabian networks were functionally differentiated as well around occupational (e.g. business), religious, educational, and social concerns. After September 11, we learned of the formidable social capital and network flows inherent in militant Islamist networks.

Network success of the Islamists

Islamist networks indeed seem to be particularly successful. Four questions for further research might explain why this is the case. First, how potent and socially pervasive is the value agenda that their leaders offer? Second, how do they recruit, retain, and deepen the commitment of members of the network? Third, to what extent can they build upon and benefit from existing kinship, occupational, educational, or financial networks? Fourth, does the information technology revolution extend political networks beyond face-to-face relationships; or to put it another way, can social capital (and trust) be effectively transmitted through cyberspace?

A casual survey of formal Islamist political networks such as the Organization of the Islamic Conference; clandestine movements such as the Egyptian *gama'at*; the Shi'a networks of Lebanon, Iran and Iraq; the Palestinian Islamist groups; similar organizations in North Africa; and even the notorious Al-Qa'ida suggest that on all four counts they can advance their agendas. First, with respect to the symbolic agenda, one observes that the array of projects encapsulated by the slogan "Islam is the Solution" resonates deeply with individuals mired in the tensions and contradictions of contemporary Arab societies. Moreover, the pervasiveness of these symbols, especially when associated with longstanding nationalist concerns, extends throughout society. To employ this metaphor, thus, a network like Al-Qa'ida swims in a nutritious societal "sea." Despite Al-Qa'ida's commission of morally atrocious acts, it enjoys at least passive support across transnational social strata.

Second, as Wickham observes of Islamists in Egypt, the network itself produces the social capital rewards for membership in addition to the instrumental agendas being put forth.[21] Codes of dress and deportment are among the social cues designating membership. Peer pressure consolidates commitment to the cause. During the repressive regimes of Anwar Sadat and Hosni Mubarak, the Islamists migrated into the subaltern spaces in Egyptian society to find sanctuary and launch new initiatives to participate in High Politics. Third, Islamist networks "piggy-backed" on existing social and cultural networks. Al-Qa'ida, as noted above, rode the *hawala* financial networks. Some say it free-rides on Arabian honey trading networks. Did Osama bin Laden's family and business networks indirectly enable the development of his political network? Some Islamist networks appear to originate in the "old school ties" of schools and universities. The Taliban founders were alumni of the Deobandi seminary. The Shi'a network organizers of Amal, Hizballah, and the Da'wa formed lasting bonds in the seminaries of Qom and Najaf. Many Egyptian networkers first crossed paths at Al-Azhar. Similarly, American Muslim extremists networked in the storefront mosques of Jersey City and Brooklyn. Non-Islamist opposition networks also "piggy-back." Batatu's work on the Iraqi Communists and the Syrian Ba'thists reveals their sectarian and regional interconnections.[22] The founders of the Syrian Social National Party and the Arab Nationalists' Movement utilized alumni and student networks of the American University of Beirut as a platform for their own transnational projects.

Finally, the internet and satellite television networks vastly extended the global reach of transnational Islamist networks. Whether it is Shaykh Qaradawi's call-in program on Al-Jazeera or the substantial participants of the Islam OnLine Internet portal, these cyberspace communities may constitute an enormous recruitment pool for future political networks.

The Arab region exhibits an impressive record of regime stability. The forces of globalization, however, affect the socio-cultural-economic status quo. The relative inability of the Arab world to develop in the new global order has created severe economic and societal imbalances, which are well described in the recent *Arab Human Development Report*.[23] On the "subjective" level of legitimacy, political culture, and public opinion, the information revolution and the impact of America's global hegemony are generating tensions. As the Bush administration pursues its "war on terrorism," it exacerbates these tensions. Can the Arab Gulf region deal with them?

Conclusion

Where does the leadership of the Gulf go from here in managing and directing, as much as possible, the forces of globalism? Zanoyan asserts that

> The Gulf region is at a crossroads. Its leaders and governments can either choose a minimalist approach, aimed at marginal and superficial damage control, or they can choose to secure the future ... The main dimensions of a viable strategy include drastic reforms aimed at (a) strengthening and broadening the domestic political support base of each government; (b) constructing and articulating a positive vision for the region; (c) re-engaging the world.[24]

This is much to ask of the leadership of any state or collective of states like that of the GCC. The prosperity and tranquility of our surroundings might lead one to think that is exaggerated. But, in the deeper structural trends outlined above, this diagnosis deserves careful consideration. Our conventional understandings about the stability, efficacy, and durability of the region's political structures surely need re-examination. Can the states described by Ayubi as "fierce," steeped in the traditions of competition and conflict in the Arabian peninsula, effectively cope with the demands of the liberal global ideology and behaviors, not to mention the pressures arising from stagnant economies and burgeoning populations?[25] The rise and apparently popular acquiescence in the violent activities of Al-Qa'ida suggest a certain social malaise. The information technologies give additional "reach" and amplification to such organizations. Communal identities are more easily and quickly constructed and reconstructed. Political legitimacy is more difficult, especially if governments are not linked to their societies beyond their factional webs. The sober *Arab Human Development Report* calls for attending to the problems of governance, the marginalization of the female population, and the lack of a "knowledge-based society."[26] Blessed with natural resources, small populations, and stable governments, perhaps the Gulf states can present themselves as a model to the greater Arab region. Indeed, the Crown Prince of Saudi Arabia proposes an "Arab Charter" to "end the silence that has gone on for too long" about "the explosive situation in this area."

Coping with globalization might be easier for the Arab world if globalization did not have such a pronounced American accent. I have already indicated how the United States dominates globalization. And, remember how September 11 galvanized an administration into a tough, preemptive "forward policy." In Washington, the debate continues between those who believe that national security requires an assertive response to threats and those who favor a multilateral approach in cooperation with other governments. While talk of "empire" is in the air, there is also talk of how and why empires collapse. For the Arabs, the American-accented globalization is particularly frustrating for the interrelated Palestinian question and the unwillingness to face the proposition that Americans are "hated" for US policies but not for their values. This dichotomy intensifies the dilemma for the Arab world. When American officials prescribe reforms to bring the Arabs into a globalized world, the reputation of the messenger makes the message hard to accept. Even as Washington promotes "partnership" in bringing liberal democracy to the Arab world, previous experiments in political liberalization seem to have withered because incumbent regimes feared that those opposed to American-accented globalization might emerge.

Since the 1960s – a time of exuberant Arab nationalism, when "Western imperialism" was being rolled back and that "dignity," independence, sovereignty and social justice were within reach – it seems astonishing that the Arab world appears to have fallen into a new dependency. The will to resist the sometimes hostile forms of "globalization" seems diminished. The optimism of "the nationalist project" of the 1950s and 1960s, and the expectations that a developed, prosperous Arab future following the oil price increases of the 1970s, has given way to a future that seems to be beyond control. I realize that such an ominous conclusion is related to the potential trouble from the globalization "engulfing" the Gulf.

Notes

* Georgetown University. This paper was presented to the Globalization and the Gulf Conference at American University of Sharjah, January 26, 2003.
1 Vahan Zanoyan, "Time for Making Historic Decisions in the Middle East" (paper presented at the Center for Strategic and Future Studies Conference, Kuwait, November 2002).
2 "Measuring Globalization," *Foreign Policy* (January–February 2001): 56.
3 "Globalization's Last Hurrah?" *Foreign Policy* (January–February 2002).
4 Benjamin R. Barber, *Jihad vs. McWorld* (New York: Times Books, 1995). Mohammed A. Bamyeh, *The Ends of Globalization* (Minneapolis, MN: University of Minnesota Press, 2000), 80–81.

5 Jon W. Anderson, "The Internet and Islam's New Interpreters," in *New Media in the Muslim World*, ed. Dale F. Eickelman and Jon W. Anderson (Bloomington, IN: Indiana University Press, 1999).

6 Michael Hardt and Antonio Negri, *Empire* (Cambridge, MA: Harvard University Press, 2000), 15.

7 Stephen Brooks and William Wohlforth, "American Primacy in Perspective," *Foreign Affairs* 81 (July–August 2002): 22.

8 Jon W. Anderson, "Cybarites, Knowledge Workers and New Creoles on the Information Superhighway," *Anthropology Today* 11 (August 1995): 13–15.

9 See Smith in this volume (Chapter 2).

10 Cf. Malcolm Kerr, *The Arab Cold War: Gamal 'Abd al-Nasir and His Rivals, 1958–1970*, 3rd edn (New York: Oxford University Press, 1971).

11 Augustus Richard Norton, ed., *Civil Society in the Middle East* (Leiden: Brill, 1995).

12 Nazih Ayubi, *Over-stating the Arab State* (London: Tauris, 1995).

13 Manuel Castells, *The Rise of Network Society*, 2nd edn (Oxford: Blackwell, 1996, 2000), 410.

14 *Ibid.*, 411.

15 James S. Coleman, "Social Capital in the Creation of Human Capital," in *Social Capital: A Multifaceted Perspective*, ed. Partha Dasgupta and Ismail Serageldin (Washington, DC: The World Bank, 2000), 16.

16 Richard Rose, "Getting Things Done in an Antimodern Society: Social Capital Networks in Russia," in Dasgupta and Serageldin, *Social Capital*.

17 David Ronfeldt and John Arquilla, "Networks, Netwars, and the Fight for the Future": http://www.firstmonday.org/issues/issue6_10/ronfeldt/index.html, 2001.

18 Guilain Denoeux, *Urban Unrest in the Middle East: A Comparative Study of Informal Networks in Egypt, Iran, and Lebanon* (Albany, NY: State University of New York Press, 1993).

19 Robert Springborg, *Power and Politics in Egypt: Sayed Bey Marei – His Clan, Clients and Cohorts* (Philadelphia: University of Pennsylvania Press, 1982).

20 Diane Singerman, *Avenue of Participation: Family, Politics and Networks in Urban Quarters of Cairo* (Princeton, NJ: Princeton University Press, 1995).

21 Carrie Wickham, "Constructing Incentives for Opposition Activism: Islamist Outreach and Social Movement Theory" (paper presented at the Middle East Studies Association Annual Conference, Chicago, IL, December 5, 1998).

22 Hanna Batatu, *The Old Social Classes and the Revolutionary Movements of Iraq* (Princeton, NJ: Princeton University Press, 1978); *Syria's Peasantry, the Descendants of Its Lesser Rural Notables, and Their Politics* (Princeton, NJ: Princeton University Press, 1999).

23 *Arab Human Development Report 2002* (New York and Amman: United Nations Development Programme and the Arab Fund for Economic and Social Development, 2002).

24 Zanoyan.

25 Ayubi.

26 *Arab Human Development Report* 2002.

References

Abd al-Bari Atwan. *Al-Quds al-Arabi*. June 26, 2002. Quoted in "Views from Abroad," *The Washington Post*, June 30, 2002.

Abu Jaber, Kamel S. *The Arab Ba'th Socialist Party: History, Ideology, and Organization*. Syracuse, NY: Syracuse University Press, 1966.

Ajami, Fouad. *The Vanished Imam: Musa al Sadr and the Shia of Lebanon*. Ithaca, NY: Cornell University Press, 1986.

Anderson, Benedict. *Imagined Communities*. London: Verso, 1983, 1991.

Anderson, Jon W. "Cybarites, Knowledge Workers and New Creoles on the Information Superhighway." *Anthropology Today* 11 (August 1995): 13–15.

——. "The Internet and Islam's New Interpreters." In *New Media in the Muslim World*, edited by Dale F. Eickelman and Jon W. Anderson. Bloomington, IN: Indiana University Press, 1999.

Arab Human Development Report 2002. New York and Amman: United Nations Development Program and the Arab Fund for Economic and Social Development, 2002.

Ayubi, Nazih. *Over-stating the Arab State*. London: Tauris, 1995.

Bamyeh, Mohammed A. *The Ends of Globalization*. Minneapolis, MN: University of Minnesota Press, 2000.

Barber, Benjamin R. *Jihad vs. McWorld*. New York: Times Books, 1995.

Batatu, Hanna. *The Old Social Classes and the Revolutionary Movements of Iraq*. Princeton, NJ: Princeton University Press, 1978.

——. *Syria's Peasantry. The Descendants of Its Lesser Rural Notables, and Their Politics*. Princeton, NJ: Princeton University Press, 1999.

Brooks, Stephen and William Wohlforth. "American Primacy in Perspective." *Foreign Affairs* 81 (July–August 2002): 20–33.

Byford, Grenville. "The Wrong War." *Foreign Affairs* 81 (July–August 2002): 34–43.

Castells, Manuel. *The Rise of Network Society*. 2nd edn. Oxford, UK: Blackwell, 1996, 2000.

Coleman, James S. "Social Capital in the Creation of Human Capital." In *Social Capital: A Multifaceted Perspective*, edited by Partha Dasgupta and Ismail Serageldin. Washington, DC: The World Bank, 2000.

Conesa, Pierre, and Olivier Lepick. "The New World Disorder." *Le Monde Diplomatique* English edition (July 2002).

Crocker, Chester A., Fen Osler Hampson, and Pamela Aall, eds. *Herding Cats: Multiparty Mediation in a Complex World*. Washington, DC: United States Institute of Peace Press, 1999.

Dasgupta, Partha. "Overview: Economic Progress and the Idea of Social Capital." In *Social Capital: A Multifaceted Perspective*, edited by Partha Dasgupta and Ismail Serageldin. Washington, DC: The World Bank, 2000.

Dasgupta, Partha and Ismail Serageldin, eds. *Social Capital: A Multifaceted Perspective*. Washington, DC: The World Bank, 2000.

Denoeux, Guilain. *Urban Unrest in the Middle East: A Comparative Study of Informal Networks in Egypt, Iran, and Lebanon*. Albany, NY: State University of New York Press, 1993.

Devlin, John F. *The Ba'th Party: A History from its Origins to 1966*. Stanford, CA: Hoover Institution Press, 1976.

Dodge, Toby and Richard Higgott. *Globalization and the Middle East: Islam, Economy, Society and Politics*. London: The Royal Institute of International Affairs, 2002.

Donnelly, John, "Cheney States Case for Action on Iraq." *Boston Globe*, August 27, 2002.

Donnelly, John and Susan Milligan. "Cheney Speech Seen Setting Path to War." *Boston Globe*, August 28, 2002.

Eickelman, Dale F. and Jon W. Anderson, eds. *New Media in the Muslim World*. Bloomington, IN: Indiana University Press, 1999.

Fandy, Mamoun. "Information Technology, Trust, and Social Change in the Arab World." *Middle East Journal* 54 (Summer 2000): 378–394.

Fukuyama, Francis. "Social Capital, Civil Society, and Development." *Third World Quarterly* 22 (2001): 7–20.

Galston, William A. "Why a First Strike Will Surely Backfire." *Washington Post*, June 16, 2002.

Ghareeb, Edmund. "New Media and the Information Revolution in the Arab World: An Assessment." *Middle East Journal* 54, no. 3 (2000): 395–418.

"Globalization's Last Hurrah?" *Foreign Policy* (January–February 2002).

Haass, Richard N. "Defining U.S. Foreign Policy in a Post-post-Cold War Period." The 2002 Arthur Ross Lecture, Foreign Policy Association, New York, NY, April 22, 2002.

Hardt, Michael, and Antonio Negri. *Empire.* Cambridge, MA: Harvard University Press, 2000.

Haynes, Jeff. "Transnational Religious Actors and International Politics." *Third World Quarterly* 22, no. 2 (2001): 143–158.

Henry, Clement M. and Robert Springborg. *Globalization and the Politics of Development in the Middle East.* Cambridge: Cambridge University Press, 2001.

Hirsh, Michael, "Bush and the World." *Foreign Affairs* 81, no. 5 (2002): 18–43.

Kazziha, Walid W. *Revolutionary Transformation in the Arab World: Habash and His Comrades from Nationalism to Marxism.* New York: St Martin's, 1975.

Kerr, Malcolm, *The Arab Cold War: Gamal 'Abd al-Nasir and His Rivals, 1958–1970.* 3rd edn. New York: Oxford University Press, 1971.

Marks, Gary T. and Douglas McAdam. *Collective Behavior and Social Movements.* New York: Prentice-Hall, 1994.

"Measuring Globalization." *Foreign Policy* (January–February 2001): 56–64.

Murden, Simon W. *Islam, the Middle East, and the New Global Hegemony.* Boulder, CO: Lynne Rienner Publishers, 2002.

Norton, Augustus Richard, ed. *Civil Society in the Middle East.* Leiden: Brill, 1995.

O'Hanlon, Michael E. "A Flawed Masterpiece." *Foreign Affairs* 81, no. 3 (2002): 47–63.

Piscatori, James, "Religious Transnationalism and Global Order, with Particular Consideration of Islam." Ch. 3 in *Religion and Global Order*, edited by John L. Esposito and Michael Watson. Cardiff: University of Wales Press, 2000.

Putnam, Robert D., Robert Leonardi, and Rafaella Y. Nanetti. *Making Democracy Work: Civic Traditions in Modern Italy.* Princeton, NJ: Princeton University Press, 1993.

Ronfeldt, David, and John Arquilla. "Networks, Netwars, and the Fight for the Future." http://www.firstmonday.org/issues/issue6_10/ronfeldt/index.html, 2001.

Rose, Richard. "Getting Things Done in an Antimodern Society: Social Capital Networks in Russia." In *Social Capital: A Multifaceted Perspective*, edited by Partha Dasgupta and Ismail Serageldin. Washington, DC: The World Bank, 2000.

Scowcroft, Brent. "Don't Attack Saddam Hussein." *Wall Street Journal*, August 15, 2002.

Singerman, Diane. *Avenue of Participation: Family, Politics and Networks in Urban Quarters of Cairo.* Princeton, NJ: Princeton.

Springborg, Robert. *Power and Politics in Egypt: Sayed Bey Marei – His Clan, Clients and Cohorts.* Philadelphia: University of Pennsylvania Press, 1982.

"Top American Official: Hezbollah the 'A-Team of Terrorists'." *Haaretz* (Tel Aviv), September 5, 2002.

Wallerstein, Immanuel. "The Eagle Has Crash-landed." *Foreign Policy* (July–August 2002): 60–68.

Wickham, Carrie. "Constructing Incentives for Opposition Activism: Islamist Outreach and Social Movement Theory." Paper presented at the Middle East Studies Association Annual Conference, Chicago, IL, December 5, 1998.

Wiktorowicz, Quintan. "The New Global Threat: Transnational Salafis and Jihad." *Middle East Policy* 8, no. 4 (2001): 18–38.

Zanoyan, Vahan. "Time for Making Historic Decisions in the Middle East." Paper presented at the Center for Strategic and Future Studies conference, Kuwait, November 2002.

Zuwiyya Yamak, Labib. *The Syrian Social Nationalist Party: An Ideological Analysis.* Cambridge, MA: Harvard Center for Middle Eastern Studies, 1966.

Part IV
Globalization in the Gulf

9 Saudi Arabia's role in the global economy*

Rodney Wilson

Introduction

Saudi Arabia was once regarded as an open economy, but, in many respects, a closed society. The challenge for the House of Saud was to modernize the economy while maintaining traditional values and safeguarding the power structures of the state. To a considerable extent this balancing act between economic progress and social stability worked, despite the great changes that oil wealth brought through rapid urbanization and the arrival of millions of migrant workers in the Kingdom.

By the 1990s, the twin-track policy of combining economic modernization with the perseverance of the social status quo started to break down. This partly reflected domestic pressures, notably the rise in youth unemployment as the high birth rates but rapidly declining infant mortality rates of the 1970s and 1980s resulted in swift population expansion along with large numbers of Saudi Arabian citizens seeking to enter the workforce. It was also a result of high but largely frustrated expectations, as Western materialism had an increasing impact on the wealthy families, but the poorer sections of society were increasingly marginalized.

Closer integration with the global economy is consequently a divisive issue in Saudi Arabian society. Most of the royal family and the merchant elite favor economic liberalism, but others, perhaps the majority, are more doubtful about any benefits in a "trickle-down" system. These inherent contradictions of the past two generations have reached an apex in an increasingly tumultuous regional context, with demands for democratization by the United States and a not unsubstantial backing of the hard right of the Islamists.

This chapter explores the implications of globalization for the Saudi Arabian state and the economy. The government faces both conflicting international and domestic pressures. The special relationship with the United States that has been the linchpin of Saudi Arabia's foreign policy has come under severe strain. This has economic consequences in terms of the Kingdom's bid for World Trade Organization membership, which requires American support. It also has implications for foreign investment policy, notably the opening up of the Kingdom's gas resources to multinational companies, with the US energy giant ExxonMobil as the major player. The IMF is increasingly critical of the lack of fiscal discipline in the Kingdom. Saudi Arabia's governmental indecision on these three crucial issues demonstrates its reluctance to make hard choices. The balancing act has become increasingly difficult to maintain. Procrastination is only making matters worse as the economy continues its decline in GDP per capita, and the government debt continues to rise.

Regional hegemony could be one alternative to global integration, especially since Saudi Arabia is the dominant economy in the Gulf Cooperation Council. Wider Arab economic integration is problematic and may not serve Saudi Arabia's economic or political interests, but the GCC has established a viable free trade area, and in January 2003 it became a customs union. The extent to which GCC economic integration is a stepping-stone or an alternative to global integration will be considered in the final section of this chapter.

Saudi Arabia's economic openness

The peg between the riyal and the US dollar and the riyal's free convertibility were and continue to be major stabilizing factors for the Kingdom's economy. Oil prices are denominated in dollars, and most imports are paid for in dollars. The only significant protective tariffs are applied to goods manufactured in Saudi Arabia in order to give protection to infant industries, but otherwise trade was and remains relatively free.

There are no controls on capital movements, and investment flows freely both outward and inward. However, there are major restrictions on foreign ownership of assets in the Kingdom. Foreign companies could only participate in a limited range of investments as a joint venture with Saudi Arabian shareholders having a majority stake. Nevertheless there were pressures for liberalization of foreign investment laws, partly because it was recognized that with lower oil revenues, recurrent fiscal deficits, and increasing government debt, the state could no longer finance the major projects needed to reinvigorate and diversify the economy.[1] Consequently, in 2000 the Saudi Arabian General Investment Authority (SAGIA) was established, with one of the younger, more business-oriented members of the royal family as its chairman, Prince Abdullah bin Faisal bin Turki Al-Abdullah Al-Saud.

The new policy provided corporate tax reductions for foreign investors – from 45 percent to 30 percent – and has enjoyed some success. In 2001 Saudi Arabia attracted US $4.8 billion in foreign investment. This is over half of the total dispensed to the Middle East, despite the uncertainties resulting from the events of September 11, 2001, and their aftermath.[2] Nevertheless, this represented less than 0.5 percent of total global foreign direct investment flows, illustrating the scope of the total. Foreign investors were attracted by the Kingdom's resource base (mostly oil) and the size of its domestic market, which is the largest in the Middle East. However, licensing and visa hurdles, sponsorship rules, the tax regime, and legal uncertainties put them off.

The law was changed in 2002 to allow foreign ownership of property and to permit foreign investors to sponsor their own employees, but there remains considerable uncertainty as to how this will work in practice. There is also a lengthy list of sectors in which foreign investment is unwelcome, notably oil, communications and telecommunications, banking, and insurance. Saudi ARAMCO, the state oil company, is reluctant to cede control of its oil monopoly, and few want to see a return to the pre-1973 era when US multinational oil companies largely determined oil pricing and production levels with the Saudi Arabian government as a mere onlooker. Since the controversy over the major gas development schemes highlights many of the issues dividing those in favor and those against globalization in Saudi Arabia, it is perhaps pertinent to consider it in some detail.

The gas initiative

The gas initiative announced in the spring of 2001 was viewed as crucial for the future industrialization of Saudi Arabia and as a test of the Kingdom's willingness to become more open to foreign investment. The Kingdom has the world's fourth largest proven gas reserves, which are estimated at 6.6 trillion cubic meters.[3] A consortium led by ExxonMobil and including Royal Dutch Shell, British Petroleum, and the US company Phillips was keen to get involved in the exploitation of these huge resources. However, arguments over the terms and conditions impeded the negotiations, and these became overshadowed by events involving Iraq and continuing strains in Saudi–American relations. Nevertheless, the position of the Western oil companies would strengthen with regime change in Iraq, a fact that economic advisors in Riyadh and the Saudi Arabian government were well aware of. Therefore, as the situation in Iraq was coming to a climax, there were time pressures to quickly conclude a deal to ensure that many of the projects (worth $25 billion) associated with the gas initiative would get implemented.[4]

The failure of the gas initiative would be a major setback for economic diversification in Saudi Arabia. The schemes involved not only the harnessing of gas, but projects that include its use for electricity generation, water desalination, and petrochemical production. This would help the development of downstream industries in Jubail and Yanbu, and create much needed employment for Saudi Arabian citizens and investment opportunities for local businesses. If the present negotiations fail, and new bids are invited for a restructured scheme, it is likely to require a much longer time to implement and be on a more limited scale.[5]

There were three major factors that caused the impasse. First, the Western oil companies were expecting returns on their investments of up to 18 percent per annum to reflect the risks involved. But, on the most generous estimate, the initial terms offered by Saudi Arabia were unlikely to result in returns exceeding 10 percent. Second, the areas offered by the government for gas exploration and exploitation were deemed by ExxonMobil and its Western partners to be too limited in area to produce the quantities needed for the planned electricity, desalinization, and petrochemical plants. The companies estimated that the fields offered were incapable of producing more than 6 trillion cubic feet, less than half of the output they envisaged. Finally, Saudi ARAMCO opposed Western oil companies becoming directly involved in resource exploitation within the Kingdom again. Although the project involved gas rather than oil, there were fears that their penetration would reach into oil again.

Furthermore, Saudi ARAMCO is itself involved in gas exploitation. It has already developed a Master Gas System without the involvement of foreign companies, apart from contracting for limited technical tasks. Its Hawiyah gas plant became fully operational in December 2001, the fourth major plant to open. Saudi ARAMCO's gas production already amounted to 5.4 billion cubic feet per day by 2002 and was projected to rise to 7.0 billion cubic feet per day by the end of 2003.[6] Its executives argue that they can manage the gas expansion themselves with much more limited involvement by foreign companies that does not necessitate an ownership stake. In addition, Saudi ARAMCO can raise capital on favorable terms. For example, in September 2002 it raised US $2 billion from a consortium of banks at 25 basis points over LIBOR, with the condition that this be raised to 30 basis points if more than half the facility were used. It plans to build an $800 straddle plant using gas from the core area of interest to ExxonMobil and build an East–West link (parallel to the present oil pipeline) to carry gas to the western region.

Ali Naimi, the Oil Minister, has consistently supported Saudi ARAMCO. Consequently, he has been less than enthusiastic about the gas initiative. He was persuaded by Saudi ARAMCO's arguments that it needed more access to gas itself and that it was capable of undertaking many of the projects envisaged under the gas initiative. However, the projects would proceed at a slower pace than proposed by the Western oil companies. Saudi ARAMCO's impressive record of employing nationals also factored in its favor.

Gas in the wider context

Crown Prince Abdullah wants to see progress on the gas initiative, as he recognizes that if it fails the new investment policy would be threatened and its credibility undermined. Furthermore, given Saudi Arabia's rapidly growing population, the expansion of electricity generation capacity and desalinization cannot be postponed. The further development of petrochemicals is of some urgency; otherwise, other countries will build market share. In addition, given the conflicting views within the Bush administration on Saudi–American relations, the Crown Prince realizes the importance of strengthening ties with those who adopt a more friendly posture toward the Kingdom. Cementing relationships with business interests such as the Texas oil lobby and ExxonMobil would facilitate this process.

As a consequence, Foreign Minister Prince Saud al-Faisal has handled the negotiations rather than Ali Naimi. Both individuals accompanied the Crown Prince on his visit to the United States in May 2002. However, it was Saud al-Faisal who was more receptive to the points offered by Lee Raymond, the head of ExxonMobil. Although the gas returns estimated by the Western companies were raised modestly in the so-called "final offer" in September 2002 to between 10 to 12 percent, a guaranteed return rate of 15.5 percent has been offered on the downstream elements of the scheme (involving power generation, water desalinization, and petrochemicals). These higher returns are attractive to the Western companies. The major remaining issue is the quantity of gas needed for the schemes, a technical matter that should be readily resolved.

Foreign Minister Prince Saud al-Faisal has been able to see the gas initiative in the broader context of Saudi–American relations and Saudi Arabia's relations with the West more generally. He knows there is much domestic dissatisfaction, even anger, with some of the measures the United States has introduced since September 11, 2001, such as requiring fingerprints and photographs of men and women with their heads uncovered for visa applications. The interrogation of Saudi Arabian postgraduate students in the United States has also fueled resentment. Threats to reciprocate and introduce similar measures for American citizens entering Saudi Arabia, including oil company employees, further exacerbates matters.

Against these short-term difficulties, however, Prince Saud al-Faisal has to balance the long-term costs of not striking a deal with leading American oil companies. Gas could be developed more rapidly elsewhere, notably in a post-Saddam Hussein Iraq, at the expense of Saudi Arabia. Other GCC countries are also pushing ahead with petrochemical developments, as in Iran, which could undermine Saudi Arabia's position as a supplier. The electricity grids of the GCC countries are being interconnected, and there will be links to Egypt, Jordan, and even Turkey. Saudi Arabia has the potential to be a substantial exporter of electricity, but unless generating capacity is increased significantly, it could just as easily become a net importer. The stakes are clearly very high with the gas initiative. It will require political statesmanship to see beyond the present difficulties and realize the future gains.[7]

Privatization

The procrastination over the gas initiative has been paralleled by attempts at privatization. Although this might be regarded as merely a domestic matter, it has implications for globalization. In this regard, privatization implies a loss of state control and a possible takeover of the newly privatized companies by multinational corporations. In addition, those who are broadly favorably disposed toward privatization prefer a liberalization agenda and globalization, whereas those against represent more conservative and nationalistic forces.

The decision by the Saudi Arabian Cabinet on November 11, 2002, to privatize 20 key economic sectors has been widely welcomed by Western business interests. However, there was much skepticism over how quickly this will happen in the absence of a timetable for its implementation. The publication of the list of companies to be privatized has been long anticipated. The wide scope of the areas included caught observers by surprise, especially the inclusion of water, postal services, and the outsourcing of the maintenance of public buildings, including schools and universities.[8]

There is much opposition to privatization from Saudis employed in the public sector, as they fear the consequences for their jobs and the working practices of more commercially driven management. There is also some public concern that privatization will bring higher prices for basic services such as water and electricity. Also, there is opposition to the highway tolls proposed to pay for road maintenance. Yet, budgetary pressures are forcing the agenda forward, as the government faces unpalatable choices over how to deal with its large debts, with privatization seen by many as the least bad option.

Dr Ibrahim Al-Assaf, the Minister of Finance and National Economy, admitted in November 2002 that the privatization agenda was driven by the pressure of debt. The state owes US $63 billion to citizens who have purchased government bonds, US $32 billion to the local commercial banks that have given it loans, US $37 billion to its own pension fund, US $18 billion to the General Organization for Social Insurance, and US $24 billion to other organizations and companies, including contractors and farmers.

This debt overhang is severely limiting the government's power over public spending, as servicing the debt costs $10 billion each year. In addition, with increasing calls on the social insurance fund to cover sick leave in the Kingdom, where one-quarter of the population are diabetic, and with a large rise in the number of civil service and state-sector pensioners, the continuing depletion of the social insurance and pension funds to finance current spending is becoming unsustainable.

Although Saudi Arabia enjoyed a budgetary surplus in 2000 as a result of favorable oil prices, the slippage of the oil price in 2001 and its weakness in 2002 mean that there is once again a fiscal deficit. The surplus that amounted to 3.2 percent of GDP in 2000 became a deficit of 3.9 percent of GDP in 2001, and the expectation is that the final 2002 figure will be worse.

The only obvious solution was to diversify revenue sources and reduce oil dependence. In a report released in early November 2002,[9] the IMF urged the Saudi Arabian government to impose income tax and widen its revenue base given the continuing uncertainties over oil.[10] There is much opposition to income tax, however, and fears that although it can be easily collected from government employees, it will be difficult to ensure compliance by the private small business sector. The religious authorities also argue that as most Saudi Arabian citizens pay *zakat*, a type of alms giving, there is no need for income tax. Value added tax might prove more acceptable, as this is imposed on consumption rather than income. This means the burden is shared more widely, rather than being concentrated on politically influential high-income earners.

The privatization debate

The government's declared intention is to have a deficit-free budget for 2005. As debt has increased from 92 percent of GDP in mid-2001 to almost 100 percent by the end of 2002, radical measures are clearly needed. This is recognized not only by the ministries, but also by members of the Shoura Council, the appointed body that may, with political evolution, eventually function as an elected assembly. In the past, the role of the Shoura Council was largely reactive, but the council is starting to play a more proactive role in economic affairs. Its economic and financial affairs committee can call ministers to account. Although the government is not obliged constitutionally to follow the council's advice, it cannot simply ignore the council's deliberations.

One of the Shoura's most influential members, Ehsan Bouhaleeqa, an economist by training, has called on the government to reduce public debts by increasing non-oil revenue.[11] He argues that since non-oil income only accounts for 7 percent of total revenue at present, it is imperative that this figure be increased, especially if the government is to meet its commitments on health and education spending. Bouhaleeqa, like most members of the Shoura, is opposed to privatization, and indeed is even against the state reducing its stake in the Saudi Arabian Basic Industries Corporation (SABIC). He points out that the private sector has a poor record of hiring nationals as compared to the public sector, which employs a much higher proportion of nationals. Bouhaleeqa is doubtful that unemployment among Saudi Arabian nationals will be reduced if the state withdraws from economic activity.

Despite opposition from some Shoura Council members, the government is more likely to take the advice of the IMF report and proceed with its privatization plans. Ibrahim Al-Assaf, the Minister of Finance and National Economy, believes that if the private sector can offer services previously offered by the state, this will result in expenditure savings. Local newspaper editorials, which are becoming increasingly outspoken on economic matters, are also supportive of privatization, largely because they believe consumers will get a better deal and more efficient services.[12]

Although the November 2002 privatization announcement was described as the Saudi Arabian "sale of the century," only one date was actually set.[13] The sale of 30 percent of Saudi Telecom Company (STC) took place on December 17, 2002. This was a relatively easy sale, as STC has a monopoly of both fixed line and mobile communications in the Kingdom, which is unlikely to be challenged for the foreseeable future. The share price was fixed at US $45 per share. With 90 million shares being sold, this raised over US $4 billion. As STC made a profit of US $750 million in 2001, the issue was oversubscribed. One-third of the shares was allocated to the General Organization for Social Insurance, and one-third went to the state pension fund through a debt-to-equity swap.

More difficult privatizations include the over-manned postal services, supposedly second on the list. Since international courier firms have much of the profitable business and internal post is loss making, postal services are a much less attractive proposition for potential shareholders. Other problematic privatizations include *Saudia*, the national airline. Despite its services being recently repackaged to replace economy class with "guest" class, it continues to lose out to foreign carriers on its international routes. Furthermore, there are several Saudi Arabian businessmen who would like to establish cut-price airlines on busy domestic routes, such as Jeddah to Riyadh, to challenge the domestic monopoly of *Saudia*. Given continuing complaints over ticket prices, *Saudia* has little chance of preserving its monopoly after privatization.

With conflict between government ministers, Shoura Council members, and public sector bosses, the Supreme Economic Council under Crown Prince Abdullah will have to make the final decisions on the timing and methods of privatization. Compromise seems inevitable, with, for example, Build, Operate, and Transfer (BOT) schemes more likely in industries such as electricity rather than Build, Operate, and Own (BOO) schemes. This will ensure that ultimate ownership and control remains with the state rather than with multinational companies. Foreign companies are wanted on a temporary basis for their management skills and access to capital. However, this is more a matter of expediency rather than representing an ideological commitment to privatization.

World Trade Organization accession

Saudi Arabia has aspired to become a WTO member since its inception in 1993. Membership could bring substantial benefits to the Kingdom, not least in getting petrochemical exports to Western markets and reducing the prices of imports, as those trading with the Kingdom could obtain finance on more favorable terms because of greater certainty over trading rules. There has been reluctance to make concessions that would undermine local interest groups, however, not least in telecommunications and banking services. The Kingdom's negotiators also see it as unfair that those Arab countries, such as Egypt, that were already General Agreement on Tariffs and Trade (GATT) signatories were admitted to the WTO almost as a matter of course, despite having much more restrictive trading systems than those of the Kingdom, which has always been a relatively open economy. Saudi Arabian negotiators feel that the "goal posts" are constantly being moved without justification and that the WTO rules for accession are far from clear.[14] However, some Saudi Arabian observers have expressed concerns about the skills and understanding of their own negotiating team.[15]

A working party of Saudi Arabian and WTO officials has been laboring on the Kingdom's application for accession since July 21, 1993,[16] but progress has been slow on securing agreement on agricultural subsidies, pre-shipment inspections, trade related intellectual property (TRIPS), and sanitary and phyto-sanitary measures (SPS). Trade related investment measures (TRIMS) also remain a problem despite the liberalization of the Kingdom's investment laws.[17] At the full meeting of the working party in October 2000, limited progress was made. Despite negotiations being resumed in earnest following the fourth WTO Ministerial Council Meeting in neighboring Qatar in November 2001, talks seem to have stalled. WTO accession in the short or even medium term still seems unlikely, despite the other five GCC countries already being members.[18]

Bilateral market access agreements are seen as essential pre-requisites to WTO entry, as these ensure the support of WTO members. So far, Saudi Arabia has secured such an agreement with Japan, which supports the Kingdom's entry. The EU has also been supportive despite the Kingdom's insistence that it could not open its market to goods deemed offensive to Islam, such as alcohol or pork products, of which the EU is the world's largest supplier.[19] The re-entry of American oil companies into the Saudi Arabia energy sector would help ensure support from the Bush administration, even if there are continuing reservations about the failure to completely open up the oil sector and allow international banks and telecommunications companies market access. The strains in US–Saudi Arabian relations since the events of September 11, 2001, have undoubtedly delayed entry, which is impossible without strong American support. The Saudi Arabian ban on companies that have forged certificates of origin to disguise goods originating in Israel has not helped, even though most were Jordanian and Cypriot rather than American.[20]

It is recognized in the Kingdom that the WTO affects Saudi Arabia even though it is not a member, as the organization has 141 members that control 85 percent of world trade.[21] With the admission of China into the WTO in 2001, Saudi Arabia has become one of the four largest economies still excluded from the organization. Despite domestic opposition, a number of measures are being instigated to facilitate membership, most controversially the creation of special-ized commercial tribunals to replace the *shariah* religious courts for settling trade disputes.[22] Saudi Arabia's trade partners have long complained of the lengthy delays in resolving disputes and the uncertainties of the *shariah* court system. Privatization of the telecommunications industry and the opening up of the banking system would facilitate membership, although Saudi Arabian negotiators point out that Kuwait was admitted to the WTO with a banking system under protected majority local ownership similar to that in the Kingdom.

Some observers argue that Saudi Arabian products should be able to compete in the local market after WTO entry without significant protection, as the infant industries of the 1970s and 1980s have matured and proved their commercial viability.[23] Furthermore, the competitiveness of the petrochemicals industry might be improved by WTO membership. For example, the EU's unilaterally imposed tariffs on Saudi Arabian petrochemical exports could be challenged under WTO rules with the issue referred to an arbitration panel that might well rule in favor of the Kingdom. By being excluded from the WTO, Saudi Arabia does not have access to such arbitration. These gains for industry are likely to offset any losses suffered by local vested interests by the further opening of the economy. In the long run, a competitive environment locally as well as internationally should serve the interests of Saudi Arabia's consumers.

An "Arabian shield" policy as an alternative to globalization

The countries that comprise the Gulf Cooperation Council have limited domestic markets, but the creation of a single market through the customs union provides a greater opportunity to pursue policies of regional self-sufficiency rather than being small players in a global market. The EU is often depicted as having the option of pursuing a "fortress Europe" policy because it has a high degree of economic integration. Given the much weaker level of GCC integration, it would be misleading to talk of an "Arabian shield" policy in the economic sphere. However, it must be considered as a long-term strategic option.

Is such a policy desirable and feasible? The implications of an outward-oriented development strategy based on export promotion and an open door to foreign investment can be contrasted with a policy of import substitution with production geared primarily to the single GCC market. This used to be limited, but as the population of the GCC already numbers over 30 million and the Saudi Arabian gross national income is almost 50 percent greater than that of Egypt and 20 percent greater than that of Iran,[24] there is clearly much scope in being more inwardly focused.

An "Arabian shield" policy could offer a measure of protection from the uncertainties of reliance on international markets, whether these are commodity markets, notably those for oil and gas, or Western capital markets, in which GCC citizens have over US $1.3 trillion invested.[25] Replacing expatriate labor with local citizens can also be viewed as part of such a policy. Re-focusing on domestic investment and building human capital through increasing the level of education and the skills of the indigenous population can increase the domestic supply capacity of the GCC. Ultimately, it is this that will determine the region's natural rate of economic growth. Reliance on primary extractive activity would be reduced, with greater local value added in the energy sector, and increasing diversity in domestic provision of goods and services.[26]

Adopting an "Arabian shield" policy may imply a degree of protectionism, but this is very different from being isolationist. The so-called "Washington consensus" of the IMF and World Bank favors open economies, and the WTO, of which five out of the six GCC states are members, strongly encourages free trade. Indeed, supporters of the "Washington consensus" point to the considerable body of empirical evidence that supposedly demonstrates that liberal economies enjoy higher rates of economic growth than those adopting protectionist policies.

The evidence from the Arab World is more mixed, however, as throughout the region growth has been disappointing. Per capita gross domestic product (GDP) growth in Egypt and Syria, two rather protected economies, amounted to 2.4 percent and 2.7 percent per annum respectively during the 1990s. For Saudi Arabia and the UAE, both more open economies, per capita GDP contracted by 1.1 percent and 1.6 percent per annum respectively.[27] The "Washington consensus" attributes the low growth in Egypt and Syria to their protectionist policies, but their performance is superficially better than that of the major GCC economies. Not much can be read into this evidence however, as the level of GDP in the GCC economies continues to be dependent on oil pricing developments and the volume of crude oil exports.

Gulf Cooperation Council economic integration

Ministers from six Gulf countries meeting in Muscat, Oman, on December 31, 2001, agreed on far-reaching proposals to irrevocably strengthen their economic and military ties. The 22nd GCC summit was the most important since the 1981 Unified Economic Agreement was signed, as this has now been replaced by a much more ambitious program that aims to make the Arabian Peninsula the region's major economic power, with a gross domestic income that will dwarf that of its neighbors, including Israel, Iran, and Egypt.

The economic integration of the six GCC countries (Bahrain, Kuwait, Oman, Qatar, Saudi Arabia, and the UAE) will create an economic giant in Western Asia and transform the region into the economic hub of the Middle East and Arab world rather than being on the periphery. With a young, reasonably well-educated population exceeding 31 million (over 300,000 of whom are dollar millionaires), more than one-third of global oil and gas resources, and a modern industrial base that will include over 10 percent of world petrochemical capacity by 2010, the region has huge economic potential as well as the skills and finance to achieve a high rate of sustainable growth.[28] Oil prices have been the major factor driving economic activity over the last half century, but until around the mid-twenty-first century GCC market growth will bring about the rapid development of the service economy and diversified light manufacturing. Dubai has already become a world-class service and distribution center; its role in West Asia is comparable to Singapore in South East Asia. Other centers are following, with Bahrain as the region's financial center, Doha as the media center, and Riyadh as the institutional and diplomatic center.

The timetable for the transformation of the GCC from a free trade area to a customs union was brought forward from January 1, 2005, to January 1, 2003. Bahrain had already proposed 2003 at a previous summit in 2000, but the UAE was opposed to early implementation because its tariff levels were lower than those proposed for the customs union of 5.5 percent for basic commodities and 7.5 percent for luxury goods, which included most consumer durables and cars. Saudi Arabia reduced its highest 20 percent tariff level in 2000 to 10 percent, and signaled that it was prepared to go further. Consequently, rather than continuing the lengthy process of deciding which goods should be classified as luxury, the GCC Ministers in Muscat agreed on a single tariff rate. This was set at a mere 5 percent as a concession to the UAE, with commodities such as foodstuffs and energy free from any tariffs. The tariff reduction to 5 percent was implemented by Saudi Arabia in May 2001.[29]

Since January 1, 2003, goods entering Dubai and re-exported to Saudi Arabia and other GCC states are not subject to any further tariffs, creating in effect a single market comparable to that of the EU. The GCC entry point is determined solely by commercial and logistical considerations such as port fees and transportation charges. Due to the excellent network of highways linking the GCC states, cross-border road freight transport is expected to increase considerably, with containers from the EU arriving through the Suez Canal in Jeddah, and then been sent by road to Riyadh and the Gulf. Jabal 'Ali near Dubai serves as the major entry port for containers from East and South East Asia.

In addition to the single market for goods, there is also a single market for labor and capital. No work permits are required at present for GCC nationals working in member countries, although these are required for foreign workers from South Asia or the Mediterranean Arab countries. In practice there has been relatively little mobility, however, partly due to a reluctance to relocate, but also because of educational differences. Work has started on a joint GCC educational curriculum that would replace varying national curricula based on Egyptian and Jordanian models. In the past many teachers in the GCC came from these countries, but now most teachers are GCC citizens. The joint curriculum will bring a mutual recognition of qualifications at all levels. Universities in the GCC already organize many joint conferences, usually discipline based, with academics from departments in particular fields debating their research and teaching methods. This wider interchange is much more fruitful than would be possible within individual GCC countries.

Capital also moves freely between GCC states. Since 2000, locally owned banks in one GCC country are free to open banks elsewhere in the region. Bahrain's Gulf International Bank was the first to take advantage of this with the opening of a branch in Riyadh. Trans-border bank mergers are already being explored with, for example, two Islamic financial institutions, the International Investor of Kuwait and Albaraka of Saudi Arabia attempting to merge their operations and be listed on the Bahrain stock exchange. However, this failed due to personality factors and differences in corporate culture. Companies quoted in one GCC stock market can now cross-list on other markets, which improves access to capital without undermining share prices.

GCC monetary union

Adopting a common currency for the region will enhance the GCC market. At the meeting in Muscat, GCC Ministers agreed that a new common currency would be introduced on January 1, 2010, replacing the Saudi Arabian and Qatari riyal, Omani rial, UAE dirham, and Kuwaiti and Bahraini dinar.[30] Like these existing national currencies, the new common currency will be freely convertible into dollars, euros and yen, and is likely to emerge as the major currency of the Islamic world. It has also been agreed that the new currency, designated as a dinar, will be pegged to the dollar. There was some debate about whether the new currency should exchange on a one-for-one basis with the Islamic dinar, which is used as the Islamic Development Bank's unit of account. The existing Islamic dinar trades at parity with the IMF's special drawing right (SDR), which is in turn valued on the basis of a weighted basket of the dollar, euro, and yen. Since most trade of the GCC countries is based on these currencies an SDR peg had some merits, but with the oil price dollar denominated, the decision was made to keep the peg with the dollar.

A common Gulf currency will mean that stock market prices can be more easily compared, which will enhance the prospects for stock market integration and development. Saudi Arabia's new *Tadawul* real-time trading system has been successfully operating since October 2001 with all the Kingdom's banks linked into the system so that they can provide speedy and efficient brokerage facilities. Compatible systems are likely to be introduced by other GCC countries and should facilitate cross-border trading. Currency union should also facilitate the expansion of derivatives markets, most likely to be located in Bahrain. This may extend to oil and gas options and futures.

GCC integration and globalization

Overall, the pace of integration appears to have quickened considerably in the GCC, spurred on by the events of September 11, 2001, and their implications for regional security. The last major obstacle to the customs union was overcome in May 2002 with agreement on how revenue from the common external tariff should be shared. Saudi Arabia will receive between 45 and 47 percent of the total revenue, and the UAE from 20 to 23 percent.[31] The completion of the GCC customs union in 2003 also paves the way for progress on the much discussed free trade agreement between the GCC and the EU.[32] The EU saw a common GCC external tariff as a necessary precondition for wider trade liberalization and the establishment of an EU office in Riyadh.[33] Free trade would result in the elimination of EU tariffs on Saudi Arabia's petrochemical exports as well as on aluminum exports from Bahrain and Dubai and possibly help reduce the region's substantial trade deficit with the EU.

It is premature to answer the question of whether GCC integration will facilitate globalization, or whether it is a meaningful alternative to globalization. Humayon Dar and John Presley have pointed out how trade within the GCC remains limited, with external trade still dominant for exports and imports.[34] Further, they identify many non-tariff barriers as obstacles to regional trade and investment, notably the differing investment laws, limited standardization of products, bureaucratic formalities and the lack of a unified policy on the role of the public versus the private sector. Other GCC members may have reservations about Saudi Arabian economic hegemony, although there is no doubt a Riyadh–Abu Dhabi axis can achieve as much for the GCC as the Paris–Bonn axis did for the EU from the 1960s until the 1980s.

Notes

* Paper presented at the Conference on Globalization and the Gulf at the American University of Sharjah, United Arab Emirates, January 26, 2003.
1 The debt was estimated at US $171 billion, mostly financed domestically, with the banks holding around one-fifth. Brad Borland, *The Saudi Economy at Mid-year 2002* (Riyadh: Saudi American Bank, August 2002), 13.
2 Javid Hassan, "New Rules Spur Foreign Investment," *Arab News*, August 9, 2002.
3 BP Statistical Review of World Energy, http://www.bp.com.
4 Justin Keay, "Gas Hope for Troubled Economy," *The Times Focus on OPEC* (London: 2002), 7.
5 "Saudis May Restructure $25 Billion Gas Scheme," *Gulf News*, July 18, 2002.
6 "Rapid Strides Made in Securing Gas Supplies to Domestic Market," *Arab News*, July 28, 2002.
7 "Saudi Gas Initiatives Talks Push into 2003," *Middle East Economic Digest*, November 22, 2002.

8 Omar Al-Zobaidy, "Privatisation Move Dubbed 'Historic, Encouraging'," *Arab News*, November 13, 2002.

9 "IMF Concludes 2002 Article IV Consultation with Saudi Arabia," www.imf.org:80/external/np/sec/pn/2002/pn02121.htm.

10 Nadim Kawach, "IMF Urges Saudis To Impose Income Tax, Lift Barriers," *Gulf News*, November 8, 2002.

11 Mutlak Al-Baqami, "Privatisation Drive to Cut Public Debt, Says Al-Asaf," *Arab News*, November 14, 2002.

12 Editorial, "Privatization," *Arab News*, November 13, 2002.

13 "STC Set to Start Sale of Shares from December 17th," *Arab News*, November 19, 2002.

14 Badr Al-Nayyif, "Faqeeh Blames Lack of Clear WTO Rules for Delay in Entry," *Arab News*, April 19, 2002.

15 Muhammad Omar Al-Amoudi, "Saudi Agenda and WTO," *Arab News*, June 13, 2001.

16 World Trade Organization, "Current Status of Individual Accessions," www.wto.org/wto/english/thewto_e/acc_e/status_e.htm.

17 Mohammed A. Al-Sahlawi, "Saudi Arabia and WTO in the Light of MENA Experience," World Bank Working Paper, 1999, p. 6, www.worldbank.org/mdf/md3/papers/global/Al-Sahlawi.pdf.

18 Jamal Banoon, "Kingdom's Accession to WTO Still Some Way off Says Faqeeh," *Arab News*, October 2, 2001.

19 "Kingdom Can't Open Market to Banned Goods," *Arab News*, April 22, 2001.

20 "Saudi Arabia Bans Companies over Israel Imports," *Saudi Times*, August 5, 2002.

21 Wahib Binzagr, "WTO: The Good and the Bad," *Arab News*, June 25, 2001.

22 "Saudi's Plan Tribunals to Settle Trade Disputes," *Gulf News*, January 20, 2002.

23 Khalil Hanware and Abdul Wahab Bashir, "Saudi Products Will Compete Well in Global Markets," *Arab News*, May 2, 2001.

24 *World Bank Atlas* (Washington: 2001), 44–45.

25 Brad Borland, "Outward Flows, Inward Investment Needs in the GCC," *Arab Banker*, Autumn 2001: 49–51.

26 Nadam Kawach, "GCC States Hold Talks to Push for Customs Union," *Gulf News*, February 14, 2002.

27 Figures from *World Bank Atlas*.

28 Ghazanfar Ali Khan, "GCC Ministers to Review Progress on Customs Union," *Arab News*, October 10, 2002.

29 Abdul Wahab Bashir and Javid Hassan, "Kingdom Cuts Import Duties to 5 percent," *Arab News*, May 28, 2001.

30 "King Calls for GCC Common Currency," *Arab News*, December 30, 2001.

31 "GCC Customs Chiefs Set to Hold Key Talks Next Month," *Arab News*, May 4, 2002.

32 Ghazanfar Ali Khan, "Kingdom in New Bid for Strategic Business Partnership with EU," *Arab News*, August 6, 2002.

33 Rodney Wilson, *The Gulf-EU Trade Relationship: Challenges and Opportunities* (Abu Dhabi: Emirates Centre for Strategic Studies and Research Lecture Series, 37, 2002).

34 Humayon A. Dar and John R. Presley, "Ideals and Reality of GCC's Integration Programme," *Arab Banker*, Autumn 2002: 35–38.

References

Al-Amoudi, Muhammad Omar. "Saudi Agenda and WTO." *Arab News*, June 13, 2001.

Al-Baqami, Mutlak. "Privatisation Drive to Cut Public Debt, Says Al-Asaf." *Arab News*, November 14, 2002.

Al-Nayyif, Badr. "Faqeeh Blames Lack of Clear WTO Rules for Delay in Entry." *Arab News*, April 19, 2002.

Al-Sahlawi, Mohammed A. "Saudi Arabia and WTO in the Light of MENA Experience." World Bank Working Paper, 1999, p. 6, www.worldbank.org/mdf/md3/papers/global/Al-Sahlawi.pdf.

Al-Zobaidy, Omar. "Privatisation Move Dubbed 'Historic, Encouraging'." *Arab News*, November 13, 2002.

Banoon, Jamal. "Kingdom's Accession to WTO Still Some Way off Says Faqeeh." *Arab News*, October 2, 2001.

Bashir, Abdul Wahab and Javid Hassan. "Kingdom Cuts Import Duties to 5 percent." *Arab News*, May 28, 2001.

Binzagr, Wahib. "WTO: The Good and the Bad." *Arab News*, June 25, 2001.

Borland, Brad. "Outward Flows, Inward Investment Needs in the GCC." *Arab Banker* (Autumn 2001): 49–51.

———. *The Saudi Economy at Mid-year 2002*. Riyadh: Saudi American Bank, August 2002.

BP Statistical Review of World Energy, http://www.bp.com.

Dar, Humayon A. and John R. Presley. "Ideals and Reality of GCC's Integration Programme." *Arab Banker* (Autumn 2002): 35–38.

Editorial, "Privatization," *Arab News*, November 13, 2002.

"GCC Customs Chiefs Set to Hold Key Talks Next Month." *Arab News*, May 4, 2002.

Hanware, Khalil, and Abdul Wahab Bashir. "Saudi Products Will Compete Well in Global Markets." *Arab News*, May 2, 2001.

Hassan, Javid. "New Rules Spur Foreign Investment." *Arab News*, August 9, 2002.

"IMF Concludes 2002 Article IV Consultation with Saudi Arabia," www.imf.org:80/external/np/sec/pn/2002/pn02121.htm.

Kawach, Nadim. "IMF Urges Saudis To Impose Income Tax, Lift Barriers." *Gulf News*, November 8, 2002.

———. "GCC States Hold Talks to Push for Customs Union." *Gulf News*, February 14, 2002.

Keay, Justin. "Gas Hope for Troubled Economy." *The Times Focus on OPEC*. London: 2002.

Khan, Ghazanfar Ali. "Kingdom in New Bid for Strategic Business Partnership with EU." *Arab News*, August 6, 2002.

———. "GCC Ministers to Review Progress on Customs Union." *Arab News*, October 10, 2002.

"King Calls for GCC Common Currency." *Arab News*, December 30, 2001.

"Kingdom Can't Open Market to Banned Goods." *Arab News*, April 22, 2001.

"Saudi Arabia Bans Companies over Israel Imports." *Saudi Times*, August 5, 2002.

"Saudi Gas Initiatives Talks Push into 2003." *Middle East Economic Digest*, November 22, 2002.

"Saudis May Restructure $25 Billion Gas Scheme." *Gulf News*, July 18, 2002.

"Saudi's Plan Tribunals to Settle Trade Disputes." *Gulf News*, January 20, 2002.

"STC Set to Start Sale of Shares from December 17th." *Arab News*, November 19, 2002.

"Rapid Strides Made in Securing Gas Supplies to Domestic Market." *Arab News*, July 28, 2002.

Wilson, Rodney. *The Gulf-EU Trade Relationship: Challenges and Opportunities*. Abu Dhabi: Emirates Centre for Strategic Studies and Research Lecture Series, 37, 2002.

World Bank Atlas (Washington: 2001), 44–45.

World Trade Organization, "Current Status of Individual Accessions," www.wto.org/wto/english/thewto_e/acc_e/status_e.htm.

10 The impact of globalization on Arab Gulf States

Abdulkhaleq Abdulla[1]

Introduction

The Arab Gulf States (AGS) of Kuwait, Bahrain, Qatar, Oman, Saudi Arabia, and the United Arab Emirates have been exposed to direct global forces for the last three decades. They have also remained critically important to the global economy and security. At the turn of the new century, they are still at the top of much of global attention just as they have been ever since 1973. Their global geopolitical and strategic nexus will only continue to increase in importance. Indeed as world demand for oil continues unabated, the AGS will continue to be integral global centers of economic and political power.[2] These states have developed effective strategies for accommodating global pressures, feel quite confident with their role of global management, and know how to seize global opportunities as well as mitigate global risks.[3]

Yet, while worldwide attentions and connection are not necessarily novel to the AGS, globalization is. Globalization is ushering a new era in human history. At the turn of the twenty-first century, globalization is a mighty and decisive force that is shaping events and creating new social realities on world scale. Like most other states, the AGS are now encountering these new ideas and realities that are implanted by the uncontrolled forces of globalization[4] and attempting to figure out what and how to do, if anything: basically, if they participate in the global market then they must accept the cosmology-changing advertising and the political pressures from the West of guaranteeing capital investments in the Gulf and the resulting profit margins. Gulf states acknowledge that they are in the grip of forces over which they have little power. They are also aware that the world around them is changing at an exceptionally rapid pace. There is a new historical juncture, new world order, as well as new power relationships, new forces at work, and certainly new opportunities and unfamiliar challenges. This is the new world of globalization and the realities of the early twenty-first century, which seem to be as different in form as in substance from the cultural period that had just ended.

At this point, it is too early to ascertain for sure whether globalization is a positive or negative development in the course of human history. The only sure thing is that the process of globalization has already started and is rapidly unfolding.[5]

The forces are too strong to stop. While it is creating greater material benefits for the rich countries that are becoming even wealthier,[6] globalization poses threats of unprecedented proportions to most other countries – those that are called the periphery and semiperiphery by world systems theorists. Less developed and poor countries fear that they would be drastically poorer. There are sufficient reasons for many to oppose globalization, just as there are solid reasons to welcome its seemingly manifold benefits.[7] Some countries are already relishing the bountiful rewards of globalization; others however, are rightly frightened of perpetual servitude to the needs of capital in the foreseeable future.

The AGS are among those few regions that have developed mixed fairly positive attitudes about the ongoing process of globalization; for the Gulf states, the material benefits of being high on the hierarchy far outweigh the detrimental aspects. And these are strong states that can reduce the negative aspects through policy. They accept the fact that globalization is underway. The topic is much debated in public. As it is usually the case with all new events and developments, the official position towards globalization seems to be one of "wait and see." Yet, there is a qualified yes for economic globalization; some AGS, such as the UAE, are more receptive than others.

However, none of them is entirely ready for the more engulfing cultural and political aspects of globalization. Political and cultural globalization is perceived by the rulers of these relatively conservative Arab states as an unwanted intrusion and a menace to deeply held social values. Yet, none has flatly rejected globalization in all of its manifestations, which is practically impossible while most of their children are educated in English speaking preparatory schools and are exposed to the mind-altering foreign advertising of the consumer lifestyle. The next generation of rulers will be even more drawn into the cultural reality of globalism.[8]

This chapter tries to describe how the AGS are dealing with globalization. How do they view it? More specifically: (1) Do the various governments view it as largely positive or negative aspects of development? (2) How are the Gulf states responding, if at all, to the different representations of globalization? (3) How relevant are such widespread concepts as borderless world, shrinking world, and the end of the nation states to political strategies and long term realities of the AGS? (4) How do small yet oil-rich states respond to the demands of the "global village" and interact directly with different cultures? (5) How do they experience the new political space where politics everywhere relates to politics everywhere else? (6) What is the impact of the new global politics on domestic and foreign policy of the AGS? (7) What kind of political reordering, if any, is needed in response to the economic and cultural changes associated with globalization? (8) And, in short, will the AGS change or remain the same from the processes of globalization?

Taken together, these questions raise issues that deal with the prospects and risks of political globalization for the wider Gulf area. The chapter argues that the AGS are coming to understand catching on with the various forms of globalization quite unevenly. Some AGS are responding more enthusiastically, while others are clearly hesitant to receive globalization at full strength. The UAE stands out as the most globally embracing of the AGS and the city of Dubai is a global city par excellence, especially as a regional financial and service hub.[9] Nonetheless, signs of globalization are to be found all over the region. Some of the AGS are among the most open and perhaps the most integrated into the world market.[10] Many of the AGS are among the most ardent subscribers to privatization and free market ideas that underlie globalization. Yet, most AGS remain uncertain about the political consequences of globalization. Hence, these states may not be as receptive if it comes to democratization, or giving up their sovereignty. Importantly, the AGS have not lost control over their destiny.

Globalization

Roots aside, globalization can be conceived as a new world system and decisive economic and technological force is a recent development.[11] It is a new phase that has just come to world attention and with enhanced currency since 1990. As such, this intensified globalization seems to be the product of the collapse of the Cold War rivalries and "battle lines." It also relates to profound technological innovations that revolutionize thinking and acting.[12] Yet despite its relative youth, globalization has already unleashed potent ideas and economic forces that are beyond the control of single states.[13] It has shaped the world in new ways and in manners that are yet to be adequately comprehended. The globalized world seems to be closer, smaller, faster, freer, and somewhat easier for goods, information, and people to cross international borders toward the first truly borderless world.[14] But this borderless world is also a runaway world, whereby nations and individuals might feel that they are powerless to resist the forces of change.[15]

We are more conscious of our belonging to one world than before. Robertson asserts that globalization refers to two simultaneous processes.[16] The first is compression of the world into a greater material interdependence and interconnection that will reproduce the world as a single system. The second process is the intensification of the consciousness of the world as a whole, which is the more novel and serious aspect of globalization. According to this process individuals everywhere are able to internalize the global whole as they now relate to their immediate local and national surroundings. This global awareness along with greater socioeconomic integration, is spurring the development of a single economy, a single society and a global culture, but not necessarily one central government.[17] More importantly, without borders and spatial boundaries, relationships between people in various parts of the world will be as easily formed as between people living in the same neighborhood.[18]

If anything, economic globalization is creating a world of winners and losers. The AGS have decided to be among the winners in this rather tantalizing and overwhelmingly complex process of globalization.

The AGS and economic globalization

The AGS are aware that information technology is creating the first-ever wired century with all the prospects for prosperity.[19] They realize that globalization will profoundly restructure the way they used to live. Also, they have not tried to ignore or underestimate the transformation taking place in the economy. These realizations have been quickly absorbed by government officials and elites, not to mention large social segments in the AGS.

Sheikh Abdulla bin Zayed Al Nahayan, UAE Minister of Foreign Affairs, articulated this awareness to a conference on e-business during which he warned the AGS "must not be left behind in this global transformation of ideas and attitudes. 'To be e-active is no longer a matter of choice, (but) a necessity' to compete in the global economy."[20] The UAE, perhaps more than the rest of AGS, "possesses the necessary ingredient to thrive in the age of globalization." With its state of the art telecommunications, a well-educated multinational workforce, and a society based on the rule of law and free enterprise.

When compared to other Arab States, the Gulf states initially are making globalization work and are showing more confidence in dealing with its risks. This can be related to history, geography, and oil. Oil involves the AGS in global affairs and global influence. Oil has also made these relatively small states massively wealthy, which in turn made them more cosmopolitan and integrated into the international system than their Arab neighbors. Most of the AGS are increasingly involved in globalization but seemingly they do not have any other choice. Indeed, the Gulf crisis of 1990–1991 epitomized how closely interconnected the world system, local decisions, and regional actions triggered global responses and how the fate of Kuwait became intractably linked with the superpowers.[21] This crisis showed that economic and political globalization is an inescapable fact of life and that the conventional separation between the internal and external is something in the past.

Since 1990, the AGS have been coping with increasing globalization. These states have gained enough experience since the 1970s to deal with internal and external challenges. They have naturally affirmed open markets, free trade, and the World Trade Organization, which promotes free trade and economic liberalization. They fully agree about the benefits of free trade and privatization. They were the most committed free marketers well before globalization.

At the same time, these capital surplus states have quickly gravitated to the benefits of the information technology, such as computerization, miniaturization, satellization, and internetization.[22] The AGS are creating the first dot com and the first www world that unites them economically and culturally. Most of the AGS want to "seize the future"[23] like the West and become fully wired in the information technology rush. They are racing to hook up with the new economy and the e-commerce, as the wave of the future, well ahead of the Arab states outside of the Gulf.

The UAE has done most in terms of actually building the infrastructure, allocating the necessary investment, promoting its potentialities, and taking serious initiatives in the e-commerce market. The UAE, which is already the Middle East hub for business, shopping, and tourism, is launching the Internet City, the Media City, the Incubator City, the Sillicon Oasis, and the Internet University, which are part of a vision to establish the Dubai free zone for technology and media.[24] This is the first of its kind in the Arab world, which could determine not just the UAE's future but also the future of the region.

The UAE, especially its dynamic city of Dubai, is no longer dependent on oil that dominated events and developments since 1973. It is time for the new economy based on human and social capital, which is now comparable in magnitude to the earlier transformation from barren desert and subsistent economy to oil-rich country. Dubai is aspiring to be a be a visionary and pioneering global city. All across the city can be found global brands, names, events and issues and transnational companies. Dubai is a center with the greatest connections to the operations and many transnational corporations which have also been assuming a global role and turning into an essential unit in the chain of global command and control over input and output of services and products.

No other city in the Middle East probably has such tolerant, easy going and conspicuously liberal social lifestyles as Dubai, which includes entertainment, shopping malls, cinemas, hotels, leisure facilities, and resorts of world standard. Dubai possesses information and accumulated knowledge and is the preferred place for many consulting and legal firms, news agencies, advertising houses, television networks, and international journalists covering events in the wider Gulf and Middle East region. The city agglomerates professional talents in legal services, technicians, managers, and computer experts. These are highly paid professionals; wealth is made and spent in large quantities. A global city like Dubai is where a disproportionate share of world's most important business is conducted, especially in banks. Dubai is diligently preparing itself to play a high-profile global role as a command point in the organization of global economy.

AGS and political globalization

Yet political globalization has not been widely embraced by the AGS. These largely conservative oil-rich countries more easily deal with the economic and technical but not necessarily the political aspects of globalization and liberalization. Political globalization characterized by such threatening features as: (1) trusting the market and its invisible forces to regulate relationships between people and countries, so that local governments cede control to outside forces; (2) gradually losing their power to govern and eventually surrendering their natural sovereignty to the people as consumers who become responsible for the way their own community is governed, so that people sovereignty replaces state sovereignty; (3) the breakdown of the state to collective decision making of many states to address global issues; (4) the failure of the states to live up to the requirements of an open and globalized society where citizens are freely connected through global networks, which replace national structures and loyalties; (5) the emergence of larger political units, with their own supranational administrative apparatuses[25]; and (6) states are forced to democratize and embrace liberal democracy which is in conflict with the traditional ruling dynasties prevailing in the AGS. Any of these possibilities threatens the nation state, so that political globalization is not welcomed by the AGS.

Yet political globalization forces do not necessarily mean an irreversible decline of the state, nationality, and sovereignty. Most states will benefit from globalization. While dynastic sovereignty is affected, political and geographic sovereignty will remain established as it has during the last three hundred years. Moreover, many segments in AGS do not see political globalization as negatively as some critiques and government officials with ties to the current elites claim it to be. Many opportunities may arise with the development of the new world order and its democratic reforms. The new world order (*c.*1990) is palpably more liberal and committed to individual rights than its predecessor. Human rights are definitely high on the new world order agenda where people should be able to decide their destiny and governmental accountability. Political globalization also instigates global civil society, which is mostly comprised of non-governmental organizations to realize political and societal goals beyond the level of the single state.[26] Civil society organizations are building a more humane global order.[27] As such, political globalization seems to be a step toward a closer interdependent world with enhanced collective handling of global issues and problems. Moreover, political globalization not only brings more democratization but also could create more efficient government through better application of new technologies. The new e-government can ideally now connect with citizens online and hence become more responsive to a broader base of people, especially with little wealth and influence.[28]

Clearly the opportunities of political globalization are just as numerous as risks. The AGS are comparatively small and are still young. But what we should keep in mind, at least theoretically is that, even in a partially globalized world, almost all states lose control over their own affairs. The process of integration into the wider global economics and politics, even if benign, introduces stresses that demand considerable adjustments. Perhaps most immediately is the question of the role of states in the possible breakdown of what is inside and outside their borders – that is, what is within and what is beyond domestic affairs.

As the processes of economic and cultural globalization widen, the political space automatically shifts to the wider world order, in which the state can no longer control the flow of ideas and products. As a result, the internal policy instruments of the state become ineffective, and many areas of its responsibility must be coordinated with transnational actors. In one view, this is but one step towards the eventual death of the nation state. This futuristic scenario could also be feasible for some but not all parts of the world.

Let us keep in mind that the death of the state syndrome is nowhere to be seen in the AGS. The state in the Arabian Gulf is still the pivotal political actor. It is in control of its destiny and its sovereignty is untouched. Their internal policy institutions are more effective than before. The state continues to provide all the essential services: feeding its people; providing them with the maximum care, welfare, and education; addressing their social problems; and not deflecting any of its responsibility on to the global arena. The state controls much of what goes in and out as it has been doing since its inception. In this region, the state in its pure Westphalia form is alive and well, defying all predictions about the end of sovereignty and the eventual demise of the nation state.

This does not mean that the AGS are immune from the other implications of political globalization, especially democratization. The AGS have yet to address this first political tenet of globalization. Democracy is spreading all over the world and the viability of the democratic political system is universally recognized. Authoritarian practices are becoming antiquated in this world of fast and open communication. As the collapse of the Berlin Wall showed, governments that are used to heavy handed control of their people – "how they live, where they live, where they travel, what they say and even what they think" – are dwindling in number and becoming obsolete. Information technology is ending this kind of authoritarian rule. It is creating opportunities to experience freedom to communicate, which has not been there before. This is disconcerting for many authoritarian regimes still operating in the Arab world, especially those that do not insure the material well-being of their populations with the surpluses from oil extraction. The holiday is almost over for all the remaining authoritarian and dictatorial regimes that still believe they can control what their citizens think and say.

Many of the AGS will await the coming of age of the next generation to stop resisting this movement toward democracy. All, however, realize that the world is becoming more liberal and that democracy is not the dominant model of decision making. They are quietly responding to the worldwide call for democratization. Hence some liberal and democratic ideas are already flourishing in the AGS, but with considerable hesitation and trepidation. Most of these states look more democratic and more tolerant than a decade ago.[29] There has been some movement toward constitutionalization and democratization reform and even some relaxation of the old-style heavy-handed government control of the press. Elections, however controlled, have been taking place recently in many AGS. Local human rights organizations are allowed to attend to their business more freely. And women's rights and women's participation is becoming a public issue.

On the other hand, the AGS have not gone through the major shift toward being democratic regimes as seen in the former Soviet Union and Eastern Europe, for example since the late 1980s. If democracy means a system of government involving effective and periodic competition between political parties for positions of power, this kind of democracy would be a long-term project for the AGS. Yet democracy in these states seems to have shallow roots and can be easily swept away. But beyond this mixed picture, there are of course considerable differences in the nature of democratic initiatives underway in various AGS. One can place AGS along a continuum from Kuwait at one end to Saudi Arabia at the more conservative end with the rest in between. Kuwait, which already has one of the oldest democracies in the region, is deepening its democratic institutions. Oman is steadily moving in this direction. Bahrain has surprisingly taken practical initiatives and is experiencing democratic reawakening. At this stage Qatar is merely talking about democratic reform. The UAE, which is by far the most tolerant socially, is still waiting for some crucial political decisions. Saudi Arabia while making some constitutional reform is still resisting the global movement toward democracy. All in all, the AGS now have the choice of either opening up and democratizing or else resisting the movement to political liberalization. The latter scenario approach would eventually leads to stagnation or social disruption in this writer's opinion.

Visible sign of new cultural globalization. Globalization according to its opponents refers to the process whereby the people in the AGS and throughout the third world are incorporated into the capitalist market as passive consumers of standard products and nothing more. But the very heart of criticism of globalization is one that has to do with who is in control of this process and what control small states such as AGS have as they welcome it and go along with it, supposedly all the way? Nobody in the AGS has any definitive answer, or maybe there isn't one. When it comes to dealing with globalization we are all, for better or worse, seemingly blindfolded.

Notes

1 Professor, Department of Political Science, Emirates University, Al Ain, UAE.
2 Abdulkhaleq Abdulla, "The Arab Gulf States: Old Approaches and New Realities," *The Emirates Occasional Papers* 40 (Abu Dhabi: The Emirates Center for Strategic Studies and Research, 2000).
3 For more on the Gulf's importance to global economics and politics see, Ken Mathews, *The Gulf Conflict and International Relations* (London: Routledge, 1993); Tareq Ismael and Jacqueline Ismael, eds, *The Gulf War and the New World Order* (Tampa: UPF, 1994).
4 Sulayman Khalaf, "Globalization and Cultural Identity: A Theoretical Conceptualization for the Study of the Gulf and Arabian Peninsula," *Arab Journal of Humanities* 61 (Winter 1998): 52–93; "Globalization and Heritage Revival in the Gulf: An Anthropological Look at Dubai Heritage Village," *Journal of Social Affairs* 19, no. 75: 2002.
5 John Beynon and David Dunkerley, eds, *Globalization: The Reader* (New York: Routledge, 2000).
6 Stephen Haseler, *The Super Rich: The Unjust New World of Global Capitalism* (Great Britain: Mcmillan, 2000).
7 Jay Manzur, "Labor's New Internationalism," *Foreign Affairs* (January 2000): 1–11.
8 Mohammed Bin Rashid Al Maktoom, *My Vision Challenges in the Race for Excellence*, 2006, Motivate Publications, Dubai.
9 The Gulf Development Forum devoted its twenty-first annual conference, held in Dubai February 3–4, 2000, to the issue of the Gulf States and globalization. The proceedings were published in Ahmad Bishara, ed., *The Gulf States and Globalization* (Kuwait: Development Forum, 2000) (in Arabic).
10 Abdulkhaleq Abdulla, ed, The Gulf Strategic Report 2004–2005, Dar Al Khaleej, Sharjah.
11 Thomas Friedman, *The Lexus and the Olive Tree: Understanding Globalization* (New York: FSG, 1999).
12 Eugene Skolnkoff, *The Elusive Transformation: Science, Technology and the Evolution of International Politics* (Princeton, NJ: Princeton University Press, 1993).
13 For more on global trends and forces see Ingomar Hauchler and Paul Kennedy, eds, *Global Trends* (New York: Continuum, 1994); David Held, ed., *Global Transformation* (Oxford: Polity Press, 1999); Gerald Celente, *Trends 2000* (New York: Warner Books, 1997).
14 John Allen and Chris Hamnett, *A Shrinking World* (New York: Oxford University Press, 1995).
15 Anthony Giddens, *Runaway World: How Globalization Is Shaping our Lives* (London: Profile Books, 1999); Saskia Sassen, *Losing Control: Sovereignty in an Age of Globalization* (New York: Columbia, 1996).
16 Ronald Robertson, *Globalization* (London: Sage, 1992).

17 Malcolm Waters, *Globalization* (London: Routledge, 1995).
18 *The Report of the Commission on Global Governance: Our Global Neighborhood* (New York: Oxford University Press, 1995).
19 James Slevis, *The Internet and Society* (Cambridge: Polity Press, 2000).
20 Abu Dhabi, WAM, May 27, 2000 and September 29, 1999.
21 Anthony McGrew states that "the Gulf crisis of 1990–1991 stands as powerful evidence of the remarkable intensification of patterns of political globalization in the late twentieth century. It exhibits vividly the implications of a shrinking world." "World Order and Political Space," in *A Global World*, ed. James Anderson and Allan Cochrane (Oxford: The Open University, 1995), 14.
22 John Anderson, "Arabizing the Internet," *The Emirates Occasional Papers* 30 (Abu Dhabi: The Emirates Center for Strategic Studies, 1998).
23 Allan Oxley, *Seize the Future* (Sydney: Allen and Unwin, 2000).
24 It is worthwhile to visit the website for the Dubai Internet City to explore the diversity of its activities and future plans: http://www.dubaiinternetcity.com.
25 Kenichi Ohmae, *The End of the Nation States* (New York: Free Press, 1995).
26 Jeremy Brecher, Tim Castello, and Brendan Smith, *Globalization from Below* (Canada: Southend Press, 2000); Paul Ekins, *A New World Order: Grassroots Movements for Global Change* (London: Routledge, 1992).
27 Richard Falk, *On Humane Governance: Towards a New Global Politics* (Oxford: Polity Press, 1995).
28 The literature on e-government is expanding, including books on how to use the Internet to participate in politics and interact with government. See, for example, Allison Hayward, *E-Politics* (Indiana: SAM, 2000).
29 This seems to be the general consensus reached at the twenty-second annual conference of the Gulf Development Forum held in Dubai in February 2001, which was wholly devoted to the issue of democratization in the AGS. The proceedings were published in September 2001.

11 An overview of international relations from the Arabian Gulf

Fred Halliday*

In this chapter, I offer a generalized view of how the Gulf states fit into the wider picture of an internationalization globalization of the arenas of political interaction. This presentation and general analysis is taken from the views of Arab Gulf nationals.[1] The argument is constructed by observations, some seemingly anecdotal, on the changing position of the Gulf states in the continually shifting international sphere. The period since the 1960s was an especially tumultuous time of change in the Gulf and, indeed, throughout the Middle East. In this I include the GCC states, plus Iraq and Iran. The citizens of the Gulf have come to manage and dispose of enormous sums of oil revenues in the building of the infrastructures of modern states, but with fairly small populations (except Iraq and Iran). However, buildings and airports are easy to develop as the physical plants of society; the values, motivations, beliefs, and mental skills of an "informational society" basic to production in a globalist world necessitate more subtle and deeply penetrating strategies of development. With the current information revolution, the more information present, the more there needs to be a definition of quality, and the more there needs to be an absolute standard. Standards evaluating the information or the sources should be considered in a world with many voices and sources of authority. The same ethic applies to universities as official information producers. Everybody knows various educational institutions are not all of the same level. Standards allow evaluation and classification.

At a meeting in the early 1980s in New York, Professor Edward Said laid down a challenge. What he said was this: "In the Arab World we have built wonderful international airports, we have built wonderful palaces, we have built wonderful state-of-the-art hospitals, we have built wonderful roads but nowhere, not from Casablanca to Baghdad, have we built a single world class library!" (parenthetically, at least since Umayyad Cordoba, a thousand years ago). Gradual change in this regard is a recognition of what the difficulties of running a library are, that it takes time and commitment. Other problems of development are personnel and freedom of opinion. People can't say, "You have a book by Mr So-and-so on the shelf and cannot take it out. You are not allowed to study this work because it is subversive." In our case in point, you can have a world-class library, and in one or two years, if you haven't continually invested the money and the time, it will no longer be world class. This is to say that development requires not just physical infrastructure that can be purchased and installed readily enough, but that it takes an interconnected web of a myriad of trained people to keep it running and functioning.

To return to Cordoba, not only did it have the world's largest library at the time, it also had one of the world's first universities, the largest urban population in the world, the most scientists and book copyists. This is a critical mass of talent, what the geographers call agglomeration.

The relation of social science to this region also correlates. In the late 1960s, there were virtually no social science books about the Arabian Peninsula. While there were books on the rise of Islam and on travel, the social science books that you could use in a university course were virtually nonexistent. The first modern volume of social sciences that I read about the Arabian Peninsula was by the Yemeni economist Dr Said Al-Attar, entitled *The Economic, and Social and Underdevelopment of Yemen*. It was his thesis from the Sorbonne and was published in 1964 in Algeria. Since then many books have appeared, and there is now an extensive literature in anthropology, political science, foreign policy, economics, and gender studies. This literature is often written by scholars from the region as well as from outside. Probably the most authoritative history of Saudi Arabia was written by a Russian, Professor Alexei Vassiliev, who certainly considered that he would never be allowed to go to Saudi Arabia. However, he did manage to visit after the book was published. We are now in a situation much richer than when I was a student. Even in those days there would be books about the economics of Gulf States or Peninsula States. Yet, they weren't really books about the economics of these states; rather, they described what the finance ministry said. They wrote about subjects that were available as "hands on." This has considerably changed.

However, issues of judgment and quality remain: the kind of challenge that you face in teaching about the Middle East in Europe or that you face in the Gulf is not so much the question of accumulating information, data, and studies. It is about challenging the misunderstandings from both the East and the West that is the crux of education. Many well-read, well-traveled professionals do not know that Persians and Arabs have different languages, cultures, and traditions.

Other misconceptions, of course, prevail. One well-kept secret about this part of the world is when people relax together, they often tell each other political jokes. To illustrate, I have heard Gulf expatriate couples complain, asking, "What's wrong with England? You don't have any jokes," and, of course, jokes express something about the culture and politics of the country. Of course, the most obvious, old-fashioned explanation as to why these political jokes flourish is that they do so where there are limits on freedom of speech. Yet, even when you do have the freedom of speech, as in the Gulf, people still tell you political jokes.

Understanding the cultural other as inherent in globalization

On the other side, in addition to explaining about the Gulf in the West, there is a challenge of explaining the West to the people of the Gulf. Yet, the Gulf is well connected to the United States and the European Union. If you're going to understand what's happening here, you have to know what's happening in Washington. After the events of September 11, 2001, a lot of people said, "Let's stop relying on Gulf oil. These people are too unstable and you have to get out of that." Clearly, to evaluate the question and how far it affects Western oil imports requires knowing about the West and understanding its economic and political makeup.

The following anecdote explains how the West might be seen through local eyes. While in Dhofar in 1970, the tracks through the mountains were very narrow, and groups of people couldn't easily pass each other. When people meet coming from other directions, the custom of the region requires that you exchange greetings: "Kayf halukum?" and "Kayf antum?" and then they would reply meaning "What's the news?" "Kayf al Arab?" meaning "How are the Bedouins?" and then "How are the tribes?" An old man asked me "Al akh min wain?" (Arabic for "Where are you from?"). I said from England, and he asked, "Kayf al qaba'il fi inglatera?" (Arabic for "How are the tribes in England?"). I said as one always does, "They are all fine." Thus, studying the region is a two-sided job, and it is very important to maintain both sides of it. I am often struck by how little Westerners know about people in these countries even when sufficient information is available.

In the 1970s, there was an understanding, at least among the elites in the East and the West, about constituted progress and freedom of opinion. Since then, we have seen the rise, in both the West and the East, of ideas of difference and identity; now, it is no longer possible to argue in terms of universal principles and universal categories. Some of this is fueled by both religion and by nationalism. But this plays into the "Clash of Civilizations" thesis by Samuel Huntington, which emphasizes the limited possibility of knowing the other. Taken to the literal logical extreme, it would not be possible for Westerners to study the culture of the Gulf and it would be impossible for Arabs to study and know the West. However, I do think that every culture contains the possibility, the universal, and the particular. We need to continue making the case for universalism.

In his book *Season of Migration to the North*, the Sudanese novelist Tayeb Saleh relates a story of a Sudanese who goes to train in England.[2] After six or seven years he goes back to Sudan, and answers the question "What's it like in the North? What is it like in the land where fish freeze in winter?" and he says, "More or less, they are the same as we are, they are born, they grow up, they die. Some of them have hopes, some of them are fulfilled, some are not; as with us some of them are crooks, most of them are honest." And he goes on like this. This message is important for those who endlessly pressure us to believe in unbridgeable cultural differences.

International relations only arose as a discipline after World War I, and it was almost exclusively concerned with the relations between states, between governments, and between foreign ministries. It was concerned ideally with great states, with great powers – imperial powers – and, during the Cold War, with the West, Russia, and China. A course that I now teach called "The Great Powers in the

Middle East" downplays the role of smaller states who always had room for maneuver, and, indeed, there are certain benefits from being a small state. Basically big powers only have to give them a little aid. It is a mistake, thus, from World War I on to ignore the role of local states. But there is a third dimension: "transnational" means relations that are not controlled by states; things such as the flow of money, migration, smuggling, family links, the movement of ideas, and not dating since the internet and an advent of globalism that has been going on for hundreds of years. Both Islam and Christianity spread through transnational activities as much as through the actions of states. The challenge of international relations is to keep the role of states versus transnational flow in perspective. If you look at the history of Europe in the nineteenth century, for example, big events such as the unification of Germany and the unification of Italy were carried out by nationalist movements and nationalist leaders, much of it from below. But the rise of nationalism in Europe was as important as the Industrial Revolution and more important in the diplomacy of states for what happened.

More recently, during the wars in the Balkans, many in the Western power structure wished to keep Yugoslavia together so as to avoid much trouble with its fragmentation. But in spite of all the diplomatic planning and pressure, Yugoslavia did break into three different states. Thus, frequently people exaggerate the role of great powers and exaggerate how much they can really affect things, and ignore the role of local states and the role of transnational and social movements.

Greater Arabia as one cultural and political entity

Applying these generalizations to the Arabian Peninsula and the Arab Gulf in particular, the Arabian Peninsula (Jazeera al Arabia) is a political unit. There are separate states and oil has made the states more separate, but the tribal groups, the elites, and the migrants of the peninsula interact with each other as they have done throughout history. This "Arabian unit" has the potential to become a single political, cultural, and economic player of considerable world importance.

Before Islam, the peninsula was united by trading routes. Makkah and Madina were important trading cities, which explains part of what happened there. Although no unified states existed in the Arabian Peninsula since the death of Omar or Othman, the societies have continued to interact. The Ibadi tribes of Oman around the Jabal Akhdhar came from Yemen in the second century, and they are still aware of this fact. Ibadism as a form of Islam in Oman came from Basra in the eight or ninth century. If you look at Kuwait or Bahrain or Qatar, you are looking at social and tribal family interactions with Saudi Arabia. With the rise of the modern economy, thousands of Yemenis have migrated to the Gulf states and people have come from one part of the Gulf to another. People are quite aware of what's happening in the neighboring states. If there is an experiment in parliamentary democracy or a lessening in press control, the other states, big and small, will take notice of this. If Qatar allows women to drive, this is noticed by the Arabian Peninsula.

The fascinating interaction between Yemen and the rest of the peninsula provides another case in point. The 1962 revolution in Yemen sent a shockwave through the Arabian Peninsula. Yemeni president Abdulluh a-Sallal called for a "United Republic of the Arabian Peninsula." King Faisal of Saudi Arabia was moved to introduce certain important changes in Saudi Arabia, and he seized that moment to do so. This pattern of interaction continues to this day.

The interaction between the oil-producing states and the non-oil-producing states speaks to the unity of the Arabian Peninsula. Yemen wishes to join the GCC, although there will be other forms of arrangements to continue the political and social links. There have been very significant changes in the role of religion and attitudes toward religion in certain Arabian Peninsula countries. Kuwait and Yemen are seeing a greater influence of Wahhabi ideas and practices.

This unity of the peninsula is matched by a second factor, which is the way in which it as a unit is affected by what's going on around it. When I began studying the peninsula, I questioned how people write about the politics of the Arab world and never mention the peninsula. This is what I call "Mashreko-centrism" – only writing and talking about Iraq, Syria, and Lebanon and not about greater Arabia. Yet, the Arabian Peninsula is the epicenter, in some senses, of the Middle East. This has been the case since the rise of the Islam and continues in present politics.

Think of the Hashemites of World War I from the Hijaz, when they allied with the British against the Ottomans. Think of the role of the Palestine issue in the history of the peninsula. Any treatment of Arab nationalism within the Arabian Peninsula would consider the impact of dates like 1948, the first Arab–Israeli war, 1956, 1967, 1973, and the Egyptian and Israeli Syrian war. These dates impacted the Arabian Peninsula enormously among intellectuals, among oil workers, and among ordinary people. The advent of the radio in the late 1950s also impacted the region. Presently, Al Jazeera and Al Arabiya broadcast live footage from Palestine. What that is doing to the people's feelings, to their sentiments in the peninsula, and the people's view of their own countries is incalculable. The same is true with the influence of Egyptian nationalism. In 1956 huge demonstrations broke out in support of Egypt in Aden and Bahrain. The same happened in 1967, and the nationalist movements in Yemen in the north and in the south were very strongly influenced by Egyptian nationalism. This feeling grew in the 1950s.

An incident will illustrate to the wider social current of the times. Some Yemeni students of mine returned from Cairo. When they were coming back to Hudaidah on the boat from Egypt, they were singing a song called "Hurriya" (*"freedom/liberty"*). The first thing they had to do when they returned was to see the imam. Yet, they took a vow among themselves that when they saw the imam, they would refuse to kneel down and kiss his hand, for modern people shake hands in revolutionary Egypt. However when they went into the imam's greeting room, and he was seated with Sudanese guards behind him with their swords, the first student went up to him, the imam put out his hand to be kissed. The student tried to shake his hand but the imam hit him over the head and gestured to him to kneel down. And so he did. That is an instance of the conflict between the young educated people in Yemen and the imam, a conflict fueled by Nasserism.

Nasserism went into crisis after the 1967 war and was discredited among many Arab leftist nationalists because it was said Egypt couldn't fight Israel and couldn't defend the Palestinians. There was a phrase that described this as "the crisis of the petty bourgeoisie." Nasserism would be rejected, which was associated with the Palestinians and Jordanians then. The Yemenis asserted that they were not going to surrender to the royalists and were not going to surrender to the British, as Nasser desired. An anti-Nasserist outbreak ensued among Yemeni radicals, which was a pity, because Nasser gave good counsel. When a South Yemeni delegation visited his house in Alexandria in 1969, he said, "You started arresting your political opponents in the party. My impression is you're going to kill them. If you kill them then somebody else is going to come up and kill you." And that is what happened.

The relationship continued between Nasser and the peninsula in the 1960s on the historic links across the Red Sea between Egypt and Yemen and between Egypt and the Hijaz. On the southwest, Yemen is affected by the Horn of Africa and its wars. Indeed, you see around the peninsula different degrees of influence from external factors. For example, Oman has been closely linked to Africa since the time when it was a major maritime power. Perhaps 20 percent of Omanis who came primarily from Zanzibar in the 1960s speak Swahili as their first language. South Asia also influences Arabia. There are also Indians and Pakistani merchants there due to the geographical proximity to Pakistan and India. In recent years, the speedboats smuggle drugs at night from Pakistan.

What is happening in Iran and Iraq also is of fundamental importance in the Gulf and will continue to be so. The history of the Arab Gulf states has been shaped in many ways by what happened in Iraq after 1958 and in Iran after 1979. I remember talking to a Saudi official about relations with Iran. I was advocating the position that it is important to talk to Iran and he said, "That's true, but there is one problem. In Iran you don't know who you're talking to."

The power of the state

The third dimension of the international relations of the Gulf is its integration into the global system. While it is obvious that the Gulf has become increasingly integrated into the world market and into world society, this has been going on for decades through travel, trade, and education. One obvious consequence is the strengthening of peninsula states. The state machinery and the state apparatus have become much more powerful from oil money. The security is guaranteed by outside powers, analogous to the days of the Trucial States.

However, the strengthening of the state with oil money has complicated the unification of peninsula states. Simply put, if one can survive on one's own with all the oil revenues, then why should you share this with other people? It is best to garner the oil revenues exclusively. However, it is the state that has been able to employ people and that has been able to fund trade and banks. It is the state that has been able to build an educational system. It is the state that is the dominant actor in this part of the world whether in the monarchic GCC countries or in the republican countries, including, of course, Iraq and Iran. This returns to my earlier example of a large library needing a human infrastructure.

That role of the state is both positive and negative. Clearly, with the pressure for trade liberalization and the drive towards joining the WTO and conforming to Western norms, the role of the state has been questioned. It can help, but it can also distort economic development. Allow me to illustrate the problems of state-directed economics with a vignette concerning Iraq. A noted Palestinian economist went in 1974 to Baghdad, to a conference on Arab economic development. One evening something happened to the participants, typical of other dictatorships like those of Stalin and Fidel Castro. Suddenly people from the foreign ministry came and said, "We all need to get into the bus immediately. We're going somewhere." They were taken to a building, where they sat around the table. A few minutes later, a young man came in with a big moustache and a pistol on his side; it was Saddam Hussein. He put the pistol on the table and he said, "I want to know about economic development." Nobody said anything, then finally my interlocutor said, "Look! I'm a Palestinian, I will be the *fidaee*," and stopped. Why? First of all this man was not educated and could not understand what was being communicated. He simply wanted to know "How he could strengthen the state, his state?" He did not want to know about levels of illiteracy; he did not want to know about urban-rural relations; he did not want to know about agricultural programs. He just wanted to strengthen the state. By the late 1970s Baghdad and Basra had lots of cars, houses were re-painted, and shops were full. The money was re-distributed. But the priority of political power then came in to dominate during the wars against Iran (1980–1988) and Kuwait (1990–1991), which had such negative consequences for the Iraqi economy and society.

As mentioned the Gulf has witnessed an increased power of the state in all domains. This is therefore another major contrast between the Arabian Peninsula and the Gulf that I first studied in the early 1970s and the Gulf as it is now. Another personal citation will illustrate a point about introducing political pluralism (*ta'adudiya*) into the country. I said to the official at that time, "Why did you introduce the *ta'adudiya*?" He said, "What do you think? The President has told us to introduce *ta'adudiya*. That's the way it is."

Regarding the international relations of this region, it has seen major wars since the 1980s. It is one of the major focuses of world anxiety presently and will continue in Iraq. Yet, in comparison there are no major issues in dispute between the peoples in the Arabian Gulf compared to those that divide India and Pakistan, Eritrea and Ethiopia, China and Taiwan, or the Congo and its neighbors in Africa. There remain certain territorial questions. These include the islands (i.e., the islands of Greater Tunb, Lesser Tunb and Abu Mussa) for one, the Shatt al-Arab for another. The antagonistic prominence that these issues have had since the 1970s has been one that has been chosen by states.

Regarding the Shatt al-Arab dispute, the 1975 agreement between Iran and Iraq settled the dispute reasonably. Under Saddam Hussein, Iraq accepted the agreement and settled the disputed waterway and land areas. It also required agreement about mutual non-interference in each others' affairs. Of course, that ended with the Iranian revolution, when Iranians denounced Saddam as Yazid, the Sunni tyrant, or as a new heathen god, a new *taghout*. As such, the people of this region can relatively easily settle problems, as Bahrain and Qatar demonstrated through arbitration.

The final general point about the relations between the Arabs and the Iranians arises out of my own experience. As neighbors, the Arabs and Iran had relations before the Americans, the British, and the French ever appeared and will continue to have relations long after these Westerners have disappeared. Many cultural features are held in common, whether food, humor, or ways of life. These peoples also influence and enrich each other. While I have noticed an almost complete lack of interaction between the elites of the Arab Gulf and Iran, good relations continue among academics, security people, and journalists. At the time of the Shah and of Khomeini, the elites were more interested in visiting Paris, London, or New York than the Arab world. While Khomeini used the term *istikbar-il jahani* (world arrogance) for the United States, Iran's own *istikbar* exists vis-à-vis the Arab world.

From the Arab perspective, there is very little first-hand knowledge of Iran and the events that shape its policies. For example, when I queried the faculty from the University of Basra in the 1980s, no faculty from the Centre of Arab Gulf Studies had been to Iran, even though it was only a half-hour taxi ride away. They also didn't have many books on Iran. One Palestinian faculty could speak Persian and was an authority on Iranian medieval literature. Tellingly, none of the faculty members were *au courant* about current events in Iran even though they were neighbors and both countries were gearing up for war.

This is a deep-seated problem on both sides of the Gulf and speaks to historic patterns. The lack of familiarity with Arabic is endemic in Tehran. Soon after the revolution (1979), I was with the liberal National Democratic Party, which was organizing a demonstration against press censorship by the Khomeini government. They were designing their posters in Persian, French, and English; when queried about who could write Arabic as well, I was the only one available. I wrote at first in Arabic *Ash nidaal asha'ab al filisteeni* ("Long live the struggle of the Palestinians"). Khomeini was regarded as too Arab in his own culture because he introduced many new Arabic words into Persian. This lack of communication between the Arab and Iranian worlds will not be resolved by the occasional ministerial exchange.

I would like to point out certain problems that pertain to the academic study of the Gulf as well. Regarding the use of history, it is quite important that we understand the historical and cultural origins of contemporary states. There is also the use of history to confuse. For example, during the conflict between Yemen and Saudi Arabia, Yemeni officials would go on radio and appeal to the "Sons of Himyar and Saba'a." Saudis on the other hand would say "The sons of Adnan and Qahtan are fighting again." Please bear in mind that such rivalry has nothing to do with Adnan or Qahtan but simply with contemporary factors and especially with the fact that the Gulf states have lots of oil and the Yemenis did not. As such, the past does not explain the present.

Similarly, when the Iraqis invaded Kuwait in 1990, there were many explanations and, legitimately, many different interpretations. We do not know because we didn't know what was in Saddam's mind at the time. Yet, an Egyptian journalist claimed all this political conflict is the product of ancient rivalry, between the brown and the green, *a-asmar wa al-akhdhar*. So, such invocation of history really does not explain current events.

Similarly the Iran and Iraq war in 1980 was couched in the ancient conflict between Sunni and Shia. From an actual historical perspective there have been some conflicts between the Sunnis and the Shia in the Gulf, but most of the time they have lived reasonably peacefully next to each other. Moreover, after 1500, when the Safavi state ruled Iran and the Ottoman state ruled Turkey, they had fought occasionally but most of the time they did not. Thus, this war between Iran and Iraq in 1980 was not a product of some ancient rivalry. It was a product of two modern states, both of which bought into nationalism as a way of legitimizing themselves. In Iraq this took a form of anti-Persian nationalism and in Iran this took a form of anti-Arab nationalism.

There remains the question of the link between local actors and the great powers. On one hand, it is believed by some that local actors act at the behest of great powers. For example, when King Faisal of Saudi Arabia was assassinated in 1975, the reaction was: Was one of the great powers involved? The fact was that there was only a deranged Saudi prince involved. But the problem of attributing foreign culprits persists. However, sometimes there are conspiracies. For example, conspiracies in the Gulf abound (e.g., the 1953 coup in Iran and the 1956 war over the Suez Canal). Therefore, a way must be found of evaluating how far external actors really do control events. In this regard, they generally tend to control things much less than people often imagine. During the Cold War there was a lot of talk about the Russians having their bases in the Gulf, especially in Iraq and in South Yemen. Yet, the Russians did not control the Ba'ath Party in Iraq. The Russians also did not have control over what was happening in Yemen. In fact, they often became annoyed with the Yemenis, who they regarded as "adventurists" for their aggressions. This holds for the Western side as well; people say very blithely that Saudi Arabia is an American client and the Shah was an American client. They may have been more correctly identified as junior allies. The Saudis had a considerable margin of freedom, and they used it for their own purposes. Setting the price of oil would illustrate such a margin.

Conclusions

In conclusion, let us keep in mind that all states are part of international structures that limit their power. Even the United States, China, Britain, and Russia are limited as states. The Canadian Prime Minister Trudeau was once asked, "What percentage of freedom does Canada have?" He thought for a minute and he said, "Five percent." Yet, all states have some margin of freedom and, usually, a greater margin of freedom than they appear to have. The British historian Paul Kennedy wrote that however dependent the country is, there are three things that any state can do for which it is responsible: (1) the quality of its education, (2) the position of women, and (3) the honesty of its government. Although it is difficult to quantify education, the position of women, and the honesty of government, they are indicators of development. Basically, everybody in a society knows whether the government is corrupt or not. The countries in the Gulf with their oil wealth, and with their educated elites are in a very good position to use their very considerable margin of freedom. I would also add a fourth issue, freedom of the press, as another area of potential enhancement carried out by each state.

The long-term challenge of the Gulf is to produce a working understanding between the Arabs and Iran. From the Iranian side, I have to say both the Shah and the Khomeini people did far too little to promote it because they were resorting to nationalism of various kinds. If you look at the Gulf region since the 1980s, there have been conflicts between Iran and the Arab states that have side tracked much of longer-term collaborative efforts. The goal is to get an understanding between the three major powers in the Gulf at the same time – Saudi Arabia, Iraq, and Iran. At the moment, if you have an understanding between two, then you have hostility toward the other.

Finally, let us return to the theoretical system of international relations and its three analytical dimensions – the great powers, the local states, and internal change. It belabors the obvious that these societies are changing and have been changing for a long time. There have been protests and revolts and critiques by intellectuals in the Gulf; some of it has succeeded and much of it has not. But one cannot write about the history of the Gulf simply by writing about the history of the governments and rulers. There is a history from below, usually constructed through anthropology and sociology, and a history from above, constructed by historians and political scientists. I see all my own work largely as history from below. The decades of revolt and radical transformation that began with the Yemeni revolution in 1962 went through the OPEC challenges of the early 1970s. A new period of political negotiation has begun, which is referred to as globalism and is the crux of this volume. This movement from below is going to continue and is going to affect the foreign policy of states. The demands of people for competitive education and then for employment are not going to be something that the states can ignore. There are growing requirements externally, such as WTO compliance, but also demands internally for transparency of statistics and oil revenue that have hitherto been outside of the normative expectations of governmental accountability. Therefore, the future of the Gulf is going to depend upon how the social and the political change are managed. There are some rulers who have been sagacious and others who have been less wise. Those changes will in part be affected by the outside world but they will largely be determined on what's going on internally within the Gulf societies. It remains to be seen if a stable political system can emerge in Iraq. What happens in the GCC countries, all of which are experimenting with various reforms? Things are moving and, without overstating it, each one will be affected by the others. There is no way that one GCC country can suddenly experiment with elements of democracy and its neighbors not react. There is an element of coordination and mutual stimulation between them all. I don't argue that foreign policy or external relations of states are solely determined by the internal dynamics. However, internal social and political change is going to be important in the coming years. That will determine how far it is possible for Gulf States to take a margin of the freedom that they have and use it well, both at home and on the international stage.

Notes

* Professor of International Relations, London School of Economics.
1 This chapter is adapted from a lecture given at the Gulf Research Centre, Dubai, UAE, October 20, 2003.
2 London: Quartet Books Ltd (1980).

12 Foreign matter

The place of strangers in Gulf society

*Paul Dresch**

The GCC states, by comparison both with neighbors and with states elsewhere, have a large percentage of foreign residents. Oman counts almost 30 percent foreigners in its total population; Saudi Arabia counts a little over that, and in some states, such as Qatar, the figure is more like 80 percent.[1] Official or quasi-official figures are probably underestimates. Obviously, distributions are uneven within certain states, as for instance the foreign presence in Ras al-Khaimah or Fujairah is less striking than that in Dubai or Abu Dhabi. It might be argued, also, that the effect is most marked in the region's cities, which have become, in Bourgey's now famous phrase, "towers of Babel."[2] But everywhere a great deal turns on the distinction between national or citizen (*muwāṭin*) and expatriate or migrant (*wāfid*).

This distinction between citizen and foreigner is a social phenomenon, a question of arbitrary self-classification, which recurs throughout the modern world. It takes different forms, however, and the implications differ. The usual pattern with European states in recent decades, for instance, has been to draw a line coincident with physical boundaries, placing foreigners notionally "outside" the polity: the corresponding problem in public rhetoric is of immigrants and border controls. The Gulf states, with large non-citizen populations inside their frontiers, must draw the line by other means, which I suspect prefigure what we all face as part of globalization or *al-ʿawlamah*.[3] The rule with modern states seems to be that the greater the degree of economic and political interconnectedness, the greater the stress on exclusivity, expressed often in essentialized terms of "culture."

Foreigners as a structural feature

If gross population figures for the Gulf states are often striking, those for the workforce are even more so. In Kuwait, for instance, 92 percent of Kuwaitis who work at all do so for the government;[4] in the UAE, as well, nationals show a marked preference for government employment, whether federal or local, and they make up only 10 percent of the workforce overall.[5] As for Saudi Arabia, Prince al-Walīd bin Ṭalāl – himself no stranger to global commerce – has said that, excluding the small efficient oil sector, over 98 percent of the local (i.e., citizen or national) workforce is "relatively unproductive."[6] The private sector, on which hopes are pinned, employs mainly foreigners in most Gulf states. The public sector employs a great many also, and overall, for each working national or citizen in 1997, there were two foreign workers in Bahrain, five in Kuwait and Qatar, and nine in the UAE.[7]

In Bahrain, Oman, and the UAE, over 80 percent of foreigners are now Asian, and even in Kuwait, which long showed a preference for Arab workers, 63 percent of all foreigners were Asian by 1996. This drift from Arab to Asian labor precedes the upheavals of 1990–1991:[8] it does not reduce to short-term political decisions. Analyses of the Gulf economies' effects on the Arab world[9] have meanwhile rather died away, and patterns of global connectedness must often be sought in specialist journals concerned with migration. Regional implications have not disappeared, however. Yemenis, for instance, who before 1990 had privileged access to several Gulf states,[10] were delighted, at Muscat in December 2001, to gain membership of certain GCC committees and some thought this prefaced full membership.[11] But if the rights and status of GCC citizens were given to what potentially is an "internal" working class (an Arabian population as large as the rest combined), the existing structure of Gulf societies would evaporate.

The large foreign presence is dealt with conventionally by the Gulf press as a "demographic imbalance" as if somehow, with a few twists of policy, it would go away.[12] One might suggest instead that these are rather specialized polities, to which the distinction between citizen and migrant is integral. Indeed, the import of non-citizen labor is the structural mirror image of, say, the US outsourcing manufacture to Third World countries, and it illustrated something like "globalization" before the term was ever coined. The disjunction between identity and territory, however, makes comprehension difficult at local level:

> Most Kuwaitis I talked to about the immigrants ... assumed they would soon be on their way. The labourers would have to return home once the construction work was finished, while young Kuwaitis now at school or in universities abroad would soon be able to take over the work of the better educated ... it would not be many years before most of the population would again consist of Kuwaitis.[13]

The field-notes from which that passage derives were written some fifty years ago. That is not to say things will go on unchanged for another fifty. It is to suggest, however, that a large on-shore foreign presence has long been a part of Gulf society and its structural significance usually remains unthought.

Analysis of the Gulf's position in a world economy has meanwhile focused on the way in which wealth (and thus power) is concentrated in a few hands. Something like this long ago informed the work of Muḥammad al-Rumayḥī and Khaldūn al-Naqeeb, and more recently, in adapted form, it occurs in Sulaymān Khalaf's analyses where the stress falls on consumerism in a distinctively cultural approach to Gulf realities.[14] In political science, of course, "rentier state theory" was long dominant. The theory itself has lost ground among Western writers primarily as a matter of academic fashion, though some of the substantive criticisms are fair. The idea of "buying off" political dissent, for instance, which one finds in Luciani's and Beblawi's formulations,[15] is far too simple. But, just as important for the present purpose, rentier theory treated local economies as mere epiphenomena of the world trade in hydrocarbons, where in fact these economies sustain an important part of citizens' income and themselves are sustained in part by on-shore non-citizen labor.

Whatever the significance of direct handouts, initial prosperity was encountered in related ways by all the Gulf states and rulers. First, whatever land was not *milk* (personal "property" in something close to the sense in Islamic legal theory) was declared to be that of rulers and was then apportioned to and redistributed among citizens, not least as *ta'wīd* or compensation in urban improvement schemes. Citizens were everywhere established as privileged landholders. The second distinctive innovation of Gulf societies was the system of *kafālah* or "sponsorship," whereby citizens were established as privileged employers and business-owners, drawing surplus from the foreign presence as they do from real estate. Many of the national population are themselves therefore minor rentiers.[16] Their interests may well be at odds with "national" economic planning, just as may those of British mortgage-holders, American investors in company stock, or stakeholders in the French state-pension scheme.

To reduce the number of foreigners seems attractive in general terms, much dwelled upon by the Gulf press;[17] more reflective work concerned with local identity and values makes a similarly general appeal to reduce the foreign presence and thus reassert control.[18] In specific terms, however, as one finds rent for property or one's income from little stores declining, pressure is brought to reverse the process and the foreign population again rises. The contradiction is only sharpened as global pressure is brought on the state economy and we enter the logic of what Henry and Springborg call "globalizing monarchy."[19]

The ability of Gulf elites to interact as they do with global pressures depends not only on control of localized resources (hydrocarbons are still of huge importance, at first hand or second hand) but on speaking for nation states whose people they represent and whose territory they control. They have, so to speak, constituencies. Indeed their care for these constituencies might be thought rather greater than that of North Atlantic elites for their own fellow-citizens, though the wishes of citizens are everywhere fraught with paradox. Throughout the Gulf, there have been campaigns to "nationalize" certain areas of employment, for instance. The wish has been vigorously expressed, though seldom pursued with vigor, for Saudization, Kuwaitization, Omanization, and Emiratization,[20] and progress has been made in specific cases, but the overall balance of demography hardly shifts in the local populations' favor, for the reasons outlined above. Yet whichever strategy is chosen or avoided, the nation state is pushed always to the fore. Adaptation to global economic constraints requires governmental action – whether on quotas, exclusions, or access to forms of training – if citizens are not to be marginalized by foreign capital and the polity in effect dissolved.

Kinship and closeness

In these circumstances the importance of citizenship does not dwindle away, as proponents of globalization would predict or wish, but increases over time, and the line around the privileged status of "national" or *muwāṭin* is drawn ever more tightly. This is not to deny the enormous inequalities among citizens themselves. But the smaller polities of the Gulf may be seen as "ethnocracies,"[21] in which all citizens enjoy a certain privileged status, and the distinctive identity of citizens is protected in sometimes unusual ways, which emphasize, again, the place of governments. The process is little noticed because the terms employed are usually so familiar, as for instance in the case of marriage.

Saudi Arabia, Oman, and Qatar have all imposed laws that restrict nationals' marriage choices if the prospective spouse is from elsewhere than the GCC, and debates about "marriage with foreigners" have recurred more widely.[22] What used to be archetypically a matter of family choice and of status concerns among families has in several Gulf states become a matter of public concern and of government intervention, centered on, for instance, the Interior Ministry, with the aim of preserving national identity.[23] Though this now seems for many people to have the value of common sense, to have suggested such a thing even fifty years ago would have been eccentric. The present arrangements suggest a profound, if tacit, shift of moral order.

If marriage as an axis of relationship (or potential relationship) among persons has quietly become subject to public laws, so has the axis of shared descent. In an older world, genealogy was constructed as one went along, and Gavrielides spells out the implications for Kuwait in the late 1980s: "Noble tribes ... never publish their genealogies. To crystallize such an important part of the oral tradition would deprive it of one of its most important features, its flexibility, which responds to popular opinion and changing circumstances."[24] The management of such ambiguity was once the very stuff of political life locally, and nowhere was there full agreement as to family or collective history. Though ambiguity has not disappeared, the arbiter is now a state apparatus, which rules upon genetic facts.

Kuwait, in 1959, thus defined nationality through shared male descent and residence at a critical date, and the result, notoriously, was a large, ill-defined group of people "without" nationality (the *bidūn*), who claimed connection with Kuwait and Kuwaiti families but possessed no documented status as part of Kuwait or of its neighbors. Though less written of, or even spoken of, the phenomenon recurs elsewhere, in sometimes surprising places such as Sharjah. The continuing suggestion from intellectuals that long-term Arab residents should be given citizenship[25] meanwhile makes little headway, while families resident for generations remain in limbo. And the new claims to exclusivity use the old terms of genealogy. They are not quite the same, however, as the old "relatedness" or the theory of *nasab* in Islamic law. The process is most advanced, as usual, in Kuwait's case, where DNA samples might be taken to see who is and who is not Kuwaiti,[26] and to paraphrase Freud, biology becomes destiny.

One important result is that what was previously judged by diffuse public opinion is now judged by state bureaucracy. An anthropologist, meanwhile, cannot help noticing a shift from agnatic to bilateral or cognatic reckoning: instead of counting only male descent, one now counts on both sides of the family and reckons kinship relatedness to, for instance, "the fourth degree" (*al-darajah al-rābiʻah*).

It always mattered, of course, who one's mother was, but it mattered in local ways. Now the terms are generalized. The practice of female hypergamy (girls always marry up, ideally) allowed for status claims to be managed subtly and for successful groups to absorb or redefine their neighbors, associates, and erstwhile rivals in a network of potential relatedness that extended from Africa to Southeast Asia, and indeed beyond. The shift to generalized cognatic claims means an essentialized, bounded identity of a kind that was simply not there before. Not least in Kuwait, one sees something like European ideas of "race" evolving.

The old distinction was between *qarīb* and *gharīb*, those "close" as kin or neighbors and those "strange" – whether on account of distance and unfamiliarity or on account of some inherited social difference. There were no clear lines, and all was a matter of degree and interpretation. What now we are usually dealing with are claims to a bounded identity threatened by a foreign presence,[27] as if the number of obvious "strangers" had forced on Gulf societies a way of thought described by Adam Ferguson for Europe in the eighteenth century: "The titles of *fellow citizen* and *countryman* unopposed to those of *alien* and *foreigner*, to which they refer, would fall into disuse and lose their meaning."

Space and identity

The distinction between *qarīb* and *gharīb*, like modern arrangements, was shot through internally with ideas of hierarchy, moral status, and control. Important families or groups always had retainers who were not kin; the fact that people shared a house or *farīj* (a "quarter" of a town or village) did not make them equals. The relation between moral separation (or self-definition) and spatial separation was therefore complex. But outright strangers who were resident in Gulf society were conceived of as the protégés of rulers.[28] With the development of oil wealth, and then with the boom or *tufrah* of the 1970s, the number of strangers in the Gulf grew exponentially. These strangers were no longer merely guests or retainers, and their presence came to be felt threatening,[29] which itself has come to be expressed in terms not only of biology but of "culture" and also of geographic space.

An early result of immigration was the social distance established between locals and foreigners.[30] The effect is not limited, however, to foreigners in the simplest sense (that is to *ajānib*, the non-Arabs), for non-GCC Arabs are often excluded also,[31] and fellow nationals may divide out among themselves, their sensitivity to difference perhaps heightened by modern circumstance. The Bahraini village of 'Askar, on the southeast coast, provides a case from as late as the 1980s, where 200 or so "local" families, of the Āl Rumayḥī and Āl Bū 'Aynayn, expelled a newly arrived baker of (distant) Iranian descent, preferring 10–15 minutes' drive for a loaf of bread to having their privacy disturbed by a resident *gharīb* or "stranger." In none of these cases are we looking at simple admixture of populations.

Philipe Fargues drew attention in the Kuwaiti case to the way that the overall ratio of foreigners to nationals is seldom reproduced at the level of city districts, which tend to be predominantly one group or another.[32] That would be so in Abu Dhabi, too, where villas make up only about 6 percent of the rental market. The logic of local rent, which we touched on earlier, is apparent in the fact that the vast majority of Abu Dhabi citizens are housed in villas, whether gifted them by their emirate's government or built themselves, and foreigners cannot own property; the majority of rental properties are apartments. Villas, of course, relate to a status one can analyze in class terms or ethnic-cum-national terms, but Khālidīyah is perhaps the one area of Abu Dhabi full of villas and yet also full of foreigners.[33] Meanwhile the so-called Central Business District and, say, Baṭīn, which is very much a villa-zone, provide a striking contrast between high-rise and low-rise areas, which maps closely onto housing density, employment patterns, and national status,[34] the dwellers in high-rise areas being those who pay rent. "Cultural" difference is then attributed easily to the places where people live.

Sharjah's development shows a different rhythm but in some ways a similar result. As roads and building-plots were developed in the 1970s, so compensation (*ta'wīd*) and a tendency to rent what one had to foreigners, moved the national population slowly inland.[35] As of 2000–2001, one found a line roughly along Ḥamad bin Saqr street: south of there were predominantly nationals, but north of there most nationals had rented out their property and themselves had moved on to Shahbā'. The course of development is more visible in Sharjah than in Abu Dhabi. Older housing projects, whether rented to foreigners now or occupied by nationals, are still standing;[36] in some places, such as Ḥazānah (Riqqah), national families have demolished old houses and rebuilt on the same plots. But, partly as a result of formal zoning, one has little difficulty marking most of the city's areas as either national or foreign, and though not as dramatic as in Abu Dhabi, the same distinction is evident between low-rise and high-rise zones.

Dubai is a slightly different matter. The mobility of families is often striking, and as in most Gulf cities, citizens have moved outwards from the old center. An acquaintance, for instance, began life in al-Barāhah (near the center of the old town in Deirah), then moved to al-Maṭīnah in the mid-1970s and grew up largely in Hawr al-'Anz, before moving out to Mizhar 2 in 1997 taking with him his ageing parents. Commercial developments, such as Murdif, add a twist to the pattern, but recolonizing the center has not begun, and there is little sign yet of the Creek as a high-cost residential zone on the model of the Thames waterfront. Almost all of one's Dubai acquaintances continue moving further out.[37] What distinguishes Dubai, however, is the vast, still spreading, expanse of suburban villas that puts casual visitors in mind of southern California, for the low-rise world of Dubai comprises much more than citizens.

Nationals used to predominate in, for instance, Ṣafāh, Rāshidīyah, Abū Hayl and Hawr al-'Anz down to perhaps the mid-1980s; the old town center (Deirah) had by then been given over to Arab or Asian migrants, and some ambiguity attached to al-Ḥudaybah.[38] A relatively recent detailed report shows certain further areas being left to foreigners: Abū Hayl and Hawr al-'Anz West, for instance, now figure in the bracket 21–40 percent nationals.[39] New developments at Ṭawār 2 and 3 fall in the bracket 81 percent or more nationals. Most interesting, however, are the areas listed as roughly 50–50, such as al-Barshā', Saṭwah, Hawr al-'Anz East, Ṭawār 1, Rāshidīyah, Murdif and Mizhar 1.[40] As anyone who knows Dubai will recognize, these represent a wide spread of socioeconomic circumstance. The practical integration of people from different countries is not, however, a great deal more striking than in Kuwait, or for that matter Abu Dhabi.

Social space and physical space are two different things, though easily mistaken for each other by theorists and city planners. In terms that "postmodern" theorists might themselves have used, an advertisement in Dubai asked recently, "Could a shopping mall be a destination in itself?" Plainly, it could: "More than just a shopping mall," says the advert, "Bur Juman is a bona fide cultural phenomenon." But the mixture of persons in a setting like this lasts for most purposes only as long as the experience of shopping. Certain cafés around town are meanwhile colonized by locals (often men, but sometimes women, too) as Kuwaiti, Qatari, or Emirati space, and corners of the lobbies of grand hotels often serve for men as a cross between market and *majlis* or *dīwān*, transformed for the moment into temporary "national" space. Yet fixed national space of a collective sort seems usually to be confined to "heritage" zones such as Bastakīyah in Dubai, where all but, I think, one or two local families in fact sold their houses years ago.

Togetherness

Almost everywhere in the modern Gulf an image recurs of an older world where everyone knew everyone else. Old *sūqs* or markets are remembered fondly, and life in the past is depicted often as within the *farīj* or quarter, where networks of kinship and personal acquaintance governed interaction.[41] That is largely gone now. To take a Saudi case, fairly far removed from "globalizing" forces, 'Unayzah's memory is in this respect typical: "Each area had its own mosque or mosques. Rich and poor were mixed within any neighborhood; ... and the ties of neighborliness were highly valued."[42] In many places people have since then migrated of their own volition or been resettled in housing that is organized by other patterns.[43] "The new residential areas do not form neighborhoods,"[44] and trying to build the old style of network in modern settings is often difficult.

A whole industry of nostalgia thus develops around notions of authenticity and imagined neighborhood. Clive Holes describes a typical Gulf example in Bahraini television's depiction of the local past.[45] Symptomatically, the series was called *al-Bayt al-'Awd*, "the Big House," and the theme of thwarted domesticity was recuperated in the simplest sense, whereby those who interacted with each other in the series' imagined past really were all kin, or dependants to whom the language of kinship could be applied, or long-term neighbors whose "closeness" (*qarābah*) was just as marked. The foreign domestic staff so widely blamed for present faults[46] are conspicuously absent from images of this sort; more powerful foreigners appear as marginal and absurd figures. Yet the greater the means to realize such visions of homogeneity in real life, the further from the vision reality seems to grow. There is more at issue than an outside presence or even, in strict terms, outside pressure.

The original Abu Dhabi plan, it seems, was to keep tribal groups together, each with its own quarter, but the plan "fell apart after a couple of years because of the economic differences that arose."[47] Economics, in fact, is not unconstrained. Where land is allotted by the *dīwān*, or ruler's office, there seems still to be an effort made to group relatives together. The truth of Arnaud Boot's contention, just cited, is most marked in the vast new projects run by Public Works, where a formal bureaucracy interprets the wishes of those in power: the rows of identical villas that stretch for miles from Bahiyah and Shahāmah through Raḥbah to Samḥah are allotted, if not at random, then without regard for genealogy or shared history. These are *masākin sha'bīyah* or *buyūt sha'bīyah*, "popular houses" provided by government, as decades ago they were on Abu Dhabi island.[48] On the island itself the old *buyūt sha'bīyah* have disappeared in favor of private villas, and the distinction is now less of one tribe against another than of generation, whereby younger men, whose fathers and uncles live still on the island, gained plots "between the bridges" (*bayna l-jisrayn*), off the end of Abu Dhabi island, or further out in the new developments such as Khalīfah A and Khalīfah B. On the island itself, though some families have clustered successfully, there are few obvious "communities" of the kind once planned.

An obvious exception might be al-Za'ab. A large group of Za'abīs decamped from Ra's al-Khaimah in 1968 and arrived in Abu Dhabi, where they were granted space by Shaykh Zayed and housed at first in tents. They are now very much part of Abu Dhabi life, and are conspicuous in for instance the foreign ministry. Through the mid-1980s, however, as a great wave of rehousing and redevelopment set in, they were still rather marginal to local politics and their community was somewhat left behind by urban planning. It is now, almost by mistake, the one predominantly "national" area on Abu Dhabi island where one sees people outside their houses in the evening talking to neighbors. The same might be said of far less prosperous areas inland, such as Banī Yās or Wathbah. Yet themes in domestic architecture override in some degree the differences between rich and less rich, the dispersed and the still neighborly.

Almost everywhere, in all the emirates, one finds *buyūt sha'bīyah* ("popular houses") with walls of 2–2.5 meters.[49] Of a sample in Abu Dhabi, though the date is unclear, 4 percent had new rooms added and 89 percent had the walls raised to a height of 2.5 or 3 meters.[50] In al-'Ain, 79 percent of a sample of owners of *buyūt sha'bīyah* had done the same.[51] Despite adventurous exceptions to the rule here and there, most private villas show the same concern, and a recent report even on Dubai speaks of "local customs and traditions that emphasize the need to realize the principle of privacy."[52] The semi-privacy of the *farīj* or quarter, less obvious to the eye, is meanwhile lost, for where courtyards and compounds in pre-oil towns were separated by narrow alleys, the villas of the modern suburbs, whatever their scale, are separated by wide roads that are not under the neighborhood's special care.[53] Within the distinctively family privacy of the individual courtyard, one is left to address a less than immediate set of relationships that seem all but imaginary or virtual. Architects' drawings for private villas in

Abu Dhabi, for instance, often show a *majlis* taking half of the whole ground floor. Yet, apart from the occasional wedding or funeral, there are few visitors.

One has to be careful "reading" these spaces, for whatever is going on may be specific to the Gulf. Coffee shops and restaurants in 'Unayzah, to return to a Saudi case, are places mainly for foreigners, and the market is no longer an obvious meeting place for local men.[54] Such meetings in the old days, however, were not unstructured. The market was a matter of personal relations, the booths or shops were a place to be invited by the owner, and the Western fascination with "unregulated public space"[55] found little echo. "Even poor people in the Gulf regarded sitting about in cafes as a weakness."[56] New things may indeed be happening: the unlikely nostalgia sites of Shindagah in Dubai or the Breakwater in Abu Dhabi, for instance, do attract at times a distinctively Arab crowd and even a distinctively Emirati crowd. But social life is in most places fragmented and dispersed. Streets are often dominated by the foreign presence, and urban layout "does not fill the gap between lived domestic space and a space that overwhelms the city in a sort of nomadism stretched out by jet to the world's four corners."[57]

Local ethnicity, global class

If citizen groups are mixed in with each other, so to speak, horizontally (*al-qarīb* may now be quite a long drive away; *al-gharīb* may live next door), the foreigners may be separated out vertically by income and occupation. Longuenesse argues that throughout the Gulf class relations of the kind expected in Europe are displaced in part by communal or "ethnic" identities,[58] and the local division of labor can certainly be complex, as it was in Kuwait some years ago:

> Christians from Goa in India work exclusively as maids and governesses for urban Kuwaiti families ... Baluchis are employed as door keepers by Kuwaiti families, while Egyptians from lower Egypt are employed as door keepers in apartment buildings owned by Kuwaitis but inhabited by non-Kuwaitis. Nubians are employed as cooks ... Syrians from Houran operate tire repair stores; Armenians from Aleppo who were previously brass workers now operate car body repair shops. Sikhs from India maintain car spare parts stores.[59]

Sociologists or anthropologists might be drawn to parallels with caste as much as class. But however one labels them, economic and social relations existing on a global scale are imported or reproduced locally, a long-standing aspect of globalization that few recent authors have faced up to. South Asia contributes a great many laborers for instance, who at home are farmers; Europe contributes many well-paid managers, who at home are nothing much. Among the stereotypes, the vast Indian middle class now working in the Gulf is often not clearly noticed. These various relations and definitions are exaggerated in Gulf settings but they are not of the Gulf states' making.

The famous Jabal 'Ali Free Zone, west of Dubai, aims to attract global commerce with minimal restrictions and thus imports global difference socially. Its promotional *Business Guide* (1995) suggested wage rates for unskilled labor (in practice nearly all from the Indian subcontinent) of $140–200 per month, and housing for these laborers at $40 each per month with eight men to a room, not including meals, laundry, or air-conditioning. This is the world not only of Jabal 'Ali itself but of, for instance, Quṣayṣ and al-Qaws, the areas labeled frankly on Dubai's bus route maps as "labor camps." On the opposite page of the Jabal 'Ali brochure, as if to point out the contrast, were a group of Europeans disporting themselves on exercise machines above the caption "Health and fitness clubs are abundant in Dubai"; these people would be housed in rented villas in Jumeira, which the *Business Guide* says started at $16,000 per annum "including servants quarters."

Such villas, of course, are owned by nationals. So, too, are most of the accommodations where poorer Asian families live, and not a few single Asian workers. An internal Dubai Municipality report concludes that assessing this statistically is near impossible.[60] What matter for our purpose are the different forms of separation and control. As of the year 2000, the overall statistics from the UAE were something like this: about 400,000 non-citizens present as domestic servants, about 300,000 in labor camps, and beyond that more than a million housed in anything from a shack to a minor palace paying rent to a national population not much over half their number. The million or so foreign renters are sociologically the most intriguing. They are neither excluded neatly like the laborers in camps nor controlled like domestic staff, yet certainly they are not citizens; the difference between their position and that of nationals, meanwhile, does not always show in geographical surveys or statistics on gross income. Again, we come back to the logic of local rent.

In Abu Dhabi, 71 percent of national families claim an income of over Dhs 15,000 per month (Dhs 5 equals approximately 1 GBP: more accurately Dhs 1 equals 3.6 USD), and almost 32 percent claimed an income over Dhs 30,000 per month, though the overall amount of wealth within the higher brackets deserves noting.[61] In Dubai, 22.5 percent of national families claim a monthly income of Dhs 30,000 or more. The corresponding figure for Asian families is 1.5 percent, and for Europeans 30 percent:[62] the typical European household in Dubai, if the calculation be found meaningful, is thus wealthier than the typical national household, though a gross average would show nationals far richer as a group. Broad census categories obscure a great deal. The distinguishing line between nationals and migrants, however, is less average income than the source of such income locally. Thus, 48 percent of national families' incomings in Dubai is from rents and shares.[63] Some 20 percent for national families in Abu Dhabi emirate comes specifically from building rent, another 18 percent from "private activity and work"; and sundry smaller headings add up to a picture not unlike Dubai, although the overall sums are larger.[64]

Not everyone receives rent directly, of course, or even income from foreign workers. But structurally the foreign presence permeates the whole society in far more important ways than who fills the streets at which time of day. The moral aspect is bound to be ambiguous where so little of these relations is visible from any one point of view. Key relations of class exist largely offshore, for instance; at home, foreign groups appear more like castes, each with a specialized place and function. The basis of ranking among fellow citizens may also be hard to see.

But the special status of citizen is defended against a sea of change and of foreign residents, and that status takes explicit form where ideas of physical space, of dependence, and morality intersect.

Several writers, following Ghassan Salamé,[65] have drawn parallels between the states of the GCC and polities of the classical Mediterranean. But certain divergences are also striking. In imperial Rome the *domus* or courtyard-house (very much the equivalent of current villas) was the privilege of the well established, wherever they came from, while the *insulae* or apartment blocks housed the less well off, whether citizens or non-citizens. Romans rented from Romans. Gulf citizens, by contrast, do not on the whole rent from fellow citizens, and the modern equivalent of *insulae* are intended for foreign renters. In Dubai if we add modern villas to *masākin shaʿbīyah* and add both to the self-deprecating category *buyūt ʿarabīyah* we come up with a figure of only 2.6 percent of nationals living in apartments.[66] If we add up the figures for Abu Dhabi – a special case as the federal capital and thus the work place of civil servants from other emirates – we come up with only 2.5 percent of nationals renting on the open market.[67]

As a rule (very nearly a definitive rule), citizens do not rent from citizens; the typical sort of rental property, that is, the flat or apartment, is strongly marked as unsuitable for national families. Stereotypically, in discussion, newspaper letters, and short stories, an apartment is a temporary arrangement for young couples waiting for their own house, or else a place of assignation and a site for wild young men to do their illicit drinking.[68] A private villa or a *bayt shaʿbī*, by contrast, is respectable, and associated with security and independence.[69] This transcends simple economics and even caste-like ranking. Not to live in a villa or a *bayt shaʿbī* (not to have one's own walls, in brief) is to be less than fully a citizen,[70] and the threat to that status is often seen as involving foreigners in ways most citizens can avoid within a family compound. The obvious exceptions, to prove the rule, are the many civil servants from other emirates who work in Abu Dhabi but cannot own land there:[71]

> Most of them live in apartments whose rent is arranged by where they work, and this situation is reflected in the social relations connecting these families to other national families, such that [in effect] they are isolated from the society of nationals ... This isolation leads to their children making closer contact with the inhabitants of these [apartment] buildings, most of whom would be a mixture of nationalities, Arab or otherwise, who each have their peculiar customs and traditions, which leads [in turn] to a weakening of ties and relations within the families of those nationals who live in this type of accommodation. The children ... are given the idea that they are not part of this country (*waṭn*), that they are strangers in their own land.[72]

Public order

Before the great transformation brought on by oil wealth, Gulf societies were not wholly isolated from the world.[73] Even Buraydah and ʿUnayzah, for instance, were on trade routes and Najdi trade reached India, while young men from 'Unayzah would later seek fortunes in Kuwait or Basra, or further off.[74] But Greater Najd, despite 'Unayzah's depiction as a local "Paris," was a by-word among neighbors for its exclusivity: on the Gulf littoral, the proverbial "go to al-Qasīm" still means to attempt something hazardous or trying. Coastal Arabia seemed to offer a different model, as a visitor noted of Oman's main port in the late nineteenth century: "The population of Muscat, drawn by trade, belongs to the most diverse races. With the Arabs of the coast and interior, who make up most of the inhabitants, are mixed Baniah from India, Baluchis, Persians, Abyssinians and blacks from the whole coast of Africa."[75] This was not, however, mere admixture but a system of priority and ranking based on something like patronage.

Arabs "of the coast and interior" are no longer the majority in Muscat; nor are they alone in 'Unayzah. The extent of the foreign presence in much of the UAE is huge. And despite the continued prominence of *kafālah* or "sponsorship," the old forms of control through personal and family patronage no longer suffice to maintain moral hierarchy. Rather, public order, in as disparate spheres as dress codes and employment law, devolves upon governments. Government itself, meanwhile, is not displayed *in* cities, as it might be in Paris or Washington (throughout the Gulf, in fact, administrative buildings tend to be dispersed), but instead is displayed *by* cities, whose progress is measured against foreign standards and whose upkeep requires a foreign staff. Abu Dhabi, for instance, has its famous grid of wide streets, high-rise buildings, and its greenery and fountains. A laudatory picture book from the Public Works Department describes the "garden city of the Gulf" in English that has plainly been translated: "It's sincerely a new pulse for civilization vainglory among other cities, going ahead towards promising future of hope, blessing and welfare." This keen awareness of foreign eyes, just as much as the use of foreign labor, supports a style of development that citizens by themselves might not have chosen.

A marker of planners' progress was reached in the mid-1980s when the inhabitants of Abu Dhabi were forbidden from keeping animals outside their houses. Until then, it seems, many national families tethered camels where they could feed them and make much of them, but such informality was at odds with the planners' spirit and was duly banned: "The decision aims at preserving the urban outlook of the city, where, under the current modernization programme, gardens are springing up everywhere, including residential areas."[76] Real life thus disappears within compound walls, while the high-rise areas (where foreigners live) are disciplined in the same spirit. As of early 2000, the following affiche from Abu Dhabi's *baladīyah* or municipality could be found in the lobbies of downtown buildings:

In order to maintain the civilizational peculiarity and beauty of our city and to preserve the harmonized features of the buildings of the Emirate of Abu Dhabi, kindly observe the following:

1. It is absolutely prohibited to hang washing on a clothesline at the windows/balconies overlooking the main road, whether out of the

window/balcony or hang the same inside in such a way that makes it
apparent for the public.

2. It is absolutely prohibited to fix clotheslines out of the windows/
    balconies on any side of the building that overlooks the main roads.

3. It is absolutely prohibited to clean or put rugs/covers etc., on the
    windows/balconies overlooking the main roads.[77]

In other domains, the conflict of orderly appearance with sociability is more
nuanced. Many young Emiratis agree with fellow Arabs from further west and
north that this is somehow "the age of the *sheeshah*" or water-pipe: whether or not
they are cigarette addicts, many people enjoy the ritual of water-pipe and mint
tea that now enlivens the Edgware Road in London as much as the Levant or
Cairo. It comes as a surprise to find that, *au pied de la lettre*, outdoor *sheeshah* cafes
have been illegal in Abu Dhabi since at least 1996.[78] In fact, as of 2000 there were
somewhere between 400 and 500 *sheeshah* cafes in Abu Dhabi city, and some of
the outdoor ones were famous, quite respectable, meeting places: the "Folk
Restaurant" at the Breakwater and "Layālī al-Zaman" on the Corniche are well-
known cases. Indoors, one gathers, in other parts of town were some women-only
venues. The original decree was aimed mainly at male-only Egyptian sidewalk
cafes whose presence can only have seriously disturbed non-Emiratis, if even
them; but the result is an image of an ideal city, where real life even among
citizens proceeds as a set of arbitrary exceptions to the public rule.

In Sharjah, a ban on *sheeshah*s outdoors has been enforced. Here the language of
public health is prominent in almost the manner one finds in New York or
California, while signs in public places offer exhortations to show one's "civilized
personality" by behaving nicely. Public order more generally is promoted in the city
itself and inland, towards Dhayd, in rural areas such as al-Malīhah, where a citizen
says that new police stations are needed "to ensure the security of the area because
of the presence of many Asian nationalities, who conduct themselves in improper
ways" (*tartakab sulūkiyāt ghayr sawiyah*).[79] As always, the concern with security is oddly
prominent, as it is in much Gulf literature on housing.[80] The complement is an ideal
aesthetic order, so trees should be planted in Sharjah to complete "the beautiful,
civilized appearance (*sūrah hadāriyah jamīlah*) of the emirate."

> As for taxis, although they provide a good service for the citizens they have
> become a source of unrest and disturbance because of the lack of awareness
> (*wai*) among the drivers, most of whom are from uneducated Asian
> nationalities so they bring to our conservative society their uncivilized customs.
>
> Also the appearance of grocery-shops spread about in the midst of resi-
> dential areas has begun to mean disturbing gatherings and meeting places for
> the Asian work force who work in citizens' houses. These have turned into
> places where the secrets of citizens' houses may be passed on.[81]

The speaker's concern here is with security and moral order: these shops, he
argues, should be closed or else supervised closely by the *baladiyah* or municipality.[82]

He does not, however, suggest that Asian domestic workers be removed, which is surely what might be said in comparable European cases. If the state can discipline public space, then nationals' domestic space can be ordered by themselves. What cannot be done within this logic of the foreign presence is to reproduce the sense of community so longingly remembered in memoirs and reproduced on television.

Sharjah is an interesting case. Not only does zoning often separate rented from owned property, and even property gifted from property bought, but it separates service areas from residential areas such that new developments for citizens mean driving to the store in the Californian manner. At the center of what was once the old town, meanwhile, stands the famous Rawlah tree, a symbol of integrated social life. The tree itself has gone. A statue of a tree now represents the spot where meetings were once held, horse races run, and where at festivals a young man might perhaps "see the girl of his dreams."[83] Rawlah Square is these days the starting point for *hajj* and *'umrah* parties made up mainly of South Asians. What on occasion was communal space – indeed, in this case, a focus of local identity – seems always to turn into foreign space. One wonders could it be otherwise. Let us look briefly, therefore, at a case that tries to avoid such conspicuous foreign dominance.

While Abu Dhabi intersects with a "globalizing" world in ways many citizens find uncomfortable, the second city of Abu Dhabi emirate, al-'Ain, represents, so to speak, a free play of collective imagination.[84] How old the name itself may be is unclear. Those who lived or worked there in the 1950s remember the particular settlements having names, though not the region, and al-'Ain being one of several neighboring oases. From the famous Buraimi dispute onwards, however, this cluster of oases featured heavily in the Emirates' self-definition. The late UAE President Shaykh Zayed was once governor here, and when means became available he nurtured al-'Ain as carefully as he did Abu Dhabi: by the late 1990s some 9,500 *buyūt shaʿbiyah* had been distributed,[85] and al-'Ain became a showpiece, a rural idyll, to which many who work in Abu Dhabi now retire on weekends. But something like 6,000 staff (nearly all of them foreigners) attend to the public gardening chores.

One of Shaykh Zayed's early great deeds, before he became ruler, was organizing the renewal of *aflāj*, the channels bringing water to date gardens. A pipeline was built in Shakhbūt's time, bringing water from al-'Ain to Abu Dhabi; in the 1980s the flow reversed, however, and massive pipelines now lead from desalination plants near al-Ruwais and Abu Dhabi to al-'Ain, allowing huge water consumption per capita, much of it for gardens, farms, and ornamental greenery. Work is under way to bring pipes from further desalination plants on the Indian Ocean coast. To most inhabitants of al-'Ain the costs of this are invisible as, in a less literal sense, are the foreigners cutting grass on road islands. In rather the manner of Western suburbia, the town appears to float free of outside connections and constraints.

Al-'Ain will become, as in some degree it already has done, a city no less and more real than others. Its planners envisage an economy based partly on "internal tourism" (Hili Fun City is a feature of local life); in practice, government salaries will surely remain the major source of citizens' income. The industrial – or workshop – area of Ṣanāʿiyah, a little south of the town center, is meanwhile very much the domain of Indian and Pakistani workers, and "for this reason al-Ṣanāʿiyah is subject to close and constant health and security surveillance."[86] As in Sharjah, the concern for security is matched with a claim to aesthetic order: streets are thus "planted with numerous varieties of flowers and trees, which fill them in a beautiful and organized way."[87] The central square of al-ʿAin has colored lights and a "music fountain." But this is scarcely Emirati space, let alone a space dominated by al-ʿAin's own families. And to those not involved in the family links that inform life locally (for instance, to nationals from Sharjah or Dubai who work in al-ʿAin's schools or hospitals) the abiding impression is simply of anonymous, endless walls.

Local reactions to a global world

Long before mass labor migration and the changes brought on by oil, houses and town-quarters throughout the Gulf were characterized by architectural privacy.[88] Walled compounds are still a domestic ideal, and until quite recently the presence of an unaccompanied stranger in a city quarter was almost a contradiction, as indeed it was in eighteenth-century Paris. But regional and local order has been threatened in the Gulf more than most places since the mid-twentieth-century by flows of trade, imagery, and foreign persons. Some of the reactions are those one finds elsewhere in the current world; some are more specific. The issues suggested by space and architecture recur in other domains where borders of some kind are being drawn.

The idea of an external threat to culture is common, and the Gulf states' concerns with, for instance, the internet and satellite television might be found in many countries. Certain local twists to the theme are perhaps not fundamental: both Saudi Arabia and Qatar, for instance, banned the children's collecting craze of "Pokemon," and some Saudi clerics detected in this commercialized fantasy no less than a plot by world Zionism.[89] The worry, of course, is for morality at home. In the UAE, national youth seem to be the main traffic offenders[90] but juvenile delinquency is put down to "the openness of the UAE society [*sic*] to other cultural influences."[91] On occasion, the foreigners themselves are denounced *en masse* not only as venal or lazy but as a source of both disease and crime.[92] This kind of thing can be found in most countries. What is more unusual in the Gulf case, because of the specific structure of economy and population, is the way in which general and particular complaints are often contradictory and policy becomes hard to formulate. If we focused earlier on cities as the points most obviously exposed to globalization, here we might take a rural case: the fishermen based mainly in the northern emirates.

Some years ago now, having absorbed the language of ecology and conservation, owners of fishing boats accepted that limitations on their catch were in order, for the grounds were in danger of being fished out. The damage was attributed to

"Asian fishermen." It is only going through old newspaper files that one realizes, first, how long this has been going on and how often a law has been passed that has then not been applied, and second that the "Asian fishermen" in question are actually the employees of citizens. It could not be otherwise. They are not sailing over from the Malabar Coast or the Comoros Islands but are resident on the Gulf coast and therefore have local *kufalā'* or "sponsors." Finally a law was passed (Federal Law No. 23 of 1999) insisting that local owners be present on these boats at sea to supervise what was done; the owners, having denounced the generalized Asian presence at length, then protested volubly that they had other things to do and could not spare time to bob around on the ocean supervising individual crews.[93]

The same kind of paradox is apparent as we saw with the management of cities. The very source of citizens' livelihood, in a concrete sense, is treated in abstract terms as a threat from elsewhere, and the practical coherence of citizens as a group against others is difficult to realize as consistent policy. This kind of paradox runs deep in local society.[94] If one wants to know how a Gulf company works, one usually does better to befriend the American lawyer, the British accountant, or the Indian office-manager than the owner's relatives. Yet the importance of the line between citizens and others, not least in legal terms, continues growing.

A place in the wider world

As early as the 1950s, "it proved unexpectedly difficult to think of the local population of Kuwait, indigenous and immigrant, as anything coherent enough to be called a society ... though there was certainly a Kuwaiti community at the center of things."[95] To the foreigner in most Gulf states, some fifty years later, locals or citizens (*muwāṭinīn*) seem both everywhere and nowhere. But citizens themselves now worry whether a community of the kind that Lienhardt mentions still exists. It is precisely in this kind of circumstance that the stress falls on essentialized ideas of culture and cultural identity. Nor are the countries of the Gulf alone in this, though they may provide extreme cases.

Globalization, in the form so much talked of since the 1990s, rests on a claim first of all to free flow of investment capital; then, less consistently, to free movement of goods; then perhaps to flows of persons, though the last of these is by far the most ambiguous and is problematic nearly everywhere (one has only to think of Western Europe). Certain notions of identity and order rest very much on control of specific places, a control which globalization threatens to remove in favor of a uniform economic space in which capital and labor flow without hindrance. A "policy of the open door" always looks attractive to those least exposed to its consequences. But everywhere, at present, one's position in a global system can be hard to judge from a purely local viewpoint, as much in a United States economy that exports manufacture as in a small Gulf economy that imports labor.

The implications of the two forms of globalization – exporting manufacture and importing labor – are not very different. People move in one case, jobs in the other. In both, however, the citizen is forced to consider rights and obligations based very much on place and territory in a world that in some ways claims to be non-territorial. The issue in each case is less "culture," though that is where we all first feel the pinch if large numbers of people move, but rather status, control, and moral order.

Notes

* University of Oxford.

1 A. Kapiszewski, *Nationals and Expatriates: Population and Labour Dilemmas of the Gulf Cooperation Council States* (Reading, UK: Ithaca Press, 2001), 39–40.

2 A. Bourgey, "Les villes des émirats du Golfe sont-elles encore des villes Arabes?" in *Les Migrations dans le Monde Arabe*, ed. G. Beaugé and F. Buttner, 69–92 (Paris: CNRS, 1991), 73–74.

3 For a sample of local press commentary on *al-'awlamah*, see *al-Khalīj*, January 30, 2000; February 19, 2000; March 6, 15, 18, 2000; and April 4, 13, 26, 2001. As elsewhere on earth, economic and political vulnerability is seen primarily as a threat to culture or to local values.

4 *al-Wasaṭ*, no. 488, June 4, 2001; *Middle East Economic Digest*, June 28, 2002.

5 *Gulf News*, August 7, 1999, and March 31, 2001.

6 *Arab News*, January 21, 2002.

7 Kapiszewski, 70.

8 P. Fargues, "La migration obéit-elle à la conjoncture petrolière dans le Golfe? L'exemple du Koweit," in *Les Migrations dans le Monde Arabe*, ed. G. Beaugé and F. Buttner, 41–66 (Paris: CNRS, 1991), 56.

9 E.g., Nādir Farjānī, *al-Hijrah ilā l-nafṭ: ab'ād al-hijrah li-l-'amal fī l-buldān al-nafṭiyah wa-athar-hā 'alā l-tanmiyah fī l-waṭan al-'arabī* (Beirut: Markaz dirāsāt al-waḥdah al-'arabīyah, 1983); Sa'd al-Dīn Ibrāhīm and Maḥmūd 'Abd al-Faḍīl, Intiqāl *al-'amālah al-'arabīyah: al-mushākil, al-āthār, al-siyāsāt* (Beirut: Markaz dirāsāt al-waḥdah al-'arabīyah, 1983).

10 P. Dresch, *A History of Modern Yemen* (Cambridge: Cambridge University Press, 2000), 131, 153, 185.

11 *al-Wasaṭ*, January 21, 2002, 521; cf. *Ibid.*, 486, May 21, 2001.

12 See e.g. *Gulf News*, October 28, 1996; *al-Bayān*, August 25, 1997; and *al-Khalīj* April 15, 1990, April 4, 2000, April 18, and June 11, 2001. This is not the place to pursue the issue, but the nature of the rhetoric has hardly changed in decades.

13 P. Lienhardt, *Disorientations: A Society in Flux: Kuwait in the 1950s*, ed. Ahmed Al-Shahi (Reading, UK: Ithaca Press, 1993), 50.

14 Muḥammad al-Rumayḥī, *al-Khalīj laysa nafṭan: dirāsah fī ishkālīyāt al-tanmiyah wa-l-waḥdah* (Beirut: Dār al-jadīd, 1995); Khaldūn. al-Naqīb, "al-Uṣūl al-ijtimā'īyah li-l-dawlah al-tasalluṭīyah fī l-mashriq al-'arabī," *al-Fikr al-'arabī al-mu'āṣir* 27–28, (1983): 217–232; S. Khalaf, "Gulf Societies and the Image of Unlimited Good," *Dialectical Anthropology* 17, no. 1 (1992): 53–84.

15 G. Luciani, "Allocation vs. Production States: A Theoretical Framework," in *The Rentier State*, ed. H. Beblawi and G. Luciani, 63–82 (London: Croom Helm, 1987); H. Beblawi, "The Rentier State in the Arab World," in *The Rentier State*, 85–98.

16 Cf. Fargues, 53.

17 Some idea of the disjunction between rhetoric and practice is given by the rhetoric's stability: "Asians Blamed for Nationals' Unemployment" says *Emirates News*, March 17, 1996 (cf. *Ibid.*, May 28, 1996; *Gulf News*, May 30, 1996). Much the same complaint recurs four years later (*al-Ittiḥād*, April 10, 2000).

18 E.g., Muḥammad al-Murr, *Āmāl waṭanīyah; maqālāt fī ḥubb al-imārāt* (Sharjah: Dār al-khalīj, 1997).

19 C. Henry and R. Springborg, *Globalization and the Politics of Development in the Middle East* (Cambridge: Cambridge University Press, 2001).

20 For a sample of comment in the Emirati case, see *Zahrat al-Khalīj*, January 10, 1998; *al-Imārāt al-Yawm*, October 10, 1998; *Gulf News*, August 7, 1999, and March 31, 2001; and *al-Khalīj*, January 28, 2000. The word often used to describe "nationalizing" jobs is *tawṭīn*. Well within living memory, the same term was used to describe "settling" the Bedu. A very great deal has happened in a short time.

21 See A. Longva, *Walls Built on Sand: Migration, Exclusion and Society in Kuwait* (Boulder, CO: Westview, 1997) and "Neither Autocracy nor Democracy but Ethnocracy: Citizens, Expatriates, and the Socio-political System in Kuwait," in *Monarchies and Nations: Globalization and Identity in the Arab States of the Gulf*, ed. Dresch and Piscatori, 114–135 (London: I.B. Tauris, 2005).

22 *al-Wasat*, no. 383, May 31, 1999.

23 For a fuller treatment of contemporary marriage debates, see P. Dresch, "Debates on Marriage and Nationality in the United Arab Emirates," in Dresch and Piscatori, 136–157.

24 N. Gavrielides, "The Anatomy of Parliamentary Elections in Kuwait," in *Elections in the Middle East: Implications of Recent Trends*, ed. L. Layne, 153–183 (Boulder, CO, and London: Westview, 1987), 162.

25 See, e.g., *al-Khalīj*, April 30, 2001.

26 *Gulf News*, September 21, 1998, and February 25, 2000.

27 See, e.g., al-Murr, *Āmāl waṭanīyah; maqālāt fī ḥubb al-imārāt*.

28 C. Allen, "The Indian Merchant Communities of Masqat," *Bulletin of the School of Oriental and African Studies* 4, no. 1 (1981): 390–354; Gavrielides.

29 See, e.g., Fawzīyah al-Badrī, "al-Taḥawwulāt al-ijtimāʿīyah fī mujtamaʿ dawlat al-imārāt," *al-Buḥūth al-fāʾizah bi-jāʾizat al-ʿuways li-l-dirāsāt* (Dubai) 7, no. 2 (1996): 79–80.

30 Lienhardt, 35, 39.

31 al-Rumayḥī, 278–279.

32 Fargues, 61–63.

33 ʿAbd al-Ḥamīd Ghanīm, "al-Khaṣāʾiṣ al-sakanīyah fī madīnah abū ẓabī," *Dirāsāt fī mujtamaʿ al-imārāt* 11 (1995): 70.

34 cf. Ghanīm, 69–70, 82 ff.

35 Here we touch on a whole unwritten history of Gulf cities, but for a useful sketch of Sharjah at a critical period see G. Anderson, *Mushkilah ḥafẓ al-mabānī al-turāthīyah* (Sharjah: Dāʾirat al-thaqāfah wa-l-iʿlām, 1995), 92 ff.

36 An obvious case would be the Ghubaybah area near the Sharjah sports club. Tucked away behind some large, though not extravagant, villas are many early *buyūt shaʿbīyah* with distinctive double-barreled roofs. The equivalent "living history" in Abu Dhabi seems all to have been swept away.

37 This is very much a broad-brush picture. For a detailed account of citizens' lives in two neighborhoods on the Deira side of Dubai, one quite prosperous and the other less so, see Amina Abu Shehab, "The UAE in the Era of Affluence: An Anthropological Study of Consumption" (Ph.D. thesis, London School of Economics, 2000).

38 E. Gabriel, *The Dubai Handbook* (Ahrensburg: Institute for Applied Economic Geography, 1987), 83–84.

39 Dubai Municipality. Dubai Urban Area Structure Plan. Working paper 4A, phase 2; housing (unpublished report, Dubai Municipality Planning and Survey Department, 2000).

40 *Ibid.*, 3–1 ff., and section F-1.

41 S. Khalaf and H. Hammoud, "The Emergence of the Oil Welfare State: The Case of Kuwait," *Dialectical Anthropology* 12, no. 3 (1988): 347; al-Badrī, 33, 56.

42 S. Altorki and D. Cole, *Arabian Oasis City: The Transformation of ʿUnayzah* (Austin: University of Texas Press, 1989), 22. Altorki and Cole stress the mixed origins of residents in some of ʿUnayzah's quarters (*Ibid.*, 209). But closeness or *qarābah*, does not reduce to North Atlantic versions of "blood-relatedness." To say people are relatives

(*aqribā*) is to say they are close, and the measure of local control (hence of moral coherence) is a settled view of who can and cannot rightly marry whom.

43 Cf. S. Nagy, "Social Diversity and Changes in the Form and Appearance of the Qatari House," *Visual Anthropology* 10, nos. 2–4 (1998): 281–304.

44 Altorki and Cole, 217.

45 C. Holes, "Dialect and Bahraini Identity: The Cultural Politics of Self-Representation in Bahraini *musalsalāt*," in Dresch and Piscatori, eds, 52–72 Articles on old Shindaghah, in Dubai, paint a similar picture of "a society tied together by mutual responsibility" (*al-Khalīj*, April 23, 2001). The complement is a supposed breakdown of family ties under "modern" pressures. For Emirati examples of such discourse, see al-Badrī and *Gulf News*, November 26, 2000.

46 E.g., al-Badrī, 56–57.

47 A. Boot, "Tribes and Families of Abu Dhabi," (typescript produced for the Dutch embassy, Abu Dhabi, UAE, n.d.), 46.

48 Khalfān Jāsim al-'Abdūlī, *Taṭawwur al-ittijāh al-ma'āmiñ li-dawlat al-imārāt al-'arabīyah al-mutaḥḥidah* (no publisher listed, 1989), 72, 115 ff. and passim. The high point of such provision in the Emirates was probably in the late 1970s, though they are still provided particularly for national families with limited incomes.

49 *Ibid.*, 116.

50 Ghanīm, 77.

51 al-Sayyid al-Aswad, *al-Bayt al-sha'bī: dirāsah anthrūbūlujīyah li-l-'amārah al-sha'bīyah wa-l-thaqāfah al-taqlīdīyah li-mujtama' al-imārāt* (Al-'Ain: Jāma'at al-imārāt, 1996), 70.

52 *al-Bayān*, April 17, 2000.

53 Cf. Nagy; N. Fuccaro, "Visions of the City: Urban Studies on the Gulf," *MESA Bulletin* 35, no. 2 (2001): 175–187.

54 Altorki and Cole, 225.

55 M. Naciri, "Le role de la citadinité dans l'évolution des villes arabo-islamiques," in *Sciences sociales et phenomènes urbains dans le monde arabe*, ed. M. Naciri and A. Raymond, 131–147 (Casablanca: Fondation du Roi Abdul-Aziz Al Saoud, 1997), 140.

56 Lienhardt, 43.

57 Naciri, 144.

58 E. Longuenesse, "Raports de classes, solidarités communautaires et identité nationale dans les pays du Golfe," in *Les Migrations dans le monde Arabe*, ed. G. Beaugé and F. Buttner, 123–133 (Paris: CNRS, 1991).

59 Gavrielides, 161.

60 Dubai Municipality, Dubai Urban Area Structure Plan, 2–13.

61 Emirate of Abu Dhabi Planning Department. *al-Natā'ij al-nihā'iyah li-mash mīzānīyat al-usrah* (Family Income and Expenditure Survey), 3 vols. (Statistical Section, 1998), iii, 210.

62 Dubai Municipality. *Natā'ij baḥth dakhl wa-infāq al-usrah* (Income and Expenditure Survey) (Administrative Affairs, Department of Statistics, 1998), 91 ff.

63 Dubai Municipality, Income and Expenditure Survey, 130. Earlier estimates (1993) were even more striking: 20 percent of nationals' income came from real estate, 66 percent from companies, and only 14 percent from salaries and wages. Average pay for nationals at the time was estimated at Dhs 9,596 per month. Laborers make up about 30 percent of the population, which is unusual in the modern world.

64 Emirate of Abu Dhabi, iii, 2. The category national here includes citizens from other emirates, who do not derive rent from Abu Dhabi property. All these calculations omit foreign assets, which in the case of wealthy national families may be large, nor are income surveys of their nature accurate. Nonetheless, it is noteworthy in the Abu Dhabi case that building rent comes to 22.8 percent of total income for families based in Abu Dhabi city, almost 26 percent for those living in al-'Ain, and only 6.7 percent for al-'Ain's rural areas.

65 Ghassan Salamé, "Small is Pluralistic: Democracy as an Instrument of Civil Peace," in *Democracy Without Democrats? The Renewal of Policy in the Muslim World*, ed. Salamé (New York: I.B. Tauris, 1994), 100.

66 Dubai Municipality, Income and Expenditure Survey, 84–5: *buyūt 'arabīyah* are houses in supposedly "traditional" style (most date in fact from the 1960s or 1970s), which are usually not in good repair. Old or broken-down housing is usually what is meant.

67 Emirate of Abu Dhabi, i. 36.

68 An obvious source in which to explore the values attached to different forms of housing is local imaginative literature [e.g., Muhammad al-Murr, *al-A'māl al-qiṣaṣīyah*, 3 vols. (Beirut: Dār al-'awdah, 1992)], and, of course, the press. But the dubious character of apartment life is contrasted clearly with the respectability of having one's own walls and compound. See, e.g., a series on local housing problems in *al-Khalīj*, December 11–21, 1990.

69 al-Aswad, 68–69.

70 Cf. Ghanīm, 94.

71 Emirate of Abu Dhabi, i. 38.

72 *al-Khalīj*, January 5, 2000.

73 Fuccaro, 176.

74 Altorki and Cole, 57, 90, 108.

75 Quoted in Bourgey, 76.

76 *Emirates News*, January 11, 1986.

77 The text itself dates from some years earlier: "hanging clothes out to dry…blemishes the civilized look that should be maintained on the buildings of Abu Dhabi, and that's why we have decided to ban it altogether" (*Gulf News*, June 12, 1996).

78 For an overview of the *sheeshah* controversy, see, e.g., *Emirates News*, September 22, 1996; *Gulf News*, January 16 and 20, 1997; *Gulf News*, January 20, 21, 30 and October 13, 2000; *Khaleej Times*, October 11, 2000; and *al-Khalīj*, February 15 and April 4, 2000. Sharjah seems to have been the only place where a ban succeeded.

79 *al-Khalīj*, April 27, 2001.

80 E.g., M. Saleh, "Privacy and Communal Socialisation: The Role of Space in the Security of Traditional and Contemporary Neighborhoods in Saudi Arabia," *Habitat International* 21, no. 2 (1997): 176–184.

81 *al-Khalīj*, April 27, 2001.

82 A member of Sharjah's advisory council, praising the ruler's perspicacity and the energy of the crown prince, says "safety and security have spread to all parts of the emirate and Sharjah has become safe and tranquil to an enviable degree" (*al-Khalīj*, April 27, 2001). An outsider might ask, when was it not? As far as one can gather, Sharjah was always a model of civility.

83 *al-Khalīj*, May 11, 2001. Of particular interest is the accompanying illustration of a symbolic funeral for Gamāl 'Abd al-Nāṣir (so, presumably 1970) with a crowd wearing Gulf *thawbs* and the sports jackets one would later associate with Yemenis. It is hard to imagine so "Arab" a scene these days.

84 For al-'Ain, see 'Abd al-Ḥamīd Ghanīm and Sayf al-Qāyidī, *al-Namū al-'umrānī fī iqlīm al-'ayn* (Abu Dhabi: al-Mujamma' al-thaqāfī, 2001). I have also drawn on two public lectures, one by Ṭalāl al-Salmānī at the Sharjah urban planning conference, and the other by Sayf al-Qāyidī at the Cultural Foundation, Abu Dhabi, both in April 2001. Al-Aswad reckons that in al-'Ain's new housing complexes, 65 percent of neighbors are from the same tribe; in the adjoining villages, the figure may be 69 percent (Al-Aswad, 56).

85 Ghanīm and al-Qāyidī, 106.

86 *Ibid.*, 108.

87 *Ibid.*, 104.

88 Altorki and Cole, 22; Lienhardt, 32, 68; Saleh; Nagy.

89 *Gulf News*, March 26 and April 9, 2001.
90 *Gulf News*, March 23, 1995.
91 *Emirates News*, May 21, 1995; cf. *Gulf News*, May 20, 1995.
92 al-Badrī, 80.
93 For part of the story, see *al-Khalīj*, February 1, 2000, and April 30, 2001; *Gulf News*, November 19, 1996, and May 6, 2001; and *al-Ittihād* May 3 and 9, 2001. It is not unusual that an article in May 2001 should announce that "the Ministry of Agriculture and Fisheries will tomorrow begin to implement" a law passed two years earlier.
94 See Fox *et al.* in the introduction to this volume.
95 Lienhardt, 35.

References

al-'Abdūlī, Khalfān Jāsim. *Taṭawwur al-ittijāh al-ma'āmirī li-dawlat al-imārāt al-'arabīyah al-mutaḥḥidah.* No publisher listed, 1989.

Abu Dhabi, Emirate of. *al-Natā'ij al-nihā'īyah li-mash mīzānīyat al-usrah* (*Family Income and Expenditure Survey*), 3 vols. Statistical Section, Emirate of Abu Dhabi Planning Department, 1998.

Abu Shehab, Amina. "The UAE in the Era of Affluence: An Anthropological Study of Consumption." Unpublished Ph.D. thesis, London School of Economics, 2000.

Allen, C. "The Indian Merchant Communities of Masqat." *Bulletin of the School of Oriental and African Studies* 4, no. 2 (1981): 390–354.

Altorki, S. and D. Cole. *Arabian Oasis City: The Transformation of 'Unayzah.* Austin, TX: University of Texas Press, 1989.

Anderson, G. *Mushkilah hafẓ al-mabānī al-turāthīyah.* Sharjah: Dā'irat al-thaqāfah wa-l-i'lām, 1995.

al-Aswad, al-Sayyid. *al-Bayt al-sha'bī: dirāsah anthrūbūlujīyah li-l-'amārah al-sha'bīyah wa-l-thaqāfah al-taqlīdīyah li-mujtama' al-imārāt.* al-'Ain: Jāma'at al-imārāt, 1996.

al-Badrī, Fawzīyah. "al-Taḥawwulāt al-ijtimā'īyah fī mujtama' dawlat al-imārāt." *al-Buḥūth al-fā'izah bi-jā'izat al-'uways li-l-dirāsāt* (Dubai) 7, no. 2 (1996): 21–102.

Beblawi, H. "The Rentier State in the Arab World." In *The Rentier State*, edited by H. Beblawi and G. Luciani, 85–98. London: Croom Helm, 1987.

Boot, A. *Tribes and Families of Abu Dhabi.* Typescript produced for the Dutch embassy, Abu Dhabi, UAE. n.d.

Bourgey, A. "Les villes des émirats du Golfe sont-elles encore des villes arabes?" In *Les Migrations dans le Monde Arabe*, edited by G. Beaugé and F. Buttner, 69–92. Paris: CNRS, 1991.

Dresch, P. *A History of Modern Yemen.* Cambridge: Cambridge University Press, 2000.

Dresch, P. "Debates on Marriage and Nationality in the United Arab Emirates." In *Monarchies and Nations: Globalization and Identity in the Arab States of the Gulf*, edited by P. Dresch and J. Piscatori, 136–157. London: I.B. Tauris, 2005.

Dubai Municipality. *Natā'ij bahth dakhl wa-infāq al-usrah* (*Income and Expenditure Survey*). Dubai Municipality, Administrative Affairs, Department of Statistics, 1998.

Dubai Municipality. Dubai Urban Area Structure Plan. Working paper 4A, phase 2: housing, unpublished report. Dubai Municipality Planning and Survey Department, 2000.

Fargues, P. "La migration obéit-elle à la conjoncture petrolière dans le Golfe? L'exemple du Koweit." In *Les Migrations dans le Monde Arabe*, edited by G. Beaugé and F. Buttner, 41–66. Paris: CNRS, 1991.

Farjānī, Nādir. *al-Hijrah ilā l-naft: abʿād al-hijrah li-l-ʿamal fī l-buldān al-naftīyah wa-athar-hā ʿalā l-tanmīyah fī l-watan al-ʿarabī.* Beirut: Markaz dirāsāt al-waḥdah al-ʿarabīyah, 1983.

Fuccaro, N. "Visions of the City: Urban Studies on the Gulf." *MESA Bulletin* 35, no. 2 (2001): 175–187.

Gabriel, E. *The Dubai Handbook.* Ahrensburg: Institute for Applied Economic Geography, 1987.

Gavrielides, N. "The Anatomy of Parliamentary Elections in Kuwait." In *Elections in the Middle East: Implications of Recent Trends,* edited by L. Layne, 153–183. Boulder, CO, and London: Westview, 1987.

Ghanīm, ʿAbd al-Ḥamīd. "al-Khaṣāʾiṣ al-sakanīyah fī madīnah abū ẓabī." *Dirāsāt fī mujtamaʿ al-imārāt* 11 (1995): 65–99.

Ghanīm, ʿAbd al-Ḥamīd, and Sayf al-Qāyidī. *al-Namū al-ʿumrānī fī iqlīm al-ʿayn.* Abu Dhabi: al-Mujammaʿ al-thaqāfī, 2001.

Henry, C., and R. Springborg. *Globalization and the Politics of Development in the Middle East.* Cambridge: Cambridge University Press, 2001.

Holes, C. "Dialect and Bahraini Identity: The Cultural Politics of Self-representation in Bahraini *musalsalāt.*" In *Monarchies and Nations: Globalization and Identity in the Arab States of the Gulf,* edited by P. Dresch and J. Piscatori, 52–72. London: I.B. Tauris, 2005.

Ibrāhīm, Saʿd al-Dīn, and Maḥmūd ʿAbd al-Faḍīl. *Intiqāl al-ʿamālah al-ʿarabīyah: al-mushākil, al-āthār, al-siyāsāt,* Beirut: Markaz dirāsāt al-waḥdah al-ʿarabīyah, 1983.

Kapiszewski, A. *Nationals and Expatriates: Population and Labour Dilemmas of the Gulf Cooperation Council States.* Reading, UK: Ithaca Press, 2001.

Khalaf, S. "Gulf Societies and the Image of Unlimited Good." *Dialectical Anthropology* 17, no. 1 (1992): 53–84.

Khalaf, S. and H. Hammoud. "The Emergence of the Oil Welfare State: The Case of Kuwait." *Dialectical Anthropology* 12, no. 3 (1988): 343–357.

Lienhardt, P. *Disorientations: A Society in Flux, Kuwait in the 1950s.* Edited by Ahmed Al-Shahi. Reading UK: Ithaca Press, 1993.

Longuenesse, E. "Raports de classes, solidarités communautaires et identité nationale dans les pays du Golfe." In *Les Migrations dans le Monde Arabe,* edited by G. Beaugé and F. Buttner, 123–133. Paris: CNRS, 1991.

Longva, A. *Walls Built on Sand: Migration, Exclusion and Society in Kuwait.* Boulder, CO: Westview, 1997.

Longva, A. "Neither Autocracy nor Democracy but Ethnocracy: Citizens, Expatriates, and the Socio-political System in Kuwait." In *Monarchies and Nations: Globalization and Identity in the Arab States of the Gulf,* edited by P. Dresch and J. Piscatori, 114–135. London: I.B. Tauris, 2005.

Luciani, G. "Allocation vs. Production States: A Theoretical Framework." In *The Rentier State,* edited by H. Beblawi and G. Luciani, 63–82. London: Croom Helm, 1987.

al-Murr, Muḥammad. *al-Aʿmāl al-qisasīyah* (3 vols.) Beirut: Dār al-ʿawdah, 1992.

al-Murr, Muḥammad. *Āmāl watanīyah; maqālāt fī ḥubb al-imārā*t, Sharjah: Dār al-khalīj, 1997.

Naciri, M. "Le role de la citadinité dans l'évolution des villes arabo-islamiques." In *Sciences sociales et phenomènes urbains dans le monde arabe,* edited by M. Naciri and A. Raymond, 131–134. Casablanca: Fondation du Roi Abdul-Aziz Al Saoud, 1997.

Nagy, S. "Social Diversity and Changes in the Form and Appearance of the Qatari House." *Visual Anthropology* 10, nos 2–4 (1998): 281–304.

al-Naqīb, Khaldūn. "al-Uṣūl al-ijtimāʿīyah li-l-dawlah al-tasallutīyah fī l-mashriq al-ʿarabī." *al-Fikr al-ʿarabī al-muʿāsir* 27–28 (1983): 217–232.

al-Rumayḥī, Muḥammad. *al-Khalīj laysa nafṭan: dirāsah fī ishkālīyāt al-tanmīyah wa-l-waḥdah.* Beirut: Dār al-jadīd, 1995.

Salamé, G. "Small is Pluralistic: Democracy as an Instrument of Civil Peace." In *Democracy Without Democrats? The Renewal of Politics in the Muslim World*, edited by G. Salamé, 84–111. New York: I.B. Tauris, 1994.

Saleh, M. "Privacy and Communal Socialisation: The Role of Space in the Security of Traditional and Contemporary Neighborhoods in Saudi Arabia." *Habitat International* 21, no. 2 (1997): 176–184.

13 Ambivalent anxieties of the South Asian–Gulf Arab labor exchange*

*John Willoughby***

Introduction

No region in the world economy has experienced more profound economic and social changes than the Arabian Peninsula. Once an economic backwater, the Arabian Peninsula now boasts high living standards, rapidly rising literacy rates, and a modern infrastructure of roads, airports, and mobile phone and internet networks.[1]

An ethnographer in the 1950s might have expected that outsiders' images of the past would fade with this rapid and unprecedented modernization. However, it is my experience that Arabs and non-Arabs alike continue to view the Gulf Arabs as almost pre-modern, enriched by unearned oil wealth, but not productively contributing to the society in which they live. They are thought to be enjoying extraordinary luxury while others work around and for them.

This culturally constructed picture distorts a more complex Arabian reality, although certain distinct political, social, and economic features of the labor market do distinguish the Arabian Peninsula from almost every other section of the world. This paper focuses on the anxieties resulting from the Gulf's heavy reliance on expatriate labor from South Asia. It concentrates on the regions most heavily implicated in this labor exchange: the emirates of Sharjah and Dubai in the United Arab Emirates and the state of Kerala in South India. I interpret empirical data and accounts of labor market experiences through microeconomic theory to explain this labor exchange, which breeds concern and worry on both sides of the Arabian Sea. The chapter concludes by assessing the stability of the South Asian–Gulf relationship. While political events may lessen in-migration from India, strong economic reasons suggest that Gulf Arab societies' reliance on Indian labor will continue and even deepen.

Empirical overview

One significant feature of the economic and social developments since the mid-twentieth century is the rapid population growth in the Arabian Peninsula due to high birth rates and significant in-migration.

Tables 13.1 and 13.2 suggest that the nation states of the GCC rely heavily on expatriate labor. Nevertheless, there are important differences among the states.

Table 13.1 Population growth of the Arabian Peninsula, 1950–97 (000s)

	1950	1960	1970	1980	1990	1997
Bahrain	116	156	220	347	503	620
Kuwait	152	278	744	1,357	2,143	2,153
Oman	413	505	654	988	1,524	2,256
Qatar	25	45	111	229	490	522
Saudi Arabia	3,201	4,075	5,745	9,372	15,800	19,500
UAE	70	90	223	1,015	1,589	2,696
GCC total	3,977	5,149	7,697	13,308	22,049	27,747

Source: Kapiszewski, 2000.

Table 13.2 Population of nationals and expatriates, 1997 (000s)

	Nationals	Expatriates	% expatriate	Total
Bahrain	384	236	39	620
Kuwait	744	1,409	66	2,153
Oman	1,642	614	28	2,256
Qatar	157	365	67	522
Saudi Arabia	13,500	6,000	31	19,500
UAE	658	2,038	76	2,696
GCC total	17,085	10,662	39	27,747

Source: Kapiszewski, 2000.

While the internal population growth has been high in all countries, per capita GDP seems to regulate the degree to which expatriate labor is used (Table 13.3). Thus, those nations with lower per capita GDP rely more on their national workforce, while the more wealthy nations of Kuwait, Qatar, and the United Arab Emirates manifest both greater expatriate presence in their society as well as higher internal population growth (Table 13.4). Despite Saudi Arabia's relatively less reliance on foreign labor, approximately 66 percent of expatriate workers within the GCC are employed there.

Based on these broad data, I hypothesize that two types of demand stimulate labor migration to the Gulf. First, the creation of an infrastructure for exploiting the petroleum riches required both highly trained professionals and manual laborers. Neither the skill levels nor size of the indigenous population were adequate for this export-led growth. Second, as per capita GDP rose, the demand for durable consumer goods, leisure services, educational and health services, and information technology generated a powerful employment multiplier effect that pulled foreign workers into a broad array of occupations.[2] There is no doubt that expatriate workers are crucial for the functioning of the GCC economies.

To delve further into this dependence on expatriate labor, the UAE provides an instructive case in point. Its reliance on foreign workers highlights in the extreme

Table 13.3 Per capita GDP and the presence of expatriates in the national population

GCC countries ranked by per capita	Per capita GDP (PPP* 1999)	% of expatriates in total population	% growth of national population (1950–97)
Qatar	$18,789	67	528
UAE	$18,162	76	840
Kuwait	$17,289	66	389
Bahrain	$13,688	39	231
Oman	$13,356	28	298
Saudi Arabia	$10,815	31	322
GCC total		39	330

Sources: Kapiszewski, 2000, and United Nations Development Program, 2001.

Note
* Purchasing power parity.

Table 13.4 Nationals and expatriates in the workforce, 1995–97 (000s)

	Nationals in workforce	Expatriates in workforce	Total in workforce	Expatriate workforce as % of total workforce	Expatriate population as % of total population
Qatar	22	98	120	82	67
UAE	124	1,165	1,290	90	76
Kuwait	189	991	1,180	84	66
Bahrain	104	169	272	62	39
Oman	270	496	766	62	28
Saudi Arabia	2,500	4,500	7,000	64	31
GCC total	3,209	7,419	10,628	70	39

Source: Kapiszewski, 2000.

the differences between national and non-national workers characteristic of all the Arabian Peninsula. Most UAE nationals work for the UAE government.[3] It is reported that a notable portion of national workers fails to perform their tasks with much alacrity or efficiency, at least according to Western standards of performance.[4] Absenteeism in the government sector is a constant problem. Yet, the average government salary reported in 1996 was AED 107,600 – approximately US $30,000 per year. However, it is likely that UAE nationals received an average amount significantly higher than that, since non-nationals within the government tend to cluster in the lower salary echelons. With the exception of the crude oil sector – which employs only 2 percent of the workforce – and the finance and insurance sectors, no other employment sector offers compensation that equates to half the amount of the government sector (Table 13.5). Most governments are now encouraging private banks and other financial enterprises to employ more national citizens in this high-wage sector. Even if nationals

Table 13.5 Average annual compensation by economic sector in UAE, 1997 (000s of dollars)

Economic sector	% of workforce	Annual compensation	% of government services compensation
Crude oil	1.6	24.2	82
Agriculture	7.6	3.8	13
Mining and quarrying	0.3	7.2	24
Manufacturing	11.8	6.7	23
Electricity, gas, and water	1.8	13.2	45
Construction	19.1	10.4	35
Wholesale and retail trade	17.3	7.3	25
Restaurants and hotels	3.8	6.0	20
Transportation, storage, and communication	7.3	10.2	35
Finance and insurance	1.5	26.5	90
Real estate	2.5	7.6	26
Government services	10.9	29.5	100
Social and personal services	4.6	7.9	27
Domestic services*	10.0	2.8	10
Weighted average		10.4	35

Source: International Monetary Fund, 1998.

Note
* Does not include room and board expenses borne by employer.

completely supplanted expatriate labor in the financial sector and saturated this industry, it would be unlikely that UAE nationals would then move into the low-wage retail trade or manufacturing sectors.[5]

The UAE's highly unequal compensation structure suggests a profound bifurcation between the national population and the non-national population. It is not that nationals do not work in "blue-collar" occupations; they work for the government as security guards or in public safety. Rather, the evidence suggests that this work is protected and rewarded with disproportionately high compensation. Moreover, the bifurcated wage structure even understates the difference in the two labor forces, since nationals receive subsidized supplies of energy, free medical care, free higher education, and free land. In addition, many families receive substantial cash transfers through programs such as the "marriage fund" during key stages of their lives.[6]

This snapshot of labor segmentation ignores the very real divisions within the expatriate workforce. While it is difficult to find precise empirical data on the employment location and compensation of different national groups, I propose a quadripartite ranking of the workforce, which follows as:

- European and American professionals.
- Non-national Arab and Asian professionals and business people.[7]
- South and East Asian clerks.
- South Asian laborers.[8]

The Indian subcontinent and the out-migration of Keralite workers[9]

Historical accounts suggest that starting with the oil price boom of the early 1970s, Gulf countries began to turn away from employing low-wage Arab labor from Yemen and Egypt and toward the even cheaper labor reserves in Pakistan.[10] Toward the end of the 1970s, in-migration from India increased as the presence of Pakistani workers diminished.[11] The Gulf War of 1991 intensified this trend, especially with the expulsion of large numbers of Arab workers from Egypt and the Levantine states.

B.A. Prakash, who has studied Indian migration to Gulf countries during the past two decades, notes that emigration of Indians to the Gulf divides in four stages:

1   1976–79: Beginning of out-migration.
2   1980–83: Rapid growth.
3   1984–90: Declining growth.
4   1991–94: Revival and intensified growth.[12]

Data from the Indian Ministry of Labor support Prakash's migration typology. Out-migration from the Gulf slows when in-migration falters. This synchronicity of labor import and export has resulted in a steady rise in the pool of Indian migrants to the Gulf since the 1980s (Tables 13.6 and 13.7).

A comparison of Table 13.7 with the earlier figures presented by Kapiszewski implies that Indian workers comprise slightly less than 40 percent of the total expatriate population. Since the mid-1990s, evidence suggests that at least until

Table 13.6 Annual labor outflow from India

Year	Number in 000s
1977–79	263.7
1980–82	751.7
1983–85	401.9
1986–88	409
1989–91	460
1992–94	1,325.5

Source: Prakash, 1998.

Table 13.7 Indian migrants in the Arabian
Peninsula and Gulf

Year	Number in 000s
1979	501
1981	599
1983	916
1987	957
1990	1,235
1991	1,650
1996	2,800

Source: Prakash, 1998.

the year 2000, the in-migration of South Asian workers continued at an intense pace. Zachariah, Mathew, and Rajan report that between the late 1980s and late 1990s, the annual rate of migration from the state of Kerala increased by 120 percent.[13]

In a comparative perspective, the export of labor to the Gulf is far less significant to Kerala than to the Gulf States. As one of the smallest states in India, Kerala's population is larger than all the Gulf States and Saudi Arabia combined. Moreover, this aggregate Arabian population includes the resident Keralite expatriate population (which is probably between 5 to 10 percent of the total.)[14]

Much of the out-migration emanates from a few specific regions of India. Kerala is the leading exporter of labor, supplying one-half of all Indian workers to the Gulf. Moreover, a small number of districts within Kerala provide much of the exported labor.

The economic and sociological impact of out-migration on Kerala

The effects of out-migration on Kerala are less well known than the impact on the host Gulf countries. If macroeconomic and labor market conditions approximate W. Arthur Lewis's model of unlimited labor services being supplied at subsistence wages, then any outflow of workers would benefit the home country.[15] Even if wages did not rise from the outflow, the inflow of remittance payments would boost living standards of Kerala. If, on the other hand, the quite finite professional labor permanently leaves the home country, then such a "brain drain" could cripple its productive capacity.

Unlike those of most of the Indian sub-continent, the social indicators of Kerala show that female and male literacy rates are over 90 percent; life expectancy is over 70; and birth rates have recently fallen below replacement levels. In other words, while economic indicators would place Kerala in the Third World, social indicators suggest a more developed society than the Gulf States.[16] As such, Kerala does not epitomize Lewis's model of a land peopled by desperate, impoverished, and unproductive workers. Nevertheless, the economic circumstances of the migrants suggest that unemployment along with the demand for temporary workers to fill "unskilled" jobs describes Keralite workers employed in the Gulf.

To provide a picture of the workers from Kerala in the Arabian Peninsula, the Center for Development Studies in Trivandrum and the Indo-Dutch Program on Alternatives in Development sponsored a survey of 10,000 households to assess the reasons for and consequences of migration. Tables 13.8 and 13.9 summarize data on the destination and origins of Keralite workers.

The migrating workers are overwhelmingly (90 percent) young males in their mid-20s. They tend to work as laborers or in other low-wage jobs; 26.5 percent

Table 13.8 Emigration destination of Keralite workers, 1998

Destination	Number (000s)	%
Saudi Arabia	519	38.1
UAE (total)	405	29.7
Abu Dhabi, UAE*	133	9.7
Dubai and Sharjah, UAE*	272	20.0
Oman	142	10.4
Bahrain	77	5.7
Kuwait	69	5.1
Qatar	64	4.7
USA	30	2.2
Other	57	4.2

Source: K.C. Zachariah *et al.*, October 2000.

Note
* Abu Dhabi, Dubai, and Sharjah are the three largest emirates of the UAE. The UAE figures do not include emigration to the other emirates of the UAE and thus are a slight underestimate.

Table 13.9 Occupational distribution of emigrants (by %)

Occupation	Before migration	After migration
State/government employee	2.2	2.5
Semi-government employee	0.6	0.9
Private sector employee	15.4	40.8
Self-employed	13.9	4.4
Unpaid worker	0.8	0.0
Agricultural laborer	1.8	0.1
Non-agricultural laborer	34.1	47.5
Job seeker	26.5	0.7
Voluntarily unemployed	0.2	0.2
Student	1.5	0.4
Household work	3.2	2.6

Source: K.C. Zachariah *et al.*, October 2000.

Table 13.10 The intensity of Keralite migration

District of Kerala	Migration prevalence ratio	Household migration rate
Pathanmthitta	98.6	59.4
Thrissur	88.5	49.8
Malappuram	78.1	52.2
Alappuzha	72.7	38.9
Palakhat	65.1	37.1
Thiruvananthapuram	61.6	44.9
Kasargode	60.7	38.1
Kollam	59.4	41.7
Koshikode	48.4	37.7
Kannai	42.4	35.4
Ernakulam	37.3	25.4
Kottayam	35.9	27.5
Wayanad	19.6	16.0
Idukki	11.5	7.6
Total for Kerala	59.0	38.5

Source: K.C. Zachariah *et al.*, October 2000.

are listed as job seekers in Kerala, and 47.5 percent work as non-agricultural laborers in the Gulf. Approximately half of them are married. While 27 percent of the households in Kerala were Muslims, 51 percent of the emigrants are Muslims. Although functionally literate, two-thirds of the migrants have no higher or technical training.[17] These workers come from the state's poorer districts.

Zachariah, Mathew, and Rajan have constructed a measure of the intensity of migration by district (Table 13.10). The Migration Prevalence Ratio (MPR) measures the number of people who have migrated and/or returned per 100 households.[18] In addition, the Household Migration Rate (HMR) measures the number of households per 100 that have members who are presently working outside Kerala or who have returned.

These data show that while migration to the Gulf may have minimal impact on the huge Indian economy, it profoundly affects the society and economy of Kerala. Fifty-nine percent of all households have at least one member who has worked outside of the state.[19]

Aggregative and disaggregative measures also assess the impact of out-migration on the Keralite economy. The remittances rose sharply per capita income above the gross domestic product. For example, in the early 1980s, the district of Malappuram reported a per capita income figure 69 percent higher than the gross domestic product.[20] Moreover, more recently Kerala's per capita consumption levels are among the highest in India, while the per capita domestic product is near the middle.[21] A disaggregative approach shows more precisely how out-migration has changed the living standards of Keralite workers. Table 13.11 lists key consumer durables and calculates the percentage of households that have such items. The table also indicates both the general poverty of Keralite citizens and the positive impact that out-migration has had on living standards.

Table 13.11 Percent of households possessing selected household consumer durables, by migration status, 1998

Consumer durables	Return emigrant households	Emigrant households	Non-migrant households
Motor car	7	6	2
Motor cycle	18	12	8
Telephone	31	32	11
Television	54	53	34
VCR	28	28	6
Radio	28	28	6
Water pump	46	52	22
Sewing machine	24	21	14
Refrigerator	41	40	13
Washing machine	20	16	4
Fan	80	83	47
Mixer	60	66	28
Gas stove	39	38	15
Clock	88	91	76
Iron	72	76	37
Stereo	52	51	21
Watch	95	91	79
Cycle	33	27	25
Sofa	34	34	15
Toaster	5	3	1

Source: K.C. Zachariah *et al.*, Working Paper II, 2000.

Economic analysis: rent-seeking by surplus labor and the scramble for jobs

The data from both the Gulf and Kerala indicate that participants in this labor exchange receive significant economic benefits. While the data on consumer durables indicate considerable gains in material benefits for Keralite workers, the mental health costs of prolonged separation are high (although the ethnographic and survey data are ambiguous). Some of the women left behind gain considerable autonomy and improve their marital relations.[22] On the other hand, the Gulf economy clearly benefits from the supply of tractable and productive low-wage labor.

Given this benefit, it is surprising to note a constant drumbeat for the "nationalization" of the Gulf workforce, which has included reliance on the increased participation of national women in the labor market. As Kapiszewski states:

> The employment of national women acquires special importance. In addition to the fact that their numbers can make a difference in itself, some experts think that national women are more cost-effective compared to national men or even expatriates. They can also take some jobs that national men would be reluctant to accept – such as secretarial or administrative positions in

schools or hospitals. Therefore the authorities in several GCC countries [have begun] to promote the employment of national women, seeing it as a significant means of limiting the size of the expatriate labor.[23]

Many nationals clearly view the large South Asian workforce as a threat to the cultural integrity of their nation.[24]

On the Keralite side, commentators express their anxiety about the labor exchange in two ways:

- That Indian workers suffer extreme exploitation in the Gulf that the Indian government is not able to prevent.
- That any halt in the flow of labor from Kerala will seriously disrupt the domestic economy.

These two concerns are clearly contradictory. If the Indian government complains about the treatment of its citizens in the Gulf, then the Gulf states can seek low-wage labor elsewhere. The economic crisis in Indonesia, for example, could permit labor there to supplant South Asians.

The worries of both Gulf nationals and Keralites, paradoxically, come from the same source: Gulf enterprises acquire labor within a buyer's market. Even though the income offered to many laborers is low, high unemployment and even lower wages in South Asia push large numbers of excess workers to "bid" for jobs. That surplus labor bids for scarce jobs is an all-too familiar aspect of the global migration experience. Central Americans also experience this when coming to the United States.

If institutional barriers, wage-setting customs, or efficiency wage calculations prevent the offering of lower wages that might limit the inflow of workers, then other administrative and market-based institutions facilitate this rationing of labor.[25]

Both the UAE and Indian governments have attempted to implement administrative regulations to halt the movement of excess labor. For a worker to receive a visa for employment in the UAE, the UAE government must issue a work permit or a "no objection certificate." In addition, the Indian government also requires evidence of employment before issuing an exit permit.

These rules could in principle reduce the number of migrants to the desired amount. In fact, however, such measures fail to limit in-migration. Accordingly, a market in permits and "sponsorships" has emerged. Workers compete against each other for the papers necessary to obtain a visa, and this allows the seller of such certificates to extract rents through discriminatory pricing for agent services and "cheating" – the payment for services that are not delivered. (See the appendix for a description of this rent extraction process.)

Behind this supply–demand analysis lies extraordinary risk-taking and its consequences. One Keralite informant of ethnographer Leela Gulati describes the initial travails of her husband, Basheer.

> Things did not move fast for Basheer. It took almost two years after our marriage to locate an agent who promised to obtain an employment permit

for Basheer. According to him, we would require Rs. 15,000 (U.S. $319) to cover the cost of the employment permit as well as the return air ticket.

To put together the money, several sources had to be tapped. But my jewelry came first. There was also the cash that my parents had given in my dowry. My mother-in-law and sister-in-law also gave up their gold.

Once the money was ready Basheer became impatient and started pestering the agent. That, it turned out, was a big mistake. He was sent to Bombay on the promise that he would be given the employment voucher and ticket. But this turned out to be false. After waiting for nearly four months in Bombay where one lives on one's own, usually in a mosque and in extremely difficult conditions, he returned home empty-handed. He was angry with himself and the agent. We thought he would never make it.[26]

Figure 13.1 explains the most common method of recruiting labor or selling jobs. The sponsors who begin to search for expatriate workers may represent large corporations, owners of small businesses, or even individual Gulf national householders. In all cases, these "sponsors" of expatriate workers must obtain the necessary certificates from the UAE government. Large businesses or institutions normally do not inflate the number of positions required. They seem content with the potential profits by employing the workers. On the other hand, it is not unusual for heads of households or owners of small businesses to overstate their labor requirements and then sell the excess permits to eager individuals attempting to "crack" the UAE labor market.

The sponsors with excess permits often market them. The buyers could be licensed labor recruitment agencies, unlicensed agencies, or private individuals

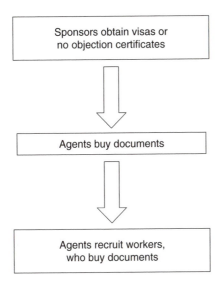

Figure 13.1 Gaining entry to the Gulf labor market.

such as workers returning to Kerala on leave or because their contract and residence visa have expired. Often these permits are resold to other agents before finding a would-be emigrant. Once a worker arrives in the UAE, his travails may not have ended. Despite guarantees, it often happens that employment is not available for the worker. A search for further employment by the worker requires the expenditure of more funds to new sponsors and agents so that the worker's employment status can be regularized.

Another method of obtaining employment is to enter the UAE as a tourist and then search for a job and purchase work permits there (Figure 13.2). As Nair states, this method also leaves the worker vulnerable to exploitation.

> Though this method of job search is hazardous and land many of the aspirants in jail, thousands do manage to get jobs and regularize their travel and employment documents with the help of their employers. It is understood that some of the employers in the host countries find it more economical to make such on the spot recruitment because in these cases they don't have to incur the cost of making recruitments either directly or through recruiting agents. Further they could also get recruits on terms and conditions much inferior to those they would otherwise have to agree to.[27]

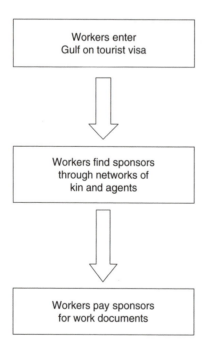

Figure 13.2 Alternative method of gaining entry to the Gulf labor market.

Table 13.12 Per capita costs of emigration

Type of cost	US dollar expense	% share
Ticket	$279	17.0
Visa	$627	38.1
Agent commission	$299	18.2
Cheating	$439	26.7
Total	$1,644	

Source: K.C. Zachariah, *et al.*, Working Paper I, Chapter 5, 1999.

Note
Rs. 47 = US $1.00.

How much rent is extracted from the worker? Survey data collected by Zachariah, Mathew, and Rajan suggest that ignoring the ticket expense, workers spent on average Rs. 64,178 or US $1,365 to obtain a job from agents (Table 13.12). If each emigrant loses Rs. 20,654 or US $439 through "cheating" (the selling of false documents and misrepresenting employment prospects), this absorbs 32 percent of total rent payments made by impoverished Keralite workers and 27 percent of total job-seeking costs.

The social categories of those who extract the rent from the job-seeking workers are Gulf nationals, expatriate business people in the Gulf, and licensed and unlicensed recruitment agents in Kerala. This largely private network of rent-seeking agents involves both Indians and Emiratis and is only imperfectly controlled by the UAE, Indian, and Keralite governments. Indian government officials weakly attempt to limit the exploitation of job-seeking agents by Indian nationals. UAE officials know that they are limited in controlling the visas overall because Emirati citizens gain considerable revenue from sponsoring expatriate workers. Nationals may either use their influence to obtain visas that can be sold to formal and informal recruiting agents in Kerala (or to Keralite workers who sell visas on their return home) or they can receive funds from agents or workers who have access to visas but need a sponsor to formalize their employment in the UAE. Yet, within the wider framework of nationalizing the UAE workforce, often referred to as "Emiratization," the drive by UAE entrepreneurs to sponsor expatriate workers clearly frustrates efforts for such nationalistic aspirations for the workforce. National business people attempt to subvert government policy for their own gain, while at the same time complaining about the high wages they would have to pay to their own citizens. As Addleton suggested, large-scale migration undermines the regulatory capacity of the state to direct economic life and shows the strength of globalization processes in thwarting the goals of the state.[28] This applies to both the South Asian and Gulf States.

The ambivalent control of surplus labor in the Gulf

The immigration control process is flexible and open to manipulation partly because enforcement costs are significant and partly because citizens within each state profit from this ambiguity. I would hypothesize, however, that an additional reason for the toleration of a surplus labor pool in the UAE is that it also furnishes a reserve that facilitates the control of labor. Because the labor market is slack, workers have diminished bargaining power. Moreover, the presence of a surplus labor pool leads the UAE government to impose extra regulations that facilitate the tracking of immigrant workers who have no legal right to reside in the UAE without a job. These extra controls tie workers more tightly to particular jobs. For construction and clerical work, the governments throughout the Gulf operate a twenty-first century version of indentured servitude. However, such servitude may be long established and reciprocal in the minds of the Emiratis, who may have family members who served in the households of Indians prior to the oil boom. Unlike colonial America, however – where indentured servitude arose to prevent workers from escaping into the hinterland – the effort to tie workers to a particular job in the Gulf is a national security response to the destabilizing threat of large numbers of unemployed non-citizen workers within a sparsely populated country. The UAE government is constantly struggling with constructing appropriate policies that simultaneously permit the flexible distribution of labor according to economic need, the maintenance of the "correct" amount of surplus labor in the country to stabilize economics, and the close observation of all expatriate workers to dissipate potential unrest. It is not surprising that these efforts often appear confused and contradictory.

The *Gulf News* publishes a weekly column entitled "Ask the Law" that provides legal advice to the expatriate community. Many of the letters revolve around the legal complexities that inevitably arise when non-citizens marry, divorce, have sex, or traffic accidents.[29] A large number of letters, however, appear to lament the peculiarities of the UAE labor market. For example on March 8, 2002, A. Haroon of Dubai writes:

> The company that has sponsored me gave my passport to another company as guarantee without my knowledge. I now need my passport. My sponsor is out of the country and my passport has been with the other company for four months. The company that has my passport needs a bank guarantee from my sponsor company. This is not possible in the absence of my sponsor and without his signature.
>
> Can a company who is sponsoring an employee give an employee's passport to someone else without the employee's knowledge? If so, how can the employee get his passport? Can the employee take legal action?

It is impossible to know exactly the reasons behind the complex exchange that Haroon describes. Most likely, the original sponsoring company agreed to transfer Haroon to another company and simultaneously transferred the passport. Now, however, he cannot transfer to another company or leave the region without his original sponsor paying the other company some compensation for the loss of his services. Until that payment is made, Haroon must work in his new company.

Whatever the precise circumstances, the *Gulf News* columnist writes:

> A company which keeps its worker's passport may not use the passport for any purpose without permission from the passport's holder. A passport is kept as a security measure and may not be submitted as guarantee to a third party because there is no relationship between the worker and that party.
>
> The worker can submit a complaint to the police or the prosecution demanding that his passport be returned to him because there is no relationship between him and the company which holds the passport as a guarantee.[30]

Haroon thus has legal recourse, but it is certainly possible that Haroon does not wish to complain to the police or endure the psychological and financial strain of litigation. Further investigation could reveal that Haroon is working in a job that does not correspond to his visa. Moreover, a complaint to the police might deprive him of his sponsor's protection.

It is not unusual for employees in any labor market to lack leverage over their employers and thus be reluctant to complain or protest heavy-handed practices. In the UAE, strict laws against labor organization combined with the poor fallback position of many individual workers weaken labor's bargaining power further. For example, E. Lising of Dubai writes in the February 15 issue of the *Gulf News*:

> I have a friend working in a company in Jebel Ali. In April, the company sent him and several others a letter saying that they would have to take four months' leave since the company did not have enough projects to support their employees. Only one month was paid for. Six months have gone by and the company has not recalled them. Is this legal?

Once again, the newspaper's columnist assures the correspondent that the workers should be compensated: "It is the responsibility of the company to find jobs for its workers."[31] Nevertheless, this story and many others that nearly all professional and expatriate workers know about testify to the difficulties associated with the enforcement of these laws and the real vagaries of the global market.

Arbitrary behavior allowed of employees can further facilitate the control of the expatriate labor and increase productivity. There are limits, however. If the UAE government made no effort to control immigration or regulate working conditions, the pressure of large pools of unemployed workers combined with erratic and unfair labor practices could threaten social stability and seriously demean the "guest" workers. The government clearly recognizes the range of possibilities for abuse. Laws are on the books to protect workers from unscrupulous employers. Moreover, the government does occasionally attempt to enforce these laws. The sporadic nature of this intervention, however, leaves a contradictory body of practices and understood ambiguities that both protect and exploit workers.

Conclusion

It is difficult to predict the future contours of the Gulf Arab–South Asia relationship. One can say, however, that the small rich Gulf States such as the UAE, Kuwait, and Qatar will rely on foreign labor into the indefinite future. The only question is from where the labor will come.

One scenario would be that the slow unification of the GCC combined with the relative decline of large-scale construction projects would eventually create a single Arabian labor market. This would allow workers and their families from Saudi Arabia and Oman to immigrate to the richer states of the peninsula. Such a movement could be supplemented by a rise in females in the labor force and perhaps a return to the Yemeni labor of earlier times.

Despite the possibility of such a scenario, great cultural and political barriers will probably block such developments. The experience of the first Gulf War suggests that rulers will avoid the political challenges to authority that the presence of low-wage Arab workers might pose. Moreover, ideological based cultural resistance to a pronounced expansion of female labor into the clerical and retail sectors remains strong.[32] Finally, the unification of labor markets might lead to pressures to unify social and welfare policy. It is highly unlikely, however, that the richer energy states will share their bounty with poorer, non-citizen Arabic-speaking brethren.

Southeast Asia could be an alternative source of labor, rather than South Asia. Filipino labor already figures importantly in the retail and leisure service sectors of the UAE economy. In addition, Muslim Indonesia might be an obvious source for labor requisite for future large construction projects. Certainly, managers of expatriate labor within Gulf countries want not to be solely dependent on one national group. And, commentators have already noted an increase in the inflow of female labor from Southeast Asia into domestic service.

On the other hand, if infrastructural construction projects decline, there would probably not be a significant shift in the origins of workers. Rather, it is more likely that the recruitment of clerical and service workers into large and small enterprises would use pre-existing channels. The large presence of a settled South Asian business and professional population and the ability of workers to sell the documents for entry into the Gulf labor markets facilitate the recruitment of workers of similar nationality.[33]

As GDP per capita grows within the Gulf region, the demands for service and professional workers will increase. Short of a major disruption in the political economic framework of the Arabian Sea economy, labor and financial flows between South Asia and the Gulf states in general and Kerala and the UAE in particular should continue. The ambivalent anxieties unleashed by the intensive utilization of South Asian labor in the Gulf are a permanent political economic product of the labor networks, remittances and capital flows emanating from a still emerging Arabian Sea economy.

APPENDIX

Workers decide whether or not to immigrate to the Gulf by comparing the income they expect to receive over the contract period with their opportunities in

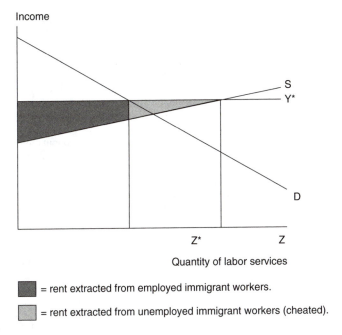

Figure A13.1 The extraction of rents from immigrant workers.

the home country. A higher expected income will induce more workers to leave their home country. Because South Asia has a large pool of surplus labor, this graph depicts a relatively horizontal or elastic supply curve. Demand is regulated by the employers' calculation of wage costs over the life of the contract in comparison to the workers' projected economic productivity. If custom or law sets expected income (or wage costs) at Y*, then this disequilibrium income level will generate a permanent labor surplus. Unemployed immigrant workers in the Gulf and workers in South Asia waiting for entry after having paid the necessary "entry" fees constitute this surplus, which on the graph is equal to the line segment between Z* and Z.

The graph also indicates that many workers will be willing to pay the difference between the income they need to induce them to immigrate to the Gulf and the income they expect to receive. Most of these payments to agents and sponsors are rent (or employee surplus) that the workers would have received but have instead transferred to these intermediaries. A portion of the payment may be for actual job finding services provided by the agent. Economists would not classify this payment as a rental payment. Unemployed workers who make these rental payments have clearly been cheated. It is possible as well that employed immigrants feel cheated because they have taken jobs less remunerative and attractive than what had been promised. This type of cheating is not illustrated on this graph (Figure A13.1).

Notes

* An amended version of this chapter was published by Revista Economia Mundial.

** Professor of Economics, American University. The Office of the Provost of American University provided important funding for this research. The author would like to thank the faculty and staff of the Centre of Development Studies in Trivandrum, Kerala, for their hospitality. Dr S. Irudaya Rajan of the Centre was of great assistance and generously shared the results of his investigations. Thanks also to Rich Burchett, Mary Ann Fay, Garay Menicucci, Mustapha Pasha, B.A. Prakash, David Spielman, and members of American University's Globalization and South Asian seminars for insightful and helpful comments on earlier drafts of this paper.

1 Many poor Gulf Arabs reside in the region, and a part of the population, both male and female, have embraced the rigors of contemporary work and/or higher education as well.
2 El Musa has argued that the oil economy provided no backward or forward linkages to Gulf economies. The absence of backward linkages – that is, the development of industries to supply the technologically sophisticated oil industry – is a plausible claim. On the other hand, the huge rise in living standards has spawned enormous forward linkages indicated by the development of service industries that require significant technological capability [Sherif S. El Musa, "Technology and the Dynamics of Socio-Economic Change," *The Middle East Journal* 51 (Summer 1997): 358–72].
3 There is significant presence in the oil industry, the financial sector, and the state-owned telecommunications sector.
4 While commenting on the problem of the unemployment of national citizens, Kapiszewski (2000, 10–11) states that, "Another reason for unemployment is nationals' work ethic. Nationals are often disinclined to enter low-skilled posts while, at the same time, the educational systems are not well equipped to deal with the problem of how to reorientate traditional work values. In the majority of cases, nationals are ready to enter only occupations that are culturally acceptable, high in social status, typical 'modern' and connected with the white-collar environment."
5 By comparison, the poorer male citizens of Oman, Bahrain, and Saudi Arabia do work in relatively low-paid jobs. In these countries, the percentage of expatriate workers is significantly lower.
6 The only exception to the pattern of the national workforce receiving high pay for labor services is in the agricultural sector, where Emiratis tend land in the oil-poor emirates of Ras Al Khaimah and Fujairah. Most of the nationals in the police force and military come from these emirates as well.
7 Most Asian professionals hail from South Asia. There is also a significant presence of Filipino and South Korean professionals, who enjoy higher prestige. This hierarchy is malleable and differs according to one's perspective. For an excellent discussion of issues of class, ethnicity, and status in Kuwait, see Anh Nga Longva, *Walls Built on Sand: Migration and Exclusion in Kuwait* (Boulder, CO: Westview Press, 1997).
8 An exception is the relatively large number of female domestic workers from Southeast Asia, rather than South Asia, who work in the households of nationals and richer expatriates. Countries such as Indonesia are increasingly the suppliers of domestic work, although Filipino women labor in the high end of the market. Part of the reason for this difference in the market for low-wage women workers can be found on the supply side; the Indian and Pakistani governments have banned the out-migration of women to the Gulf as a result of earlier scandals over mistreatment. On the demand side, evidence suggests that national households prefer young women workers from Southeast Asian Muslim countries. Yet, the hierarchy of national expatriate workers varies by gender.
9 It is difficult to be more precise about the national composition of the expatriate workforce. The governments of the region are sensitive about their dependence on expatriate labor and do not publish the labor force data that are undoubtedly available to them.

10 Sharon Stanton Russell and Muhammad Ali Al-Ramadhan, "Kuwait's Migration Policy Since the Gulf Crisis," *International Journal of Middle East Studies* 26 (November 1994): 569–87.

11 For data on Pakistan, see Jonathan S. Addleton, *Undermining the Centre: The Gulf Migration and Pakistan* (Oxford: Oxford University Press, 1992).

12 B.A. Prakash, "Gulf Migration and Its Economic Impact: The Kerala Experience," *Economic and Political Weekly* December 12, 1998: 3210.

13 K.C. Zachariah *et al.*, "Impact of Migration on Kerala's Economy and Society," *International Migration* 39 (2001): 66.

14 If we accept Kapiszewski's report that 39 percent of the total population in the GCC countries is expatriate and that 40 percent of the foreign presence is Indian, this means that between 15 and 16 percent of all residents in the GCC countries are Indian. It is commonly estimated that half of all Indians in the Gulf and Saudi Arabia hail from Kerala. Thus, approximately 7.5 percent of the total population is Keralite. The figure for the UAE would be approximately 15 percent.

15 The class statement of the Lewis perspective is in W. Arthur Lewis, "Economic Development with Unlimited Supplies of Labour," *The Manchester School* 232 (1954): 139–91.

16 Data and analysis that highlight the unique nature of Kerala's development path can be found in Jean Dreze and Amartya Sen, *India: Economic Development and Social Opportunity* (Delhi: Oxford University Press, 1995).

17 *Ibid.*, 75–81.

18 This includes migrants to other parts of India as well as international emigration. In recent decades, emigration has outweighed internal migration by Keralites.

19 K.C. Zachariah *et al.*, *Dynamics*, 89, and I.S. Gulati and Ashoka Mody, "Remittances of Indian Migrants to the Middle East: An Assessment with Special Reference to Migrants from Kerala State," *Working Paper* 182 (Trivandrum: Centre for Development Studies, November 1983).

20 *Ibid.*

21 Joseph Tharamangalam, "The Perils of Social Development with Economic Growth: The Development Debacle of Kerala, India," *Bulletin of Concerned Asian Scholars* (January-March 1998).

22 See the accounts of Leela Gulati, *In the Absence of Their Men: The Impact of Male Migration on Women* (New Delhi: Sage Publications, 1993).

23 Kapiszewski.

24 An Emirati student of mine once admitted that he became scared while once riding an elevator with a group of South Asians. He realized for the first time that, "They could take our country over."

25 It is not certain that market-clearing wages can be established in an environment of unrestricted migration since development theorists have long noted that the presence of surplus workers in urban areas is a common feature of Third World economies. See Michael P. Todaro, *Internal Migration in Developing Countries* (Geneva: International Labor Office, 1976).

26 Gulati, 66.

27 P.R. Gopinathan Nair, "The Process of Migration," in *Indian Migration to the Middle East: Trends, Patterns and Socio-economic Impacts*, ed. B.A. Prakash (Rohtak: Spellbound Publications, 1998), 42.

28 Addleton.

29 For example, Ashraf Iqbal asks: "Is it a crime to have sex with someone without getting married?" The columnist answers by noting that, "The United Arab Emirates is a Muslim country. Premarital sexual intercourse is illegal under the UAE laws … According to the UAE Penal Code, he who indulges in sexual intercourse with a woman to whom he is not married even if it is with her consent, will be sentenced to no less than a year in jail" ("Ask the Law," *Gulf News*, March 15, 2002).

30 "Ask the Law," *Gulf News*, March 8, 2002.
31 "Ask the Law," *Gulf News*, February 15, 2002.
32 See Eleanor Abdella Doumato's perceptive analysis of the strict limits that continue to be placed on female labor force participation in "Women and Work in Saudi Arabia: How Flexible are Islamic Margins?" *The Middle East Journal* 53 (Autumn 1999): 568–83.
33 This chapter has not explored the position of near permanent South Asian residents in the UAE. I would hypothesize that the rise of cultural and professional South Asian institutions in the Gulf helps stabilize the South Asian presence in the region and facilitates the continued presence of "temporary" Indian workers. Social scientists of the region should study this affluent group more intensively.

References

Addleton, Jonathan S. *Undermining the Centre: The Gulf Migration and Pakistan*. Oxford: Oxford University Press, 1992.

Doumato, Eleanor Abdella. "Women and Work in Saudi Arabia: How Flexible are Islamic Margins?" *The Middle East Journal* 53 (Autumn 1999): 568–83.

Dreze, Jean and Amartya Sen. *India: Economic Development and Social Opportunity*. Delhi: Oxford University Press, 1995.

El Musa, Sherif S. "Technology and the Dynamics of Socio-economic Change." *The Middle East Journal* 51 (Summer 1997): 358–72.

Gulati, I.S. and Ashoka Mody. "Remittances of Indian Migrants to the Middle East: An Assessment with Special Reference to Migrants from Kerala State." *Working Paper* 182. Trivandrum: Centre for Development Studies, 1983.

Gulati, Leela. *In the Absence of Their Men: The Impact of Male Migration on Women*. New Delhi: Sage Publications, 1993.

International Monetary Fund. *United Arab Emirates: Recent Economic Developments*. IMF Staff Country Report no. 98/134. Washington, DC: 1998.

Kapiszewski, Andrzej. "Population, Labor and Education Dilemmas Facing GCC States at the Turn of the Century." Paper presented at the conference Crossroads of the New Millenium, Abu Dhabi, UAE, April 9, 2000.

Lewis, W. Arthur. "Economic Development with Unlimited Supplies of Labour." *The Manchester School* 232 (1954): 139–91.

Longva, Anh Nga. *Walls Built on Sand: Migration and Exclusion in Kuwait*. Boulder, CO: Westview Press, 1997.

Nair, P.R. Gopinathan. "The Process of Migration." In *Indian Migration to the Middle East: Trends, Patterns and Socio-economic Impacts*, edited by B.A. Prakash, 42, Rohtak: Spellbound Publications, 1998.

Prakash, B.A. "Gulf Migration and Its Economic Impact: The Kerala Experience." *Economic and Political Weekly*, December 12, 1998: 3210.

Russell, Sharon Stanton, and Muhammad Ali Al-Ramadhan. "Kuwait's Migration Policy Since the Gulf Crisis." *International Journal of Middle East Studies* 26 (November 1994): 569–87.

Tharamangalam, Joseph. "The Perils of Social Development with Economic Growth: The Development Debacle of Kerala, India." *Bulletin of Concerned Asian Scholars* (January-March 1998).

Todaro, Michael P. *Internal Migration in Developing Countries*. Geneva: International Labor Office, 1976.

United Nations Development Program. *Human Development Report 2001*. New York: Oxford University Press, 2001.

Zachariah, K.C., E.T. Mathew, and S. Irudaya Rajan. "Migration in Kerala State, India: Dimensions, Determinants and Consequences." Working Paper I. Thirunananthapuram: Centre for Development Studies, Indo-Dutch Program on Alternatives in Development, September 1999.

——. *Dynamics of Migration in Kerala: Dimensions, Differentials and Consequences*. Thiruvananthapuram: Centre for Development Studies, Indo-Dutch Program on Alternatives in Development, October 2000.

——. "Migration in Kerala State, India: Dimensions, Determinants and Consequences." Working Paper II. Trivandrum: Centre for Development Studies, 2000.

——. "Impact of Migration on Kerala's Economy and Society." *International Migration* 39 (2001): 66.

14 The evolution of the Gulf city type, oil, and globalization

*Sulayman Khalaf**

Once upon a time Harran was a town of fishermen and returning travelers. But now the town belongs to no one. Its people have no common features, they are from all races, they lack a distinguishing type. They have come from everywhere yet it seems that the human in them is missing. Languages live next to dialects, colors next to colors, and religions next to religions. Wealth in it and beneath it is different from all types of wealth. Harran does not resemble any other city. It does not resemble itself. The people in it got here together by accident, and they will not stay long.[1]

Introduction

This chapter provides a panoramic description of the evolution of the Arabian Gulf oil city as a particular city type. More specifically, the paper explores the most salient factors, forces, and characteristics related to the Gulf city's physical make-up and functions. Its social formation is manifested in rapid development with a multi-ethnic character and housing patterns. My argument is that these emerging urban characteristics and socioeconomic formations have produced a city type that, in the words of Munif, "does not resemble any other city."[2] The definitive aspects of the Gulf city type are viewed within the context of the dynamics of the oil economy and globalization processes.

The paper primarily synthesizes existing studies and introduces new empirical data. My field observations on the Gulf city came through everyday "participant living" while teaching anthropology and sociology courses during decades in Kuwait and the United Arab Emirates. My numerous visits to Bahrain, Oman, and Saudi Arabia also provided relevant field observations on the changing urban structures of these cities. However, I draw more data from Emirati cities.

Since I construct a composite picture of the Gulf city as an evolving type, I combine my own field observations with findings from existing writings on the Gulf urban phenomenon. Obviously, the aim is ambitious, entailing the descriptive/analytical treatment of each of the constituents and conditions that comprise the Gulf city. Each of the urban features is an invitation for future research. The methodological approach differs from the technical statistical approaches often used by urban sociologists, social geographers, city planners, and architects, who concentrate on particular aspects of urban development.

Theoretical note

Since the mid-twentieth century, the making of Arab Gulf societies in Kuwait, Bahrain, Qatar, the UAE, and Oman has been associated primarily with the factor of oil. Locals often label their societies *al-mujtama't al-naftiya*m, which translates as oil societies.[3] However, as an energy resource and a base of wealth, oil is not uniformly causal here across human societies. Other factors particular to individual societies often render specific patterns and directions. Hence is the significance of detailed comparisons to identify what is common and what is particular in the various Gulf societies and their cities.[4]

Yet, the dominant features that underpin Arab Gulf societies as one societal type far outweigh those that create diversity. To wit, they all share a similar climate and ecology, common history, language, demographic features, religion, and culture. Moreover, they found themselves recently possessing huge oil reserves. The export of this national treasure has brought about great prosperity, which in turn has generated similar transformations, development, and challenges. Yet, the oil economy did not only generate similar economic conditions and social and cultural patterns in the Gulf. It also greatly integrated this region within the world economic order and its transnational global culture. In less than half a century, oil wealth brought somewhat uniformly broad transformations to the Arab Gulf's entire way of life.

These transformations are interconnected and embedded within the region's oil political economy and the global condition encapsulating it. Firstly, the transformed economic infrastructure is reflected in the accelerated integration of the new oil economy within global capitalism. In the words of Al-Fahim, material life conditions in the Gulf region have gone from "rags to riches."[5] Secondly, political transformations have changed the ruling sheikhs' material support structure so that they have become the controllers of national oil wealth, the massive bureaucratization of authority, and mechanisms of governance. The traditional sheikhs have emerged as benevolent distributors of oil wealth and the builders of cities with their modern welfarism and good life. Thirdly, demographics have transformed, as evidenced in the rapid population increase primarily from the flow of expatriate laborers needed to modernize society. This massive influx of expatriates made the nationals of Kuwait, Qatar, and the UAE minorities in their homelands.

Taken together, these factors have transformed socio-cultural life. Rapid modernization, massive urbanization, and exposure to global forces and culture affect local cultural lifeways, which have been undermined in varying degrees by oil wealth. By the beginning of the twenty-first century, these transformations have forged a societal type that is unique to this region. This urban social formation differs markedly in its sociological characteristics and evolution from other societal types dominant in most industrialized capitalist societies or the least industrialized (Third World) developing countries, as well as those found in other oil-producing Islamic Middle Eastern societies. For example, this society type differs from oil exporting countries such as Iran, Iraq, Algeria, Nigeria, and Venezuela in standards of wealth, income per capita, population size, and particular developmental needs such as reliance on massive imported expatriate labor.

Accordingly, the urban oil-rich Gulf societies have each emerged as a particular type of "oil city" – not an industrial oil city but one in which oil wealth has shaped both physical structure and social composition. The main cities that have evolved in the Gulf since the mid-twentieth century, such as Kuwait, Manama, Doha, Abu Dhabi, Dubai, Sharjah, and Muscat, reflect similar political economies and share more common features than differences. Commonalties lie in both the indigenous local and the exogenous global constituents that have produced specific similar urban configurations. The wider societal and historical contexts in which these cities evolved are strikingly similar. These contexts relate to their political economies and to the geographical, ecological, sociocultural, and demographic factors that are specific to their making in comparison with other urban settlement types in our contemporary world. Qutub noted the uniqueness of the development of the Gulf city: "It is difficult to make any comparisons with the urbanization process of other developing countries where urbanization was slow and was associated with industrialization and sound economic development."[6]

In his proposed typology of Middle Eastern cities, Khuri identifies Gulf ones as the "industrial city" type.[7] He sees that "cities such as Kuwait, Doha, Abu Dhabi, Riyadh, Al Khobar, and the two cities of Yumbu and Jubail in Saudi Arabia are built around the industry of oil and are in this sense classified as industrial."[8] Yet, most Gulf cities have evolved not only as the capitals of their countries but also as urban centers where multiple functions are performed, such as managing all aspects of the "political economy" of oil wealth, which itself is encapsulated within the global capitalist economy and culture. Therefore, Khuri's label "industrial" is not an adequate term to describe these still-developing cities, as they are "industrial" only in one sense of the word. However, Riad's term "petro-urbanism" seems more appropriate to describe the emerging urban character and ethos of the Gulf oil city.[9]

As such, the Gulf oil city is viewed within the macro globalization dominated by transnational corporations and propelled by "flexible accumulation of capital."[10] Similarly, economic globalization relates to city design and culture that is generating specific spatial patterns that organize lifeways of local cultures throughout the world.[11] The increasing "economic globalization is compelling world cities to respond physically by adopting universal standards of urban planning in standard street widths, standard plot area, standard provision of infrastructure, and standard zoning criteria. This trend is encouraged by the failure of local urban forms and processes to provide quality floor space area for global economic activities."[12]

Contemporary Gulf cities are now sprawling urban fields in which forces and scenes of globalization continue their flow. In the words of Appadurai, global forces represent the flows of "ethnoscapes, mediascapes, technoscapes, financescapes, and ideoscapes."[13] The reception, negotiation, and management of these global flows in the Gulf city are generating a meek counter trend of localization. Together, these flows and counter cultural forces build and evolve oil cities. The global "scapes" *à la* Appadurai continue to provide the essential modern infrastructures and services required for the modern "El Dorados" of the Gulf. Despite the recurrent pride-inspiring nationalistic songs and commentaries in local media, the modern Gulf cities have traveled far from the traditional urbanism of the region in their design, features, tempo, and ethos.

Evolution of the Gulf oil city

Speedy evolution, distorted demographic composition and functions, and intense emerging characteristics have combined to configure the Gulf oil city in space and time. The following are specific characteristics, functions, and social formations that distinguish the Gulf oil city from other urban phenomena.

Coastal locations

Life along the coast has provided more opportunities for livelihood through the centuries than the harsh desert interior. The cities of Kuwait; Al Muharraq and Manama in Bahrain; Doha in Qatar; Abu Dhabi, Dubai, Sharjah, Ajman, Ras Al Khaimah, and Fujairah in the UAE; and Muscat, Oman, were pearling, fishing, and sea trading towns. Pearling and long-distance sea trade also account for the cultural tolerance and wider outlook on the world, which characterize the attitudes of those living on the coast as compared to the fierce conservatism of their nomadic Bedouin kin in the desert. This historical proclivity has affected the acceptance of change recently. Again in comparison, the few towns in the desert interior, such as Al-Jahra and Al Ahmadi in Kuwait, Al Ain and Beda Zayed in Abu Dhabi Emirate, UAE, and Nizwa in Oman reflect staunch social and cultural conservatism.

Exponential growth

In Abu-Lughod's words "what Gulf countries lack in population, however, they make up for in interest, for seldom has the world seen a more striking *in situ* experiment of instant urbanization and hot house forced social change."[14] Oil-generated growth has literally demolished mud-walled small seaports and villages. In just four decades, these cities transformed into glittering commercial capitals and sprawling suburbs integrated within the global economy and culture. The speed, pattern, and policies of urban development have been fairly similar across the Gulf. While slight chronological variations reflect different advents of oil exportation in each country, each city has reproduced similar urban processes.[15]

In this rapid urbanization, sequential phases delineate the ontology: traditional phase, initial phase, rapid urbanization phase, and the final gradual phase. Each phase actually parallels the socioeconomic and political developments of the Gulf oil societies at large.[16]

The traditional phase

The "pre-oil phase" ended in the 1950s in Kuwait, Bahrain, and Qatar and in the 1960s in the UAE and Oman. The Gulf cities were then small seaside towns with populations ranging between 2,000 and 15,000 inhabitants. Some were fortified and surrounded by mud walls with watchtowers, city gates, and citadel-like forts for the rulers. Dotting the length of the Arabian shoreline, these old urban cores (see Chapter 15) reflected a sea-orientation. Their size and prosperity seemed calibrated to their fresh water supply, their proximity to pearling grounds and inland trade, the properties of their harbors, their economic symbiosis with neighboring oasis farming communities, and their relationship with nomadic tribal groups. Building materials were derived from local sources (as described in Chapter 15), although some wood for roofing was imported from India and East Africa. The houses were usually compounds of modest structures, accommodating extended patrilineal families, and the courtyard was large enough to add on rooms for newly wed sons (patrilocal residence). With one kitchen for the family compound and sons following their father's trade, we have the nucleus of the old socio-economic organization.[17]

Images of the pre-oil towns have been reproduced in the form of heritage villages (*qura turatheyyah*) close to the sea in the midst of modern skyscrapers built of shining concrete, glass, and steel. These reconstructed villages represent frozen slices of the region's history. What is worth noting here is that the reconstruction of the cultural past appears as heritage shrines in similar ways in all of the modern Gulf metropolises. The reproduction of this eclipsed city life now preserves local roots that were bulldozed away under the frenzy of the oil boom.[18]

The initial phase

The Gulf states were financially empowered by oil revenues to modernize state and society, as evidenced by the building of modern infrastructure. Modernization included the construction of houses, roads, hospitals, schools, markets, ports, airports, communication systems, mosques, universities, parks, and recreational facilities. While the pearl divers, seamen, and semi-nomads *en masse* were filling the burgeoning state bureaucracy and its emerging welfare institutions, the leading old merchant families were transformed into business agents for international companies that began pouring in consumer goods. Subsequently, commercial institutions with global links developed rapidly; light industries and contracting companies sprouted up without overall planning. Meanwhile, the oil industry continued to modernize and expand, thus offering great employment opportunities for both nationals and expatriates.

The capital cities attracted most of the modernization processes, and their populations grew rapidly. Both internal and external migration continued to fuel this rapid growth. During this phase, the nationals represented more than half of the total population in their respective countries. The open-door policy toward foreign labor created an ethnic/cultural mosaic, and the flood of foreigner workers was not yet a national political or cultural issue.

The rapid urbanization phase

The initial phase lasted about two decades in Kuwait, Bahrain, and Qatar, and only one decade for the UAE and Oman. Multiple factors created the right environment for the rapid and massive urbanization in the capital cities. The most important was greatly increased oil revenues during the oil embargo of the Arab–Israeli war in 1973. This phase halted at the end of 1980s due to the rapid depreciation of oil prices and because most modernizing state infrastructure had been built.

The late gradual phase

Starting in the late 1980s and continuing to the present, a phase of slow economic growth and development set in. While the capital cities grew, quality instead of quantity was emphasized. Better roads were constructed, greater attention was paid to the greening of the urban environment, and more specialized hospitals, universities, and technical colleges were (and are being) built. Locally oriented tourism and industry diversify the economies. Scores of international chain hotels stud the shoreline of the Gulf cities; for example, Dubai alone boasts about forty five-star hotels and resorts. The building of large American-style shopping malls is the latest trend in the Gulf cities. Almanma in Bahrain has three large malls while Dubai prides itself on having more than twenty such urban wonders, many built on specific themes (e.g. Mercado features an Italian theme and the ancient Egyptian-themed Wafi Center has three pyramid roofs and sphinxes guarding the front entrance). High, prestige-inspiring towers, grand exhibition and conference centers, internet cities, media cities, knowledge cities, American and British universities, recreational theme parks, golf courses, wider and more efficient highways, and beautified seafronts are recent urban development projects common in the Gulf cities. Information technologies are widely implemented in institutions of higher education, schools, and homes.

The relatively modern buildings constructed during the early phases of development in Kuwait and Qatar have been demolished. In Abu Dhabi, hundreds of 12-storey buildings from the early 1970s are now being replaced by residential and commercial towers at least twice as tall. Land value has increased, but the longevity of buildings has decreased in the excessively hot and humid weather. City roads are continuously expanded and redesigned. Many highways and intersections built only a decade ago are increasingly obsolete due to the burgeoning traffic. To illustrate, but with some hyperbole, "the intensifying road activity has turned Abu Dhabi's traffic network into a virtual workshop. Visitors to the city will quickly notice the transformation of the capital's famous clean streets into what looks like a war ravaged area. At major intersections, the serenity of traffic lights alternating quietly has been murdered by the deafening drills and roar of massive cranes."[19]

The Gulf city as a metropolis

For Riad, the Gulf city has rapidly grown with the proportions of a "megalopolis."[20] Coined by the French geographer Jean Gottmann, a megalopolis is an urbanized region combining several metropolitan areas.[21] The megalopolis of Dubai–Sharjah and Ajman may approximate this form, although trends toward megalopolis-type of urban growth more characterizes the Gulf. The Gulf city represents "a process of agglomerating people in a limited urban space and a virtual evacuation of the greater part of the country leaving it unused or ill-used."[22]

At the height of the oil boom (1970s to 1980s) along with the rise of "wealth-fairism" and "welfarism," the capital cities were perceived as "El Dorados" or oases of "unlimited good" where the benevolent ruling sheikhs and emirs supervised the distribution of all good things to create affluence.[23] Factors that account for the rapid metropolitan growth in terms of structural/spatial expansion and population size include: (1) the cities as seats of power for the dynastic ruling families, who control the state and distribute oil wealth; (2) new employment opportunities in the cities; (3) migration from the resource-poor desert interior combined with the extensive welfare inducement; (4) a large influx of laborers from across the world, particularly Arab and Asian countries; (5) migration from the old city center into suburban development (in the desert); (6) widespread dissemination of communication and transportation technologies (e.g. automobiles, the mobile telephone, and the internet); (7) the almost total reliance on the private car as the primary transport, leading to wide streets and a system of highways and ring-roads; (8) the cities functioning as ports and industrial centers, political and diplomatic capitals, and educational centers; (9) nationals' strong preference for fully detached villas as opposed to high-rise apartment living; (10) open desert surrounding these cities; and (11) state ownership of the desert, which has facilitated the rulers' ambitious plans for the growth of their cities. Together, these factors have contributed to a low-density horizontal expansion of the city into the adjoining desert in ways that do not proportionately mirror its population size.

By the end of 1980s the greatest percentage of the national population was found within these metropolises, which became termed "city-states." This indeed characterizes Kuwait, Bahrain, Qatar, and the seven emirates of the UAE. The expansion of Doha illustrates this city-state type well. In 1959, the population of Doha (about 15,000) constituted 37.5 percent of the total population of Qatar. In 1980, Doha's population alone (190,000) constituted 86.3 percent of the population of Qatar.[24] Similarly, in the emirate of Dubai, 97.3 percent of the population live in the city of Dubai, with the remainder living in the nine outlying villages.[25]

The multi-ethnic migrant character

Multi-ethnic diversity and segregated housing patterns are urban features not particular or unique to the oil-rich Gulf cities. Yet, in worldwide comparison, these cities exhibited an unprecedented pace of change, greater population heterogeneity, and greater magnitude in development, leading to demographic imbalances (e.g. nationals versus non-nationals and gender ratios) and disparities in privilege and life conditions among the various ethnicities and classes.

Rapid urban growth from migration has provided a multi-ethnic character. The majority of migrants are foreign guest workers, referred to in Arabic as *al-wafedeen* (the in-comers) while the nationals are *al-muwateneen*. The now permanent ethnoscapes in the city have produced a multi-ethnic global social and cultural make-up. The still expanding Gulf city harbors now within it more than a hundred nationalities and ethnicities, all with their own physical types, languages, religions, and other cultural particularities. The non-national component of the city population is now overwhelmingly large, reaching in Kuwait City, Doha, Abu Dhabi city, Dubai city, and Sharjah city some 70 to 90 percent. Visitors to Dubai may comment that they actually feel they are in an Indian rather than Arab city.

Beyond this, the foreigners are also represented by multiple crisscrossing divides and boundaries that give separate ethnicities their own national identifications. First, the major ethnic divide is between nationals and expatriates. The expatriates subdivide according to various criteria such as regional origin, nationality, language, religion, sect, social class, roots, and genealogies of origin. As such, the categories are recognized as Asians, Arabs, Europeans, Africans, North Americans, Indians, Pakistanis, Iranians, Muslims, Hindus, Christians, Sunnis, and Shias. Relations among nationals and migrants are affected by specific laws and conditions that relegate most migrant groups to subordination.[26] This in turn has created a psychology of caution and ambivalence both between these two major population groups as well as among the migrant ethnic groups themselves.[27] While this multi-ethnic character is found in many large American, Asian, and Middle Eastern cities, this feature of the Gulf oil city is more accentuated with its own socio-political particularities. Only the Gulf oil city has up to 80 percent of its population as transient guest workers with few equal legal rights and privileges as compared to the nationals.

Segregated housing patterns of the migrants

The multi-ethnic population of the Gulf city is segregated by housing areas and neighborhoods. One may analyze the housing patterns within the context of global trends as well as within the local rentier oil state with its politics of welfarism and privilege, exclusion, and urbanization. A number of social scientists have commented on the "social formations" of the Gulf cities with their social and economic segregation patterns.[28] I synthesize the following five characteristics in the migrants' housing patterns:

(1) The construction and industrial workers arrive in Gulf cities on temporary contracts for specific projects and live in residential camps and ad hoc shanty housing compounds. The workers are often single males, and more recently, single women for the growing garment industry, who arrive in large groups and are housed in work camps or compounds that are isolated on the edges of communities.

(2) With the onset of oil wealth, the old traditional neighborhood houses were deserted by their owners, since they generally lacked modern amenities and conveniences. Now they appear sunken in the jungle of modern high-rise

concrete and glass buildings. The new residents of these old quarters are primarily bachelors, unskilled and semi-skilled migrants, particularly from the Indian subcontinent. Each room typically houses 4 to 8 men; an old 5-bedroom house may have 40 to 50 people crammed in far beneath any standards of hygiene and human dignity. Many old houses are hidden behind high-rises and function as derelict structures behind the shining facades of modern streets and commercial complexes. Given the poor living conditions in these inner city "old quarters," they are viewed by nationals as the foci of unpleasant and unwanted problems that distort their idealized image of their new cities. Newspapers publish letters bemoaning these old quarters and asking the authorities to remedy a worsening and embarrassing facet of otherwise elegant cities. Since the 1990s, the Gulf municipalities have renovated and preserved many traditional quarters as heritage monuments.

(3) According to Al-Najjar, the high-rise residential buildings and suburban villas rented by foreign middle-class professionals represent a specific housing pattern.[29] In physical structure, these apartment buildings and towers with facades featuring some distinctive architectural embellishments are designed to evoke images of Manhattan or other large US cities. These deluxe residence complexes have many modern features that ostensibly appeal to the bourgeoisie with young, urban, Western taste and lifestyle. They are usually spacious, with two or three bathrooms and often a special maid's quarter. Many of these buildings have swimming pools, gymnasiums, recreation rooms, banquets/party halls, parking, reception/security desks, mini-markets, and laundry services. The average rent is between US $20,000 to 30,000. These apartment complexes are owned by nationals, who may be kindred of the ruling family. As such, the rent revenue would be another governmental subsidy, since the residents usually get this quality housing as part of their international employment contracts. By and large the residents are European, American, and Canadian professionals. Arab, Indian, and Pakistani businessmen and professionals employed in the private or government sectors also usually live in the same category of housing.

(4) Villas and townhouse residential compounds are a rapidly growing residential pattern built to house expatriate families of middle-class professionals, technocrats, consultants, and businessmen who are usually older than the residents of the high rises. Dubai city prides itself on having about a hundred of these large estate residential compounds. Most of them are located in Jumeira, Umm Suqueim, and a few other suburbs like Satwa, Rashidiya, Al Garhoud, and Mirdif. These compounds vary in size from 20 to 120 villas or townhouses; the village-like compounds of detached houses are usually large and often walled, with gates and security officers.[30] High-quality primary and secondary schools staffed by American, British, and Canadian teachers, and supermarkets and mini-malls are found nearby.

(5) Other residential zones have rows of modern buildings of much lower quality. These buildings are uniformly repetitive and seem to lack character (they are reminiscent of the apartment buildings in former communist Eastern Europe). They were built some around the 1970s to house lower middle-class

families from the Arab world and the Indian subcontinent. Such migrant professionals and/or skilled technical employees work as schoolteachers, medical technicians, nurses, clerks, surveyors, foremen, policemen, accountants, and specialists in government public institutions. They are the ones who keep the modern welfare institutions of the oil state running.

Income, ethnicity, and culture seem to place immigrant families in specific neighborhoods. To illustrate, Al Karama in Dubai is inhabited almost entirely by Indians and is nicknamed Little Bombay. Similarly, the Hawalli neighborhood in Kuwait is nicknamed *Al-Dhifah Al-Gharbeya* (the West Bank in Palestine) since more than 90 percent of its residents are (or once were) Palestinians.

The existing immense Asian expatriate labor force in the Gulf stems from preferential policies in both the private and public sectors. The Arab component of the migrant population in the Gulf cities have played, and still play, a modernizing role in these once quite tribal societies.[31] The financial investment and rent profits are a major component in the prosperity of the business elite, the ruling sheikhs, and increasing numbers of nationals. Gulf nationals clearly benefit from the existing economic-political system as rentiers using their names as sponsors (*kafeels*) or business partners to facilitate business for expatriates and as landlords (*mullak*) who collect rent from foreign tenants in their residential or commercial properties.

Housing patterns of the nationals (al-muwatineen)

In the Gulf, nationals dwell in spatial properties primarily according to wealth and social power. I identify three main types of national housing, each associated with a particular social class: houses of the (1) political and economic elite, (2) new middle class, and (3) low-income social strata.

Houses of the political and economic elite

Each of the ruling families in the Gulf comprises large maximal lineage, which itself is subdivided into minimal lineages, and, at its most basic level, individual extended and/or nucleated families. The sheikhly families live in separate palace-like dwellings or in a number of individual mini-palaces within a huge compound built by the old sheikh for his sons. Many of the grand palaces of the emirs are located on sea fronts with their own private beach. They are distinguished by their immensity, high encircling walls, arched gates with cannons or statues bespeaking grandeur and power, and lush landscaped gardens. Many of the sheikhs have more than one *qaser* (palace). The Al Ain oasis city in the interior of Abu Dhabi has about 30 large palaces; the circumference of the fenced grounds of each typically is 300 to 1,000 meters. Many of these spacious palaces are empty most of the year, as their residents prefer living in the capital city of Abu Dhabi closer to the political action and international diplomatic community. In Abu Dhabi city, the area of *Qusour al-shuyoukh* (the sheikhs' palaces) extends 10 km along the west coastline.

Villas of the economic elite resemble the palaces of the sheikhs but are built on smaller grounds. Nonetheless they appear as modern palaces – ostentatious structures with columns, marble facades, arched windows, and high wrought-iron gates. Each is staffed with about half a dozen domestic helpers (maids, drivers, cooks, and gardeners) whose numbers may actually exceed the family members of the house. However, these compounds usually have separate quarters built for the domestic helpers so that privacy can be maintained for the family life.

The new middle class

The new and large middle class comprises thousands of relatively well-educated nationals who were born early in the oil revolution. They are middle and upper echelon state bureaucrats and professionals such as doctors, teachers, engineers, army and police officers, lawyers, bankers and managers in state and private companies, and small businessmen. The wives increasingly are employed in the public sector, thereby enhancing the family's income and its high consumer lifestyle.

Members of this homogeneous class obtained '*ard wa qardh*', land and money loans, from the state to build their modern villas. In their houses and material lifestyle patterns, such individuals emulate the elite class and often build two-story villas to reflect their new social position and quest for continued upward social mobility. The villas may have 5 to 7 bedrooms, 3 to 5 bathrooms, large living and dining rooms, and a basement used as a children's recreation area. These villas also contain separate quarters for an average of two maids, swimming pools, a 2-car garage, a high fence, and pretentiously high gates. High consumer aspirations have indebted many families to banks, and some subsequently fall victim to their own race toward heightened consumerism. Ideologically, they oscillate between traditionalism and modernity, which is also reflected in their large family sizes – 5 to 8 children. In spite of their acceptance of bourgeois consumerism, they remain sociopolitically traditional primarily as a defense mechanism against global forces that threaten their national identity (and thus privileges).

Tempted by more modern and larger villas, members of the economic elite have moved away from the old neighborhoods and traditional houses lacking modern amenities. They have benefited from the state's subsidized housing, free land plots and easy loans. In contrast, the suburban villa with a garden is a suitable stage for the nouveaux riche to enjoy what Veblen calls "conspicuous consumption and honorific waste."[32]

However, the hidden price for this shift to showy affluence is greater dependency on globalized consumer products, which in turn has produced a greater dependence on the welfare state and thus, the depowering of the middle class' political position.[33] As such, they differ markedly from the middle class of industrial capitalist countries who wield significant political power. An unabated desire to be lulled into modern villa living has meant increasing reliance on foreign live-in servants, who attend fully to the service and comfort of the family members for about 15 hours a day, 7 days a week, to create feelings of "a generalized aristocracy."

The irony of such a new social phenomenon is that nationals are the most vocal about their local culture being overrun by armies of foreigners, while their children are raised by foreign governesses.

Low-income social strata

The houses provided freely by the state to the low-income national groups, mostly recently settled Bedu tribal families, are referred to as '*al-bait al-sha-bi*' (literally, *people's house*) in neighborhoods referred to as '*sha'beyya*' (*people's community*). Most of the *sha'beyat* (pl. of *sha'beyya*) were built in the early 1970s and 1980s and were then located at the peripheries of the cities. They also are the dominant housing in the small towns and villages. However, the rapid horizontal growth of the Gulf cities, whether along the coast or into the desert, has resulted in most of these *sha'beyat* being engulfed by the new expanding suburbs.

Each *sha'beya* usually has 50 to 80 family homes of a single lineage, or sub-tribe, with repetitive uniformity in the architectural design of the single-story houses. Gulf governments have relocated members of particular tribal groups to the same neighborhoods so that the traditional social bonds can be maintained. The houses usually have palm trees growing in the open courtyard and wide metal gates color-fully decorated with local folk themes such as falcons, coffee pots, crescents, and incense burners. In his study of the "*Al-bait al-sha'bi*" (folk house) in the UAE, El-Aswad notes that the repetitive single-story low profile "gives *al-sha'beya* features of simplicity and horizontal harmony, thus identifying it as a distinct integrated social unit in which socioeconomic differences disappear. That is, kinship is more impor-tant than social ranking. The uniform architectural pattern of the *sha'beya* commu-nity as a whole symbolizes its modest social ranking within the larger society."[34]

The inhabitants of these communities are sociopolitically conservative, especially in their strong sense of tribal kinship identity and solidarity. El-Aswad found that around 65 percent to 69 percent of all the families living in one *sha'beya* community in Al-Ain belong to one lineage.[35] The large courtyard with its palm trees provides residents open space for adding extra rooms for family expan-sion. In each compound, the men's *majlis* (guest reception room) always has its own entrance and washroom to maintain family privacy. Social customs are sex-segregated, especially with male or female visitors to the house, and the women are veiled. Even the Asian live-in maids dress modestly, like the family members. Many *sha'beya* houses still keep lambs, goats, and chickens, and until recently, even camels in special corrals adjacent to the house. Some Bedu families still pitch tents next to the house to provide extra space for family life during the mild seasons of winter and spring or during Ramadan. Residents' relative wealth is shown by having one or two live-in maids and garages for luxury saloon cars and four-wheel-drive cars. However, the communal egalitarianism is evidenced by *sha'beya* families living next to mosques providing home-cooked food as religious charity at *iftar* (breaking the fast at sunset) during the fasting month of Ramadan. The food is placed next to the mosque fifteen minutes before sunset for members of the Asian Muslim urban proletariat.

The Gulf city as highly stratified society

The housing patterns of the Gulf city reflect the recent stratification according to ethnicity and social class. Laws and politics of exclusion maintain sharp economic disparities that favor nationals and render large numbers of immigrants susceptible to exploitation. While exploitation is manifested at multiple class/ethnicity levels, the semi-skilled and unskilled Asian and Arab workers experience the greatest exploitation. These workers are locally described as "the marginal labor force" – domestic servants, street cleaners, gardeners, construction and maintenance workers, and other manual laborers. This underclass earns around US $130 to $200 a month, or about one-sixth of the wages of their counterparts in the West. In a sense, the nationals are blessed twice: by the oil pipeline and the pipeline of cheap migrant labor. In reflection, the latter provides a psychological sense of self-elevation to the nationals. However, the low-income migrants view their exploited condition as an "opportunity" to be safeguarded and prolonged. It is regarded as their chance to lift up themselves and their families back home.[36]

The Gulf city as a center of consumption

Unlike large cities elsewhere, the Gulf cities are primarily "centers of consumption rather than centers of production."[37] The most diagnostic feature of Gulf capital cities is the immensity and centrality of showrooms, large malls, and exhibition centers. Presently, these cities rank among the world's top in per capita retail mall space. Dubai city, for example, ranks third after the United States and Singapore.[38] Since the late 1980s, large, ultra modern, air-conditioned shopping malls have been mushrooming across major Gulf cities. Kuwait, for example, recently has built 4 malls, and Al Manama in Bahrain has 3. Dubai prides itself on its appellation of the "Shopping Capital of the Middle East," with more than 20 large, American-style, multi-storey shopping malls with the latest technological innovations and elegance. These cool structures are welcoming havens from the torrid outside temperatures with their arcades of elegant shops, shining marble floors, escalators, postmodern fantasia color schemes, water fountains, Mediterranean-style cafés, international restaurants, food courts, soft music, and prestige German and Japanese cars as lottery prizes for the shoppers. The unpleasant hot and humid weather during half of the year make the malls' cool and colorful interiors appear as a shaded refuge, particularly with free underground parking. As such, the malls attract shoppers and onlookers by the thousands every day, and embody the goods and seduction of global capitalism. As the venues for summer shopping festivals, their wide marble arcades transform into arenas for cultural and dance spectacles by performers from all over the world. With their adventurous design and aesthetics of display and spectacle, the malls create and "focus the dream images of the global economy and help to produce global subjectivities by shaping everyday people's imagination and discourse about globalization."[39]

Modern supermarkets and co-operatives are also found in large numbers; each is staffed with scores of low-paid male and female Asian workers. Most of these stores are modeled after Safeway in America and Sainsbury in Britain. With their large air-conditioned interiors, these stores offer foods from the West, Middle East, and South Asia. For poor migrants from India, Egypt, and Syria, these modern supermarkets generate feelings indeed of oases of unlimited good.[40] As a corollary, the household waste in Gulf cities is among the highest in the world. In the UAE, for example, the municipalities have failed to achieve their target to cut waste production to 555 kilograms per person per year.[41]

High consumption in the Gulf city can be seen as a function of: (1) the high incomes of the nationals and immigrant professionals; (2) the distribution of the oil wealth to very large segments of the national population as high salaries for bureaucratic jobs (99 percent of the national labor force is in the public sector); (3) the oil welfare state, which provides its citizens with a comprehensive range of free services and provisions (e.g. free housing, education, medical care). The state welfarism helps nationals to redirect their resources toward greater consumption; and (4) perhaps "a natural reaction to the age-long deprivation" of the pre-oil life conditions.[42]

Immigrants consume at many levels. One way is buying home appliances, electronics, and other items not only for themselves but also for the family back home. The annual ritual of the migrant returning home loaded with gifts maintains his sense of social self and his symbolic standing in his/her community of origin. To illustrate, the stereotypical picture of the Egyptian (Saidi) peasants in the Gulf airports pushing carts with huge piles of suitcases filled with consumer goods informs us that immigrants here also consume for many other people in far away villages and towns in the Middle East or in Asia. Finally, consumption is an important cultural value that underpins global culture, especially within the urbanscapes of the Gulf oil city.

The Gulf city as a showcase

The physical appearance of the new Gulf city is metaphoric of large display cases of goods. It has been said that "The viewer in the Gulf cities gets the impression that their buildings have just peeled off their plastic wrapping sheets."[43] Some call these cities "too glittery, and somehow unrealistic."[44] Under the Gulf's brilliant sun along wide boulevards, the large commercial buildings, banks, five-star hotels and high-rise residential towers appear bejeweled with their glass and metallic facades. The palatial suburban villas of the elite and middle class with their high gates, impressive facades, and shiny furniture also express exhibitionist excesses of a nouveau riche consumer society. Annual shopping festivals and celebrations of national and religious holidays press the shopping centers, malls and municipalities to spend lavishly on decorating city streets, buildings, trees, and bridges with millions of colorful lights that make these cities glitter for several months every year.

The ruling elite perceive their new metropolises as monuments of modernity, progress, and national prestige. This nationalistic message is unmistakable in the popular songs on satellite television played to images of Gulf urbanscapes and national rulers. In songs, each of these cities is repeatedly described as the

"Pearl of the Gulf," "Diamond of the Gulf," and the "Bride of the Gulf." We have already discussed Dubai as the "Shopping Paradise of the Gulf." Both state and city municipalities spend generously on city beautification, expanding and modernizing their corniches, greening projects, traffic and street signs, public hygiene, cleanliness, and public safety. In comparison, the Gulf cities rival Singapore as a model to be envied and emulated by most world cities, particularly in the developing regions of the world. Remember, though, that the Gulf city's cleanliness and polished showcase image has been achieved not only because of oil wealth and newness but also by armies of cheap Asian laborers.

Again, it is paradoxical that the citizens view the migrants as blemishing their new and beautiful cities, particularly when this migrant labor force has built and maintained all the urban services. Since the early 1990s, most Gulf municipalities (*baladiyyahs*) prohibited the hanging of laundry on balconies overlooking main roads. These laws were obviously directed to the underclass migrants, as nationals do not usually live in apartments, which would represent an infringement on their full citizenship (i.e. to have land and a house). Even when young Emirati couples temporarily live in an apartment, they feel embarrassed until their own houses are built. A social/cultural dimension is seen in the numerous letters in the newspapers that reflect both the citizens' displeasure at Asian taxi drivers and grocery shopkeepers who, because of their uneducated and poor backgrounds, bring uncivilized customs to the clean and conservative Gulf society and also call attention to their lifestyle and gatherings that are regarded as unsuitable and potentially harmful for the health and image of the city. Houses of bachelor migrants (*masakin al uzzab*) are seen to represent unpleasant social conditions. One Abu Dhabi citizen recommended that the bachelors, the low-paid Asian laborers, should be moved to the fringes of the city in special houses for bachelors (*masakin liluzzab*). According to this writer, such a solution means cheaper rent than in overcrowded city apartments.[45] Government officials also tend to view certain social pathologies – such as crime, drugs, suicide, and illicit sex – as foreign imports brought along with *al amala al wafida*, the migrant labor force.[46]

In broad comparisons, the showcase image lends credibility to the idea that the Gulf cities have evolved recently into "megacities" (cities such as Cairo, Baghdad, and Jakarta). According to Amirahmadi, the uneven global urbanization is manifested in these "megacities," poor and rich alike with demographic repression, global exploitation, functional hollowness, socio-cultural dislocations, politico-institutional underdevelopment, environmental degradation, loss of carrying capacity, and loss of buffering capacity.[47] The oil cities, due to the special niche of their political economy and recent evolution, have, to a great measure, been saved from these negative global consequences.

The car as a dominant feature of city life

Expansion into large areas of desert has created urban sprawl instead of cities with delimited boundaries and specific characters. This feature is functionally connected to the intensified use of private cars. As in the case of Los Angeles, priorities in city planning were given to facilitate the daily use of the car on a large scale by individual commuters. Public transportation in Gulf cities remains underdeveloped. The city public bus service is associated with low-status, low-paid Asian and Arab migrants. It is indeed rare to see a citizen using public transport. Greater attention is given to building first-class road systems and is exemplified by the disproportionately large space for wide roads and super highways like those of southern California. Pedestrian shopping areas, which generate a friendly and interactive human experience, have indeed become tiny pockets within the car-oriented urbanscape. The psychology is of a transient world, very much like that which Munif described in his *Cities of Salt*.[48] The small-scale shaded *souqs* and neighborhoods of the former old towns are now only nostalgic images for the constructed heritage villages.

This global primacy of the car has contributed to generating the consumer life in Gulf oil cities. The city's far reaching horizontal growth, the glorification of the role of the car in daily life, and the design of large villa-type houses with garages that accommodate two to six cars reflect a human ecology that drives people to consume high levels of energy and to stimulate their appetite for high consumerism. Therefore, the construction of this car-dominated urban type in the Gulf is symbiotic with the leading industrial capitalist countries, which redirect their own metropolises in different ways than the capital surplus generated in these oil countries.[49]

The Bahraini writer Madan described the impact of the car on the Gulf city when he returned from visiting Cairo, known for its pulsating pedestrian street life.

I did not notice before that the modern Gulf city lacks the concept of *al-shari'*, the street, in terms of dense social activity, as I have experienced it in Cairo. It is true that our streets are wide, well-organized, comfortable for drivers as they can accommodate fast flowing car traffic through their multiple ring roads and flying intersections. Yet they remain streets for cars only. The sidewalks paralleling these roads cannot be compared in their vitality, pulse, gregariousness and human details with its counterpart in the world's great cities.[50]

The Gulf city as a stage of segregated multicultural lifeways and identities

During the post-oil development of Gulf societies, social groups of power and influence did not present a national political ideology accepting multi-ethnic or cultural pluralism as a national goal. Multiculturalism has entered into the very making of the city and shaped it in its present-day particular form. Because of its large multi-ethnic social makeup, the Gulf city lacks a dominant, integrated, and homogeneous cultural ethos or character that one can find in metropolises such as Cairo, Beirut, London, Bombay, or Hong Kong. The urban culture of the Gulf city is rather a constellation of urban subcultures representing multiple ethnic groups and lifeways. It can be argued here that it is indeed this cultural diversity that has become a distinguishing feature of the Gulf oil city culture, which manifests itself in the simultaneous performance of multiple ethnic characters. This generates a cultural kaleidoscope of urban lifeways and identities, all with their different nationalities, religions, physical types, dress, food, music, smells, and even localized suburban environments. It is in the scale and intensity of such cultural diversity that the cities of Dubai, Abu Dhabi, and Kuwait differ from Cairo, Damascus, Bombay, Chicago, New York, and Tokyo.

Yet, the numerous ethnic groups display their activities against the backdrop of the indigenous Arab Gulf culture. However, the nationals increasingly are expressing their anxiety over the threats facing their own culture. In various public and private discourses, the nationals express a psycho-cultural state of being under siege by the huge presence and effects of such diverse immigrants and their cultures.[51] The increasing ethnic multiplicity with its varied manifestations has created, "a strong sense of self preservation among the indigenous Gulf communities. This has resulted in increased consciousness of their societal identity by upholding their age-old customs and traditions as identificational factors."[52] Indeed since the early 1990s there have appeared decorative elements along the roadsides that depict traditional cultural themes – coffee pots, old forts, dhows, falcons, etc. – that are aimed at generating symbols of local cultural identity. Some monumental buildings embody in their architectural design both the dynamic spirit of tradition and the utilitarian aspects of modernity.

Conclusion

I have delineated the dominant features, variables, and constituents in the evolution of the Gulf city as a particular city type. This is illustrated in all major Gulf capital cities, which share striking features of the particular urban configuration identified here as the "Gulf oil city." The composite picture shows how the evolving Gulf city acquired its features, which set it apart from other city types in the Middle East, the Third World, or Western countries.[53] This overview required that an "underview" – snapshots of the social formations of the Gulf city – be presented to illustrate its social groups, classes, and segregated housing patterns.

The Gulf oil city manifests urban parameters characteristics which relate to: (1) universal constituents of urbanization, (2) Arab/Muslim constituents, (3) third world elements and global capitalist western constituents, (4) local pre-oil constituents and features, and (5) local post-oil constituents of super-rich globalized societies. The dynamic interplay of these constituents within the particularities of the oil political economy of Gulf societies and global forces and trends account for the making of this particular city type. What has given the Gulf oil city its particular features does not reside in the simple addition of these constituents, but rather in the ways they have functionally coalesced and, at times, counteracted to produce a particular urban configuration.

Notes

* Associate Professor of Anthropology, University of Sharjah, UAE.
1 Abdul Rahman Munif, *Muden Al-Milh (Al-Ukhduod) (Cities of Salt)* (Baghdad: Al-Maktaba Al- alamiyya, 1986), 182–184.
2 *Ibid.*, 182.

3 Abdul-Khaliq Abdulla, *al-Nizam al-Iqliemi al-Khaleeji (The Regional Gulf System)* (Beirut: University Establishment Publications, 1998).

4 Further research is required to compare Arab Gulf cities with other oil cities such as Bacu, Nigeria; Caracas, Venezuela; and Baghdad, Iraq.

5 Mohammad Al-Fahim, *From Rags to Riches: The Story of Abu Dhabi* (London: London Center for Arab Studies Ltd, 1996), 11.

6 Ishaq Qutub, *Khasa es al-Numuou al-Hadari fi Dowal al-Khaleej al-Arabi (Characteristics of Urban Growth in Arab Gulf States)* (Kuwait: Kazima Publications, 1985), 175.

7 Fuad Khuri, "Urbanization and City Management in the Middle East," in *The Changing Middle Eastern City*, ed. H. Riviln and K. Helmer (Binghampton: SUNY Press, 1980), 1–15.

8 *Ibid.*, 6.

9 Mohammad Riad, "Some Aspects of Petro-urbanism in the Arab Gulf States," *Bulletin of the Faculty of Humanities and Social Sciences* 4 (1981): 1.

10 David Harvey, *The Condition of Post-Modernity* (Oxford: Blackwell, 1989).

11 Mike Featherstone, ed., *Global Culture: Nationalism, Globalization and Modernity* (London: Sage Publications, 1990).

12 Ahmed Salah Ouf, "Creating a Sense of Place in Sharjah City"(paper presented at the Second Sharjah Urban Planning Symposium, Urbanization, Urban Theory and Planning in the Middle East: The Role of Visible and Invisible Factors in the Next Millennium, April 10–11, 1999), 38.

13 Arjun Appadurai, "Disjuncture and Difference in the Global Cultural Economy," in Featherstone, *Global Culture*, 296.

14 Janet Abu-Lughod, "Urbanization and Social Change in the Arab World," *Ekistics* 50, no. 300 (1983): 227–228.

15 One advantage that Muscat, Oman, gained from a relatively late start in modernization was the opportunity to learn from the mistakes of others. The result is a capital city that has retained much of its traditional architecture and beauty. Muscat and its neighboring port of Mutrah have been modernized without being bulldozed out of existence, as has happened to kin cities in the Gulf. However, the creation of Greater Muscat does reflect global city development and modernization patterns similar to those in the other major Gulf cities.

16 Qutub, 174.

17 Riad.

18 Sulayman Khalaf, "Globalization and Heritage Revival in the Gulf: An Anthropological Look at Dubai Heritage Village," *Journal of Social Affairs* 19, no. 75 (2002): 13–42.

19 *Gulf News*, 14 August 2003, p. 4. Municipality officials say that the current plan covers most of the city streets and also includes tunnels, parking, and flyovers. They justify the chaos motorists are facing now by pointing out that "these are large projects and you can't guarantee perfection in their planning." Although known for its large and neat streets, Abu Dhabi can no longer handle the sharp increase in car numbers. Planners say previous projects costing around AED 800 million were intended for a population of 300,000. However, the population of Abu Dhabi city reached 1.2 million in 2002 (*Gulf News*, 12 May 2003, p. 7).

20 Riad.

21 Hans Blumenfeld, "The Modern Metropolis," in *Cities*, ed. Dennis Flanagen et al. (New York: Alfred A. Knopf, 1965), 40–57.

22 Riad, 20.

23 Sulayman Khalaf, "Gulf Societies and the Image of Unlimited Good," *Dialectical Anthropology* 17 (1992): 53–84.

24 Riad, 21.

25 Dubai Municipality, *Comprehensive Statistical Survey: Emirate of Dubai*, Book 2 of Socio-economic Survey 1993, July (1995): 19.

26 Roger Owen, "Migrant Workers in the Gulf," *Minority Rights Group Report No. 68* (1985); Sulayman Khalaf and Saad Alkobaisi, "Migrants' Strategies of Coping and Patterns

of Accommodation in the Oil-rich Gulf Societies: Evidence from the UAE," *British Journal of Middle Eastern Studies* (1999, 26(2), 271–298).

27 Nader Farjani, *al-Hijra ila al-Buldan al-Naftiyya (Migration to the Oil Countries)* (Beirut: Center for Arab Unity Studies, 1983).

28 Abu-Lughod; Farjani; Qutub; Owen; Khalaf (1992); Abdul Raouf Al-Jardawi, *al-Hijra wa al-Uzla al-Ijtema yya fi al-Mujtama al-Kuwaiti (Immigration and Social Isolation in Kuwaiti Society)* (Kuwait: Al-Robaian Publications, 1984); Mohammad Al-Haddad, "Ethnic Groups and Ethnic Stratification in Kuwait City," in *City and Society*, Leiden Development Studies no. 7, ed. A. Southall, P. Nas, and G. Ansari (Leiden: University of Leiden, 1985), 105–126; Abdulrassol Al-Moosa and Keith McLachan, *Immigrant Labor in Kuwait* (Kuwait: Dhat As-Salasil Publications, 1990); Saad Alkobaisi, "Keralites in Abu Dhabi: A Study of Unskilled and Semi-skilled Keralite Migrant Workers in the City of Abu Dhabi" (Ph.D. diss., University of Hull, UK, 1992); Baqer Al-Najjar, "Al-Khaleej: al-Medina al-Muta ditatu al-Jinsiyyat. al-Dhaqafa, al-Hawiyya-Muhawala bilbahdh fi al-Takween al- Ijtima i lil Madina al-Khaleejiyya ("The Gulf: Multinational, Multicultural, Multi-identity City; Research into the Social Formation of the Gulf City") in *The City and The Country*, Al-Rafed Book no. 5, 28–37 (Sharjah, UAE: Ministry of Culture and Information Publications, 1996); Tim Catchpole, "Sustainable Urban Environment: The Quality Dimension (Comparing UK and UAE Experiences)" (paper presented at the Sixth Sharjah Urban Planning Symposium, Innovative Urban Development: Intelligent Cities, Smart Growth, Sustainable Futures, June 1–2, 2003).

29 Al-Najjar.

30 In the townhouse compounds, usually each house is a two-story structure, has its own entrance and two-car garage open to the outside. These compounds have communal facilities for the residents located in landscaped central courtyards and include swimming pools, shaded lounging areas with a variety of trees, flowering shrubs, and green lawns. More modern compounds could have additional sports and recreational facilities like tennis and squash courts, large recreational rooms (with table tennis, sauna, fitness room, etc.).

31 Al-Najjar.

32 Thorstein Veblen, *The Theory of the Leisure Class* (London: Unwin Books, 1970), 5.

33 Lewis Mumford noted in the 1960s how state ruling groups can actually exercise greater control over citizens living in mass suburbia "The present means of long-distance mass communication and sprawling (housing) isolation has proved an even more effective method of keeping a population under control" [*The City in History* (New York: Harcourt Brace & Company, 1989, 1961), 512].

34 El-Sayed El-Aswad, *al-Beit al-Sha bi (The Folk House)* (Al-Ain: UAE University Press, 1996), 54.

35 *Ibid.*, 56.

36 Khalaf and Alkobaisi.

37 Abu-Lughod, 229.

38 *Gulf News*, August 15, 2003, p. 30.

39 Ahmed Kanna, "Dream Images of the Global: Dubai as an Ethnographic Site in the Global Economy" (paper presented at "Dubai Conglomerated: A Conference on Dubai at Harvard Graduate School of Design," April 18–19, 2003), 9–10.

40 Khalaf, 1992.

41 *Gulf News*, August 17, 2003, p. 6.

42 Mohammad Al-Muttawa, "Factors Influencing the Consumer Process in UAE Society." *International Sociology* 11, no. 3 (1996): 349.

43 Hassan Madan, "Al-Shari (*The Street*)," *Al Khaleej*, February 28, 1999, p. 34.

44 Katakura, personal communication, January 23, 2003.

45 *Al Khaleej*, October 27, 1997, p. 40.

46 *Al Khaleej*, October 23, 2001, p. 11.
47 Hooshang Amirahmadi, "Uneven Global Urbanization and Megacities: Challenges for a Global Urban Policy" (paper presented at the Fifth Sharjah Urban Planning Symposium, The Future of Cities in an Uncertain Global Environment, April 7–9, 2002), 292–294.
48 Munif.
49 Anthony King, "Architecture, Capital and Globalization of Culture." In Featherstone, *Global Culture*, 397–411.
50 Madan, 34.
51 Mohammad Al-Mur, *Amal Wataniyya (National Aspirations)* (Sharjah: Dar Al-Khaleej Publications, 1997); Frauke Heard-Bey, "Labor Migration and Culture: The Impact of Immigration on the Culture of the Arab Societies of the Gulf" (paper presented at BRISMES Conference, Oxford, UK, 1997); Said Harib, "al-Tanmiyya al-Dhaqafiyya fi al-Imarat" ("Cultural Development in the Emirates") in *Studies in UAE Society*, 125–167 (Al-Ain: UAE University Press, 1996).
52 Ghaus Ansari, "Urbanization and Cultural Equilibrium in the Arabian Gulf States," *Bulletin of the International Committee on Urgent Anthropological and Ethnological Research* 28 (1987): 22.
53 Robert Potter and Sally Lloyd-Evans, *The City in the Developing World* (London: Longman, 1998).

References

Abdulla, Abdul-Khaliq. *al-Nizam al-Iqliemi al-Khaleeji (The Regional Gulf System)*. Beirut: University Establishment Publications, 1998.

Abu-Lughod, Janet. "Urbanization and Social Change in the Arab World." *Ekistics* 50, no. 300 (1983): 223–231.

Al-Fahim, Mohammad. *From Rags to Riches: The Story of Abu Dhabi*. London: London Center for Arab Studies Ltd, 1996.

Al-Haddad, Mohammad. "Ethnic Groups and Ethnic Stratification in Kuwait City." In *City and Society*, Leiden Development Studies no. 7, edited by A. Southall, P. Nas, and G. Ansari, 105–126. Leiden: University of Leiden, 1985.

Al-Jardawi, Abdul Raouf. *al-Hijra wa al-Uzla al-Ijtemayya fi al-Mujtama al-Kuwaiti (Immigration and Social Isolation in Kuwaiti Society)*. Kuwait: Al-Robaian Publications, 1984.

Alkobaisi, Saad. "Keralites in Abu Dhabi: A Study of Unskilled and Semi-skilled Keralite Migrant Workers in the City of Abu Dhabi." PhD diss., University of Hull, UK, 1992.

Al-Moosa, Abdulrassol and Keith McLachan. *Immigrant Labor in Kuwait*. Kuwait: Dhat As-Salasil Publications, 1990.

Al-Mur, Mohammad. *Amal Wataniyya (National Aspirations)*. Sharjah: Dar Al-Khaleej Publications, 1997.

Al-Muttawa, Mohammad. "Factors Influencing the Consumer Process in UAE Society." *International Sociology* 11, no. 3 (1996): 337–357.

Al-Najjar, Baqer. "Al-Khaleej: al-Medina al-Muta ditatu al-Jinsiyyat. al-Dhaqafa, al-Hawiyya-Muhawala bilbahdh fi al-Takween al- Ijtima i lil Madina al-Khaleejiyya." ("The Gulf: Multinational, Multicultural, Multi-identity City: Research into the Social Formation of the Gulf City.") In *The City and The Country*, Al-Rafed Book no. 5, 28–37. Sharjah, UAE: Ministry of Culture and Information Publications, 1996.

Amirahmadi, Hooshang. "Uneven Global Urbanization and Megacities: Challenges for a Global Urban Policy." Paper presented at the Fifth Sharjah Urban Planning

Symposium, The Future of Cities in an Uncertain Global Environment, April 7–9, 2002, 274–296.

Ansari, Ghaus. "Urbanization and Cultural Equilibrium in the Arabian Gulf States." *Bulletin of the International Committee on Urgent Anthropological and Ethnological Research* 28 (1987): 19–23.

Appadurai, Arjun. "Disjuncture and Difference in the Global Cultural Economy." In Featherstone, *Global Culture*, 296–308.

Blumenfeld, Hans. "The Modern Metropolis." In *Cities* (Scientific American book), edited by Dennis Flanagen *et al.*, 40–57. New York: Alfred A Knopf, 1965.

Catchpole, Tim. "Sustainable Urban Environment: The Quality Dimension (Comparing UK and UAE Experiences)." Paper presented at the Sixth Sharjah Urban Planning Symposium, Innovative Urban Development: Intelligent Cities, Smart Growth, Sustainable Futures, June 1–2, 2003.

Dubai Municipality. *Comprehensive Statistical Survey: Emirate of Dubai.* Book 2 of Socio-economic Survey 1993, July (1995): 19.

El-Aswad, El-Sayed. *al-Beit al-Sha bi (The Folk House)* Al-Ain: UAE University Press, 1996.

Farjani, Nader. *al-Hijra ila al-Buldan al-Naftiyya (Migration to the Oil Countries).* Beirut: Center for Arab Unity Studies, 1983.

Featherstone, Mike, ed. *Global Culture: Nationalism, Globalization and Modernity.* London: Sage Publications, 1990.

Harib, Said. "al-Tanmiyya al-Dhaqafiyya fi al-Imarat" ("Cultural Development in the Emirates.") In *Studies in UAE Society*, 125–167. Al-Ain: UAE University Press, 1996.

Harvey, David. *The Condition of Post-modernity.* Oxford: Blackwell, 1989.

Heard-Bey, Frauke. "Labor Migration and Culture: The Impact of Immigration on the Culture of the Arab Societies of the Gulf." Paper presented at BRISMES Conference, Oxford, UK, 1997.

Kanna, Ahmed. "Dream Images of the Global: Dubai as an Ethnographic Site in the Global Economy." Paper presented at "Dubai Conglomerated: A Conference on Dubai at Harvard Graduate School of Design," April 18–19, 2003.

Khalaf, Sulayman. "Gulf Societies and the Image of Unlimited Good." *Dialectical Anthropology* 17 (1992): 53–84.

———. (2002) "Globalization and Heritage Revival in the Gulf: An Anthropological Look at Dubai Heritage Village." *Journal of Social Affairs* 19, no. 75 (2002): 13–42.

Khalaf, Sulayman and Alkobaisi, Saad. "Migrants' Strategies of Coping and Patterns of Accommodation in the Oil-rich Gulf Societies: Evidence from the UAE." *British Journal of Middle Eastern Studies*, 1999.

King, Anthony. "Architecture, Capital and Globalization of Culture." In Featherstone, *Global Culture*, 397–411.

Khuri, Fuad. "Urbanization and City Management in the Middle East." In *The Changing Middle Eastern City*, edited by H. Riviln and K. Helmer, 1–15. Binghampton: SUNY Press, 1980.

Madan, Hassan. "Al-Shari (The Street)." *Al Khaleej*, February 28, 1999, 34. Sharjah, UAE.

Mumford, Lewis. *The City in History.* New York: Harcourt Brace & Company, 1989, 1961.

Munif, Abdul Rahman. *Muden Al-Milh (Al-Ukhduod) (Cities of Salt)* Baghdad: Al-Maktaba Al- alamiyya, 1986.

Ouf, Ahmed Salah. "Creating a Sense of Place in Sharjah City." Paper presented at the Second Sharjah Urban Planning Symposium, Urbanization, Urban Theory and Planning in the Middle East: The Role of Visible and Invisible Factors in the Next Millennium, April 10–11, 1999.

Owen, Roger. "Migrant Workers in the Gulf." *Minority Rights Group Report No. 68* (1985).

Potter, Robert and Sally Lloyd-Evans. *The City in the Developing World*. London: Longman, 1998.

Qutub, Ishaq. *Khasa es al-Numuou al-Hadari fi Dowal al-Khaleej al-Arabi (Characteristics of Urban Growth in Arab Gulf States)*. Kuwait: Kazima Publications, 1985.

Riad, Mohammad. "Some Aspects of Petro-urbanism in the Arab Gulf States" *Bulletin of the Faculty of Humanities and Social Sciences* 4 (1981). University of Qatar.

Veblen, Thorstein. *The Theory of the Leisure Class*. London: Unwin Books, 1970.

15 Heritage revivalism in Sharjah

John W. Fox, Nada Mourtada-Sabbah,
and Mohammed al-Mutawa*

In this last chapter, we examine how globalization has elicited the remaking of a historical and ethnic identity in the emirate of Sharjah in the United Arab Emirates. This will complete this volume's treatment of the scales of globalization from those writ large, which are applicable anywhere in the world, to those scaled down to the local level within one country. As a local community, Sharjah exemplifies quite indigenous aspects of the community with quite foreign segments. Inflow and outflow linkages intertwine this emirate of some 400,000 persons to business concerns throughout the world. In fact, the sub-national polities like Sharjah trade and sell to separate countries or transnational corporations on their own. The federal government only attempts to intercede on the inflow into its national borders. To illustrate, while Sharjah is a primary exporter of natural gas to Japan, an overwhelming percentage of Sharjah's electronic and other technologically sophisticated goods come from the Far East and West. Thus, as a community Sharjah cannot be fully understood outside of its (1) global web, (2) symbiotic intermeshing with its large and fast-paced neighbor, Dubai, and (3) outside of the distant protective umbrella of mutual self-support in defense and border regulation that the national federation of the UAE provides.

The "cultural self" under pressure

Persons who would have been considered of once mechanical solidarity a few decades ago are now juxtaposed in global relationships with those from the long established urban states with their organic solidarities on one hand, and maintain very strong local ties based on age old patterns across the community of Sharjah on the other hand. However, the identity of Sharjah is of a fairly traditional Islamic city situated within the pulsating growth zone of the northern emirates. This chapter focuses on how the ancient identity has been consciously preserved, even resurrected from extinction in a few practices, to emblazon a sense of local traditionalism within a sea of change. Buildings and artifacts of the past have been selectively enhanced to serve new functions within multicultural contexts.

Please recall that in the summary of core values (Chapter. 1), persons within the Gulf continue to identity themselves as members of a particular emirate like Sharjah, with its close social network among the nationals, kinship bonding, and, secondly, identify themselves as a member of a specific country in the Gulf. Therefore, the kinship-based emiral units still command primary allegiance. In pan-Gulf society where one's last name immediately signals who one's kinship and thus business associates are, it matters greatly to present an official persona of the community as its public face. In fact, family honor is extended to the level of the emirate as the group of belonging second only to one's lineage. And one's lineage is embedded in a web of reciprocities with that of the royal lineage. Identity enhancement has been carried out in Sharjah through heritage revivalism.

As a construct where citizens are taught that they belong to the same ethnic nationality based on a shared past, nationalism to date has thus not taken primacy in claiming people's identities within the Gulf countries. Remember, the national federation of the UAE was initially a political creation to provide safety in numbers. It was understood that seven emirates would more likely be able to deal with foreign invasions and coups than one emirate.[1] We will briefly outline how different groups came to settle within the territory that only recently became the UAE. By so doing, the reader gains some perspective in how a sense of nationalism takes generations to mold, as is very much an ongoing project.

More directly, this chapter focuses on preserving, enhancing, and reconstructing the heritage of Sharjah as a historical identity for its citizens within the context of globalization and its multiculturalism and today. We also trace the community segments of what was to eventually become Sharjah through almost two millennia, as its family segments realigned it each location as new town sites were sought. Even with this strong continuity over the centuries, an aspect of the heritage has been a multiculturalism in each an every new setting along the way. Perhaps this is only natural, the successive communities that eventually were to give form to Sharjah were situated on the frontier between the Arabs of Arabia and the Persians of Central Asia. The populations were bound to mix along the trade conduit of the Gulf, with its yearly port of calls forming an even wider international arena stretching from India to Africa. As such multiculturalism has defined the Gulf since time immemorial. The only difference was one of degree rather than of kind.

The actual town of Sharjah gains historical visibility about two centuries ago within a context of the increasing trade among the Gulf Arabs, as well as of increasing rivalry among the European powers to intercede in that trade. Sharjah emerged as the main seaport for the northern Emirates, until it was surpassed in this capacity by Dubai when the latter's harbor was dredged in the 1960s. Since the 1970s, much of the change from globalization has spilled over from nearby Dubai.

Today, Sharjah's economic mainstays are natural gas extraction and its export. A sizeable Russian community lives on the northern shore and engages in export air freighting on huge cargo planes out of the Sharjah airport. Although Emiratis from Sharjah are likely to commute to Dubai for entertainment or other activities, their place of employment is most likely to be determined by kinship relationships within Sharjah. However, they also are landlords to apartment complexes for persons working in Dubai, so the spill over effect of organic solidarity strengthens the ties of one emirate to another. However, kinship remains an important organizing feature of the emirate, although the once family neighborhoods have dissolved into the more fragmented residence patterns typical of suburbia throughout the world. Attempts are made to lure some of the tourists from Dubai to see some of the traditional architecture and historical sights.

Symbols of traditionalism revived

In these contexts, Sharjah has consciously attempted to develop, advance, and enhance its identity as the educational and cultural center of the Gulf and perhaps even more broadly, of the Middle East. It is within the overall plan of developing some of the best tertiary educational institutions and libraries within the Gulf, plus some museums, that it has invested its gas revenues.[2] It is within this broad governmental mission, conceptualized and overseen by the Ruler of Sharjah, and a scholar in his own right, that parts of the old city were selectively, restored, rebuilt and refurbished. This conscious preservation and restoration of the historical areas and the developing of the educational, and cultural arts earned Sharjah the designation as cultural capital of the Arab world by the Arab League in the early 1990s and by UNESCO in 1998.

In this chapter we narrate and analyze how the identity for Sharjah, and by extension, the identity of the wider Gulf society, has been molded in response to increasing globalization. As we will see, the reconstruction of Historical Sharjah began in the 1990s, and was aided by its director, who sought asylum during the war fought to evict the Iraqis from Kuwait in 1991. Reconstruction proceeds to this day.

Globalization refers to multiple identities that a single individual might assume in different contexts. There is no mistaking the identity of a Gulf citizen when encountered in a luxury hotel in Cairo for example. Globalization is defined as managing multiple identities depending upon context. The Gulf Arabs dress in white flowing robes with head scarves knotted in a distinctive way so that each person may be identified with a particular emirate or country. However, in bespeaking the multiple identities of globalization, the Gulf Arabs might just as readily don jeans and a cowboy hat when visiting a race horse farm that they might own in Kentucky, or race horse stables in the United Kingdom.

To try to put our understanding of ethnic identity in comparative relief, one would ask who has a right to the Gulf identity generally and to that of Sharjah specifically, bearing in mind that a majority of residents are probably expatriates? While marriage was within the extended family group in generations past, who is it appropriate to marry these days? Are non-nationals from within the GCC acceptable to marry, or more widely are fellow Muslims from Pakistan acceptable, or are implicit in-group/out-group social boundaries to be maintained in this multicultural world where one jets for shopping and sporting events to Europe or the US?

At home with its imported technology and mass consumed images, how are the nationals culturally distinguished as people worthy of being the proprietary class of much of the world's natural wealth? One can readily recall that there were few cultures as materially deprived prior to the pumping of gas and oil only one or two generations ago, that have also become almost wholly dependent upon importing the full range of consumables, ranging from food to automobiles. Accordingly, Historical Sharjah also grounds the local nationals and distinguishes them as the main proprietors of the economy. The "placelessness" of global consumerism is thus officially resisted and identity is reterritorialized. The self-conscious sculpting and enhancing of local identity counters the overpowering forces of internationally made images and may also blend the global and local.[3]

In this study, we scrutinize in some detail how Sharjah, has revived and reconstructed its historical identity to enhance a sense of collective self and pride within multicultural Dubai-Sharjah-Ajman. Specifically, we examine: (1) how the historical and partial multicultural identity of Sharjah developed within its de facto international location along near the Straits of Hormuz over two millennia, and, (2) how the historical core of the city has been restored by the government for enhancing a sense of historical roots in a multicultural society of flows of expatriate workers, images, and foreign products in a wider metropolis known world wide for its malls. In addition to his interest in education and more broadly culture in its various forms, the Ruler of Sharjah has selected heritage to invest the government's revenues, as a formal policy of development. By bringing back to life the old buildings adjacent to the sea portage, this specialized heritage complex performs functions similar to that of Williamsburg in the US and the Tower of London in the UK, for their respective national populations.

The restoration has been underway since the early 1990s and has come to offer festivals, serve as a reception area for entertaining official guests (who sit on traditional palm reed mats called *hosor* – singular *hasirah* – in one of the old buildings) and who are treated to native foods and dances, for an ongoing tourist market that draws tourists, and as an office area of government agencies managing the development of culture. Thus, Historical Sharjah is transforming not only into an "ethnoscape" but as a government sponsored "satellite city" somewhat analogous to University City, with seven separate institutions elsewhere in Sharjah. Dubai has deployed similar efforts within no more than twenty kilometers, but these were oriented to different themes such as media and internet (Media City, Internet City), tourism (Festival City), and medicine (Medical City). While all of these satellite cities are government sponsored, each has a different theme and function within government planning. However, Sharjah's satellite cities must also be seen as providing contrast with those in neighboring although administratively separate Dubai.

Trading towns through time

To provide some background for understanding the refigured cultural forms of Historical Sharjah, we briefly discuss the Gulf trading community historically and outline the tradition-bound organizational norms of Gulf society from the beginnings of recorded history, and also examine the cultural identities of the persons who composed these communities as forerunners to the various city-states like Sharjah today. The lineage based polities recall those described by Ibn Khaldun seven centuries ago.[4] Ibn Khaldun's thesis is that the strong kinship alliances and group feelings, as an esprit de corps (*asabiya*), steadily diminish as the communities grow into cities. Since the advent of globalization, the population of Sharjah has increased some 15,000 percent, witnessed an infusion of foreign guest workers, and the ancient kin groups have dispersed largely to the suburbs of a sprawling Sharjah today. We examine how cultural, social and demographic transformations of Sharjah since the advent of globalization have necessitated a rekindling of its historical identity, not unlike the *asabiya* described by Ibn Khaldun more generally for societies throughout the Middle East. Certainly, the accentuating the traditional symbols in the built environment will contribute to feelings of belonging and solidarity. If this analogy is valid, then societies across the Middle East have maintained a distinctive culture for more than a millennium that consists of customs and idea systems to resist, adapt and syncretize aspects of intrusive culture, such as that promulgated by globalization today.

First, looking back in time, the geographical position centuries ago of open desert to the west and open sea to the east have adapted the settled peoples (*hadar*) on the Gulf coast as both partly Bedouin (*Bedu*) in outlook and lifeway and partly sedentary cosmopolitans, for they traded their few local pearls in India, and traded in Zanzibar, Africa. Nearly all wood, including the teak (*shesam*) boarding for their ships (*dhows*) was imported from India, and most woods for the doors came from Africa. Only some of the cross members of the beams in houses were built from the native palm tree. One might generalize that because the Arabian coast and indeed much of Arabia coast was so bereft of resources that the region had little to offer foreign conquerors throughout the millennia. Arabia was essentially bypassed by marauding armies from Egypt, Mesopotamia, and Rome, and was able to assert a great deal of local independence.[5] The Ottoman Turks did exert some control over parts of Arabia, but they shared Islam which closely meshed with the lifeways of Eastern Arabia. With pearls as the main tradable commodity, the orientation was directed out into the sea lanes to sell the pearls and then to return with foreign goods.

A little history will bear out that the trading town that characterized Sharjah during its two centuries prior to globalization, has existed for much of the duration of settled life along the Arabian Gulf. Perhaps a residual characteristic of the Gulf town since time immemorial has been a form of lineage-based social organization which allows peoples of many nationalities to reside as separate neighborhoods within an overall somewhat culturally heterogeneous community.

The first glimpse of town and society begins with recorded history itself, when the Sumerian cuneiform clay texts mention *c.*3200 BC the pearl merchants of Dilmun and importing timber on ships to build temples. Dilmun is identified with the stone masonry complexes, perhaps from the 3000s–1700 BC in Bahrain.[6] The archaeology of Dilmun, and indeed of much of the Gulf, shows a hybrid culture equally influenced by Mesopotamia to the north and the Indus Harappan civilization of the Indian subcontinent. A polyglot, multicultural character is certainly borne out in the material record.[7] The peoples from the Arabian and Middle Eastern worlds mixed with those from the Indus and Persian worlds; it may be appropriate to speak of the peoples of Hanaji here, which is the Arabic name for the Gulf as an ethnic mixture from times immemorial.

As another reference to the trading/pearling town prototype, Sinbad the sailor of *The Arabian Nights* fame legendarily hailed from the trading town of Sohar, which was subservient to the trading island of Hormuz (below, off of the Iranian coast opposite Ras al Khaimah in the UAE), settled and controlled by the forebears of the historic Sharjans. Sohar was of sufficient significance to be a likely candidate for the *Omania*, a commercial entrepot mentioned by the geographer Pliny.[8] Hormuz was first described to the West by Marco Polo in his epic travelogue, *Description of the World* (1299). However, that Hormuz was also prominently described in the Persian commercial records, in which the inhabitants were described as traders who wore long white robes *thob* or *disdasha*), a belt and a dagger (*khanjar*). This was reminiscent of the native dress of what was to become the UAE, and the national dress today (minus the dagger, except on ceremonial occasions in some countries of the Gulf). Thus, an already extant culture of attire, and building construction were established in the Gulf for at least a thousand years, and in the case of pearling and sea trading for at least three thousand years. The language of the Gulf during the early second millennium was probably Aramaic (and perhaps Farsi).[9]

Populations similar to the Bani Yas were recorded in the late 300s CE in the Gulf, as recently relocated from Yemen.[10] With this entry into the Gulf, notions of the pan-Arab cultural strictures of a closely bound brotherhood began to become part of the Gulf cultural tapestry. With time and success of the incoming tribes in acculturating with more indigenous peoples, these norms became established as the principal community ethic, which are outlined in Chapter 1. Perhaps it was this early amalgamation that comprised part of the basis for peoples of the Gulf to assert an Arab identity.

It should also be noted that there were Christian and Jewish communities in the Gulf, as well as pagan communities. Within a kilometer of the easternmost boundary of Sharjah in Dibba are thousands of gravestones which mark the death of Arab-speaking tribesmen from the Musandam, who had fallen in battle in 633 CE during the last of the Ridda wars signaling the reconquest under Islam.[11] With this Arab marshaling of a strong *esprit de corps* in identity and adherence to a value code that enforces a notion of brotherhood, the Gulf has been multicultural since the earliest of historical recordings.

Telescoping directly to the forebears of Sharjah, we obtain a more complete view of the pearling, sea trading, city of Julfar with a threshold of European historiography, where the Portuguese established an outpost in the early 1500s. Many of the inhabitants of Sharjah derived from Ras al Khaimah and Julfar/Hormuz before that. Thus, a case can be made that the inhabitants of the Gulf were part of the same multicultural tradition that deals with the globalized contexts of today. Significantly, some families from Julfar in the eleventh century carried the Arabic prefix *bani* meaning lineage.[12]

Julfar has gained some notoriety as the home port of the mariner, Ahmed bin Majid, who was hired to navigate Vasco de Gama to India in 1498, and who wrote the navigational treatise on navigating the Indian Ocean currents (*Al-Fawaid*, 1462), with wind and sky charts extrapolated by Columbus in his voyage across the Atlantic Ocean to the New World. Actually, the home of bin Majid has been identified a short distance inland within an ancient palm grove, and has been the site of recent archaeological investigations by the Ras al Khaimah Museum. Julfar was also interlinked with Hormuz, situated on an island eighteen kilometers away, as Sharjah and Dubai might be best understood in tandem today. Hormuz and the trading colonies established by its families contained traders, artisans skilled in metal work and fashioning of precious stones, trading families from beyond the Gulf and several notable physicians.[13]

Archaeology provides another view of the early versions of the Gulf port city, for Julfar exists (*c.*1200s–1600) as an archaeological tell (and has been a protected site since 1968, as the first site done so in what was to become the UAE).[14] Blue and white Ming period porcelain shards litter the site and speak to not only trade connections with the Far East (not necessarily China) but more probably to Malacca which was a Chinese port town in Malaysia until the Portuguese took over in the early 1500s. The archaeological site is spread along about four kilometers of coastline. Buildings were almost completely constructed of mud-brick architecture and the less permanent thatched housing of palm fronds stuck into the ground (*arish*). Lime plaster facades were introduced in the 1500s to Julfar, just before its citizens relocated about five kilometers south to modern Ras al-Khaimah, and from there to Sharjah during the 1700s. The population of Julfar probably varied by 10,000 to 30,000 persons, depending upon the season of the year, and if the traders were out to sea, and whether residences in the adjacent (landward) palm gardens are included. This range of population compared favorably to the size of Sharjah at the turn of the nineteenth century. In any event, it seems reasonable to infer that the citizens of Julfar would have maintained houses in Hormuz, and in India (probably Gujarat, as they did in Bombay during the nineteenth century).[15] Monumentality in architecture was not part even of the civic center of Julfar; the small two-roomed mosque comprised a stone foundation and mud-brick walls, although the edifice lacked a minaret (minarets were not introduced to the Gulf until the mid-twentieth century).

Nevertheless, monumental architecture was clearly known and used. For example, a massive rampart four meters high defended Julfar and its palm groves on its southern city limit. To date, this is the largest construction of antiquity known in Arabia, and could have been a prototype for the wall that fortified Sharjah during the 1700s. However, the wall outside of Julfar is constructed essentially of rounded *wadi* stones, so that the organization of labor to construct the rampart probably was not that much more involved than that needed for tending the palm orchards. We can only guess as to why such a massive wall was erected. It is noted though that there was also a sizeable concentration of Arab mountain dwellers within a few kilometers of the wall, who came to be known as the Shihuh.[16] The Shihuh seemed to have blended into the populations of the coastal plains within the past century or two.

The lure of the sea apparently outweighed the need for fresh water, which had to be carried from the palm gardens some one to two kilometers to Julfar. This was also true of the other shoreline settlements, such as Ras al-Khaimah a few kilometers south, where the citizens of Julfar relocated during the late 1500s and early 1600s. Shoreline localities were also central to the situating of Sharjah and Dubai two centuries later.

Extending back in time, however, Julfar was almost certainly settled from Kush, a mounded (tell) site about one kilometer inland as the seas receded and the merchants had a longer walk to the boats. Kush therefore provides both the historical and archaeological baseline for tracing some population segments whose descendants settled in Sharjah some fifteen hundred years later. Archaeological remains inform us that Kush was a trading center under the suzerainty of the Sassanian empire of Persia. The various archaeological markers suggest Kush as a likely candidate to be identified as the historical Emporium Persicum described by the Byzantines in the sixth century near the Straits of Hormuz.[17] Persian merchants begin to appear in the historical records in and about the Horn of Arabia during the 220s CE. Sassanian dominion was proclaimed in 242.[18]

Small Portuguese enclaves were established at Julfar and Hormuz, mostly to control trade and provision their ships with fresh water, as well as in Oman at Sohar and Muscat. A brief episode of Dutch colonization followed at Hormuz in the seventeenth century, and the French built liaisons with Muscat in the eighteenth century. Yet, the Gulf was largely bypassed by European colonization. The Qawasim fleet controlled trade as perhaps the second largest in the world by the turn of the nineteenth century with the arrival of the British, with the largest fleet.

However, at the time, the Gulf was seen by the British as simply the seafaring western flank of India; prior to the building of the Suez Canal, European invaders would have crossed Mesopotamia from the Mediterranean to Basra and then sailed to India via the Arabian Gulf. Thus, the Gulf was to be safeguarded for tactical reasons, as well as to minimize competition from the indigenous merchants, especially those of the predominant Qawasim confederation who also traded with India. The relationships with the British are outlined in Chapter 1 and extensively analyzed in other works.[19] What differences manifest in Gulf societies today may be also gauged by the degrees of autonomy that they have managed to sustain during the two centuries of British interest in the region. In this regard, the British also sought to protect their shipping along the sea lanes to and from India, and worked out a number of agreements, beginning in 1820 (the year after the British invaded and burned Ras al Khaimah). The basic arrangement was that the internal affairs of the sheikhdoms were left as before. Following a treaty in 1835 the emirates or sheikhdoms of the Horn of Arabia (the western half of the Peninsula of Oman) became known as the Trucial coast for the treaties that were in effect.

Within this context, the local emirates were able to retain quite autonomous and fairly unaltered cultural ways of organizing society. Perhaps variants of lineage organization distinguished the Bedouin dominated interior and the uplifted Musandam Plateau and Hajar Mountains from the seacoast dwelling *Hadar*. Eventually the Arabs of the desert and mountains were able to forge more polyglot communities with the coastal residents of various ethnicities. It is this common culture of what anthropologists classify as segmentary lineage organization, compounded with a common Arabic language and the dominating ideology of Islam that forms the core values of the Gulf region.[20] Yet many of the coastal towns remained bi- and tri-lingual, for their location along the Arab–Persian frontier. In comparison, perhaps the segmentary lineage organizing principles developed to be the strongest in the emirates and in Saudi Arabia, which are the two areas that seem or appear to have been least impacted by Ottoman and European influences.

However, the two groups of communities significantly differ in emphasizing religious norms to insure conformity and keep outsiders at a distance. To reiterate, this is an important dimension of globalization here today. The emirates of the Trucial coast have been fairly tolerant of individual variations in interpretation in religion, with different sects practiced within adjoining emirates. Both Sharjah and Dubai have sizeable numbers of Iranians today, whereas they have been an integral part of Sharjah extending well in history.

The seafaring Arabs have spent parts of the year in foreign entrepots, such as Bombay and Zanzibar. In contrast, the Saudis have launched the more notable purifying movements (revitalization) and have embarked on several within the past two centuries to counter intrusions of unorthodoxies as part of the development of a world system, which was intensified with the processes of globalization. The Emiratis have tend to exhibit tolerance of foreign residents, while some Saudi militants have increased cries within the past few years that there are too many foreigners within the Kingdom in proximity to sacred territory.

Identity enhancement in Historical Sharjah

We now narrate and analyze how the original downtown – recently designated as Historical Sharjah – has been reconstructed to display the "authentic self" in community identity. Specifically, selected parts of eighteenth- and nineteenth-century Sharjah, have been reconstructed or refurbished to mold a tangible sense of identity clearly visible for all to see. The historical core of the city thus provides the anchor and original place as a cultural shrine for the various Sharjans who have settled in successively more distant suburban neighborhoods stretching out in the desert, and each more spacious with larger homes than the previous neighborhood.

In the once densely packed neighborhoods adjacent to the harbor prior to independence, the private domestic quarters of many walled family compounds were set off from public life accessed by the typically labyrinthine alleys. This is a duality of identity, private family versus the public life that is manifest in a revitalized identity. Extended families and lineage alliances bound many of the social reciprocities of daily life within Sharjah. One consequence of the rapid expansion of urban Sharjah in the 1970s was vacating the old core of the walled city along the corniche for the more spacious suburban zones as each was hewn from the adjoining desert. This expansionary process today continues into an exurbia of even larger walled homes within the even more vast open tracts amid the sand dunes as the city reaches farther into the land-locked interior. Indeed, the amount of space per person may be calculated as a steady regression formula from the distant suburbs moving inwards to the old city core. In the luxurious villas being colonized by young Sharjan couples, and generously funded by allocations from the government, all one may see are other high-walled and two- and three-story villas atop sand dunes. Certainly the sense of living in closely packed neighborhoods in and amongst one's immediate relatives has given way to a sense of "distant community" where one may see a neighbor pulling out of his walled villa in a Mercedes or perhaps shopping at a mall, but that is about all. As the present generation receives a steady flow of foreign television broadcasts into the sanctity of home, and business competes internationally, the extended lineage groups of cousins and friends bound in social collectives of the old harbor-side town would seem to progressively fade.

Anthony Giddens reminds us that "the more tradition loses its hold over daily life … the more an identity is intentionally fabricated."[21] In the case of Sharjah, the former identity still exists within grandparents and may be readily revitalized. In this context, the government of Sharjah has conscientiously cultivated and promoted the history, heritage, and educational industries. In one sense, the "authentic self" has been reconstructed from archaeological and architectural residue to contrast with the "cultural other" of the foreign guest workers now spread throughout the city and engaged in their typical Western, Russian or South Asian clusters.

The government of Sharjah has set the direction for this project. This house by house reconstruction has been overseen by His Highness, Sheikh Dr Sultan Al Qassimi, the Ruler of Sharjah, and a professional historian in his own right. We trace how the "historicized" and archaeologically imbued buildings of the core of the city have been reclaimed as tenements. The buildings have been rebuilt and only slightly embellished to strengthen a historical connectedness between modern, multicultural Sharjah in the wake of incessant globalization and the more mono-cultural community of past centuries. Today, peoples of different ethnicities, native languages, religions and economic strata have come to share the same urban space.

Ideally, people retrieve an anchor in historical identities. Newly formulated identities provide a defense for this global way of imagery and new symbols and history provides symbols for formalizing a national identity. The construction of historical identity resonates with what Manuel Castells surmises – namely that "God, nation, family, and community will provide unbreakable, eternal codes around which a counter-offensive will be mounted against the culture of virtual reality."[22]

Preserving and enriching identity: dishdashas, residences and domes

The new revitalized historical identity is manifest in the white immaculate buildings of Historic Sharjah. Identity is also manifest in the white *dishdasha* (men's full body length shirt) that has come to symbolically evoke the Gulf male when encountered in Cairo, Damascus or elsewhere in the Arab World, or in broadcasts of CNN (for instance as a background figure when oil prices are being discussed). Together, the spotless white facades in dress or buildings are dimensions of a new revitalized national identity. The white dishdasha now occurs throughout much of the Gulf while head gear varies from country to country. While the circumstances in which the dishdasha became the regional dress within the past generation are not known to the authors of this chapter, it can be safely surmised that the dishdasha has been one of the distinctive garbs of the indigenous population of the Gulf for perhaps two millennia. It is thus not characteristic of other locales within the Middle East. However, the dishdasha was not widely worn in day-to-day life, judging from photographs taken of Sharjans between the wars;[23] clothing apparently was much more varied then and the numbers of foreigners were proportionately nowhere near as high as today. The dishdasha does seem to represent formal attire, perhaps like that worn when engaged in meeting persons from outside of the family or when engaged in activities with foreigners, such as in trading forays.

As the buildings of the old downtown were once variegated with the helter-skelter disorder of daily urban life (that is, with push-carts, goats, infirm elderly people, etc.), so was clothing. To generalize, both clothing and buildings of two generations ago were less than immaculately white, clean and ordered, as they are currently presented as an identity to counter globalization. The bold whiteness of the national costume and the bold white exteriors of reconstructed buildings provide the basis for the title of this section of the present chapter. That is, identity is concretized identity literally in the new coats of lime plaster, and figuratively as essentialized local identity to counter the constant cultural homogenizing forces of market-driven globalization.

The identity of Sharjah is also manifest in the white and beige domes of civic architecture across the city. As here in University City, domes signify the great tradition of Islamic scholarship which links Sharjah to the Islamic renaissance of one millennium ago at the three great centers of learning, Baghdad, Cordoba and Cairo (all of which founded universities in the 900s CE). All of the educational buildings of the half a dozen institutions of higher education within University City have the typical dome, curved arches, arabesques and tendrils except one, a police academy.[24] The dome has its origin among Roman and Byzantine architectural traditions, but was appropriated early on in the creation of Islamic authority with the Dome of the Rock mosque in Jerusalem. Among other governmental complexes that include museums and *souks* is Cultural Square (*Al-Thaqafah*); three-domed buildings there surround a monumental sculpture of an opened *Koran*, the *Moshaf*, again is emblematic of the sacred word from the holy scriptures as the basis of all knowledge.[25]

Our narrative of constructing a historical identity through restoring the historic downtown began in 1990 when an international competition was held to select the plans for restoration of Historical Sharjah by a number of international firms. In May of that year, in the midst of the international conflict over Iraq's invasion of Kuwait, the architectural archaeologist, Dr Abdul Sattar al-Azzawi, was sent by the Iraqi government to temporarily advise the Government of Sharjah on restoration of the old city core. But in the wake of this Gulf war, Dr al-Azzawi stayed and commenced work in Sharjah that is in its sixteenth year. Dr al-Azzawi brought exemplary credentials in successfully having created a monumental past for the Iraqis at a time when the Iraqi government was envisioning a modern pan-Arab although Mesopotamian-styled empire. Al-Azzawi had excavated and restored Babylon, the Parthian/Hellenistic City of Hatra, and the Abbasid palace and tower at Samara, all of which served as symbols promoting a glorious past for present and future expansionism. At great expense during the ravages of an eight-year war of attrition between Iraq and Iran in the 1980s, these reconstructions were meant to create a pride between the former and present empires; the modern Iraqis were to be celebrated as the immediate descendants of Nebuchadnezzar II and Alexander the Great and the great Abbasid caliphs, all of whom had resided in the national territory of modern Iraq. This was the sense of nationalism analyzed by Benedict Anderson in his now classic *Imagined Communities*. In this sense, the Iraqi government was able to weld together the disparate and competing religio-ethnic groups of Sunnis, Shiites, and Kurds for several decades.

The development of Sharjah during the times of globalization might also be seen as a counterpart or an alter ego for adjoining Dubai. After all, it would be difficult to tell them apart from a distance in earlier generations; both were small towns of drab architecture nestled around the mouths of estuaries. The residents of each belonged to different tribal groups, the Qawasim and Bani Yas, respectively. However, with globalization, Dubai has fashioned a shining wonder out of concrete, glass and colored flood lights to rise out of the redundant sands. As visual ecology, its awe-inspiring skyline thus stands in contrast to its undistinguished coastline that is so salty that lonely scrub vegetation grows along with a few palms. Dubai has erected an identity diametrically opposed to its surrounding environs. Indeed, the Bedouin (*bedu*) descendants in Dubai have turned the tables on the more urbane town-dwelling Arabs (*hadar*) of the traditional seaside towns with a new vigor and inventiveness reminiscent of Nebuchadnezzar (Mesopotamian king during the 600s BC), who constructed the fabled hanging gardens of Babylon. If Dubai has built the spectacular and the virtual to represent itself in one identity, then the government of Sharjah has designed quite another identity almost at the opposite pole of the continuum of possibilities; it has commissioned heritage workers to revitalize parts of its ancient past and to reconstruct a substantial shrine. If Dubai symbolizes the "virtual" then Sharjah symbolizes the concrete within a postmodern sense of complementary opposition among competing lineages.

The Sharjah government has also built official edifices in the traditional Islamic style, again harkening to time honored ways prior to the onslaught of globalization. In order to determine what should be selected for preservation among the many artifacts of downtown Sharjah and then to decide how they should appear and be landscaped, no less planning and design is required than that necessary for the creation of the hotel and marketplace complexes of Dubai. The latter tend to be manufactured using symbols of a past in the most up-to-date architecture design and technology on a far more grandiose scale than any construction in the pre-oil days. The question is, what is authentic, and of the old fragmentary buildings and artifacts, what should be saved or possibly embellished?

Conjunctive methodology for constructing authenticity

If history recreates past events, how could the goals of historiography be operationalized by city planners to reconstruct a Historical Sharjah as original to the pre-globalization past from the architectural residue still in place in the downtown? With this goal in mind on the eve of beginning work on the project *c.*1990, several methodological questions regarding chronology had to be considered: (1) What period should the authentic Sharjah come to represent, for example, that of 1800, 1900 or 1960 prior to the petroleum boom? (2) Among constructions targeted from the early nineteenth century prior to intrusion by the British? (3) How are originality and authenticity to be determined in neighborhoods with a continuous mixture of construction spanning as much as two hundred years?

First to consider a general historical baseline for the beginning of occupation of the site of Sharjah, European maps show a town of that name at least during the eighteenth century. To wit, an established community Sharjah is shown on the Niebuhr map of 1765.[26] It seems reasonable to assume that the residents were in all probability Qawasim, since they are identified in the other coastal communities of the time. When the present ruling family of Sharjah relocated from Ras al-Khaimah during the nineteenth century, clarification might be sought as to whether the Al Qassimis segment were joining a branch of their family already living in Sharjah or were simply taking over a community more distantly related within the wider grouping called the Qawasim scattered along the coastline.

Considering wider geopolitical contexts, the English established a year-round trading settlement in the Gulf during the 1760s. Certainly, the increased intensity of competition among the contending European powers for trading networks may have factored into building settlement along the particularly fine harbor at Sharjah.[27]

As to the overriding question as to what was to be preserved and enhanced to recreate the authentic precursor community, information from maps, photographs and archaeological excavation determined what had originally existed at the various periods targeted, all of which represented times when the aboriginal lifeways were in full use. At least building foundations could be identified by excavation as to original style, original location and orientation. After that, photographs of various points in the twentieth century and the memory of elderly residents also aided in determining what features formally existed, especially if walls had to be rebuilt on old foundations.

Finally, the Ruler of Sharjah made the decisions as to what of the buildings would be restored or rebuilt, in consultation with the archaeologists. Thus, not only the project itself resulted from the Ruler's vision, but actually what was to selected for manifestation in the "new" Historical Sharjah. Our guess is that some 40 percent of the standing architecture during the period sought to be preserved, *c.*1900, was slated for restoration. This estimate was arrived by comparing the restored buildings in sections within the walled area of Historical Sharjah today with the preservation plan's map of the same acreage, and also in comparison with what existed in aerial photographs taken during the 1930s to 1950s by the British. Most of the densely packed houses near the Souk Arsah exist in their original locations and have stood for perhaps two centuries. However, across the street (south) perhaps only 15 percent of the occupatial space in fact has restored buildings. Undoubtedly more structures have been removed or not rebuilt, which gives a much more spacious feel to this neighborhood today.

To answer the question as to what architectural details were to be rebuilt, the walls and other details were resurrected in the most original form that methods would allow. Fortunately, the British a map in 1820, signed by William Brooks and Thomas Remon, Lieutenants of Engineers, shows a detailed depiction of Sharjah along a deep channel some distance inland from the Gulf. The map thus furnishes a layout of the town and thus what existed at the time of the British arrival. Within the wall, running approximately 1,700 yards along the landward (eastern) side of the town on one side and the water front on the other (western) side are 22 geometric shapes. According to Dr Azzawi, the project Director, the 22 geometric shapes in all probability depict the family neighborhoods, called the *friej*. The neighborhoods seemed to be paired and color coded. Apparently they represent paired and intermarrying lineages that formed into a single larger unit through complementary opposition – eleven in all according to the map.

One aerial photograph from *c.*1940 shows a clustering of house compounds quite reminiscent of those drawn in the 1820s map. However, the most notable features evident from the slightly oblique angle of the photographic shot are the wind towers. Based on the aerial shot, the 22 compounds were probably walled complexes for single patrilineages, which would have comprised multiple generation housing for a single family of grandparents, their sons' families and perhaps the next generation as well. All housing could and usually was modified according to the needs of the residents, so that what was drawn in 1820 or photographed in 1940 was not necessarily what was in place twenty years later. The kinship custom was one of patrilineages with virilocal residence, in which males stayed within the extended family compound after marriage and daughters would relocate to their husband's family house and reside there. The ideal was to marry within the patrilineage, so that a daughter would in all probability remain after marriage within the same lineage based neighborhood (*friej*). Rooms were added when a son married, and when children were born. "Once the family was complete, all the relatives gathered to build a wall around these rooms and form one big house."[28]

In 1820, the neighborhoods are shown as spatially separated from one another and may bear out the separateness of the individual lineage compounds or neighborhoods. Oral tradition relates that each of the families tended to specialize in a specific economic activity, well into the twentieth century which represents an aspect of autarky discussed in Chapter 1. In the city maps of the 1950s through the 1970s, it seems that those individual plots also more or less conform to the residential compounds of 1820, only the degree of open space between them had been filled in.

The wall was shown with nine towers and or gates, and was soon dismantled by the British, apparently as an item of treaty. Finding and rebuilding the wall was based on using the methods of archaeology, architectural preservation techniques and ethnography (or oral history). The combining of these different methods in a single effort is termed the conjunctive method, which should yield the most exact details possible. While much of the foundation of the wall had disappeared prior to the use of photography here during the 1930s, its foundations were located through archaeological trenching. Once the foundations were encountered below the ground surface, they were then followed by trench along their original contours.

Moreover, unlike the reconstruction of walled cities in Europe or Asia from other ages, the "aboriginal period" of Sharjah was still within the memory of its still living elders. For example, the seven towers along the wall were ethnographically identified and named by elderly Sharjans; however, it has not been ascertained if they actually remembered the towers from having seen them as children, or whether the information was passed down to them orally from previous generations. When a dwelling was slated for reconstruction, often just the shell of the outer walls remained. When available photographs were used to recreate the architectural detail, such as where the doors, windows and ornamental embellishments were placed, members of the families who had once lived in the buildings, in some cases overrode the architects' decisions as to where rooms, windows, doors were situated in rebuilding their former residences.

The elderly people remembered that the original building material stone (*hajar morjani*) was coral (*morjan*) obtained from the shoals just offshore (called *fisht*), and broken while still under water. Once ashore, the coral stone of all categories was soaked in fresh water to reduce the salt content and allow the small organisms to die prior to sale in the market. The coral was covered in a gypsum plaster (*jess*).[29]

However, a local classification graded the quality of stone and the sorts of buildings in which it was employed. The most prestigious and durable stone (*al salayef*), was found in the deepest part of the Gulf, and was the most expensive to purchase. It was primarily employed in the houses (*biyut*, sing. *bayt*) of well to do merchants and other notables. Most of these houses were congregated in the *Souk Friej* neighborhood, and were among the first to be restored. Most of these substantial buildings have been restored in their original settings, with narrow labyrinthine corridors and narrow alleys winding between high and usually windowless walls (on the passages) to the corners where the doors to the interior courtyards are sometimes located.

However, today the retrieval of building material for such a massive building project in the traditional manner has not been possible since the 1990s (for one, it simply does not exist locally in the sufficient quantity necessary). Coral stone of similar composition is imported from coastal Yemen. Masons were hired from Yemen, Pakistan, and Afghanistan, among other places to shape the coral and place it in the masonry walls. However, the coral was also sliced with modern electric trim saws and set so that the sawn or smooth side of the rock faced the exterior wall. This seems to be a modern improvement in appearance.

The intricate Islamic architectural features, such as masonry lattices, were rebuilt when available or simply approximated when not available so as to create a typical impression of what buildings of the "period" might have used. In the case of ornamentation, ideas were also obtained from historic buildings in other Gulf cities. As many original iron door and shutter hinges as possible were retrieved and stored in a hinge and latch "bank." Suitable pieces of appropriate size and style were selected for reuse or were simply forged anew according to old patterns. Wood beams were naturally replaced, as they are in *shesham* (teak) from India as a prestige wood. Many beams are still constructed of the more authentic and locally available date palm wood. The roofs have been reconstructed in the original methods of lashing palm leaves (*areesh*) together with palm rope and covered in light gypsum.

What buildings symbolize identity?

Only a portion of what existed *c.*1950 was slated for reconstruction. The plan is not to bring back to life the community of that time, for we live in a different age and that would not be possible. In this section, the restoration techniques and meanings of the edifices are briefly surveyed for the houses of the wealthy merchants, the ruler's residence (fort), the market (*souk*) and the city wall. Perhaps a half a dozen of the original twenty-two neighborhoods have been reconstructed.

These large residential compounds have been rebuilt almost in their entirety, especially those with notable architectural features [such as the large square wind towers (*barjeel*) emblematic of Gulf architecture, although having originated in Persia, and imposing walls with large doors]. The round wind tower of the Al Midfa house bordering the Souk Arsah, is the only one of its kind known in the Gulf, and frequently is shown in illustrations on the historical UAE. In contrast, the small houses have not (as of yet) been rebuilt. Only one thatched house of palm leaves, which was probably the most common type of dwelling, exists in the restoration today. And the now significantly open spaces have been paved with bricks, interspersed with well manicured shade trees, so as to suggest a park. In a sense, the dwellings of the successful merchant would resonate best in revitalized identity with the global marketing of today as well as in the past.

Beside the houses of the materially better off, the civic buildings that symbolize civic-religious authority were selected for reconstruction. The *Al-Hisn* fort was originally built prior to the arrival of the British, for it is shown on the 1820 map. The fort served as the residence of the Al Qassimi family who relocated from the earlier fortified residence in Ras al-Khaimah. When touring the fort, visitors are informed that this was the first edifice rebuilt in 1969, when it was almost completely leveled during urban renewal. As the royal residence, the location of the fort outside of the city walls could bespeak the distinctive locus of the ruling lineage vis-à-vis the lineage neighborhoods within the walled city. This suggests a binary relationship of the rulers with the ruled.

The arrangements of artifacts, photographs from the 1930s and 1940s, and other accoutrements within the fort read as a text of civic and kinship-based authority. The fort tells of the historical preeminence of the ruling family, both in its architecture and within the complex. To read the architectural text, first, the entrance of the fort has twin nineteenth-century naval cannons on either side of it, facing towards the desert (obviously as a sign of authority today). This reflects what is called frontality in formal architectural analysis (where the symbolism of the front facade bespeaks or symbolizes the social position of those who live within, and whose interior symbolism is not a public statement. Frontality also guides reconstruction, where the front facade is rebuilt first, whereas the reconstruction of the interior may languish for many years. One enters the front hallway, where there is a genealogical chart of the ruling lineage from about the 1600s on. Once within the courtyard, two interior air-conditioned rooms preserve photographs of the males within the patrilineage, beginning about 1930, engaged in various civic duties.

The second major complex to be reconstructed was the *souk* or market, called then and now the *Arsah* (there is some ambiguity in translation as to whether it meant "Weasel" or "Foreigner"). It was still in use when reconstructed, and at least one merchant (of tobacco) relocated from his stall in the once fairly dilapidated old *souk* to the new air-conditioned facility. While the *souk* is worthy of a study in itself, a number of the original features have been retained, such as a corrugated floor for olive storage, in the rebuilt *souk*. Perhaps the most authentic part is a restaurant within the *souk* where as many as 15 or 20 old men congregate, fraternize, eat a meal in the traditional manner on the weekends, and smoke the water pipes (*sheesha*). Certainly the gathering of the elderly men adds authenticity and charm for the few busloads daily of European tourists who shop for souvenirs.

In the multicultural setting of today, the vendors of the *souk* are largely Iranians, Afghanis and a number of Yemenis who are brothers and cousins and one Iraqi from Bassra displaced from the recent fighting. A shop rents for about 20,000 dirhams per year (roughly $5,500) and the vendors are licensed by the government of Sharjah. The merchants mostly sell novelty items and a few antiques; the authentic artifacts were actually used within the past century by tribal peoples and mostly come from the Hadramawt district of northern Yemen and some items relocated from the recent social disruptions in Afghanistan and Iraq.

Tour groups of mostly Germans disembark from buses and file through the *souk* on the weekend mornings looking for what they perceive to be a hidden treasure in the helter-skelter decor of the shops made to look like a Middle Eastern bazaar from the orientalist paintings of the nineteenth century or from old films (and made famous at Marrakech, Morocco and Istanbul, Turkey). Most of the items for sale are recently mass-produced souvenirs (e.g. bronze horns to call camels that are made in India, *khanjars* which are silver daggers placed in the belt and made in Dubai, flintlock muskets with one or two old parts, from Afghanistan) which look traditional, and can also be found in other souvenir shops in the UAE.

The mosque was centrally situated across the street from the *souk* as the focal point of the once walled city. The last mosque was largely leveled to its foundation in the early 2000s, and the area was thoroughly excavated to identify the features of the earliest mosque. The rebuilt "ancient" mosque is nearing completion as an approximately 95 percent new construction; one small portion of a sand/clay/lime wall on the east side was left standing and incorporated into the new structure. Archaeological excavations revealed the base of pillar columns on a hard earthen floor. Rather than incorporating the fragmentary bases of original columns in the reconstruction, comparable pillars were identified in a park in India, which were in turn, transported to Sharjah and reassembled in the entrance of the mosque. The aged pillars certainly convey a feeling of ancient monumentality, a material linkage to the past. New pillars were cast of a composition mixture to match and have been erected in the interior rows; there are twenty pillars in all. Rather than roof rafters constructed of palm trunks, the beams are of finely hewn and lathed *shesham* also imported from India.

As our final monumental construction to be discussed, the rebuilding of the eighteenth-century city walls is nearly complete. Key portions of the foundations were found below the ground surface along the city's former perimeter through archaeological excavation, as were the footings of the towers (*burj*). The monumental walls, towers as well as the fort were constructed of the largest building stone available at that time, called *Abu Musa* for the small island of the same name where it was once quarried. Apparently attack would have come from the land side in centuries past, for only the west flank along the harbor was left unwalled. The wall today dramatically separates the hubbub of life in the city and its grid of planned streets from the quiet reserve of Historical Sharjah. The historic district thus has an ambience of a shrine, in which the citizens of the northern Emirates in general and those of Sharjah in particular pay their respects as a hearth area from which the new Gulf civilization sprung.

Adaptive reuse

We have already touched on a number of activities that Historical Sharjah is used for today, such as festivals, a tourist attraction, a reception area where official guests of the emirate are entertained with the traditional dance and food. The reconstructed buildings are also used for a myriad of cultural agencies, such as a center for calligraphy, a center for traditional theatre. The staff effects a quiet professionalism that you would find in a bureaucracy of any governmental complex. The Museum of Islamic Heritage here displays a collection of coins of the Abbasids of Iraq, calligraphy used in various renditions of the holy *Koran*, Arab astronomy, ornate and brightly colored Islamic ceramics of a thousand years ago, and recent archaeological finds within the Emirate of Sharjah. A second small museum complex, Al-Naboodah lineage compound (*bayt*), has rooms for the traditional crafts and occupations, such as a room for herbal medicines, clothing, etc.

However, immediately outside of the walled sanctuary to the past, is the hustle and bustle of an inner city alive with commercial activity, fumes and noise of neighborhoods of mostly South Asians, and a string of banks (on Bank Street). The centuries-old council tree (*Al-Rolah*), where the lineage elders would gather at the end of Bank Street has died, but its name has survived as the commercial center and meeting place for the South Asian community in the evenings. This constant action contrasts to a certain extent with the "authentic historical self." About a hundred meters beyond the south wall are the birds and animals market which are regulated according to encoded guidelines in effect eight hundred years ago in the cities of the Arab world.[30] Next is the much secluded old cemetery on several acres of a rolling, low hill, which is completely enclosed by a wall. This hill is shown in the 1820s map and signifies an important part of the original city. And on the southern edge of the cornice is the fish market, where *dhous* still unload their daily catch. Immediately north of the historic zone along the cornice are two alley ways, about three blocks long, called the Iranian *souk*, where about eight small shops sell a myriad of small and portable household goods for the kitchen, clothing and various herbs for folk remedies.

As a whole, the gleaming white reconstruction of Historic Sharjah is bounded by still traditionally functioning local markets. We may consider the markets of the old harbor front as unintentionally authentic from age-old practices still pursued in traditional neighborhoods of Iranians, Pakistanis and some Emiratis. We should bear in mind, however, that apart from the *souk* Arsah and the mosque, which receives worshippers of the manual laborers and from the surrounding neighborhoods, nearly all of the occupancy of the renovated historical buildings is by government agencies or government supported agencies. This speaks to adaptive reuse by city planners.

Conclusions

Today Sharjah, like its antecedent communities is quite multicultural as well as traditional. The descendant communities, as forerunners of Sharjah through the centuries were situated on the Arabian Gulf as a conduit linking Mesopotamia, Arabia, and the Indian subcontinent. In the mid-twentieth century, the Arab traders were still sailing to India and to Africa to exchange goods. In this historical frame, Sharjah's metamorphosis with globalization is thus not that novel, although certainly the rapidity and profound degree of globalization were.

In our brief study of how the authentic historical past has been constructed, the rebuilding was as historically "pure" as possible, integrating archaeological residue still in the ground, with what was recorded in photographs and maps, and what the elderly have passed on from memory and was conveyed to them through the oral history of generations now gone. The project was well served by having a copy of the map that the British drew in 1820, which was the year that they arrived. The historicity of the reconstruction is as authentic as current techniques and methods allow.

Certainly the gleaming white exteriors of the buildings and official costumes of the Emiratis, bereft of the usual disorder of daily living, is an idealized statement that is more reflective of the purity conveyed of the sacred word for a perfect world if lived according to scriptures. The activities of the *souk* Arsah indicate a very real globalization at this most local level, where goods manufactured in Central Asia and elsewhere are sold to European tourists who perceive these as authentic items from the bygone days of the Gulf or at least sufficiently exotic in their own experience to represent the Gulf. Thus, the restoration was constructed as a measure to counter multiculturalism within the Gulf, but very much fitting into the niche of tourism that the northern Emiratis have developed well beyond its neighboring countries within the GCC.

The Ruler of Sharjah has encouraged the historical-cultural-informational/ educational niche to fit within the wider Gulf regional bloc and with the linkages to the wider world beyond. Sharjah has embarked on becoming the cultural capital, as it was so designated in recognition of its endeavors in the early 2000s. We may think of resurrecting symbols of the past, such as the mosque, market and fort of Historical Sharjah, or emphasizing the dishdasha in national dress or the dome in civic architecture as material manifestations of what the social sciences call revitalization. Revitalization has been defined as reformulating the old cultural ways for strength in the adapting to the avalanche of multiculturalism that has engulfed the seaport city states since the 1970s. This version of identity reformation resurrects symbols of the past to perform new functions in an electronically networked world in its various nodes along the western shores of the Arabian Gulf. Symbols of the past are selected to keep the socio-political movement together, build a fairly impermeable defense around the polity and keep the cultural others (i.e. various forces of globalization) at a distance. We note that the government of Sharjah has revitalized a historical/cultural identity that will provide a degree of distinction within the ultramodern cityscapes that have come to characterize the Gulf.

The cultural basis or commonality for the GCC comes from a shared heritage and maritime orientation as the sea-faring Arabs of the Gulf in past centuries, as well as from similar petroleum based economies during the first generation of globalization. The traditional identity of the lineages of longstanding residency, who asserted the Arab identity in centuries past, allowed the forging of larger alliances through inter-marriage into regional blocs of allied groups. In identity, the national Emiratis define themselves with their particular emirate and by relationship to its ruling family as well as they consider themselves citizens of the UAE or as a Gulf Arab. Identities are built up and nested within larger alliances, and the countries of the Gulf self-identify as ever closer in culture and in history.

Notes

* Dr Fox is President of the Institute of International Social Research and Professor of Anthropology. Dr Mourtada-Sabbah is Associate professor of Political Science and Chair of the Department of International Studies at the American University of Sharjah. Dr Al-Mutawa is Associate professor of Sociology at the United Arab Emirates University in Al Ain.
1 Benedict Anderson, *Imagined Communities* (London: Verso, 1991), 5–6.
2 The Sharjah Natural History Museum is widely referred to as the most comprehensive and "modern museum within the Gulf," with displays on the formation of the

university, geology/paleontolgy, marine life, and terrestrial ecology. It also has a breeding center for endangered species of wildlife. *Oman and the United Arab Emirates* (Melbourne: Lonely Planet Publications, 2000), 271.

3 E. Swyngedouw "Neither Global or Local" 'Glocalization...' cited in Neil Brenner, *New Urban Spaces* (Oxford: Oxford University Press, 2004), 46.

4 Ibn Khaldun. *The Muqaddimah: An Introduction to History.* Translated by Franz Rosenthal and abridged by N.J. Dawood (London: Routledge and Kegan Paul, 1967). Originally published in 1377.

5 Colbert C. Held, *Middle East Patterns, Places, Peoples and Politics* (Boulder, CO: Westview Press, 2000), p. 22; John W. Fox. "Solutions to Water Stress in the Middle East," *Journal of Social Affairs*, 20, no. 22, 2003, p. 91–93.

6 T.G. Bibby, *Looking for Dilmun* (London: Penguin, 1970); Harriet Crawford, Robert Killick, and Jane Moon, *The Dilmun Temple at Saar* (London: Kegan Paul International, 1997).

7 John W. Fox. "The Trading Ports of Julfar and Kush, RAK, Part 1," *Gazelle*, 20, no. 6 (June 2005), 5–6.

8 Pliny. *Natural History.* H. Rackham, trans. (Cambridge, MA: Loeb, 1942).

9 Robert C. Hoyland. *Arabia and the Arabs* (London: Routledge, 2001), 19, 22.

10 *Ibid.*, p. 28.

11 Cf. Frauke Heard-Bey. *From Trucial States to United Arab Emirates* (Dubai: Motivate Publishing, 2004), 128.

12 Aqil Kazim. *The United Arab Emirates, A.D. 600 to the Present* (Dubai: Gulf Book Centre, 2000), 47.

13 Kazim, 42–53.

14 John W. Fox. "The Trading Ports of Julfar and Kush, RAK, Part 2," *Gazelle*, 20. nos. 7–8 (2005), 6–7.

15 The palm groves at Julfar are the largest in the Oman Peninsula, followed by those in Al Ain and Dibba.

16 One of the co-authors, John W. Fox, has surveyed many mountaintop Shihuh sites, and estimates about one hundred Shihuh residential complexes to exist as archaeological sites today. Each would have contained village-sized populations of about 70 to 250 persons. The housing and walls are constructed of shaped rectangular stone blocks and are perched on the higher and fortified elevations of the Musandam Plateau. The Shihuh had developed elaborate catchment systems for storing rainfall, such as cisterns, and sluiceways for distributing water to small agricultural mountain plots for wheat agriculture. The sites are richly adorned with petroglyphic carvings of camels, horses, serpents, occasionally a person attired like Yemeni and occasionally maps and cosmograms.

17 John W. Fox, "The Trading Ports of Julfar and Kush, RAK, Part 3," *Gazelle*, 20, no. 9 (2005), p. 6.

18 Hoyland, 28–9.

19 See Sultan Bin Muhammad al-Qasimi, *Power Struggles and Trade in the Gulf, 1620–1820* (Exeter: Forest Row, 1999).

20 Peter Lienhardt, *Shaikdoms of Eastern Arabia* (London: Palgrave, 2001), 98–102. John W. Fox. "Theoretical Approaches to the State, Lineages, and Women in al-Andaluis," *Journal of Social Affairs* 20, no. 79 (Fall 2003), 93–100.

21 Anthony Giddens, *Modernity and Self-identity* (Stanford, CA: Stanford University Press, 1991).

22 Manuel Castells, *The Power of Identity* (Oxford: Blackwell Publishing, 2004), 69.

23 Beginning in 1932, Sharjah was the locus of a small British airbase for refueling in flights to and from India. Frauke Heard-Bey, *From Trucial States to United Arab Emirates*, 298.

24 University City includes the American University of Sharjah, the University of Sharjah, the two Higher Colleges of Technology, a Fine Arts School, and recently a

Medical College. The Sharjah Police Academy has square towers that resemble more of a North African *kasbah* or an Arabian fort.

25 The buildings in Cultural Square are the symmetrically designed Ruler's Court (*diwan*), Cultural Palace and the Petroleum Council.

26 In Carsten Niebuhr, *Travels Through Arabia, and the Other Countries in the East* (Edinburgh: 1792).

27 Sultan bin Muhammad al-Qasimi. *Power Struggles and Trade in the Gulf*, 99–109.

28 *Gulf News*, Tabloid Section, July 25, 2002, 16.

29 The house walls were plastered in hot gypsum (*jess har*), which was burned and said to be as strong as white cement (*sarruj*). Rough gypsum (*jess khashin*) was used in floors and roofs, and soft gypsum (*jess na'im*) was used in ornamentation. Palm branches were also trimmed for use in the roofs, and bound together with ropes also made of palm fibers.

30 Ibn Abdun, *Hisba* (Manual for Muslim Seville, 1212). In *Medieval Iberia*. Edited by Olivia R. Constable (Philadelphia, PA: University of Pennsylvania Press, 1997), 174–9.

References

Anderson, Benedict. *Imagined Communities*. London: Verso, 1991.

Bibby, T.G. *Looking for Dilmun*. London: Penguin, 1970.

Brenner, Neil. *New Urban Spaces*. Oxford: Oxford University Press, 2004.

Callan, Lou and Gordon Robison. *Oman and the United Arab Emirates*. Melbourne: Lonely Planet Publications, 2000.

Castells, Manuel. *The Power of Identity*. Oxford: Blackwell Publishing, 2004.

Crawford, Harriet, Robert Killick and Jane Moon. *The Dilmun Temple at Saar*. London: Kegan Paul International, 1997.

Fox, John W. "Solutions to Water Stress in the Middle East." *Journal of Social Affairs* 20, no. 22 (2003): 83–99.

Fox, John W. "Theoretical Approaches to the State, Lineages, and Women in al-Andalus." *Journal of Social Affairs* 20, no. 79 (2003): 87–125.

Fox, John W. "The Trading Ports of Julfar and Kush, RAK, Part 1." *Gazelle* 20, no. 6 (2005): 5–6.

Fox, John W. "The Trading Ports of Julfar and Kush, RAK, Part 2." *Gazelle* 20, no. 7–8 (2005): 6–7.

Fox, John W. "The Trading Ports of Julfar and Kush, RAK, Part 3." *Gazelle* 20, no. 9 (2005): 6.

Giddens, Anthony. *Modernity and Self-identity*. Stanford, CA: Stanford University Press, 1991.

Heard-Bey, Frauke. *From Trucial States to United Arab Emirates*. Dubai: Motivate Publishing, 2004.

Held, Colbert C. *Middle East Patterns, Places, Peoples and Politics*. Boulder, CO: Westview Press, 2000.

Hoyland, Robert C. *Arabia and the Arabs*. London: Routledge, 2001.

Ibn Abdun, *Hisba* (Manual for Muslim Seville, 1212). In *Medieval Iberia*. Edited by Olivia R. Constable. Philadelphia, PA: University of Pennsylvania Press, 1997.

Ibn Khaldun. *The Muqaddimah: An Introduction to History*. Translated by Franz Rosenthal and abridged by N.J. Dawood. London: Routledge and Kegan Paul, 1967.

Kazim, Aqil. *The United Arab Emirates, A.D. 600 to the Present*. Dubai: Gulf Book Centre, 2000.

Lienhardt, Peter. *Shaikdoms of Eastern Arabia*. London: Palgrave, 2001.

Niebuhr, Carsten. *Travels through Arabia, and the Other Countries in the East*. Edinburgh, 1792.

Pliny. *Natural History*. H. Rackham, trans. Cambridge, MA: Loeb, 1942.

Al Qassimi, Sultan Bin Mohammed. *Power Struggles and Trade in the Gulf, 1620–1820*. Exeter: Forest Row, 1999.

Index